REVENUE UNIT COLUMNS

FROM

THE AMERICAN PHILATELIST

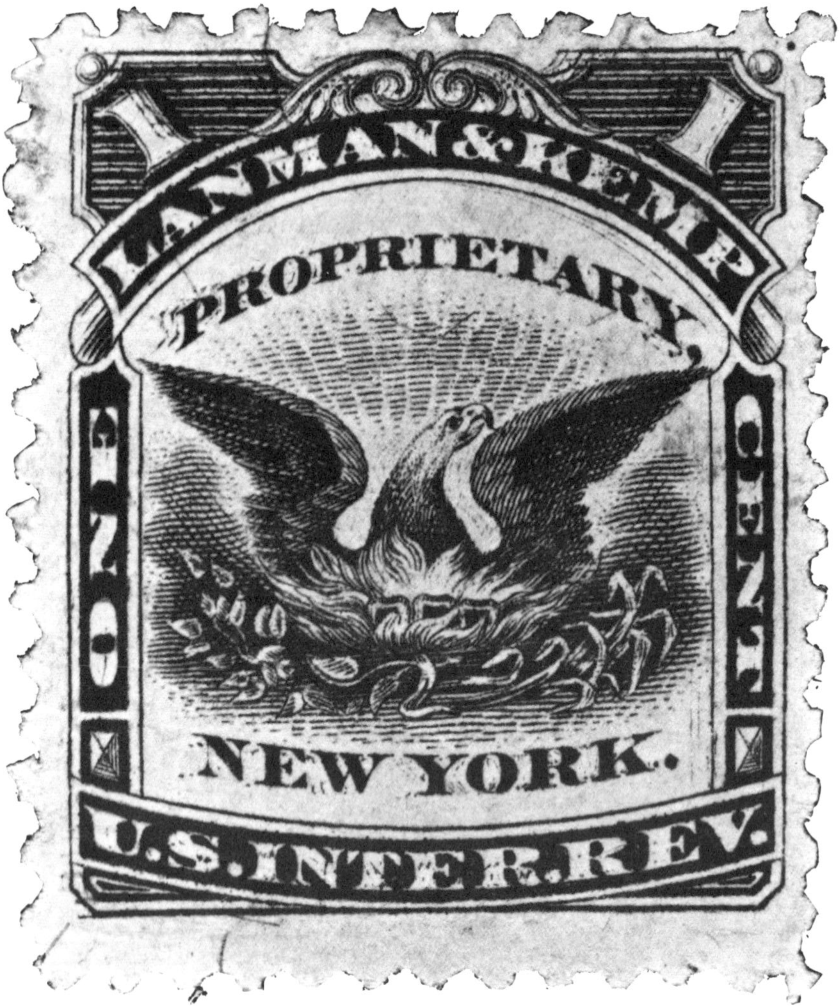
LANMAN & KEMP
PROPRIETARY
ONE
CENT
NEW YORK.
U.S. INTER. REV.

REVENUE UNIT COLUMNS FROM THE AMERICAN PHILATELIST

EDITED BY

Beverly S. King
Justin L. Bacharach
George T. Turner

QUARTERMAN PUBLICATIONS, INC.
Lawrence, Massachusetts

Copyright 1928–1942 inclusive by The American Philatelic Society, Inc.
© Copyright 1981 Quarterman Publications, Inc.

This work is a facsimile compilation of the serialization entitled "Revenue Unit" which appeared in *The American Philatelist* between February 1928 and January 1942; originally edited sequentially by Beverly S. King, Justin L. Bacharach and George T. Turner. The original text has been reproduced chronologically and the pages renumbered consecutively. A Preface, Subject Index and Author Index by Richard F. Riley have been added to this edition. The Subject Index has been adapted herein from its original publication in *Philatelic Literature Review* in 1979.

The publisher expresses its grateful appreciation to the American Philatelic Society, Inc. for permission to reprint this serialization and to the editor of the *Philatelic Literature Review*, and the author, for permission to use the Subject Index.

Library of Congress Catalog Card Number: 80-53091
International Standard Book Number: 0-88000-119-4

Printed in the United States of America.

Quarterman Publications, Inc.
5 South Union Street
Lawrence, Massachusetts 01843

PREFACE

For some years it has been apparent that many details concerning United States revenue stamps were being rediscovered by newcomers to the field who were unacquainted with the literature of decades past. This is hardly a surprising observation since philately in general is far from being the best indexed of the fields of knowledge.

Some improvements in the accessability of information about United States revenue stamps has occurred in the past several years since independent efforts have culminated in bringing considerable new material and scattered and relatively inaccessable older material on these into book form. Several examples are: *Essays & Proofs of United States Internal Revenue Stamps* by George Turner, Bureau Issues Association, 1974; *Special Tax Stamps of The United States* by Terence Hines, The American Revenue Association, 1976; *Patent Medicine Tax Stamps*, [The Collected Papers of] Henry W. Holcombe, Quarterman Publications, Inc., 1979; *United States Beer Stamps* by Thomas Priester, privately published, 1979; *A Handbook for United States Revenue Stamp Paper* by Joseph S. Einstein, Thomas C. Kingsley and W. Richard DeKay, The American Revenue Association, 1979; *The Revenue Stamps of The United States, United States Match & Medicine Stamps* and *Private Die Match Stamps,* collected columns which appeared in Mekeels) by Christopher West (Elliott Perry), Castenholz & Sons, 1979 and 1980 respectively; and the so called *Boston Revenue Book* by George L. Toppan, Hiram E. Deats and Alexander Holland, Quarterman Publications, Inc., 1980. Shorter cumulations on selected topics have appeared in recent years in the pages of *The American Revenuer.*

Another long neglected source of information consists of a series of 106 columns which had appeared under the logo "Revenue Unit" in *The American Philatelist* between February 1928 and January 1942.

A subject index to the material covered in these columns was prepared and published in *Philatelic Literature Review* in 1979. This effort acquainted a number of collectors, for the first time, with this serial account of studies of United States revenue stamps and whetted some appetites for easier access to the material than that afforded by tracking down suitable photocopies of the more difficult originals. Thus the decision was made to put together the Revenue Unit columns in the form of the present volume and thus compliment the other works mentioned above.

Acquiring tear sheets of the original columns for reproduction was solved through the exceptional offices of the Friends of the Western Philatelic Library. Mr. Matt Hedley carried out the arduous job of accumulating them as original duplicate copies of the 30-40 year-old *American Philatelist* became available to the Sunnyvale group. We are indeed appreciative of his most generous assistance. Eventually all but eight of the requisite pages had been obtained. Since none of the eight missing pages contained photographs, photocopies of them were used for reduplication. Thus the quality of the original illustrations has been maintained throughout as high as possible by working from original copy.

THE REVENUE UNIT

A small group of members of the American Philatelic Society became organized under the chairmanship of Dr. Robert Chambers of Providence, Rhode Island, as the Revenue Unit of the American Philatelic Society early in 1928. Their main purpose was the exchange of information on United States revenue stamps which was subsequently detailed in their column in the *American Philatelist* under the logo "Revenue Unit". There had been an earlier group, The United States Revenue Society, which had been founded in January of 1907, and which disintegrated in 1916, perhaps because of the general fatigue of World War I. The Revenue Unit was its direct successor. Neither society or group was ever very large. The United States Revenue Society had 143 members in its prime. The size of the Revenue Unit was not published regularly but it was hardly a much larger assemblage. Interest in the Revenue Unit declined in its turn and publication of the column ceased in 1942, perhaps in this case because of general preoccupation with World War II. The American Revenue Association started in 1947, and presently Affiliate No. 51 of the American Philatelic Society, is in some sense a successor of the preceding two groups.

Editors of the Revenue Unit columns were Beverly S. King, 1928-1935; Justin L. Bacharach, 1935-1936; and George T. Turner, 1937-1942. Beverly King the philatelist, is perhaps best known for the book: *The United States Postage Stamps of The Twentieth Century* which he authored with his friend Max Johl. King participated also in many other philatelic activities. Professionally as an architect, he created the Carnegie Library building at 564 5th Ave., New York. Justin Bacharach, a protege of Eugene Klein and Philip Ward Jr., assumed the editorial job temporarily following the tragic death of King who died the senseless victim of an accident. Bacharach is presently a professional philatelist (Lee Stamps) in Great Neck, New York. George Turner is particularly known for his book: *Essays & Proofs of the United States Revenue Stamps,* and as past curator of the Division of Philately at the Smithsonian Institution, in Washington. He was an active participant in many other philatelic activities until his death in 1979. Professionally he was a chemist. It is believed that King, Bacharach, and Turner were largely responsible for the unsigned commentary in Revenue Unit columns which are reproduced in the following pages.

Several of the signed articles are classics which evidently have never appeared elsewhere. To mention but one which nearly concludes the volume, is the extended piece written by George Turner, in a terminal effort to stimulate contributions to the Revenue Unit. Titled: Survey of United States Revenue Stamps or What Comprises a Revenue Collection?, this could serve well as a directory to anyone who might ask: where do I begin in United States revenue stamp collecting?

Pacific Palisades, California   Richard F. Riley
August, 1980

REVENUE UNIT COLUMNS
FROM
THE AMERICAN PHILATELIST

Just because we happened to have the job of Secretary-Treasurer of the Revenue Unit thrust upon us, please don't expect that we are going to run this "Colyum alone. We want help! And help with a big H.

This Unit will cover all Revenue stamps, both United States and foreign. We are fairly familiar with the Civil War Revenues, but when it comes to questions on the later U. S., any of the Canadian, Mexican, French, or other foreign revenues, we plead a dense ignorance.

It occurs to us that there might very logically be an "Editor" or "Expert" to handle Canadian Revnues, another for Mexican, one for U. S. from 1898 on, one for M. & M. and one for foreign.

Surely some of our members are "Specialists" enough on one or more of the above to be able to answer questions intelligently and prepare notes of interest for publication.

We tried to wish the job of caring for the Civil War Section on Henry L. Dean, but he just grinned cheerfully and volunteered to write some articles for us from time to time. So we will attempt to handle these first issue Revenues, until we can find some one who knows more about it—and that will not be difficult.

Who has made a specialty of Canadians and will take that section over? And who will handle those Mexican beauties?

How about you, Frank Applegate, for a section on Beer and Wine Stamps? We have been following your series of articles in Gossip with interest. It's a good write up. Then a section should be provided for those popular stamps, the State Revenues.

We are told that Charles S. Thompson of Los Angeles is a Specialist on those enticing Canadians. How about you, Brother Thompson, to handle questions and notes for the Canadian Section?

Perhaps if Mr. Thompson wont or cannot find the time, our old friend, E. R. Vanderhoof will jump into the breach, or it may be he would rather handle the Mexican end of it.

How about it, Fellow Enthusiasts, who will volunteer to help out? Please let us have your suggestions.

Of course, there are many A. P. S. Revenue Collectors who have not as yet joined this Unit. Send along your name and address accompanied by one dollar and help strengthen the Revenue cause by affiliating with us.

All suggestions and notes of interest will be most welcome. This is our first experience as "Colymist" and we need help!

BEVERLY S. KING, Secy.,
18 East 41st St., New York City.

THE IMPERFORATED REVENUES.

Dr. Clifford D. Varvey writes regarding early dates and types of cancellations on the imperforated revenues. Revenue cancellations are always interesting, and some examples are really beautiful. A handstamp in brilliant red on the $1.50 blue Inland Exchange struck squarely in the center of the stamp, or a blue cancellation similarly struck on one of the $2.50 Inland Exchange are bright spots for any collection.

Dr. Harvey gives the following early dates on some of his imperfs:

1c Telegraph, cancelled with stamp showing date Jan. 3, 1865.
10c Inland Exchange with dot and guide line above, cancelled with pen showing date 1863.
30c Foreign Exchange, pen cancelled 6/12/63.
50c Surety Bond, pen cancelled 3/13/1863.
$2.00 Probate of Will, pen cancelled with various initials and 1/20/64.

$2.50 Inland Exchange, cancelled with stamp showing date Oct. 12, 1866. Blue cancel.
$5.00 Probate of Will, pen cancelled Jan. 15, 1864.
$10.00 Charter Party, pen cancelled Aug. 13, 1864.
$10.00 Conveyance, pen cancelled Feb. 11, 1863.
$10.00 Mortgage, pen cancelled showing date Aug. 25, 1863 and showing below part of marginal imprint "RAVED BY BUTLER & C."
$200.00 pen cancelled J N L Sept. 20, 1864.

The earliest cancellation subsequent to the issuance of the stamp in this lot would be Sept. 20, 1864 on the $200. stamp which was first delivered to the Department July 7, 1864. The other stamps were nearly all printed and first delivered from September 27th on through December, 1862.

In our own collection of Imperforated we note among the 1862 cancellations:

5c Inland Exchange, pen cancelled Dec. 4, 1862.
25c Entry of Goods P. C. Dec. 12, 1862.
$2.00 Mortgage P. C. Dec. 30, 1862.

We also have the $200. imperforated dated five days earlier than Dr. Harvey's copy, viz., Sept. 15, 1863.

So far as we know most of these imperfs were issued the latter part of 1862 or the early part of 1863 though occasional sheets undoubtedly slipped out later.

It will be interesting to see who has the earliest dated cancellation on these stamps. Can you help us?

Of course the imperfs were not issued before the part perf or perforated stamps as many of us used to think. To quote from the Boston Revenue Book:

"The true facts are that THE PERFORATED STAMPS WERE THE FIRST ISSUED and, in support of this statement, we quote the following official letter from Butler and Carpenter to C. F. Estee, Acting Commissioner of Internal Revenue. It is dated Nov. 7, 1862:

"Your telegraphic communication: 'Fill all orders for stamps with utmost despatch without perforating,' is duly received and we will act at once thereon. Within two or three weeks we expect to have an adequate number of perforators in working order, and we will, in the meantime, perforate as many as possible, while we also obey your directions as above indicated—The delay is in the requisite changes of the Machinery."

"From the above it may easily be seen that, prior to Nov. 7, 1862, there was no authority for the issuance of either imperforate or partly perforated stamps and, if any were so issued, which we do not believe to have been the case, it was certainly unintentional."

It is an accepted fact that they were all issued at the same time and that under the contract made all were supposed to be issued perforated.

Mr. Theodore Steinway told the writer that in looking over many old documents of his firm he had unearthed numerous examples of the use of perforated revenues antedating the imperforate varieties.

It was only due to pressure of time that certain sheets slipped out or were delivered on rush orders in an imperforated or part perforated condition. It seems that the stamps were printed during the day and perforated in the evening.

This rush of perforating also accounts for the many so called freak perforations found on our early Revenue stamps—carelessness in placing the sheets on the perforating machines in the boys' hurry and bustle of getting their work done —for this work was done by boys. It is easy to see how a sheet might occasionally get placed askew on the perforating bed and after the off-center or diagonal perforations were discovered when the sheet was turned, to run it through again so that the holes would fall between the stamps and the sheet be not wasted.

The great majority of these stamps, however, were issued perforated in accordance with the contract and as the use was primarily for single copies rather than pairs, strips or blocks—most of the imperforated and part perforated were cut up by the users, thus accounting for the rarity of these in pairs or larger.

Some values have never been found in imperforate condition and others are extremely hard to find in pairs, either imperforate or part perforate. The writer found a pair of part perforate 30c Inland Exchange the other day, the first pair he had seen and was told by the dealer—one of the oldest in New York—that it was the second pair that had ever passed through his hands.

It is best, of course, to collect these imperforate and part perforated stamps in pairs, or larger, as there can be no question of their authenticity. They are not easy to secure and command a high price in both the open and auction markets.

Henry L. Dean, one of our best informed members on these Civil War Revenues has written several articles on the relative values of imperfs, 1st Issue, in pairs or blocks. This has been appearing in Mekeels and is well worth reading. Mr. Dean's idea of the market value of these items checks pretty well with the new Specialized catalogue. He disagrees in some instances however. To quote a few comparisons:

	Scott	Dean
$20. Probate of Will, pair	$250.00	$275.00–$300.00
$25. Mortgage, pair	200.00	200.00
$15. Mortgage, pair	200.00	175.00
$200. U. S. Int. Revenue, pair	250.00	225.00
$10. Mortgage, pair	50.00	75.00– 85.00
$5. Probate of Will, pair	75.00	60.00– 70.00
1c Playing Cards, pair	150.00	100.00+

There are seemingly no new "lots" or "finds" of Civil War Revenue stamps coming on the market except when a collection is broken up. A few dealers have a considerable stock of the more common varieties in singles, but when one asks for pairs or blocks you are met with a shrug and "There aint no such animal."

We feel sure, however, that on many old deeds, leases or whatever, that may be reposing in some odd corner or safety deposit box, there are many interesting pairs, strips and blocks, such as a block of six 50c ultramarine Surety Bond and a block of thirty-two 50c blue Surety Bond that we uncovered a short while ago. In many cases these are far more interesting on the original document, for their story is then right before our eyes.

REVENUE STAMP TAXES.

Long before postage stamps were thought of revenue stamps were in use. The most common form in the early days was the non-adhesive stamped document. Most if not all of the stamps used in connection with the celebrated STAMP ACT of 1765 were of this nature. Such were in common use in Great Britain long before the stamp tax was extended to the colonies. The crown, the royal arms and the value were generally the main feature of the design which was embossed without color on blank documents which were prepared and sold by the Government as our stamped envelopes are today. Many denominations and dies were applied to documents of all kinds in Great Britain even as early as the time of William and Mary, 1694-1702. Many of the stamps used then and throughout succeeding reigns were adhesive of a sort, semi-adhesives, as they are called in England, the embossed stamp being on a separate piece of paper stapled to the document with a piece of lead. Stamps of this nature were issued during Queen Victoria's time running up as high as £11,000!

The first revenue stamps of the United States were non-adhesive also. Dies of several denominations were appropriately inscribed for each of the first fifteen states, embossed without color on promissory notes and other documents and sold by the General Government. Each denomination showed the eagle and shield in a different position. These old documents are seldom seen nowadays but make an interesting exhibit. These were first issued in 1797. The State of Virginia issued such stamps on its own authority in 1813, and Maryland in 1845.

The earliest record I find of real adhesive documentary revenues are of those used in Holland in 1829. These too are embossed without color and circular die cut and run to thirty-one values. Colored stamps did not replace them until 1870, many years after most other important countries had been issuing colored adhesives. The colored documentary stamp issued by Austria in 1850 were beautifully engraved and executed while those of Great Britain of 1850-53 were plain, being merely a modification of the designs of the former non-adhesives, but the LIFE POLICY stamps of 1854, large and handsome, bearing the picture of the young queen, follow the best traditions of the early British postage stamps.

It took the exigencies of the Civil War to bring the possibilities of the documentary taxes again to the front in Federal legislation in this country, five years after the State of California had already adopted the system in 1857. The documentary stamps of the United States are better known and appreciated here perhaps than any other revenue stamps, yet their predecessors issued in California are in the opinion of the writer at least fully as interesting and fully as deserving of attention as the Federal issues. While they are not so beautiful they do not lack variety and they run to forty-five different monetary values. Other states have issued stamps for the collection of similar taxes which also may be classed as beautiful examples of the engravers' art.

Documents have been much more generally the subject of stamp taxes than other articles as tax collectors have found it an easy tax to enforce, and a hard one to evade, most documents subject to tax being instruments of record easily checked up by agents of government.

However stamp taxes have been applied to other things beside documents almost from the first. Great Britain put a stamp tax on dice as early as 1710, and on hats, gloves, and other articles in 1784 and these were adhesive stamps, too—and in color. All such taxes may properly be termed EXCISE taxes, a term used in England from the first. Excise taxes may be extended to cover as many different articles as the ingenuinty of governments may devise. Stamp taxes of this nature have been more consistently levied in this country than documentary taxes, and more so than in most foreign countries. The stamps we call "Tax Paids" are of this class which properly includes also the proprietary, match, wine and beer stamps. Without stopping to reflect we may fail to realize this fact, as the method adopted by our government in applying the Civil War Revenue Act was to place the documentary and proprietary stamps in the same set; yet the documentary taxes were enumerated in the act as "Schedule A" and the proprietary taxes as "Schedule B." Of course after the first issue more divergence is shown between the two classes, and in the Act of 1914 stamps for Cordials and Wines were issued in such similar form to the proprietary stamps that our cataloguers saw fit to list them also notwithstanding the fact that stamps for liquors of all kinds, also for tobacco in all forms, had been subject to stamp taxes since the time of the Civil War. There are however, two salient reasons why collectors have not taken to the so-called tax paids. The element of monetary face value has generally been lacking, and then many of them have been taboo from the government viewpoint, it having been actually illegal to remove the stamp from the container in many cases.

The beer stamps, first issued in 1866, and continued until prohibition, have always had the face value expressed in dollars and cents and are in every way analogous to the wine stamps of recent years; and the logic by which a collector cherishes the latter and ignores the former is rather obscure.

While revenue stamps antedate postage stamps by over a century it was not until well after the advent of the postage stamp that they met with the general use that now obtains. There is hardly a country in the world today that does not employ stamp taxes in one form or another. In fact the stamp tax has become a favorite device of tax collecting authority, lending itself admirably as it does to the collecting of an infinitesimal fee in great aggregate volume. It has brought in the maximum revenue with the minimum of evasion. Besides the taxing power of General Government we have municipal and provincial authority taking advantage of the same principle in a large measure. Where we have nations issuing postage stamps we have revenue stamps properly authorized by many states and cities, particularly in Europe and South America. Every province in the Dominion of Canada has its separate issues with one exception—that of Prince Edward's Island—which for some unknown reason stands out against this form of taxation.

Less popular has been the adoption of stamp taxes by State authority in this country. While ideal from the tax collectors' viewpoint they are not always so popular with the people. Following California's lead Nevada, Louisiana, Alabama, and Oregon, from time to time have adopted documentary taxes only to repeal them after a few years trial. In California the stamp taxes lasted sixteen years and this has been the average duration of such acts up to the time of the adoption of the STOCK TRANSFER TAX by New York in 1905. Massachusetts and Pennsylvania a few years later adopted the same tax as also did the Federal Government and all seem now to be established on a permanent basis.

New York also adopted a SECURED DEBT TAX in 1911 issuing in consequence a set of many interesting denominations, but the law did not prove to be such a permanent institution as the Stock transfer tax. After being amended several times during its life of less than ten years it was finally repealed altogether. Missouri tried a similar experiment in 1917. In 1921 it was knocked out by the State Supreme Court. In the face of these two failures Kansas just last year enacted a similar law which is now going strong. It is so new that none of the used stamps have yet reached the collector's hands. South Carolina is the only state having a general documentary stamp tax today.

More successful has been the operation of the state excise tax. With the exception of a sporadic experiment with a liquor tax in New York in 1903 and another in 1920 Iowa was the first to use the excise tax which she has applied to cigarettes since 1921. Noting the success of this experiment South Carolina, South Dakota, and Utah followed suit in 1923 and several other states have done the same.

State revenue stamps are of three kinds. Besides the documentary and excise taxes already described there is the INSPECTION tax, which is a very light tax levied to pay the cost of state inspection of certain products for the benefit of the consumer. Many interesting series have been issued by various states under this head. The use of inspection stamps reached its peak during the decade between 1910 and 1920. Most of the inspection taxes are now collected through the sale of tags instead of adhesive stamps. Not all, however. Our government has never seen fit to apply an inspection tax, but Canada has her WEIGHTS and MEASURES, as well as ELECTRIC LIGHT and GAS (meter) INSPECTION.

No doubt stamp taxes of one form or another will be levied by additional states in the near future, yet several great and populous states as Ohio, Michigan, Illinois and Texas have so far fought shy of stamp taxes in any form.

As a prominent fiscalist has said, "All these are grist to our mill," yet few of us would have the hardihood to attempt the revenue stamps of the entire world. This would be even a bigger job than the general collecting of the postage stamps of the world.

Much useful information is to be learned through study of the revenue systems of the various countries as revealed by their stamps, and much pleasure is to be gained through their collection.

We have yet to hear of a revenue stamp issued for petty speculative purposes. Frankly they are all issued to raise money and yet selling them to stamp collectorae rather than applying them to the articles specified in the law does not seem to have been thought of. Where you find one official who will gladly sell you what you want you will encounter a dozen who view your purchase or intended purchase with indifference if not with actual suspicion. Some of our states actually prohibit the sale of their stamps to any but dealers in the articles taxed and they are enjoined from selling to a third party.

FRANK L. APPLEGATE.

* * * * *

The March and April meetings of the Westchester Chapter of the A. P. S. were devoted to "Revenues". At the March meeting Mr. A. J. Squier showed a most interesting and practically complete collection of Beer stamps, with a side display of early Cotton and Tobacco Tax Paids, and some Hydrometer stamps.

"Beer" stamps somehow had never sounded particularly enticing to us and although we had read Frank Applegate's articles on these emissions with interest and had seen a few glasses of beer from time to time, we really had no conception of the interest and real beauty of these stamps. The entire membership was quite won over, and the "beer" had nothing to do with it, either.

Mr. Squier gave a most instructive talk and it was amusing to see how familiar many of the members were with the initial cancellations of the various breweries, the almost instant, nay, pathetic spotting of these initials showed an early familiarity with them—the breweries, we mean. But, seriously, it was a real treat for all the members and we don't blame anyone now for seriously collecting these beautiful stamps. Many of the early issues are practically unobtainable now at any price and Mr. Squier is to be congratulated on having such a complete collection.

At the April meeting general collections of U. S. Revenues were shown by Dr. Jason S. Parker of White Plains stamp fame, and Mr. Charles Taussig of Scarsdale, while the writer showed a specialized collection of the first issue in pairs, blocks and strips, with a few side items of double transfers, marginal imprints, and stitch watermarks.

One question that was discussed at some length was the comparative rarity and values of Revenue blocks vs. strips of four. It seemed to be the general feeling that in the higher values—the larger stamps—a horizontal strip of four was just as good looking a piece as a block.

It is true that owing to the long shape of these stamps a strip would more nearly fit the corner or bottom of a document that a bulky block, and the chances are that many more of the former were used. Good, uncut strips however are not particularly easy to find and though they certainly should not be catalogued at as high a figure as blocks, they should be worth more than two pairs. We therefore place them at one half the price of blocks.

This line of reasoning need not necessarily be applied to the smaller stamps—where more blocks are found—but even in these lower values a slight difference would be justified.

MINT REVENUES.

A member has written asking our opinion as to the relative value of cancelled and un-cancelled Revenues. We strongly feel that these stamps should be catalogued in both mint and cancelled condition in the Specialized Catalogue, and we further suggest that a price on cut cancellations be established for the first several issues. We would say that fewer early mint Revenues would be found in collections than early mint postage. Very likely the ratio would be one to three. These mint stamps are much cleaner and handsomer in appearance, and although the collection of gum is frowned upon by our friend, Eustace Power, we feel that when we acquire an unused copy it is much more desirable with the gum on the back. We should place at least the same ratio of difference in value on these Revenues as the Catalogue does on the early postage, which would be from four to ten times the price of cancelled copies, and possibly might go a bit higher.

* * * * *

CANCELLATIONS.

Then comes the question of cancellation. Most of these early issues were cancelled by pen strokes or written initials and dates, many by the so-called herring-bone and punch cuts, and the minority by hand stamps in various colored inks. Some of course bear printed precancels applied by various Proprietary Companies. Of these, more later.

The herring-bone or straight cut cancels might be appraised at about one-fourth or one-fifth of the current catalogue prices, and the punched copies, either round or triangular holes, at one-tenth catalogue. The pen strokes cancels, and my, my, how those old boys could spread the ink! are of course accepted as laid down by Mr. Clark and Mr. Nicklin. The hand stamp cancels certainly are worth more than the "pen strokes" and for a good clean impression we should say double catalogue would not be far off.

And there you are! No doubt many of you will disagree with us—this simply reflects the opinion of a few who have been studying Revenues for some time and we may be "all wrong."

These price suggestions will of course vary with the rarity and condition of the stamps and should not be applied indiscriminately. We bought a strip of four $200 first issue, perforated, not long ago, with a slight horizontal cut line cancellation, exactly two cuts to each stamp at top and bottom of frame, and paid only $45 for it. A strip of four of this stamp, on the above basis would be worth one half the price of a block of four or $150.—with cut cancellation one fourth or $37.50. So very likely we paid too much. But we will be glad to buy another at the same price.

What is your idea of this range of values on strips, mint copies, and cancellations? Please let us know.

EARLY DATES ON FIRST ISSUE IMPERFORATES.

Considerable interest has been shown in the early dates of Dr. Harvey's imperforated revenues. No less than six different members have written in giving us various dates from their collections so that we are able to add to the list published in the March number as follows:

1c Express, Oct. 16-62, P.C. Aug. 1-63—A. S. Yount.
2c Express, Nov. 20-62, H.S. Dec. 9-62—W. G. Saxton.
2c Bank Check, Sept. 29-62, P.C. Jan. 12-63—A. S. Yount.
2c Cert., Oct. 21-62, P.C. May 17-63—H. B. McCollum.
2c Cert. (Major shift), Oct. 21-62, P.C. Apr. 4-63—B. S. King.
5c Inl. Ex., Oct. 23-62, P.C. Dec. 1862—W. G. Saxton.

5c Cert., Dec. 3-62, P.C. May 28-63—A. S. Yount.
5c Express P. P., Nov. 20-62, P.C. Feb. 20-63—F. N. Newton, Jr.
10c Cert., Oct. 24-62, P.C. Aug. 10-63—W. G. Saxton.
10c Contract, Oct. 24-62, H.S. Mar. 2-63—H. B. McCollum.
15c Inl. Ex., Dec. 2-62, P.C. Apr. 25-63—H. B. McCollum.
20c For. Ex., Nov. 22-62, P.C. Feb. 25-63—H. B. McCollum.
20c Inl. Ex., Dec. 2-62, P.C. Jan. 8-63—A. S. Yount.
25c Protest, Nov. 15-62, P.C. Jan. 18-63—H. B. McCollum.
25c Entry of Gds., Nov. 26-62, P.C. Dec. 4-62—A. S. Yount.
25c P. of Atty., Nov. 15-62, P. C. Jan. 15-63—A. S. Yount.
25c Cert., Nov. 22-62, P.C. Dec. 6-62—H. B. McCollum.
25c Ins., Oct. 21-62, P.C. Jan. 28-63—H. B. McCollum.
25c Bond P. P., Nov. 26-62, P.C. Jan. 20-63—H. B. McCollum.
30c For. Ex., Nov. 17-62, P.C. May 9-63—S. J. Cunningham.
40c Inl. Ex., Dec. 4-62, P.C. Feb. 18-63—F. N. Newton, Jr.
50c Orig. Pro., Nov. 15-62, P.C. Dec. 8-62—F. N. Newton, Jr.
50c Mtg., Nov. 21-62, P.C. Jan. 1-63—F. N. Newton, Jr.
50c Con., Nov. 17-62, P.C. Feb. 2-63—B. S. King.
50c For. Ex., Dec. 6-62, P.C. Sept. 28-63—A. S. Yount.
50c Lease, Nov. 22-62, P.C. Jan. 26-63—A. S. Yount.
60c Inl. Ex., Dec. 3-62, P.C. Feb. 4-63—B. S. King.
$1 Manifest, Nov. 26-62, P.C. Jan. 23-63—F. N. Newton, Jr.
$1 Con., Dec. 1-62, P.C. Dec. 3-62—H. B. McCollum.
$1 P. A., Dec. 4-62, P.C. Feb. 16-63—H. B. McCollum.
$1.50 Inl. Ex., Nov. 26-62, P.C. Jan. 14-63—H. B. McCollum.
$2 Con., Dec. 18-62, P.C. Mar. 20-63—F. N. Newton, Jr.
$2 Mtg., Dec. 18-62, P.C. Feb. 26-63—A. S. Yount.
$5 Mtg., Dec. 11-62, P.C. Mar. 10-63—H. B. McCollum.
$20 Con., Dec. 18-62, P.C. Feb. 4-64—B. S. King.
$50 Int. Rev., May 15-63, P.C. Apr. 9-64—B. S. King.

Several of these are quite close to the date they were issued. The $1 Conveyance, the property of H. B. McCollum, for instance, is dated December 3, 1862 while the stamp was issued only on December 1, 1862—a lapse of three days. The next earliest would be the 25c Entry of Goods, owned by A. S. Yount, dated December 4, 1862, nine days after its issuance, November 26, 1862. The third would be the 25c Certificate of Mr. McCollum with the date of December 6, 1862, fifteen days after it was issued. The fourth is the 2c Express of W. G. Saxton, dated December 9, 1862, twenty days after its issue on November 20, 1862. The fifth is the 50c Original Process owned by Mr. Newton, dated December 8, 1862, twenty-four days after its issuance on November 15, 1862.

We wonder whether any of our members have any earlier dates than these.

DATES ON IMPERFORATES.

In further reference to early dates on imperforates it is of course quite logical to assume that many of these stamps were dated back, that is, a document calling for a certain revenue tax which was prepared before the issuance of the stamp would naturally be held, the stamp affixed as soon as it could be secured from the authorities and a cancellation date applied to conform to the date of the deed, mortgage, or what not.

Mr. Yount submits a specimen of $10 Mortgage dated Nov. 10, 1862 while the records show that this stamp was not issued until Dec. 12, 1862. This of course is a clear case of back dating.

We agree with Mr. Dean that if a serious attempt were made practically every stamp would be found dated prior to its date of issuance. It would be rather interesting to discover how many stamps we could find which have been dated back. Many of the issuing dates have been given in our last list and we shall be glad to give any others on request.

PRICES.

In the March number of the A. P. we commented on some of the prices noted in Scott's Specialized Catalogue as compared with those suggested by Mr. Dean in a recent article. Mr. Dean has written me as follows:

"Your comments are observed on the price situation and I really feel you should correct the rating you have given me for the pair of $20.00 P. W. Imperf. That top figure of $300. was my thought for the hypothetical superb horizontal pair that may exist but which none of us have ever seen. My estimate for a fine vertical pair was about the same as Scott's at 20% off for theirs is a list compilation for "good" specimens and mine was a net list for "fine" items. The two listings might tend to harmonize with the proper factors recognized but the trouble is most people just grab a figure without further thought."

"Observe you dwell a little on the scarcity of the 30c I. E. Part, Perf. pair. It certainly is not common and could list somewhat more if everything were to be in perfect balance."

If any of our members having unusual or interesting strips or blocks will send the word to this column we will be very glad to make notes or comments on the items for the benefit and interest of our general membership.

STRAIGHT EDGES ON THE 1st ISSUE PERFORATES.

Christopher West has always claimed that none of the perforated first issue revenues were issued with an imperforated margin edge—in other words that all of the stamps were perforated on all four sides. A cursory examination of your revenues may bear this out, but if you search long enough the chances are that you may discover one or more with a "straight" margin edge.

Mr. Chappell submits eleven items showing this imperforated margin, viz:

1c Proprietary
2c Proprietary
2c Bank Check
3c Proprietary
4c Proprietary
25c Bond
40c Inland Exchange
50c Life Insurance
50c Conveyance
$1 Foreign Exchange
$2.50 Inland Exchange

In looking over our own collection and duplicates, we have not found a single copy of a perforated item with a straight margin edge. If you have any such items in your collection will you kindly advise us?

THAT STITCH WATERMARK!

With fingers weary and wet,
With eyelids heavy and red,
A collector with an enlarging glass
Sat beating himself on the head—
Stitch! Stitch! Stitch!

Have you ever looked for that elusive stitch watermark? Try it on your piano some time, and after fruitlessly looking over several thousand stamps go away on a shooting trip—you'll need the rest and change of scenery.

Of course, we all know "why" the stitch, "how" the stitch, and just what it should look like. Heaven knows there ought to be enough little stitches in the felt on the rollers, and that the rollers should revolve often enough to impress the stitches into the moist paper at least every little while. But after a diligent search you will come to the conclusion that the roller felt coverings were all glued and not stitched at all.

How many examples of stitch watermarked revenues have **you** in your collection? Scott lists the 60c Inland Exchange.

We have a few and have looked for others many times but without avail. A short while ago we acquired several additional items from Mr. C. H. Chappell. Mr. Chappell in sending them to me wrote, "This little collection is the result of over twenty years searching among revenues for the elusive stitch watermark", and we can well believe his story.

We are all through looking for them, we're too old, our eyes are getting weak and we have no more hair to lose. Some of you youngsters trail them down and, having captured some, tell the Revenue Unit all about them.

Lets start a check list. We can list seventeen at present and perhaps together can increase the list to thirty or forty.

Here they are:

1st ISSUE.

2c U. S. Int. orange (J. H. Nicklin)
2c Bank Check, blue (J. H. Nicklin)
5c Inland Exchange (B. S. King)
5c Insurance (B. S. King)
25c Life Insurance (B. S. King)
25c Certificate (B. S. King)
25c Bond (B. S. King)
25c Entry of Goods (B. S. King)
30c Inland Exchange (B. S. King)
50c Conveyance (B. S. King)
50c Life Insurance (B. S. King)
60c Inland Exchange (B. S. King)
70c Foreign Exchange (B. S. King)
$1. Entry of Goods (B. S. King)
$10. Probate of Will (B. S. King)
$20. Conveyance (L. J. Flerlage)
2c brown Proprietary #4008 (B. S. King)

What can you add to the above?

U. S. Revenues Showing Stitch Watermarks.

C. H. CHAPPELL.

I note with great pleasure the listing in the 1928 Scott specialized catalogue, of the sixty cent inland exchange, with stitch watermark.

During the last twenty-five years I have examined many thousands of the first issue revenues in my search for this elusive watermark. And also great quantities of the later issues, in both the government dies and the private dies; not forgetting the match wrappers of the Civil War period. I have succeeded in locating about one hundred varieties, all told.

These varieties on the postage stamps being eagerly sought and duly chronicled, the same recognition was bound to follow for the revenue stamps, although somewhat tardy in appearance. At the request of Mr. Beverly S. King I have compiled a check list of all the varieties known to me and append it herewith.

In my studies I note two general types in the first issue, which I shall call Types I and II. In Type I the stitches are about 5 mm. wide and ½ mm. apart, while in Type II they are about 1 mm. apart. The latter type seems to be the exception, practically everything falling under Type I.

Under the 1898 issue, the letters "H.H.P." denote the hyphen-hole perforated varieties. In the match wrappers the stitch runs from 3 mm. to 8 mm. in width.

Kindly send on any unlisted varieties for correct listing in the check list. Address me at 132 Ohio Street, Rochester, N. Y.

1862   1c red, Prop., perf., thin, vertical, precancelled.
        2c blue, Bank Check, perf., thin, vertical.
        2c orange, Bank Check, perf., thin, horizontal.
        2c orange, Express, perf., thin, vertical.
        2c orange, U. S. I. R., perf.
        3c green, For. Exchange, perf., thin, horizontal, precancelled.
        4c violet, Prop., perf., thin, horizontal.
        4c violet, Prop., perf., medium, horizontal, precancelled.
        5c red, Agreement, perf., thin, horizontal.
        5c red, Certificate, perf., thin, horizontal.
        5c red Express, perf., thin, horizontal.
        5c red, Inland Exchange, perf., thin, horizontal.
        5c red, Inland Exchange, imperf., thin, horizontal, block of three.
        5c red, For. Exchange, perf., thin, horizontal, block of six.
        10c blue, B. of Lading, perf., thin, horizontal.
        10c blue, For. Exchange, perf., thin, horizontal, precancelled.
        25c red, Bond, perf., thin, horizontal.
        25c red, Certificate, perf., thin, horizontal.
        25c red, Certificate, perf., medium, horizontal.
        25c red, E. of Goods, perf., thin, horizontal.
        25c red, E. of Goods, perf., medium, horizontal.
        25c red, Insurance, perf., thin, horizontal.
        25c red, Insurance, perf., thin, horizontal, Type II.
        25c red, Life Insurance, perf., thin, horizontal.
        25c red, P. of Attorney, imperf., thin, horizontal.
        25c red, Protest, perf., thin, horizontal, hor. pair.
        25c red, Warehouse Rec., perf., thin, horizontal.
        30c lilac, Inl. Exchange, perf., thin, horizontal.

30c lilac, Inl. Exchange, perf., thin, horizontal, Type II.
40c brown, Inl. Exchange, perf., thin, horizontal.
50c blue, Conveyance, perf., thin, horizontal.
50c blue, Conveyance, perf., thin, horizontal, Type II.
50c blue, Conveyance, imperf. hor., thin, horizontal.
50c blue, Conveyance, perf., medium, horizontal.
50c blue, E. of Goods, perf., thin, horizontal.
50c blue, E. of Goods, perf., thin, vertical.
50c blue, Life Insurance, perf., thin, horizontal.
50c blue, Orig. Process, perf., thin, horizontal.
50c blue, Orig. Process, perf., ex. silk, horizontal.
50c blue, Passage Ticket, perf., thin, horizontal.
50c blue, Surety Bond, perf., thin, horizontal.
60c orange, Inl. Exchange, perf., thin, horizontal.
70c green, For. Exchange, perf., thin, horizontal.
70c green, For. Exchange, perf., medium, horizontal.
$1.00 red, E. of Goods, perf., thin, horizontal.
$1.00 red, Lease, perf., medium, horizontal.
$2.50 violet, Inl. Exchange, perf., thin, horizontal.
$10.00 green, P. of Will, perf., thin, vertical.
$20.00 orange, Conveyance, perf., thin, vertical.

1896   2c blue, Play. Cards, H. H. P., watermarked, vert., precancelled.
1898   1c blue, Doc., rouletted, watermarked, horizontal, plate No. 8087.
        4c red, Doc., rouletted, watermark, horizontal.
1899 $5.00 red, Doc., rouletted, watermark, vert.
1900 $1.00 carmine, Doc., H. H. P., watermarked, vert.
1898   ⅛c green, Prop., H. H. P., watermarked, horizontal.
        ⅛c green, Prop., rouletted, watermarked, horizontal, precancelled.
        ¼c brown, Prop., rouletted, watermarked, horizontal, precancelled.
        ¼c brown, Prop., H. H. P., watermarked, horizontal, precancelled.
        ⅜c orange, Prop., rouletted, watermarked, horizontal, precancelled.
        ⅝c blue, Prop., rouletted, watermarked, horizontal.
        ⅝c blue, Prop., rouletted, watermarked, horizontal, precancelled.
        ⅝c blue, Prop., H. H. P., watermarked, horizontal, precancelled.
        1c green, Prop., rouletted, watermarked, horizontal, precancelled.
        1¼c violet, Prop., rouletted, watermarked, horizontal.
        1¼c violet, Prop., H. H. P., watermarked, horizontal, precancelled.
        2c brown, Prop., rouletted, watermarked, horizontal.
        2c brown, Prop., rouletted, watermarked, horizontal, precancelled.
        2c brown, Prop., H. H. P., watermarked, horizontal, precancelled.
        2½c red, Prop., rouletted, watermarked, horizontal, precancelled.
        2½c red, Prop., H. H. P., watermarked, horizontal, precancelled.
        3¾ gray, Prop., H. H. P., watermarked, horizontal, precancelled.
        4c purple, Prop., rouletted, watermarked, horizontal, precancelled.
        5c orange, Prop., rouletted, watermark, horizontal, precancelled.
1914   ⅛c black, Prop., perforated postage, horizontal, block of ten.

1899 Private Dies.

1¼c v. brown, Emerson Drug Co., H. H. P., vertical stitch, precancelled "I. P. I."

1⅞c blue, Lanman & Kemp, H. H. P., horizontal stitch, precancelled "L. & K. 3-18 1901."

⅝c blue, Radway & Co., rouletted, horizontal stitch, uncancelled, vertical pair.

Match Wrappers.

Scott No.	Date.
5150	Sept. 1866, vertical, 7 mm.
	Feb. 8, 1868, vertical, 3 mm.
5152	Feb. 1, 1873, vertical, 9 mm.
	Jan. 1, 1874, vertical, 6 mm.
	Feb. 2, 1875, vertical, 7 mm.
	May 2, 1875, vertical, 7 mm.
5153	Nov. 1, 1876, vertical, 4 mm.
	Dec. 1, 1877, vertical, 4 mm.
5154	July 1, 1876, vertical, 8 mm.
	November 1, 1876, vertical, 8 mm.
	February 1, 1877, vertical, 8 mm.
	March 1, 1877, vertical, 8 mm.
	May 1, 1877, vertical, 8 mm.
	August 1, 1877, vertical, 8 mm.
	September 1, 1877, vertical, 8 mm.
	November 1, 1877, vertical, 7 mm.
	December 1, 1877, vertical, 7 mm.
	March 1, 1878, vertical, 7 mm.
	September 2, 1878, vertical, 7 mm.
	March 1, 1879, vertical, 7 mm.
	December 1, 1879, vertical, 7 mm.
	February 2, 1880, vertical, 7 mm.
	April 1, 1880, vertical, 5 mm.
	September 1, 1880, vertical, 4 mm.

DOUBLE TRANSFERS.

The first "double transfer" stamp that we ever added to our collection was the so-called "big shift" of the 10c black 1847. This was some years ago and as we remember, it made no particular impression on us at the time. Since then we have become quite keen about these curious varieties.

Have recently been investigating the various major and minor shifts of the Civil War Revenues, first issue, and have found them particularly interesting. They are, of course, an indication of poor workmanship on the part of the engraver, and for this reason are rather elusive. The engravers for these revenue stamps may have had some excuse, for the plates were prepared on "rush orders," and the stamps were printed and perforated in almost rapid fire time.

Almost a year ago there was an article in Scott's Monthly Journal, relative to these shifts, illustrated by cuts of two stamps from our collection. They are the two best known and most easily discernible transfers, the 2c bank check and the 2c certificate, but there are several other major shifts on these 2c stamps. They have never been listed so far as I know, and this is no attempt to do so. It is simply a start for our Revenue Unit and I hope that all of our A. P. S. members who have other shifts will send them to us for description and record.

In a later issue of Scott's Journal, Mr. Nicklin illustrated two other transfers —the 2c U. S. Int., "TWO" at side shifted, and the 2c U. S. Int. with a slight doubling at the top right in lettering and balls. These were from the collection of Mr. George A. Armstrong.

The following thirteen 2c stamps will give us the start of a list. **Most of the** transfers are quite clear and easily discernible without a glass.

A.

2c Bank Check, blue, perf., decided shift in lower lettering and label.
2c Bank Check, orange, perf., same.

B.

2c Bank Check, blue, perf., slight shift, upper lettering and label.
2c Bank Check, orange, perf., same shift.

C.

2c Certificate, blue, imp., decided shift in lower lettering and label.
2c Certificate, orange, perf., same.
2c Express, blue, perf., shift in lower label.

D.

2c U. S. I. R. perf., decided shift in left "TWO."
2c U. S. I. R. perf., slight shift in upper lettering and label.
2c Prop., blue, perf., decided shift in upper lettering and label.
2c U. S. I. R. perf., shift in CENTS on right.

E.

2c Prop., blue, perf., shift in lower letters and label at right.
2c Prop., orange, perf., shift in lower letters and label at right.

These double transfers are not common by any means. You may look through a thousand stamps and not find any one of them, and then again you may stumble on one at once.

Mr. Nicklin suggested to us the use of a "shift chart" based on the horizontal and vertical numbered and lettered lines found on an Atlas map for the location of cities. To determine the exact location of a transfer the stamp can be placed on the "chart" and the location described as A-3, G-7, or what not.

I had a drawing of this suggested "chart" prepared for him, which was published a short time ago. It can, of course, be used for stamp shifts other than revenues.

There are other transfers in some of the higher values, but of these, later.

We had the pleasure of a call from Mr. Philip Little, Jr., of Minneapolis, one of our members. He has been at work and has all but completed drawings and descriptions of the double transfers of the first issue. Many of these shifts he has located on the plates. His drawings and data are most interesting and we are looking toward printing his article in the Unit Column very shortly.

We are indebted to The Scott Stamp & Coin Co. for the loan of the cuts used in illustrating the foregoing list of double transfers.

JOIN OUR REVENUE UNIT.

We have received several letters from A. P. S. members inquiring how they may join this Unit. It is a simple matter.

Send us your name and A. P. S. number, together with a dollar for one years dues, and you will be registered at once. No proposer is necessary, your membership in the A. P. S. is sufficient guarantee. We are a part of the A. P. S., but a very small part at the present time. Our membership numbers only thirty-four, but an interest in Revenue Stamps is shown by these members, and others who have not yet affiliated with our Unit, that is really quite encouraging. Hardly a day passes but this Column receives one or more letters giving data or asking a question on some interesting point. Many of these letters require a personal answer, and that is what the dollar dues were voted for,—overhead.

We recently sent a "Questionaire" to the Unit members, covering their collecting activities and specialties, and asking advice and help along certain lines. The response was most prompt and we hope to print for distribution to the Unit a tabulation of the returns. This will put us in a closer touch with each other and will give us all first hand information that will be a decided benefit in Unit trading or what not.

According to our By-Laws as granted by the Governors of the A. P. S., the Revenue Unit may have an Exchange Department and this was a point in our "Questionaire" that received the unanimous vote of the membership. We have had some correspondence with President Wilhelm on this subject and hope to get such a Department started this fall.

Mr. Ackerman has suggested that we issue occasionally, printed handbooks on various Revenue items or issues. One member, Mr. O. E. Moses, made a suggestion that we bring the "Boston Revenue Book" up to date. This is entirely feasible and with the proper co-operation can be done.

The greater our membership the easier we can get results of every kind.

If you are interested in any way in Revenue Stamps and can spare one dollar a year to further a good cause,—send in your name,—and do it now.

STITCH WATERMARKS.

Our notes on the above in the July issue have uncovered several additional items.

Mr. Robert P. Chambers of Providence sent in the following from his collection,—

    2c Express—blue
    2c Proprietary—blue
    2c Bank Check—orange
    $3.00 Charter Party—green
    $3.00 Second Issue—blue and black
    $10.00 Third Issue—green and black

Mr. Don R. Bennett of Detroit adds to the list a,—

    25c Entry of Goods

He writes that he has a very fine imperforated pair of these, with a horizontal watermark across the centre of both stamps; the date is not given, other than the month, "December."

This is certainly a most interesting example of a stitch watermark, and the first we have heard of showing on a pair.

Mr. Casper J. Dorer of Cleveland writes us that in his collection he has a copy of the,—

    25c Insurance

Mr. Wm. C. Polk of Los Angeles adds six from his collection as follows,—

    1c Proprietary
    2c Proprietary
    $2.50 Inland Exchange
    $3.00 Manifest
    $5.00 Conveyance (imperforated)

    1889 Issue

    1c Documentary—blue

Now, starting with the one stitch watermark listed in the 1928 Catalogue, the—

    60c Inland Exchange

plus the seventeen items in our list as it appeared in the July issue, plus about forty-four covered by Mr. Chappell's check list, plus the fourteen examples noted above, gives us a total of about seventy-two known varieties of U. S. Revenue Stamps with the stitch watermark.

A number of these have been brought to the attention of Mr. Nicklin and Mr. Clark of the Scott Co., and will be listed in the 1929 edition of their Specialized Catalogue.

REVENUES WITH STRAIGHT EDGES.

Mr. L. Richard Harney advises us that in his collection he has the following straight edge copies of the early perforated stamps,—

    2c Bank Check—orange
    15c Foreign Exchange
    25c Certificate
    $1.00 Conveyance
    $1.00 Lease

He also has the
    50c Second Issue #3915
with straight edge and states that it is the only copy of the Second Issue that he has ever seen in this condition.

These give us to date seventeen varieties of this type. They are not common.

Election of Officers.

The annual election for officers of the Revenue Unit occurs in September of each year. During August we received the following nomination,

For Chairman, 1928-29:—

    Mr. Robert F. Chambers, Providence, R. I.
    Mr. W. M. Stone, Springfield, Mass.
    Mr. W. G. Saxton, Canton, Ohio.
    Mr. E. R. Vanderhoof, Denver, Colo.
    Judge R. S. Emerson, Providence, R. I.
    Mr. J. D. Bartlett, El Paso, Texas.

For Secretary-Treasurer:—

    Mr. Beverly S. King, New York, N. Y.

These names were submitted to the membership by mail. Mr. Saxton and Judge Emerson both requested that owing to their inability to give proper time to the Unit during the coming year, their names be withdrawn. After checking the very close vote among the four remaining candidates, it was found that Mr. Robert F. Chambers, of Providence, R. I., had been elected Chairman, to serve until October 1st, 1929, and that your overworked Secretary-Treasurer, running alone, naturally had been elected.

More Shifts.

Mr. Frederick H. Leggett, a member from Scarsdale, New York, advises us that after reading the Column for September on "Shifts" he immediately looked over his 2c Bank Check duplicates and found one copy of the major transfer that we illustrated,—the decided shift in "Bank Check" in the lower label. One interesting point in connection with this stamp is that in regular conditions it is catalogued at 2c but the "shift" gives it a value of $5.00. Better get out your glass and study your stamps.

Dr. Clifford D. Harvey of Boston, who has made a study of the 2 cent stamps has submitted several of his Bank Checks for inspection. The first is the complete re-duplication of the words "BANK CHECK" which has already been illustrated.

(2) a shift in the words "BANK CHECK" to the left which is less distinct.
(3) either a scratch across NTS or a crack in the plate.
(4) a diagonal crack or scratch in the right lower numeral "2".
(5) a crack or scratch extending from the space between E and C of CHECK and running upward and crossing the N and T of CENTS.
(6) a crack or scratch across U and 2 at upper left corner.
(7) a crack or scratch across "TWO".

These look to us more like scratches than plate cracks, though it is hard to tell. Of course, the only way to determine anything definite about them is to find another stamp with a duplication of the mark. The lines on the stamp are rather light and can be seen much more readily with a glass than the naked eye.

If any of you have 2c Bank Checks showing any of these lines will you kindly communicate with the Unit so that they may be properly established.

Dr. Harvey lists the following shifts he has found on the 2 cent Bank Checks and 2 cent Internal Revenues:—

Two cent, Bank Check, blue:—

1. Minor shift; showing in upper left hand corner in U. and S.
2. Very plain minor shift showing in CENTS and ECK of Check.
3. Very plain minor shift in CENTS.
4. Very plain minor shift in BANK CHECK.
5. Major shift showing complete re-duplication of BANK CHECK.

Two cent, Bank Check, orange:—

1. Minor shift in upper left corner.
2. Minor shift in top showing in U. S. INTER. REV.
3. Very plain shift in BANK CHECK.

Two cent, Internal Revenue, orange:—

1. Minor shift in upper left corner.
2. Minor shift in lower U. S. INTER. REV.

Other transfers, that we have seen at least two copies of, on the lower value stamps are as follows:—

A minor shift on the 3c Telegraph,—the top line of the upper label is slightly doubled.

The 3c Proprietary also shows a doubling of the upper label line "U. S." and ornament at top, this is quite distinct.

The 3c Foreign Exchange has a double frame line and ball at upper left, as also has the 4c Inland Exchange.

The 2c Bank Check has another shift. The border line of the right hand lower circular "2", the top of the label line immediately below, and the tops of letters "HECK" of check are doubled.

The 5c Inland Exchange has an excellent example of a double transfer in the lettering and lower line of the lower label. We would call it a major shift, although it is not as apparent as the 2c Bank Check, previously illustrated.

Another shift occurs o nthis stamp in the word "CENTS" in the right hand label.

The 5c Foreign Exchange has a minor doubling of the word "CENTS" in the right label.

The 5c Certificate has a fairly strong shift in the letters "CERTI" in the lower label and "REV" in the upper label. We have this in a single and also showing on one stamp of a block of four.

The 10c Contract shows a doubling of the outer line at top, at both the right and the left.

On the 15c Inland Exchange we find a minor transfer,—a doubling of the top guide line.

The 40c Inland Exchange shows a doubling of "UNITED STATES" in the upper label.

There are several shifts listed in the "Specialized" that we are not familiar with. If any of you have them or others that are not mentioned let's know about them.

Want any more about "shifts"? We don't want to bore you.

An Opportunity.

Sixty-six years ago, at the time of the Civil—or as some people call it the Un-Civil War, the United States Government as part of its taxation program, caused stamps to be issued and sold to the public for use on various papers and articles.

These are a particularly beautiful set of stamps, both as to design, engraving and color. The head of Washington in an oval surrounded by gracefully placed ribboned bands containing the necessary inscriptions, the inner corners enriched with delicately drawn leaves, gives a particularly well balanced design.

On the 41 lower values the frame lines are all curved and as a matter of fact were among the first stamps of this country to be issued without square outer frame lines or border. Yet the design is so cleverly composed that the stamps have every appearance to the casual eye of being a perfect rectangle.

The head of Washington after a portrait by Gilbert Stuart, was not the one originally contemplated for use on these stamps. The first design submitted by Butler and Carpenter, showed a profile view of Washington. This was first approved by the Hon. George S. Boutwell of the U. S. Treasury, and work started on the 1 and 2 cent Proprietary stamps.

A letter dated August 29, 1862 to Mr. Boutwell from Butler and Carpenter is interesting. It is as follows:—

"We have pushed forward the Proprietary stamps with every possible dispatch. Our Mr. Carpenter, on his return from his recent visit to Washington, found the 1 and 2 cent Proprietary stamps ready, with the exception of the wording, to be proved and forwarded to you for approval; but these designs were gotten up with the **profile view of Washington,** and you ordered Mr. C. to use the **Stuart head,** changing your former instructions.

We stopped the engravers at once, and have been pushing forward the other designs with all haste. We hope to furnish you with a proof of this new design by Monday next.

(Signed) Butler & Carpenter."

It is very likely safe to assume that the profile head of Washington originally contemplated was after the bust by Jean Antoine Houdon, similar to that used on the Proprietary issue of 1875 although there seems to be no definite record on this point. Certainly it would be hard to improve upon the design finally ordered by Mr. Boutwell.

The proofs of this series are wonderfully beautiful, the colors clear and full, and every delicately engraved line showing clearly and distinctly. Every collector who has a Revenue section should have one or more examples of these proofs, either on India paper or thin cardboard. They can be purchased from twenty-five cents up and do more to enrich an album page than anything we know of.

Owing to this irregular frame on the lower values, many curious things have occurred in either the engraving, printing or possibly the recutting of the plates as they became slightly worn.

The 1 and 2 cent Postage stamps of the early issues have been so carefully studied and written up that we have become familiar with many of the varieties and have learned to know the various types of the 1 cent 1851 issue for instance.

There is the same opportunity for study on the 1 and 2 cent Revenues of the 1st issue. Just as many varieties exist as are now known on the Postage stamps of that day. For example take a look at the 1 cent stamp. The complete design shows a continuous curved outside line at the top panel containing the word "U. S. INTER. REV." as well as a complete line at the bottom panel. Let us call this type I.

Type II will show the outer line of the lower panel broken.

Type III will have the outer line of the upper panel broken, as a matter of fact, it is more than broken, it is just gone, and all the way across from one scroll leaf to the other.

Type IV will show both top and bottom lines broken.

Type V has the start of the scroll leaf surrounding the lower numeral broken at the corners. These outer corner lines at the top are also found broken. There seems to be quite definite indications of re-cutting of the top and bottom lines, if you care to go into detail to that extent. The broken lines noted above, however, are quite distinct and you do not need a glass to see them.

The 2 cent stamps are just as prolific in types and are rather fun to look over. There are four or five quite definite varieties. Let us call No. I the perfect engraving with the four balls at the corners complete.

Type II has the upper left ball broken.

Type III lower left ball is broken.

Type IV both upper and lower left balls are broken.

Type V upper right ball is broken.

The are, of course, other combinations of these "broken balls" on the 2 cent stamps, and an interesting phase of the hunt may result in the discovering of doubled lines or lettering indicating a "shifted transfer" and if we find one of these our search is more than rewarded.

There is an opportunity right here for someone to study these 1 and 2 cent stamps and definitely establish certain types, such as above outlined. We have examples of all of these noted, and very likely there are many others.

A message from our new Chairman, Dr. Robert F. Chambers.

254 Irving Avenue, Providence, R. I.,
October 30, 1928.

Dear Mr. King:

Your letter informing me of my election to chairmanship of the Revenue Unit rather staggered me. Many of our members know more about Revenues than I do, but if the scattering votes do not elect someone else,—let's go!

I think first of all a census of the Unit should be compiled, so that the scope of each member's activities in Revenues may be known. This data I believe you have, if so, I think a copy should be sent to each member.

To amount to anything as a Unit, the members must know each others interests and help each other out with information and exchange or sale of material. If I know that John Jones wants State Revenues, I send him any that I come across, and expect him to send me anything in my special field. To do this we must know each other's desires.

I think the material you have been writing up in the Journal excellent. Also the fact that several members have contributed articles is encouraging. Dean's articles in Mekeel's are wonderful, but are of academic interest only to the majority of collectors, because they deal with pieces of which only a dozen or so examples exist. Could Dean be persuaded to tackle the same thing in the commoner values?

Regarding activities of the section the following suggest themselves:—

1—**Paper Varieties**—The first issues come on paper varieties other than the two listed by Scott, e. g., hard, soft, pelure, thin. Could we not start a list of the last two?

2—**Stitch Watermarks**—This list you have started and it will undoubtedly be extended.

3—**Double Transfer**—Lots exist that have not been noted. This list is a live one to keep going.

4—**Double Frame Lines**—e. g., 25c Entry of Goods.

5—**Cracked Plates.**

6—**Plate flaws, scratches, etc.**

7—**Recut Plates**—I know of two.

8—**Largest Pieces**—List of larger blocks of imperforated, part imperforated and perforated.

9—**Earliest Dates.**

10—**Comparative scarcity of roulette and hypenhole perfs., in Battleship Revenues.**

11—**Complete list of the Playing Card stamps of the War period, especially the local provisionals.**

12—**Colonial and Civil War stamped paper.**

13—**Tax Paids**—Many subdivisions under this heading.

Perhaps we can persuade some of our members to write on one or more of these topics. We have the information somewhere in the Unit, so let's dig it out.

Sincerely,

(Signed) ROBERT F. CHAMBERS.

Postage Used as Revenue.

In a recent issue of "Gossip" mention was made by Mr. Adler of a 2c postage stamp of the 1898 issue, surcharged "I. R." which had actually seen postal service although the stamp was intended for Revenue duty.

This "interchange" of Revenue and Postage stamps was not altogether uncommon, and every once in a while an example comes to light.

One of our members,—very likely one of our oldest, in number of years,— Mr. R. S. Nelson, recently sent us for inspection a check on which had been used a 1908 2c Trans-Mississippi instead of the Revenue stamp of that period.

In our personal collection we find a 3c Telegraph and a 5c Inland Exchange which have been used for postage, and on the postage side we have a 2c Black Jack, a 3c red of the 1861 issue, and a 2c vermilion of the 1873 issue, all cancelled and used as Revenue stamps on the original checks.

The Pre-cancelled Revenues.

In these days of pre-cancelled stamp collecting, when so many are striving not only to build up a large collection but also are on the lookout for the earliest examples of this interesting side-line, it is worthwhile to go back some sixty-five years in our stamp history and delve into about the first pre-cancels we ever had, —the first Revenues of the Civil War.

Some time ago we wrote to one of our Unit members, Judge Robert S. Emerson of Providence, who has a very complete precancelled Revenue collection, asking him for a check list. He replied that it would be too much of a proposition as he had about one thousand varieties.

The Boston Revenue Book notes only fifty-five kinds or firms with a total of two hundred and fifty-three various types or varieties, so you can see what the Judge has done.

To quote the Revenue Book,—the pre-cancel "consists of the name, or initials, of one individual or firm using them, generally accompanied with a date and in some instances, with the more or less extended advertisement of the parties whose names they bore."

These names, initials or inscriptions were usually printed, just as our present day pre-cancels are, though many of them were hand stamped.

They usually occur on the cheaper stamps and it is therefore a fairly simple matter to gather a representative collection without any great outlay.

A short while ago we had the pleasure of meeting Mr. Franklin Smith, an old time Revenue Collector, who had made a specialty of these pre-cancels. From him we absorbed a lot of information.

He gave us what he chose to call an "incomplete check list" of his collection listing eighty-one firms with a total of twelve hundred different types of printed cancellations. He said that he had also collected over one thousand different examples of the hand stamped pre-cancels.

"HAMLIN BROS."—on 4c Prop.
Five varying types of this.

"POND'S EXTRACT"—on 3c Prop.
About ninety varieties.

"DR. SETH ARNOLD"—on 1c Prop.
Twelve types.

"S. R. VAN DUZER"—on 3c Prop.
Comes in seven varieties.

We find from his list that the common 1c Proprietary, for instance, cataloging at only 5c has some 100 types of printed cancellations. They also occur on the 1, 3, 4, 5 and 10c Proprietary, the 3c Foreign Exchange, the 1, 2, 3 and 5c Playing Cards, the 2c Bank Check, the 5c Express, the 5 and 10c Certificate, the 1, 2 and 3c green and black, the 3c orange and black and all of the Proprietary Issue stamps.

Many of these can be picked out of your dealer's stock book,—and the time you spend on them is well repaid. There are comparatively few collections in existence, due principally, we imagine, to the fact that so few general collectors realize that a very interesting collection of these pre-cancels of our sixty year old Revenues can be made today.

Mr. Smith told me that his collection has been checked over by three of our Revenue Unit members, M. D. S. Ballentine, Mr. C. H. Chappell and Karl A. Pember,—the latter passed away last January.

Mr. Chappell has a collection of printed pre-cancelled Revenues of the 1898 Proprietary issue,—the "battleship stamps",—filling four volumes, so you see there is an opportunity to do something with our later Revenues too.

We will be glad to publish Mr. Smith's pre-cancel check list in this column, it is much more complete than the one in the Boston Revenue Book, if we have a sufficient number of requests for it.

Dr. Chambers in his letter of last month spoke of a 25c Entry of Goods with an outer line. We do not know just how many Revenue collectors are familiar with this stamp. Mr. Casper J. Dorer of Cleveland, wrote us in reference to it last summer. He said, "Have you ever seen a 25c Entry of Goods with an outer line at the top. I discovered six of these several years ago, two of them I have now in my collection and the other four are in Western collections. The two examples I own are imperforated. One is a single copy and the other is the second stamp from the left in a horizontal strip of four."

We have a copy, but it is perforated. Mr. Dorer asks whether any one can give him an idea as to the scarcity of this stamp. He has looked through a thousand or more and has discovered only the six he notes. How many of you have it or can tell him anything about it.

POSTAGE USED AS REVENUES.

In the December number we spoke of a few examples of postage stamps being used as revenues. Mr. Howard H. Elliott writes in reference to these stamps and says:—

"In the December American Philatelist I notice that you mention a few postage stamps used as revenues. Perhaps it may be of interest to note that I have the following in my collection, used on notes, checks and bills:

```
# 63    1 ct 1861 issue
  65    3 ct 1861 issue
  76    5 ct 1862 issue
  73    2 ct 1862 issue
  88    3 ct 1867 issue 11x13 grill
  87    2 ct 1867 issue 11x13 grill
 113    2 ct 1869 issue
 113a   2 ct 1869 issue
 114    3 ct 1869 issue
 146    2 ct 1870 issue
 157    2 ct 1873 issue
 158    3 ct 1873 issue
 182b   1 ct 1879 issue
 184    3 ct 1879 issue
```

I have also read with interest the article on precancelled revenues. These stamps interested me several years ago and I started accumulating them on the Civil War issues, the Proprietary and Playing Cards stamps of the first issue and all of the 1871 to 1881 Proprietary issues. I have never seen a check list, so have been unable to identify those with initials, and for this reason I would like to see Mr. Smith's list published.

The 1898 issues interest me but slightly, yet I have a fair collection of these stamps, not yet classified."

CRACKED PLATES.

The best known "cracked plate" variety of the early revenues is very likely the 50c Mortgage. There are two examples of "cracks" on this stamp, —the first, on a pair shows as follows:—

1—A left to right diagonal crack shown by a blue line, starting at the "I" of INTER. REVENUE and running up and to the right across the margin and through FIFTY on the adjoining stamp. It is very distinct. The copy we have is on a strip of three, perf.

2—The second, in a block of part perforated, shows a strong line starting at the "T" of FIFTY running directly upward, across the margin, between the "O" and "R" of MORTGAGE of the upper stamp, up past the "5" of 50 and dies away at the base of the oval under Washington's chin.

These are both strongly marked cracks and do not require an enlarging glass to be seen.

Any information relative to other examples of "cracks" will be appreciated by our Unit.

PAPERS.

Several questions have been asked regarding the thin, thick, and silk paper found among our early Revenue stamps. We have asked Mr. Allan P. Vestal to write us something about them.

The "Boston" Revenue Book says,—There are, for this issue, four distinct and easily recognizable papers, viz., thin, medium, thick, and silk. The first is hard, brittle, sometimes almost transparent, and generally of a yellowish or grayish appearance. The second is of various degrees of thickness, always very soft and white, and often quite porous. In this work it will be understood to embrace all varieties not included under either of the other headings.

The third, or thick variety, is very often white, hard and rather brittle. In fact it is so thick as to be almost thin bristol-board. The fourth is self-explanatory, it being merely a rather soft, thick paper, closely resembling the second, or medium variety, as described above, into the composition of which a few scattering silk fibres have been introduced. These fibres are very easily overlooked, as a general rule, they are very minute and widely scattered, so that often a stamp will show but a single fibre.

GREEN PAPER.

Mr. Philip E. Hamilton advises us that he has a two cent Bank Check stamp on a blue paper. We wonder whether this is not the peculiar green paper noted by Mr. Toppan in the Revenue Book.

Some of the three cent Postage stamps of 1861 were printed on a greenish experimental paper, that was not adopted and was never supposed to have been used. A number of copies of the two cent Bank Check have been found of this same peculiar paper. So a few sheets must have slipped out, as they did with the 1861 Postage stamp. Mr. Toppan says,—"This paper was probably an experiment and, in some unknown way, a sheet or more of each must have gotten out and been used. We have seen quite a number of specimens, all cancelled with a pen and all dated in June, 1866."

MORE STITCH WATERMARKS.

Mr. L. J. Flerlage advises us that he has uncovered a 70 cent Foreign Exchange stamp with a horizontal stitch. This has already been listed and has been placed in the Specialized Catalogue.

He also sends a copy of the six cent Inland Exchange with a horizontal stitch watermark. It is a beautiful specimen, perfectly centered and with a R. R. Co. cancellation.

"POSTAGE STAMPS USED FOR REVENUES IN SOME BRITISH COUNTRIES."

Written for the Revenue Unit by GERARD GERARDZOON.

Recently I had the pleasure of examining in detail a highly specialized collection of the stamps of the British Colonies and Dominion in Africa south of the equator. The collector who made it is one of these omnivorous chaps, who cannot be satisfied with just the postal adhesives of a country, even when he has found miscroscopic varieties that even the article in the Collectors Club Philatelist on Union of South Africa, published in 1927, disdained to chronicle. He therefore had page after page of postal stationery, telegraphs, railway stamps—and especially revenues.

I noticed with considerable interest the revenue-used postage stamps in this lot; and with the cooperation of the chap that owns the collection, have made a list of them. This article is that list written up. I strongly suspect, and the owner of the stuff definitely knows, that his material is a very incomplete representation of this field. It will serve well as a first chronicle, however.

The first group to be described here is really a bunch of false postal use of revenues. The King Edward series of the Cape of Good Hope, Natal, Orange River, and Transvaal, together with the King George series of the Union of South Africa come with the overprint "Customs Duty" in two lines of block capitals. These bear postal cancellations, but are not postally used. The Union of South Africa postal guide, issue of January 1928, has, on page 80, dealing with the importation by mail, packages of advertising matter, the following statement:—

> "The senders of such packets may, if they so desire, assess the duty at the rate mentioned and prepay it by affixing to the packet postage stamps of the Union of South Africa overprinted 'Customs Duty' to be obtained at the office of the High Commissioner for the Union of South Africa in London."

This is the only mention that I have located, in any official publication, of these customs duty stamps. In the collection there were also the last issues of the four former colonies, as I have mentioned above, with this surcharge. These are easily explained in the light of what is recorded about "interprovincials" during the first few years of the existence of the Union of South Africa. While the national issue was in preparation, the stamps of the four constituent colonies were used throughout the Union.

The "Customs Duty" stamps are found either unused or with postal cancellations. Three of those in this collection bear cancellations from England: 4d Transvaal, Liverpool 1914, 2d Natal, Bristol 1912, and 3d Orange River, London, no date visible. Another 4d Transvaal has a cancellation that may be either Stamford, England or Stanford, South Africa. Locally cancelled are the 3d Transvaal, Pietermaritzburg, Natal, 1914; 6d Cape, Germiston, Transvaal, 1912; 1d Orange River, Capetown, 1912. Uncancelled specimens include Cape 1d, 3d, 6d; Natal 2d; Orange River 1d; Transvaal 2d, 4d, 6d. The surcharge is in red on the Transvaal 3d and 4d; in black on all others. A handstamped surcharge on the Transvaal 1d also occurs.

Of the Union of South Africa postage stamps, the ½d, 2d, 4d, and 1s come with this "Customs Duty" overprint in black. Doubtless others exist, and presumably the 1926-28 issues also come thus surcharged. In this collection the ½d, 4d, and 1s bear London postal cancellations; the others are uncancelled.

From these **false** postally used revenues, we pass to the genuine thing. By this we mean stamps not bearing the double inscription "Postage and Revenue," but inscribed "Postage **only**," and used as revenues. In 1872 and thereafter the Natal current 1s stamp was printed in three colors: green, lilac and blue. The blue stamp is a revenue only. The other two were overprinted with the word "Postage" and sold for postal use only. I must add that these stamps bear only the name "Natal" in their design and no indication of their service. The 1d green, overprinted "Postage" in a straight line of capitals Scott No. 50 of 1876, is in this collection with a revenue cancellation.

The 8d inscribed "Natal Postage," the common rose Queen's Head stamp, Scott No. 67, is represented twice in this collection with revenue cancellation. One specimen bears a written cancellation with signature and 1893 date; the other part of a "Received Payment" rubber-stamp cancellation.

The 1s orange overprinted "Postage" in a semicircle of block capitals in red, Scott No. 76, is here represented by two specimens with revenue cancellations.— one a written cancellation in red, dated 1891 with initials, and one an oval "bank cancellation" handstamped in red.

From the Cape of Good Hope there are four varieties of 1d postage stamps with revenue cancellations. The 1d with seated figure, watermark anchor, Scott No. 42, occurs with an oval rubber-handstamped cancellation; the 1d standing figure, Scott No. 53, with a fine oval cancellation of a steamship Company on a pair; the 1d Table Mountain, Scott No. 61, with a portion of a handstamped and initialed "received payment" cancellation; and the 1d King's Head, Scott No. 64, with part of an oval handstamped "bank cancellation." All these, be it noted, are stamps inscribed "Postage" only; and all were paralleled by **contemporary revenue** stamps of the same denomination but entirely different size, shape and color.

The ½d and 1d King's Head stamps of the Cape come overprinted "Cigarette Duty." These are not strictly in line with the others here mentioned, as they are postage stamps converted into revenues; but they may well be recorded here.

From the Orange River Colony the 1d King's head, multiple watermark, Scott No. 71, is in this collection with a handwritten revenue cancellation.

No postage stamps used as revenues are shown from Transvaal, Southwest Africa, Rhodesia, Southern Rhodesia, Northern Rhodesia, or Nyassaland Protectorate.

In Union of South Africa, the King's Head stamps are inscribed both "Postage" and "Revenue" on the ½d and 1d values. The higher are inscribed "Postage" only. Aside from the "Customs Duty" overprints mentioned above, the collection has the 2d used as revenue on a receipt; and the owner of it assures me that the 1½d exists in similar use.

I have omitted all mention of revenue use of stamps inscribed for both postal and revenue service. This collection has a fair representation of such stamps in revenue use; but such stamps are outside the scope of this article.

U. S. SHIFTS AND WHAT-NOT.

A number of interesting Revenues were sent to us for inspection by Mr. R. A. Kremers,—the first item was a 50 cent Foreign Exchange with a double transfer in the words "United States" on the left hand side of the stamp, the straight frame line and part of the ornamental border line is also doubled. This is the first example of this shift we have seen, it is not yet listed in the Specialized Catalogue.

Another interesting variety was a copy of the 50 cent Entry of Goods showing either a crack or scratch about one half inch long. This strong line starts at the lower left hand corner and extends diagonally up through the "N" of "Entry" and up to a point between the "5" of "50." The line is just as strong as the cracked plate variety of the 50 cent Mortgage, though it is a straighter line. We have seen this stamp before and are illustrating it herewith. What is it, a crack or a scratch?

By far the most interesting item that Mr. Kremers sent was a pair of 1 cent Express showing what seems to be a decided shift in the lower right hand numeral on one stamp, and on the other what looks like a blurred transfer of the entire left lower corner of the stamp. This is also illustrated. The shift mentioned shows two complete numerals, equally distinct, forming a strong number "eleven" (11) in an oval. Mr. Kremers says that it is the most remarkable thing that he has discovered in Revenues. Both of these stamps have the top frame line broken. It is a very interesting pair and we congratulate him on discovering it. We have seen either this identical stamp or a mate to it somewhere, though we cannot place it now. Who has a duplicate?

He also sends a pair of the 50 cent Conveyance stamp in a milky sky blue color printed on thick soft paper. This is not the regular ultramarine color that the stamp usually appeared in. Most of you are familiar with this peculiar shade, it occurred only on a rather thick "blotting paper" and appeared,—from all the cancellations we have seen,—in the early part of 1870.

The shades of these ultramarine stamps vary considerably. Some of them are almost violet in color. Mr. Philip E. Hamilton sent us a half dozen shades a short while ago, each one decidedly different and all very beautiful.

* * * * *

Mr. Frederick R. Sayen submits three shifts he has found among his 2 cent duplicates. One the minor shift in words "Bank Check,"—another the shift in "Rev." and upper ribbon of the same variety and the third an upward shift in "U. S. Inter. Rev." on the 2 cent Internal Stamp,—several other specimens he sent were examples of poorly wiped plates. These are always interesting, but, of course, have no place among double transfers. One of his 2 cent Bank Check shifts was a double perforation variety which makes it even more interesting.

* * * * *

Mr. Frank Applegate is preparing an article for the Unit on the "State Revenues of Tennessee," which we hope to have for an early issue.

Minor Varieties of the $1.00 Values.

Written for the Unit by PHILIP E. HAMILTON.

There are a number of minor varieties and re-cuts on the one dollar values of the first issue that I would like to call to the attention of the Revenue Unit members. If you will carefully check the following, I feel quite sure you will find copies among your own stamps showing plainly these slight differences:

First: The $1.00 Life Insurance:

Recut line directly under bust of Washington, extending from about the middle of top bar of the letter "E" of "Life"; that is, beginning directly above the place indicated, and extending around the bottom of bust to a point opposite the extreme end of "E" of "Insurance".

Also, in the triangle directly across from "U" of "Revenue", three lines forming said triangle have been recut and extended at bottom of same across inner frame line to touch outer frame line directly across from the top of the letter "E" of "Revenue".

Also, in triangle directly below the above triangle, or opposite "c" of "Insurance", four lines within triangle are recut, only three of which cross inner frame line and meet outer frame line.

Second: $1.00 Manifest:

Recut lines in both triangles same as in $1.00 Life Insurance.

Also, same as to lower, but no lines across frame line to outer frame line in upper triangle.

Also, same as to lower, but only one line across upper inner frame line to outer frame line.

Also, same as last, but one recut line extending without line of triangle and joining triangle to main ornament underneath label containing "Manifest"; also another line extending part way across space towards same.

Also outer frame line of entire upper right triangle recut, with original line showing faintly outside recut line at right.

Also recut line above "U" of "U. S." in upper label.

Also all three outer frame lines of upper left triangle recut and two lines of lower left triangle recut.

Also outer line of lower part of right upper heart recut.

Following varieties having minor differences in upper left triangle:

    (a) four perpendicular lines,—two very fine and two heavy,—one, second from outer very heavy,—two inner very fine.

    (b) one fine line, outer,—and one heavy, inner. No lines inside latter.

    (c) bottom frame line recut.

    (d) lower part of right outer frame line recut.

Third: $1.00 Passage Ticket:

Same as $1.00 Life Insurance, and also some of first issue Manifest but not all.

Fourth: $1.00 Inland Exchange:

In upper right triangle there is a small ball cut making an "o".

Fifth: $1.00 Conveyance:

At the upper part of the right outer frame line appears the rare slip of the engraver. From the top down this slip measures exactly three millimetres and is about ¼ millimetre outside the true outer frame line. Undoubtedly due to the engraver's tool slipping. I have seen but three copies of this slip or double engraving, though others may be found. The outer frame lines of right triangles have also been recut, without extension of lines across inner line to outer frame line.

Sixth: $1.00 Power of Attorney:

Left part of upper frame line shifted or recut,—I am not certain which, —but about seven millimetres of the outer frame line is affected.
Also upper part of right frame line has been recut.
Right part of lower frame line recut.

Seventh:

All lines of upper right triangle recut, with one line extending beyond outer frame line, on inside of triangles.
All lines of lower right triangle recut and extend to outer frame line.
Line outside upper left triangle recut for 4½ millimetres, but not quite joining upper label.
Circular outer line above star at right recut.
Two lines cut at right angles above little ball at left lower corner.

In all the above varieties exist where the little balls are doubled or shifted, and some few with lines recut in balls.

I trust that a check up of the above varieties among collectors will bring to light other recuts that I have overlooked.

ODDITIES.

One of the most pleasurable phases of stamp collecting is checking over one's specimens or duplicates, looking for oddities. This phase does not often come to the junior and not as a matter of fact to the senior collector either unless he gets a real "Kick" out of his stamps. But when that point is reached and he reads or is told of some interesting "oddity", he immediately looks to see whether he hasn't a copy of it also. And if he does discover it or something near it, he gets a real thrill. We have had it and we know.

* * * * *

Mr. Don R. Bennett advises us that he has a copy of the 25 cent Entry of Goods, with the double line at the top, it is one of a pair, imperf. He also discovered that his collection contained a strip of five of the 50 cent Mortgage showing the diagonal crack. Who else has them?

He sends for inspection a block of six 50 cent Mortgage, perforated, showing on two stamps a short straight line starting at the "R" in the lower label and running diagonally down towards the right to the "E" in "Cents" of the stamp below. This is a new one to us.

Mr. J. H. Train also sends us the lower of the two stamps mentioned above, with the scratch (or crack?) across the margin and ending at the "E" of "Cents".

Another interesting stamp Mr. Bennett submitted was the $5.00 Probate of Will, perforated, with a straight marginal edge at the left.

Speaking of the cracked plate varieties of the 50 cent Mortgage,—Mr. William O. Case sends on a copy from his collection showing the upper part of the vertical crack.

Mr. Case sends two other stamps, a 2 cent Proprietary and a 10 cent Certificate, the former in blue, perforated, with a double transfer in the lettering of the lower label. It is not the clearest example of the Proprietary D. T. but it is all there. The 10 cent Certificate shows a scratch starting under the last "T" of "Certificate" and extending down across the border to the perforations.

Mr. Train has uncovered a 2 cent U. S. Int. with a scratch running from the "O" of "Two" across the margin and into the adjoining stamp on the left.

* * * * *

Mr. Henrie E. Buck sends us a perforated 5 cent Inland Exchange with a white dash or line over the top bar of the numeral "5", this occurs over each of the four numerals and he says it is constant on five copies that he has,—or rather had,—for he very kindly gave me one of them. Who has a duplicate either imperf. or perf.?

* * * * *

There is an interesting double transfer in the ⅝ cent block, 1914 issue, that we don't think we have mentioned. Practically the entire upper part of the stamp is doubled,—the border, the words "Proprietary", "United States", and the shift also shows in the numerals "⅝".

* * * * *

Mr. Eugene N. Costales shows us a perf., 3 cent Proprietary, 1st issue, with a horizontal stitch watermark,—not yet listed, but it will be.

MORE DATA ON THE 25 CENT ENTRY OF GOODS.

Mr. D. L. Ballentine writes that he has a copy of the 25 cent Entry of Goods with an outer line, this copy appears in a perforated block of four. He says,

"The two lines are very distinct but the extra line has every appearance of being inside the regular frame line,—this may not be so as my copy does not show the corners distinctly. However, I am rather convinced that the line is inside. I have had this block for many years and had made a notation calling attention to the double line. Never saw another copy."

* * * * *

Mr. Philip E. Hamilton writes his views regarding this item.

"I note by the last number of the Philatelist that collectors are requested to furnish whatever information they have as to the 25 cent Entry of Goods with double outer line at the top. I have the stamp in perforated form and have studied it carefully. I would like to examine the imperforated side by side with it for the reason that I believe it represents the sole double or possibly triple inverted transfer of a revenue stamp.

It is plainly not an example of recutting, neither is it a shift. The fact that it exists on the plate when used for imperforates proves that it existed at a very early state in the existence of the plate. My theory, which, of course, may be absolutely wrong, is that it happened when the original plate was being made, and the transfer roll was rolled in too low. When this was observed, probably before the next stamp was rolled in, the transfer roll was lifted and all parts of this relief removed with the exception of this line. The plate was then reversed and a new impression made. This would throw the unremoved line at the top of the new impression and the stamp as impressed would show two outer upper frame lines. This condition would naturally appear plainer on a worn copy of the stamp and a very late copy of this stamp might prove conclusively that it is in fact an inverted transfer.

In the copy I have, there is another interesting point which has led me to this conclusion,—in fact, it is what gave me the thought of an inverted transfer. A trifle over one-half millimetre from the outer right frame line at the top and running perpendicularly from the top label to the extra outer line, is a fine line. It has the appearance of an erased outer or inner line, or rather, the appearance of once being part of such. Then at an equal distance from the right lower rosette appears evidence of what I believe was a former entry of some kind, possibly the remains of an erased rosette, which if that be true, was originally an upper rosette. I believe this theory is more reasonable than to suppose the engraver deliberately engraved at this particular place two upper frame lines.

It is certainly interesting and reminds me of the triple inverted transfer of the 1 cent 1851. This may have happened the same way. I should think that the example imperforated of the strip of four might throw considerable light upon this question,—the question being, "Is the strip of four from the top row of the frame?" Of course, it might be from another row,—especially if it were examined side by side with a perforated copy.

Some of you may suggest that the outer frame line should have been erased or burnished out also and the only reasonable answer I could give to that would be that upon inverting the plate, the engraver would know that the new impression of the whole of the stamp would touch this line anyway and he simply did not bother to take it out. Maybe I am right, probably wrong. What do you think about it? Of course, it is a rare stamp and should be a valuable one. If it were not, many more copies would be known to be in existence. In all that I have examined, I have seen but one and that is the one in my possession."

* * * * *

We have now definitely located five copies of this 25 cent Entry of Goods with doubled top line. They are held by the following collectors:—Mr. Casper L. Dorer, Dr. Robert F. Chambers, Mr. Philip E. Hamilton, Mr. D. L. Ballentine and Mr. Beverly S. King. Has any other collector a copy? If you have, will you kindly advise the Unit? The stamp was illustrated in the January number.

This must not be confused with the 25 cent Entry of Goods with a top guide line. This guide line is very faint and extends continuously over the greater part of two stamps and the space between them. The double transfer,—or so we call it,—shows both lines of equal density and exactly the same length.

* * * * *

Mr. Dorer says:—

"Since last writing I have run across a beautiful pair of 50 cent Foreign Exchange, perforated, showing imprint and plate number on sheet margin at bottom. The peculiar feature is that the word "PLATE" shows one of the finest examples of double transfer I have ever seen. The "P" and "L" being set over toward the right a full sixteenth of an inch. In fact it is so plain that I completely overlooked it,—my wife being the one to discover it!"

What does this mean Mr. Dorer,—one of the fair sex a Revenue Collector? Good Work!

REVENUE NOTES.

A request has been made that we illustrate the 50 cent Mortgage with the diagonal crack,—and we take pleasure in doing so. This crack hits three stamps.

We also are illustrating the $3.00 Charter Party with a double transfer in the lower lettering, numerals, and outer line. It is the first re-entry that we have seen on this stamp, and incidently the writer discovered it.

32

LARGE PIECES.

Dr. Robert F. Chambers, the Chairman of our Revenue Unit, suggests that it will be interesting to list and locate the largest used blocks of the 1st and later issues of U. S. Revenues. Casper J. Dorer wrote to the Unit the other day that he has a block of six of the $10.00 Charter Party that he is rather proud of,— and we don't blame him. Don Bennett owns a strip of six of the $5.00 Conveyance.

Let us start with the 2 cent Proprietary and go right through the list. What have you?

Referring to our collection we find as a starter:

2 cent Proprietary, perf., block of forty-five.
3 cent Telegraph, part perf., block of eight.

Won't you write the Unit promptly as to what you have in blocks of four or larger in imperf., part perf. and perf.?

Let's carry it right up through the 1898-1922 issues. Some of the higher dollar values we may find in strips rather than blocks.

* * * * *

Mr. Dorer asks "to what extent do double transfers appear on the $1.50 Inland Exchange. The new Specialized Catalogue illustrates one variety, are there any more?"

We know of three. One in our collection shows a double transfer practically all over the stamp and yet neither the numerals "1" or "5" at the top are doubled as in the Specialized illustration. Our other copy seems to be doubled on both the right and left side, with an extra line at the top, and again does not check with the Specialized Cat. Who can give the Column some information on this point?

* * * * *

U. S. Postage Used for Revenue.

Mr. Dorer also lists under the above heading the:

1 cent 1861, dark blue on check.
3 cent 1861, rose on a check.
2 cent 1871, dark brown, no grill, on check.
2 cent Documentary, used as postage in 1898,—also the
2 cent surcharged I. R. used for postage in the same year.

Here, however, is the earliest one so far noted,—nothing less than a 5 cent 1847 on a note used and dated in 1866. This is the property of Mr. Howard H. Elliott our popular A. P. S. Treasurer.

Mr. Elliott also has in his collection a pair of the 1 cent 1867 with a 9x13 grill, used on a note in place of Revenue stamps.

* * * * *

SNUFF STAMPS.

Do any of you Revenue Collectors know anything about Snuff stamps? Mr. Case submits three examples. They are the size of our current postage stamps,— each one containing a head in an oval with numerals in the upper corners, and at the top, sides and bottom the wording "One Ounce", "U. S. Int. Rev.", "Series of 1875" and "Snuff". They are rather attractive stamps carefully engraved and printed and bear respectively the portraits of Washington, Dawes, and Madison. Mr. Case wants to know whether any interest is shown in these stamps. They were printed by the "Bureau of Engraving and Printing."

A New Idea For A Specialized Collection.

Mr. Robert F. Hale, of Malone, New York, has written as follows:

"In checking over a miscellaneous lot of Civil War Revenues which I have accumulated I note a considerable number bearing cancellations of Insurance Companies and Agents. I am wondering if any attempt has been made to form a complete collection of such cancellations?

It seems to me such a collection would be an interesting one to accumulate and perhaps rather unique. If anyone has worked up such a collection to the extent of forming a check list can you refer me to it?

I have never gone into Revenues except to build up my Revenue Section of the U. S. along with general issues. I have no idea as to the material available for a specialized collection of cancellations but believe I will attempt one."

We think that Mr. Hale's suggestion is an excellent one. We know that a number of our larger collectors have been quietly absorbing Revenue stamps with printed or hand-stamped cancellatons but here is still plenty of material for this sort of a collection. Have written Mr. Hale suggesting that he start such a collection of Insurance Company cancellations to get started with a check list. If any of you will help by looking through your stamps and seeing just what you can find the Revenue Unit will be glad to forward such information to Mr. Hale, and later publish the check list.

* * * * *

A number of examples of the 25 cent Certificates, showing guide lines, position dots, blurred printing and one with a slight transfer at the top have been sent to the Unit by Rev. E. Maclay Gearhart of Erie, Pennsylvania. There are a number of slight shifts on these Certificates, none of them however, are very marked.

* * * * *

Mr. J. S. Negley of Philadelphia, Pa., sent a mint copy of the 2 cent, third issue, on a very decidedly pink paper. Stirling listed this variety but Scott has never done so. The stamps of both the second and third issues appear on this pink stock as do the Match & Medicine stamps. As soon as the demand is strong enough Mr. Clark of the Scott Company tells me they will list these paper varieties.

* * * * *

During a discussion the other evening about Revenue stamps the question of No. 4126, 4⅜ cent black, perforated ten, came up. One Revenue Collector claimed that no such stamp has ever been issued and questioned the listing of it in the Standard Catalogue. None of the other men present had a copy of this stamp in his collection and we are wondering whether you can tell us something about it. Have you this stamp, either mint or cancelled, or have you ever seen it? Any information will be appreciated.

* * * * *

Our President, Mr. A. H. Wilhelm, writes us that at the Seebohm auction, held the latter part of March, the following Revenues sold for the prices noted. Mr. Wilhelm says, that, "The bidding was very spirited for these varieties and opened the eyes of those present."

2 cent Bank Check, blue, part perf. with the big shift in B label, very fine, very rare and not yet listed. (3804) ....$ 8.50
2 cent Bank Check, blue, perf. superb Horiz. Pair, L stamp with the big shift in B label, a very rare and interesting piece. (3804) 29.00
2 cent Proprietary, blue, perf. o. g. very fine with tremendous shift of entire stamp, the original impression being dropped fully 2mm and appears almost as a double impression. (3812) 37.00
50 cent blue, Entry of Goods, perfectly centered and remarkably fine on silk paper showing a big CRACKED PLATE variety at B extending into lower numerals. Very slightly thin but such should not affect the value of this rarity. (3854) 22.00
50 cent blue, Mortgage, part perf., superb with CRACKED PLATE as shown in cat. Type C58 not listed part perf. very rare. (3858) 29.00
50 cent Mortgage, blue, part perf. superb with CRACKED PLATE at T. This is the next stamp below the preceding lot and is a continuation of the crack. (3858) 53.00

* * * * *

Mr. Wm. M. Jayne of Southington, Conn., calls our attention to a copy of the 10 cent Inland with a faint outer line at the top. This stamp comes both with and without this line and sometimes half a line only will show. Who can tell us what this is, and why?

* * * * *

We crib from Mekeels the note that Mr. J. W. Wilson has recently inspected five sheets of the 1 cent carmine-rose, overprinted "Cigtte. Tubes," in which one stamp on each sheet in the same positio nis without the period. We do not recall this variety having been noted heretofore.

Revenue Notes.

Mr. Harry M. Konwiser tells us of a new find that has just come to light, nothing less than a pair of the $10.00 Probate of Will, imperforated, with fine margins on three sides. The Specialized lists a pair of these at $700.00. This figure was reached after a careful analysis of all obtainable information as to the number of known pairs of this stamp.

* * * * *

Mr. John D. Campbell, Jr., of Cadiz, Ohio, sends two copies of the $1.00 Passage Ticket, perforated, on a very thin hard paper, and a nice "peeled ink" example of the 40 cent Inland Exchange. These "lifted" or "peeled ink" stamps should not be mistaken for shifts. They are caused by the ink of the freshly printed stamps coming in contact with another sheet, and many examples can be found among both Revenues and Postage.

Mr. William O. Case presented us recently with a beautiful example of the 6 cent red orange of the present Postage issue, showing "white" or "inkless" spots all over the stamp. They are interesting to collect but are not double transfers or re-entries.

An interesting copy of the 50 cent Mortgage has been sent in by Mr. J. H. Train of Detroit, Michigan, showing a scratch running from the ornament opposite the "S" of "CENTS" out across the border line and evidently into the adjoining stamp. He also sent a copy of the 2 cent Liberty Head, fifth issue with a scratch starting at the lips of Liberty and running directly across the stamp and border line. This may also show on an adjoining stamp. Keep your eyes open for it.

* * * * *

We might just as well make up our minds that our old friend the 25 cent Entry of Goods will continue to keep bobbing up like a ghost in the dark until we definitely decide just what it is and nail it down for good and all.

Mr. Henry C. Hitt, of Bremerton, Washington, comes to bat with the terse statement that, "Your correspondents do not seem to get together on the Entry of Goods, for no one could call your illustration an extra line inside the normal line."

Mr. Hitt, in our humble opinion, is quite right, the error is the outer top line and not the inner one as suggested by Mr. Hamilton in the May number.

Mr. W. E. Booker, one of the earlier members of the A. P. S., sends us a description of the 25 cent Entry of Goods that he has in his collection. He says, "It is a perforated copy and nicely cancelled with a circular hand stamped cancellation, in blue. The two dots above the outer line show very plainly but the corners do not show distinctly as I judge they do in Mr. Ballentine's copy from his description in the May number."

Mr. C. W. Bedford makes the following pertinent and logical comments regarding this stamp:

"The stamp in question is not from the top row. I have a vertical pair the lower one of which shows this outer line at the top. The little line mentioned by Mr. Hamilton is also in the normal stamp in this pair and is not a part of this shift or error. I have three copies in my collection. Two singles and one in a pair, as above."

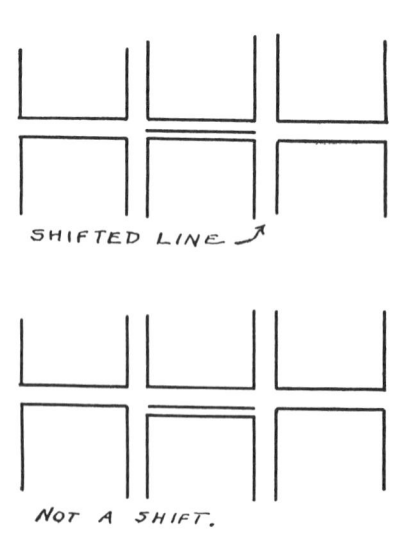

The inner line is a normal distance from the top line on all three. The side lines only go up to this line. The outer line therefore should be this error. The lines do not touch at the corners. The outer line goes right over to the right hand line. I think I have seen a horizontal pair in Mr. Dorer's collection. We should have the horizontal spacings, perhaps both top and bottom, before an absolute decision can be reached on this stamp. A block may be discovered and if this shows the outer line above the frame lines of the adjoining stamps on either side it is a shift. If on the other hand, this outer line is parallel horizontally with the frame lines of the stamps on either side and the lower frame line of this stamp as below the frame lines of the stamps on either side it means that this die was rocked in too low and an extra line was added at the top to bring back the alignment. (See illustration.) A vertical pair with this error in the upper stamp would be a valuable find, as in this way we would get the space between the upper and lower stamp.

In connection with the comment that Mr. Philip Hamilton makes regarding the lower right rosette of this stamp, I will say that the lower right rosette of all of the 25 cent Revenues is always different than the other three rosettes. This is an interesting discussion and I hope can be carried to a point so that we may determine whether this is a shift."

There, gentlemen of the Revenue Unit, you now have all the information at hand. Who can produce a block showing the spacing of this stamp? Just as soon as we have this information we feel that we can lay the ghost and place it in its proper niche in the Specialized Catalogue.

* * * * *

In one of our last numbers we mentioned that Mr. Train had discovered several 5 cent Inland Exchange stamps with a dash over the "5" which he tells us occurs on several copies which he has. He sent these on for inspection and we find that these white lines occur over each of the four fives in three copies of the stamps which he sent and also occurs on the copy which he sent some little time ago with his compliments.

Just what causes this we do not know. It does not look like an ordinary lifted ink copy as seen on some stamps.

Mention was also made of a 50 cent Mortgage with a diagonal scratch starting at the "R" in the lower label. Mr. Train has discovered the lower stamps of this sheet which shows the continuation of this line into the border and label.

He also sent 2 copies of the 50 cent Conveyance showing eight or ten light scratches in various parts of the stamp. These scratches are quite short and even. The plate was evidently not handled with a great deal of care. We have seen other copies of this 50 cent Mortgage with similar scratches.

* * * * *

There seem to be any number of light scratches and plate flaws on many of our early Revenues, lots of them too minor to note. One of the favored seems to be the 50 cent Mortgage.

Mr. W. Y. Fillebrown showed us four, one of them, however, being the lower stamp of the "vertical crack," another the middle stamp of the "diagonal crack," the third the diagonal line through "R" in lower label and margin, the one described by Mr. Train in the April "A. P." The fourth, however, is a new one to us, this shows a double line in the upper right hand corner running from the "N" of "CENTS" upward and out over the margin. These lines should show on the adjoining stamp.

Mr. Philip E. Hamilton, who has been studying the first issue dollar values, will be interested in four $1.00 Foreign Exchange that Mr. Fillebrown sent in. The first shows a broken and re-cut left corner line, the second another example of re-cutting in the same corner but the lines are continuous, though "bent." A third has a strong double outer frame line to the left from top to bottom. Dr. Robert F. Chambers, our Chairman, has this variety in his collection. The fourth $1.00 Foreign has a light diagonal scratch—not a crack—about ane and one-half inches long, starting at "U" at the left, across and out through the numeral "1" at the right. This should show on the adjoining stamp.

The Revenue Stamps of the State of South Carolina

By FRANK L. APPLEGATE.

While South Carolina was the latest state to issue documentary stamps for general use she was only preceded by one state, Iowa, in the use of excise stamps. The act providing for both became the law on May 1, 1923. Stocks and bonds were to be taxed at five cents on each $100 of face value, stock transfers and promissory notes two cents on each $100, conveyances fifty cents on each $500, proxies ten cents and powers of attorney twenty-five.

The stamps which were ready on the day the law went into effect were lithographed 17x24½ mm. exclusive of the imprint of the American Bank Note Co. below each stamp. Inscriptions are SOUTH CAROLINA at top and DOCUMENTARY at extreme bottom; state seal in circle in centre surrounded by engine work; small numeral each side.

South Carolina Documentary, First Issue, May 1, 1923, Perf. 12.

2, 4, 5, 8, 10, 25, 50 cents blue green
$1, 2, 5, 10, 30 dark brown

The sheets are of 25 subjects (5x5) with perforated margin clear around. The numerals were soon found to be too small to give sufficient distinction to the different denominations printed as they were in so limited a color scheme and it was not long before complaints were made on this score and new dies ordered to be prepared, and stamps from the new dies began to appear early in 1924. In the new die the various inscriptions are rearranged so as to allow the lower third of the stamp for the value. The engine turned background has been replaced by simpler ornamentation. The denominations and colors are the same as in the first issue except that in the dollar values the brown has more red in its composition. Soon after the change the $30 denomination was discontinued and a one hundred dollar stamp introduced, as under the amended act of 1924 most of the documentary taxes were doubled. The one cent stamp was not added to the set until 1928.

Documentary, Second Issue, 1924-8.

1, 2, 4, 5, 8, 10, 25, 50 cent, blue green.
$1, 2, 5, 10, 30, 100, chocolate.

I believe that the sheets at first were as in the first issue but they soon began to appear with imperforate margins, that is imperforate on the top, bottom and right sides of the sheet, the left margin being perforated by which the sheets are bound into books.

Used these stamps are none too common and some of them particularly the two thirty dollar stamps will be quite scarce. Used documentaries generally show a pen and ink cancellation, but are also seen cut.

About the middle of 1924 a small order was placed with the Security Bank Note Co. of Philadelphia. Stamp emanating from this firm bear their imprint on each side and are engraved. The design is very similar to the American print but the perforating is not so good.

Documentary, Security Bank Note Issue.

2c, 4c, 10c green.
$1 dark yellowish brown.

We have only the statement of the Tax Commission that the 4c stamp was included in the set. I have never been able to find one.

So much for the documentaries. The EXCISE stamps are called "Business License" stamps in South Carolina and are used to pay taxes on cigarettes, cigars, tobacco, candy and ammunition. The law of 1923 was quite complicated, and the stamps issued to comply with its provisions comprise a most interesting series of thirty denominations, many of which are unique among stamp issues. They are the product of the American Co., are lithographed and bear their imprint on each stamp as in the documentaries. They come in sheets of one hundred, not 64 as would have seemed logical, and as has been stated, ten rows of ten with perforated margin clear around. Furthermore they are almost all well centered showing what careful and experienced stamp producers can do. In the middle of each side of the sheet printed in the margin is a large numeral corresponding to the denomination, the top of the numeral being always toward the stamps, hence inverted at the top of the sheet.

Inscription at top, STATE OF SOUTH CAROLINA, around central circle bearing numeral BUSINESS LICENSE TAX. Palmetto tress on either side.

Business License Tax, First Issue, May 1, 1923, 35x21 mm., Perf. 12.

21/64, 24/64, 27/64, 30/64, ½, 36/64, 39/64, 42/64, 48/64, 54/64 and 60/64 cent all in olive gray.
1⅛, 1 1/5, 1 7/32, 1½, 2 2/5 and 12½ cent all in violet.
1, 2, 3, 4, 5, 6, 7, 8, 10, 15, 20, 25 and 30 cent, all in rose.

The values specified in the schedule for cigarettes were 1c, 1 1/5c, 2c and 2 2/5c. The rate on tobacco was six cents per lb., hence 6/16, ⅜, or 24/64c per oz., 21/64c for ⅞ oz., 1 7/32c for 3¼ oz. etc. Each one-eighth ounce required an additional 3/64c of tax. The tax on ammunition was fixed at 25c for each 1000 rounds of cartridges or shells and candy selling for 80 cents per pound or more was taxed at ten per cent. Most of the high values were used on candy or cigars. The tax on "little cigars" was one half cent on a package of ten and the half cent stamp which seems to have had no other use is quite scarce.

Exactly one year after these stamps were placed in use the law was amended and simplified although the taxes were raised. The new ratings made the fractional denominations entirely unnecessary and holders were allowed to trade them in for stamps of even value. After the bulk of them had been redeemed they were turned over to the State Bank Examiner who seems to be ex-officio auditor in South Carolina. In recent correspondence with this official he disclaims any knowledge of these stamps so their ultimate fate is shrouded in mystery. Whether they have been destroyed or not I have been unable to ascertain. If the known copies of certain of these fractionals are all that are to be left for collectors they will be good stuff. Other values which have had more general distribution and were not always turned in are more common.

There seems to have been but one printing of this entire series which in some denominations was sufficient to last several years. At the present writing the 6, 7, 8 and 30c stamps are still in use although all other values have been replaced by another issue.

In the meantime new 1 cent, 2 cent and 5 cent stamps were ordered from the Security Bank Note Co., along with the documentaries already referred to. These stamps are of the same size as the first issue by the American Co., but are engraved and come in sheets of 25 as do all subsequent issues. This issue was limited and is rather scarce.

Business License, Security Bank Note Issue.

    1c green
    2c violet
    5c scarlet

The second American issue began to replace the long stamps about this time and new values were added as the first issue ran out. A 40c denomination was added in 1926, but was soon discontinued.

One palmetto tree now grows in the centre of each stamp, flanked by numerals on each side.

Business License, Second American Issue, 1924-8, 26x19½ mm., Perf. 12.

    1c blue green
    2c violet
    3c dark brown
    4c orange
    5c rose
    10c olive gray
    15c brown red (1928)
    20c apple green
    25c blue
    40c blue

As in the case of the documentaries these stamps come in sheets of 25 imperforate top, bottom and right, with perf. margin on the left by which they are bound into books of 250 stamps.

The coil stamps were first issued in 1927 to supplement the regular issue. They are similar to the sheet stamps but smaller. The coils contain 500 stamps.

Coil Stamps, 22x19½ mm., Perf. 12 Horizontally.

    1c blue green
    2c violet
    3c dark brown
    10c olive gray

Strip stamps were also introduced about this time for tobacco and cigars in large containers. These have one palmetto tree in oval near the left end with numeral in fancy tablet at either end of inscriptions in centre of stamp; background of engine work. These are perforated horizontally also and come in sheets of 12 only imperf. at bottom. The 50 and 54 cents were issued in 1927, the 48 cent in 1928.

85x14½ mm., Perf. 12 Horizontally.

    48c turquoise blue
    50c brown red
    54c pale brown

Originally all business license stamps were required to be cancelled with pen and ink, or with rubber stamp, but cancellation is now no longer required.

The tax on soft drinks and syrups was instituted only last year. The general arrangement of the design of these stamp is more conventional than that of the business license stamps although the palmetto tree is retained as the central feature.

Soft Drinks License Tax, 1928, 22x28½ mm., Perf. 12. Litho. by American Bank Note Co.

1, 2, 3, 4, and 5c rose lilac.

In minute letters in the lower border are the letters, C. S. of S. C. Your guess is as good as mine; better I hope.

Stamps are also used on concentrated flavors and syrups in large containers. The rate is 76 cents per gallon, and stamps have been issued for containers of ¼, ½, 1, 2, 5 and 10 gal. capacity, but unfortunately the monetary denomination does not appear on these stamps.

Stamps now current may be purchased unused from the License Tax Division, South Carolina Tax Commission.

This state also issues inspection stamps for use on commercial stock feed for which there are various issues running back to 1910, and also has issued similar stamps for use on illuminatitng oil. I refrain from listing these in this article however as I fear I have taken up too much space already.

In future articles I hope to present recent revenue issues of other of our states.

Once More the 25th Entry.

Mr. Chas. S. Thompson writes that he has just found a very fine and perfect copy of the 25 cent Entry of Goods in an old collection. This one is on the very thick porous SILK paper of the 1870 printing, and is cancelled with a bank stamp "N(ov) / 20 / 1871" and seven "V" cuts which barely break the paper.

He says, "I have examined this copy most carefully for indications of a double or triple transfer, using a high-power microscope objective, but I fail to find the slightest trace of this.

Below you will find a diagram of the top lines of this stamp, of which there are THREE, not two, as generally stated. The very light line at the top is the line which was ruled on the plate for the guidance of the operator who rocked in the impression. This is evidence because it extends clear across to the perforations and shows a position dot.

The second line is the extra line of the various descriptions. On the left it does not extend quite to the end of the top frame-line, but on the right it extends to a point almost exactly over the right vertical frame-line. The top frame-line proper does not quite meet the right vertical line.

The varying thickness of frame lines on this and other 25 cent Revenues, as well as the 30 cent ones, leads us to believe that all of these lines were more or less touched up by the engravers, and that this extra top line may be the result of a trifling piece of carelessness on the part of a retoucher.

At any rate, here is the drawing, and the above explanation is as good as any of them, while the stamp under discussion, being on silk paper, is probably better! Distance between extra line and top frame line is exactly 1/10 mm. or 1/250 of an inch."

* * * * *

Mr. Frank G. Mallette of Leon, Iowa, has sent in a pair of 25 cent Entry of Goods the left hand one of which shows the outer line at the top. The interesting thing about this pair is that the outer line is parallel with the frame line at the adjoining stamp which would tend to prove Mr. Bedford's theory that this particular stamp had been rocked in too low and the line then added at the top to bring the stamp in alignment with the others.

Since writing the above we have received an imperforated block of this stamp from the collection of the Rev. E. C. Reeve. The lower left hand specimen being our old friend with the outer line. This line is parallel with the adjoining stamp on the right, and the distance between the outer line and the stamp above is exactly the same as the space between the adjoining normal stamps. This proves Mr. Bedfords theory that the stamp was rocked in too low and the outer line added later. We sent this block to Mr. Bedford for examination and he writes us as follows:

"Dear Mr. King:

"Did not realize I was "talking for publication" until the July A. P. and this letter of yours both arrived tonight.

Comments.

The extra outside line at the top corresponds to the lower diagram as shown in the American Philatelist for July. Also the bottom of the stamp extends below the lower line at the next adjacent stamp to the right. The only logical explanation is a misplaced entry, the item being too low in alignment in the horizontal row. Instead of resorting to a re-entry the engraver corrected the optical misalignment by adding an extra line. This left the stamp too low at the bottom but the human eye pays more attention to the upper half of objects, printed letters and stamps in judging alignment and the resulting effect on the eye was satisfactory. We should now look for a vertical pair with this stamp the upper stamp and a narrow spacing between it and the stamp below.

Very truly yours,
C. W. BEDFORD."

This seems to finally dispose of the 25 cent Entry of Goods and we think you will agree with us that it has been an interesting study.

* * * * *

Mr. Bedford also sent us a $1.00 Foreign Exchange showing an extra line recut at left (line split at top). The shift also shows slightly at the lower left corner. It also shows an extra frame line at the left, running from top to bottom similar to the extra top line of the 25 cent Entry of Goods. Mr. Bedford says, "It looks like extra lines to correct errors were used at least twice." (This is a duplicate of the copy Mr. Fillebrown sent us and noted in the July issue.—BSK.).

The $5.00 Probate.

Mr. A. H. Schumacher, of Houston, Texas, sent an interesting copy of the $5.00 Probate of Will. The greater part of the stamp has a series of diagonal smudge lines. It would seem as though the entire stamp had been deliberately rubbed immediately after printing and before the ink was thoroughly dry.

* * * * *

Here is an Amusing One.

Mr. Howard H. Elliott writes that he has just come into possession of a cover mailed from Sublett's Tavern, Va. to Petersburg, Va., June 29, 1870, bearing a 2 cent U. S. I. R. in combination with a 1 cent 1869, and not marked "DUE."

More Sheet Margins.

Mr. R. A. Kremers of Milwaukee, Wis., sent us copies of the 30 cent Inland and $1.00 Foreign Exchange with sheet margin. These should be added to the present list of sheet margins, first issue Revenues.

* * * * *

A New Re-cut.

Mr. Philip E. Hamilton writes as follows:

"In the May number you published certain information regarding varieties and re-cuts existing on the $1.00, 1st issue U. S. Revenue stamp that I had sent you. I realize that some of these varieties are hard to find even when ones attention is directed to the place on the stamp where the re-cut line or slip of the engraver shows, and in my former letter I called your attention to what I consider one of the real rare "slip of the engraver" under paragraph "Fifth." That occurred in the $1.00 Conveyance. I am now sending you an even rarer "slip," as manifested in a $1.00 Foreign Exchange, and I venture to state that not many of this example will be found. This "slip" is plainly visible to the naked eye, and I therefore thought you would possibly be interested in illustrating it for the benefit of the Revenue Unit Column. I personally consider it the rarest "Slip" I have ever seen, and when one considers that great care was taken by the engravers in the higher value Revenues, and that far fewer were printed from these plates than from the plates of the lower values of the regular postage stamps, one can readily appreciate the rarity of this $1.00 Foreign Exchange.

(There were 20,000 of these printed, 200 on a sheet and were first issued in 1862. Assuming that this "re-cut slip" happened during 1869,—see cancellation date,—the changes are that it occurred on not more than about 1/10 of the total number of sheets issued which will give us a total of 200 copies. The question is, how many of these were saved or are in existence today?—BSK.).

I consider it the perfect copy, and in order that you may compare it side by side with another copy not showing the slip, I am sending both to you for your examination.

Now, if you will place these stamps one on top of the other so that you may have under observation at the same time the upper two left hearts and corners you will see a most interesting case of engravers slip and re-cut combined,—on one of the stamps, not the other. An attempt was made to re-cut the outer frame line of the heart to the left side of same. Just why this was attempted is not clear to me unless this is a very late state of the plate (cancelled May 18, 1869), and at the time of the attempted re-cutting the outer frame line was broken or indistinct. However that may be, the attempt was evidently made to re-cut this particular line and in making that attempt the tool slipped and cut inside said frame line and down and across the same into the ornament below. Then, notwithstanding said slip, the engraver must have tried to trace it over again, for if you will look closely you will see another line extending above the top of the outer frame line and joining the latter, but not quite at the same place as the first slip. Then to make things more of a mess than it was, we see a diagonal line cut and almost but not quite touching the outer frame line of the stamp and running therefrom to the outer frame line of the hear,—a most remarkable example of a re-cut line or rather a bad slip in attempting to re-cut,—and so plainly visible that none ought to have any difficulty in locating it if another copy is existant. This cannot possibly be a shift. At first glance it looks as if the left side of the double frame lines of the heart had been deliberately sheared off, but that is not the case. Some of the lines at certain places on the enclosed stamps are slightly shifted, but nothing out of the ordinary has struck me except this "slip." (See illustration.

* * * * *

25 Cent Certificates.

Mr. E. F. Milliken came in to see me the other day with some ten or twelve interesting minor re-entries in the first issue Revenues. Among them were the 25 cent Certificate with a double line extending nearly all the way across the bottom of the stamp. These 25 cent Certificates come with many varieties of these minor transfers at both top and bottom frame lines, none of them however, are very pronounced.

* * * * *

We have received from Mr. Bedford two copies of the 2 cent U. S. Internal Revenue with some very curious plate marks. One of them is a diagonal line across the lower left hand corner and the other shows two strong irregular lines running almost from top to botto mof stamp right through the face of Washington. This should show on adjoining stamps and we should know more about it before making a guess as to whether it is a crack or a scratch.

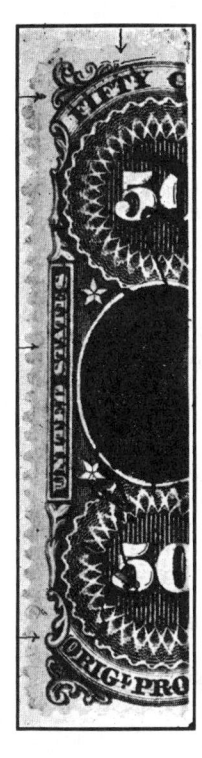

Mr. G. P. Kirshner and Mrs. C. W. Bedford have both sent us copies of an unusual re-entry in the 50 cent Original Process, which is illustrated herewith. The shift is to the top and left and shows in various parts of the stamp, most noticeable in the side panel containing the words "UNITED STATES" where there is a doubling of the letters and a strong shifted frame line. It also shows in the two numerals and rather faintly at the top border line. Illustrated herewith.

* * * * *

Mr. G. A. Doyle of Bridgeport, Conn. has discovered among some old papers a number of checks giving examples of postage stamps used as Revenues. There are several copies of the 3 cent '61 issue, a couple of 2 cent black jacks and one check bears a copy of the 30 cent orange '61 issued by "Rawson & Whipple" at the "Shetucket Bank of Norwich, Conn." on date of "May 29, 1863" and pen-cancelled "R&W" the same date. Why this 30 cent stamp was used is beyond us as the amount called for was only about $400.00.

Mr. Leon G. Young of Portsmouth, N. H. has in his collection a 2 cent 1869 Postage used as a Revenue on a promissory note.

Mr. Allen P. Vestal has sent on an envelope with a 2 cent, red, Documentary stamp in the corner used as a Postage stamp. This eminated from the town of Camargot, Ill. and is postmarked Jan. 26, 1924. It is addressed to a Mr. H. A. Stout of Indianapolis. Mr. Vestal said that there were three of these that came in to his hands all of which bore the same post mark. With this Mr. Vestal sent another envelope addressed to the same person a month later with exactly the same cancellation as that on the Revenue stamp envelope.

Gilbert M. Burr of Meshoppen, Pa. and Mr. Charles W. McLellan of Champlain, New York have both sent in copies of the $1.00 Entry of Goods showing a crack or scratch. This starts above the "O" of "DOLLAR" at the top of the stamp and runs diagonally down to the right crossing of "R" of "REVENUE." It is illustrated herewith.

Mr. Burr also sent six copies of Snuff stamps which are different than those noted by Mr. Case. They are all on blue paper and run from 1, 1¼, 1¾, and 2½ ozs. each. The higher values of course being considerably larger in size. Four of them bear the bust of Seward while the other two have a picture of a tobacco plant in bloom. They were all printed by the Bureau of Engraving & Printing and are interesting specimens.

45

Mr. Don R. Bennett has discovered a copy of the $3.00 Charter Party with the re-entry in the lower part of the stamp as illustrated in the June number. We are wondering whether any of the rest of you have found this item. Mr. Bennett also sent a list of "Postage used as Revenues" which he has in his collection:

    3 cent green on check, dated Oct. 16, 1874.
    2 cent brown on check, dated June 8, 1876.
    3 copies of the 10 cent Trans-Miss. used on a certificate of Deposit, hand stamped "The Citizens Savings Bank, Detroit, Mich." and with the letters "I. R." in red ink by pen.

* * * * *

Every once in a while an old legal document is unearthed which contains a lot of interesting stamps. The last one we have heard of was a parchment title transfer to a mine. It carried twenty fine singles and pairs of the $20.00 Probate of Will, perforated, a number of $20.00 imperforated Conveyances and one $10.00 perforated Conveyance.

It would seem too bad to break up a paper of this sort and yet it is so valuable as it now stamps,—cataloging some $800.00,—that not many of our Revenue collectors can afford to purchase it and keep it intact for his collection.

* * * * *

Mr. O. W. Mott of Jackson, Michigan has sent a number of interesting items although nothing that is new to the Unit. He sends some stamps with a fold in the paper and others with extra perforations. Among the lot were several particularly clear an dperfectly centered copies of the U. S. Internal Revenues showing the double top frame line and the double lower frame line. He also has a nice copy of the 5 cent Inland Exchange with the big shift in the lower lettering.

* * * * *

We can report one more stitch watermark item, namely:—The $2.00 Mortgage on old paper with a horizontal watermark showing about two-thirds of the way up the stamp.

* * * * *

Mr. C. W. Polk has sent us a single and a block of four of No. 4133, the ¼ cent Proprietary in black, showing a double print. This has not yet been listed in the Specialized.

* * * * *

We had the pleasure of attending the recent A. P. S. Convention at Minneapolis and thoroughly enjoyed both the sessions and the stamp show. Mr. W. L. L. Peltz of Albany joined us in New York and we went together. "Bill" Peltz, as you may recall, is the Revenue Collector who has been studying Railroad Cancellations, and he has a most comprehensive collection. We stopped off in Detroit and had a nice visit with Unit member D. L. Ballentine. Unfortunately Don Bennett and J. H. Train of Detroit were out of town so we missed seeing them.

On Tuesday afternoon at Minneapolis we had an informal meeting of the Revenue Unit, with fourteen present. There was a general discussion of Revenue activities. We agreed on the advisability of "showing" Narcotics or other "Tax Paids" at any exhibition until a ruling could be secured from the Federal Government similar to their recent decision relative to Playing Card stamps.

The question was raised as to the possibility of securing an additional copy of "Revenue Unit" notes for Unit members who might want them for reference purposes. Mr. Mosler, our new A. P. S. President, promised his co-operation together with that of Mr. Fennel, to give us any and all possible help in every way.

The exhibition was extremely well handled and presented. We had hoped for more entries of Revenue stamps, but those that were shown created a great deal of interest.

Mr. Philip Little, Jr., had the most representative exhibit, showing four frames and three albums of U. S. Revenues with a special section of double transfers and oddities. He has plated several of the lower values, locating a number of shifts.

Mr. Frank Applegate showed several frames of State Revenues, as well as a most comprehensive collection of Canadian Revenues. These are surely beautiful stamps.

Mrs. Wittmer exhibited two frames of U. S. Revenues in singles, strips, and blocks, and a very interesting lot they were.

Another exhibitor showed two frames and two albums of 20th Century U. S. Revenues practically complete and in beautiful condition together with an interesting collection of U. S. Playing Card stamps.

The next A. P. S. Convention and Stamp Show will be held in Boston and we already have the promise of Revenue entries from a number of our members who have never "showed" before. Please be rady to do your part.

* * * * *

We can report one more stitch watermark. The $2.00 Conveyance showing a horizontal stitch on thick paper.

An interesting plate flaw has come to light on the $2.00 Mortgage, first issue. This consists of a blur in the lower left hand corner, circular in shape and about ⅜" in diameter. We had four copies of this stamp sent to us recently, each one showing this peculiar flaw. The four copies check in every detail. It is therefore a plate flaw and not a blurred print.

* * * * *

Mr. Kirshner has sent several examples of the double transfer on the 2 cent U. S. Internal where the top balls and frame lines are slightly doubled. He has also sent in one of the clearest examples we have seen of the 25 cent Certificate with a double transfer, showing particularly in the lower frame lines. This copy is also a part perforated item which adds to its interest.

* * * * *

Mr. Casper J. Dorer has called our attention to an interesting double transfer on the 3 cent Proprietary. This occurs in the upper part of the stamp and shows particularly in the foliated ornaments. This is a shift that possibly most of us are familiar with, but I am mentioning it as a matter of record.

* * * * *

Mr. J. H. Train has sent in for inspection a good copy of the 25 cent Entry of Goods with the double line at the top. In addition, a copy of a part perforated 50 cent Mortgage with a plate flaw or scratch running from the "S" of "CENTS" out to the right over the frame and through the border line.

He also sent an interesting copy of the 5 cent Inland Exchange with a faint diagonal scratch starting from the "U" of "REVENUE" and running down through the stamp about to the "H" of "EXCHANGE."

The finest double transfer we have yet seen of the 5 cent Certificate has been sent to us by Mr. C. B. Dorland. The transfer is unusually strong and clear and shows throughout the stamp,—being particularly strong on the left side and top. The lines of the ribbons enclosing "FIVE" are all doubled, and the letter show a slight shift. At the top of the outer lines and balls are doubled as well as the lettering.

The numerals and medallion are clear and bright indicating that the engraver in erasing and re-entering took particular care with the central portion of the engraving but was not so fussy about the borders.

The transfer also shows slightly in the word "CERTIFICATE." The stamp is evenly centered and in mint condition.

Revenue Notes.

This "stamp game" every once in a while tends to become a bit too serious, we find ourselves discussing unimportant items most ponderously, and then unfortunately some one hands us a little jolt or a joke which makes us pause and regain our sense of humor,—and humility.

One of the writer's correspondents is a charming old Southern gentleman from Birmingham, Alabama. I feel that it would be a joy to know and talk to him, altho I have never seen him, and I am afraid never shall, for my paths seldom lead to the great Southland and I fear that New York is too much of a jump for this young Southern collector of eighty summers.

Friends and members of the Revenue Unit, may I present Judge A. H. Benners of Alabama.

The last letter that I received from him reached me a week ago,—here it is:

"Dear Mr. King:

Excuse my writing with pencil, my typewriter is out of order, and my writing with pen may become illegible,—I am 80 years old.

Revenues are with me a side line, my specialty is "Fun with stamps." I am just a philatelic Merry Andrew, but I will be glad to send any Revenue "finds"—bisects, inverts or others to you.

I enclose one of my nonsense stamps, of which I have hundreds, but this being a Revenue stamp postally used. If you care for it for your own collection, it is yours.

I keep up a vigorous exchange of fun with stampic items with Ellis Parker Butler,—the "Pigs is Pigs" man,—and have an amusing skit of his with half a dozen illustrations, anent the recent stamp washing exposure. I think it is as good as "Pigs is Pigs", and if you have time to enjoy a laugh I will send it to you, as well as some more of my own stamp nonsense.

Yours sincerely,
(Signed) Alfred H. Benners."

With this letter the Judge sent us a cover addressed to "The Butler Citizen, "News a Day Ahead", Butler, Pa.",—with a return, in the upper corner, to F. M. Baker, Butler, Pa.,—it bears a 2 cent red Documentary used as a Postage stamp. This cover had been sent to Ellis Parker Butler by the Judge, and on a slip attached to the envelope he had written:—

"The Baker's "News a Day Ahead",
Pay me cash—or you get no bread.
And he used a stamp that's Documentary
To spread the tidings elementary.
A. H. B."

Mr. Butler returned the envelope to Judge Benners and on another slip also attached to the cover he had noted:—

"That's me! "Butler, Pa." (or Papa) E. P. B."

Needless to say this cover is now in the writer's collection, just as received, with both the Judge's and Butler's notes attached to it.

This is one of the many laughs that our Southern friend has given us. We may let you in on some more of them. It will take your mind off elusive shifts and whatnot and perhaps help to save your eyesight.

As Senator Thomas H. Pratt of Tennessee wrote us:—

"I spend a whole day and about ruined my eyesight looking for shifts on the 2 cent U. S. I. R. the other day. Only found one in the lower label and I will ask you to send me on some to look at some day to see what they look like."

There you are Tom! Follow the Judge and save your eyes!

The One Dollar Foreign Exchange

By THOMAS H. PRATT.

One of the most interesting revenue stamps in regard to minor varieties is the one dollar Foreign Exchange. Although many of the other dollar values were recut it seems that this particular stamp received far more than its share. This, of course, was due to faulty transferring and we find many subjects on this plate short transferred, re-entered and others so out of alignment that an additional line was engraved beside the subject to give the plate the appearance of a better job.

No attempt has been made to study this stamp by photography—the only proper way to study recuttings, as they stand out much plainer in a photograph—but it seems that almost fifty per cent. of the subjects on the plate were recut and that there are several errors of recutting in which the tool slipped one way or the other, causing distinct minor varieties.

Four examples of recuttings are illustrated herewith and although many of the stamps have had both shields at the top as well as other parts of the design worked upon after they were "laid down" on the plate, these examples will make it clear to the student that this stamp has been sadly overlooked, while other stamps with no greater claim to fame have been exploited.

A.—Shows a slip in the recutting so that the frame line at the upper left almost touches the shield, the outer line of which has also been recut part of the way down.

B.—In recutting the left line of the left upper shield the tool slipped outwards and a line leads down from the upper left corner of the shield into the frame. Another example of a similar slip in recutting was illustrated in the American Philatelist some issues ago. This leads upward to the frame line.

C.—The upper right shield and frame line opposite it were short tranferred and were not recut but the stamp design was entered too far to the right and an additional line was laid down close to the design at the right to equalize the subject on the plate—an old trick of the trade with engravers, of which we have numerous examples in our United States stamps.

D.—Also "laid down" too far to the right and demanding an extra frame line at the left to "save face". Probably a different subject than "C", as the frame line at the right runs to the top of the stamp, although the outer frame of the upper right shield is weak and has not been recut. The position dots being slightly different on this subject tend to show that there are at least two positions with the added line at left.

* * * * *

The Fifty Cent Original Process.

We recently published a cut of the 50 cent Original Process showing a shift in the left hand label. Our old friend Don Bennett immediately went on a still hunt and discovered that he had two copies of it, one in a block of four, which he sent on for inspection, and another in a block of sixteen. Has anyone else uncovered this item?

* * * * *

Mr. L. S. Slevin of Carmel, California writes that he has a $5.00 Probate of Will and a $10.00 Charter Party, both of which were pen cancelled by his grandfather, James Slevin. He asks "Have many collectors any of these old revenue stamps cancelled by their ancestors?" We have several in our personal collections, and of course finding them in this way makes the stamps doubly interesting.

* * * * *

Mr. Philip H. Ward, Jr. sent us two copies of the 50 cent Passage Ticket showing a short crack or scratch over the "Y" of "FIFTY" in the upper border of the stamp. These two copies show that it was constant on the plate. This line should carry on upward into the stamp above.

* * * * *

The Fifty Cent Documentary.

Mr. Philip Little, Jr. sends us a 2 cent Bank Check with a vertical scratch almost from the top to bottom of stamp. He also submits a beautiful imperforated pair of the 50 cent Documentary Battleship of the 1898 issue. This is not listed and so far as we know is the only pair known. One imperforated sheet was found in St. Paul and used locally. This pair seems to have been the only one rescued. Has anyone a record of another?

* * * * *

Mr. Philip Ward, Jr. tells us of a find on the West coast of a horizontal strip of twelve of the 30 cent Foreign Exchange, imperforated.

Mr. Harry Konwiser writes us about a block of ten of the $1.00 Mortgage, imperforated, that has just been unearthed from among some old papers.

* * * * *

Mr. R. P. Sherman sent an interesting copy of the 5 cent Express which shows a slight doubling of the lettering in the lower label. Also sent two nice copies of the 50 cent Conveyance showing two of the well known plate scratches, one at the top and the other at the bottom. He also submitted two copies of the 25 cent Power of Attorney which show a slight doubling of the bottom line and lettering.

* * * * *

The Battle of Fallen Timbers.

Judge Benners looked over the recent Wayne stamps with a high power glass and wrote as follows:

> "The Indian bears the pipe of peace,
> But Anthony's fixed to kill!
> The other gent has brought a mop,
> For the blood that Anthony'll spill!"

To which Ellis Parker Butler replied:

> "Did Anthony do the Indian dirt?
> Over his arm is that Lo's shirt?"

Mr. B. A. Ashcraft writes:

"Relative to oddities among the Revenue issues of the United States I have a piece of wrapper that may be of interest to the Revenue Unit. A copy of the two cent surcharged narcotic that was used with regular postage stamps on a parcel post package.

If I have my data correct, a tax was required during that period on all parcel post packages of a certain value or on which the postage amounted to so much and this tax was to be paid by the use of the then current documentary stamp. The package in question was shipped by a wholesale druggist in New York State and the shipping clerk used the surcharged stamp in paying the tax. Whether intentionally or otherwise, I cannot say.

I also have a copy of the same issue Documentary surcharged in which the design (not the surcharge) shows a decided shift or possibly a double printing."

* * * *

Mr. C. C. Damon has favored us with the following,—the most interesting being a good clear copy of the 10 cent Contract, perforated, which shows a double transfer in the word "CONTRACT" and a doubling of the ribbon lines and lettering at both sides of the stamps.

A $1.00 Power of Attorney with the upper left corner re-cut at the side of the shield.

Also a 50 cent Surety Bond that may be a double entry but it looks to us more like a shifted print.

* * * * *

Mr. E. V. Pollack of Attumwa, Iowa, has sent an interesting copy of the $2.00 Mortgage with a diagonal scratch in the upper part of the stamp starting at the "D" of "UNITED" and running diagonally down to the "ST" of "STATES" for about ¼".

Mr. Pollack suggests that this may have been caused by the engraver's tool slipping in re-cutting. We are rather inclined to believe that it is a plate scratch although it is very distinct.

* * * * *

Mr. Casper J. Dorer has sent us a 50 cent Passage Ticket, part perforated, showing a blurred spot in the lower right corner, similar to the one noted on the $2.00 Mortgage described in the October number, though not quite as marked.

Another interesting item is a pair of the $1.00 Power of Attorney, each one showing a doubling at the left of the upper frame line, and in the word "DOLLAR" and lower outer line.

He also sends a strip of three $1.00 Power of Attorney with what at first glance looks like a doubling of the lower left shields, and lines at corner as well as the ornamental lines under "P" of "POWER." We think, however, that these are evidences of re-cutting.

Mr. Dorer sends us a copy of the $1.00 Conveyance with the right frame line doubled. This may be a similar proposition to the outer top line Entry of Goods. The line being put in to help "shape up" the plate.

Mr. Dorer also sends an interesting copy of the $1.00 Inland with the upper shields doubled and extending above the frame line. (Illustrated at left).

This is very similar, and may be a duplicate of one found by Philip Hamilton last year.

* * * * *

Mr. L. J. Flerlage has sent copies of the following stitch watermarks:

    50 cent Entry of Goods, perf.
    50 cent Conveyance, imperf.

He also submitted a reconstructed vertical pair of the 50 cent Conveyance showing a scratch on the plate running from the letter "N" of "CONVEYANCE" through the border and into the next stamp down to the right on an angle.

Another copy of the 50 cent Conveyance has a small scratch or mark through the last "C" of "CONVEYANCE."

* * * *

PLATING THE FIVE CENT INLAND EXCHANGE.

Mr. C. W. Bedford, one of our Unit members, has started plating the five cent Inland Exchange. It is a work of some importance and one that we all should help with. What he is striving to do is to locate on the plate the various double transfers and plate flaws, and we believe that they can be done within the year 1930 providing the Revenue Unit as a whole takes up the work rather than one individual.

Here is the manner in which it can be done:

1.—Will each member of the Unit send to Mr. Bedford all of his pairs, strips, and blocks, also any singles with margins or marginal data attached.
2.—Stamps not needed for re-plating will be promptly returned. Stamps retained will be mounted on small cards slightly larger than the stamps, with the owners name and address on the back and a reference number. Every item will be registered in a record book and a receipt given to the owner.
3.—All items will be returned before or during December 1930, or sooner at the request of the owner.
4.—Will all of our members who have any singles, pairs or blocks in accordance with the above kindly send these at once to Mr. C. W. Bedford, 319 Vaniman Street, Akron, Ohio.

This is an important work and we want each and everyone of our Revenue Unit members or any other Revenue collectors who have such data to help Mr. Bedford in this work.

Will you kindly take action on this at once.

The 10 Cent Contract.

There are three interesting double transfers on this stamp, the most important we mentioned a short time ago is herewith illustrated. (See Fig. 1.) This shows a complete doubling of the lower part and both sides of the stamp.

Fig. 1.

The second is a doubling of the upper frame line, ornament, and ball at the top right.

The third is a similar doubling at the upper left corner of the stamp.

Dr. Robert F. Chambers has called our attention to the second transfer and Mr. G. F. Kirshner to the third. The first shift is very clear and you have no need to use a glass to discover it.

A Shift on the $10.00 Conveyance.

Mr. Kirshner has evidently been using his glass to some advantage. He has found a slight shift on the right hand side of the 50 cent Surety in the word "INT." Also a very interesting and clear shift on the $10.00 Conveyance. This occurs in the words "INTER. REVENUE" above the medalion, also in the periods and white dots, and in "U. S." The engine turning background shows clearly at three points in the white border around the stamp, inside of the outer line. This is the first time that either Dr. Chambers or I have seen this shift although possibly some of the rest of you know of it.

* * * * *

The 5 Cent Certificate.

Mr. Howard H. Elliott has submitted an interesting double transfer on the 5 cent Certificate that does not seem to be generally known. This shows decidedly in the last three letters of the word "REVENUE," the top frame line, and in the word "CENTS."

Both Dr. Chambers and the writer have copies of this stamp in their collections. There are, of course, many transfers on this particular stamp but we do not think this one has been spoken of before.

Mr. Elliott also advises us that he has discovered that he has a copy of the 50 cent Original Process with the double transfer at the left and also has an uncancelled copy of the 50 cent Mortgage showing the crack as illustrated in the Specialized Catalogue.

* * * * *

Dr. E. M. Gearhart has also sent an interesting transfer on the 5 cent Certificate showing a doubling of the panel lines on both sides of the stamp as well as a slight doubling of the foliated ornament on the right. The shift also shows in the word "CERTIFICATE" at the bottom of the stamp.

The Two Cent U. S. Internal Revenue

By J. H. TRAIN.

About a year ago Mr. King suggested in one of his articles that the 2 cent Bank Check and U. S. Internal Revenue offered a profitable field for study for some one of the Revenue Unit members.

Since that time at odd moments I have been studying these two stamps with a view to finding as many double transfers and plate flaws as possible. I have made no attempt to plate these stamps so cannot as yet give any definite locations as to where these oddities occur on the plate. This article covers the U. S. I. R.

I have examined some 7,000 stamps and have found about 20 major or minor shifts, and plate flaws and scratches without end. It would look as though the plate from which this stamp was printed had been pretty badly handled, for a great many specimens show light or heavy scratches in various sections. Some of the stamps for instance show no scratches in their early printings and the exact same stamp, which I can spot from double transfer lines, show decided scratches or rust marks in later years. The use, of course, is checked by the dates of cancellation.

Some of the stamps that I have found show what is without question in my mind indications of plate cracks, although the number of these in comparison with the scratches are very small.

The best known major shift in the Bank Check is, of course, the downward shift in the lower label. This was illustrated in the American Philatelist sometime ago together with the well known shift to the left on the U. S. I. R.

The majority of the double transfers that I found occur in the top and bottom frame lines, in the ribbons enclosing the letters "TWO" and in both the upper and lower panel lettering.

Mr. King has prepared some drawings showing the most interesting of these double transfers which I will list as follows:

T-14 and T-14-a as illustrated in the Specialized Catalogue were found. T-14 has a double to the left in a direct horizontal line. T-14-a is a straight upward shift.

T-14-b (illustrated) is a combination of T-14 and T-14-a but the D. T. instead of being to the left or straight up is toward the N. W. corner and shows clearly in all parts of the stamp. (Two found.)

T-14-c (illustrated) has a south west shift, and shows in the left side and left lower corner and inscription. (Six found.)

T-14-d (illustrated) is an upward shift, differing from T14-a inasmuch that it shows in only the four letters of "U. S. INTER" and the pto line and balls, and is very clear on the left side ribbon and "TWO" as well as the lower balls. (Six found.)

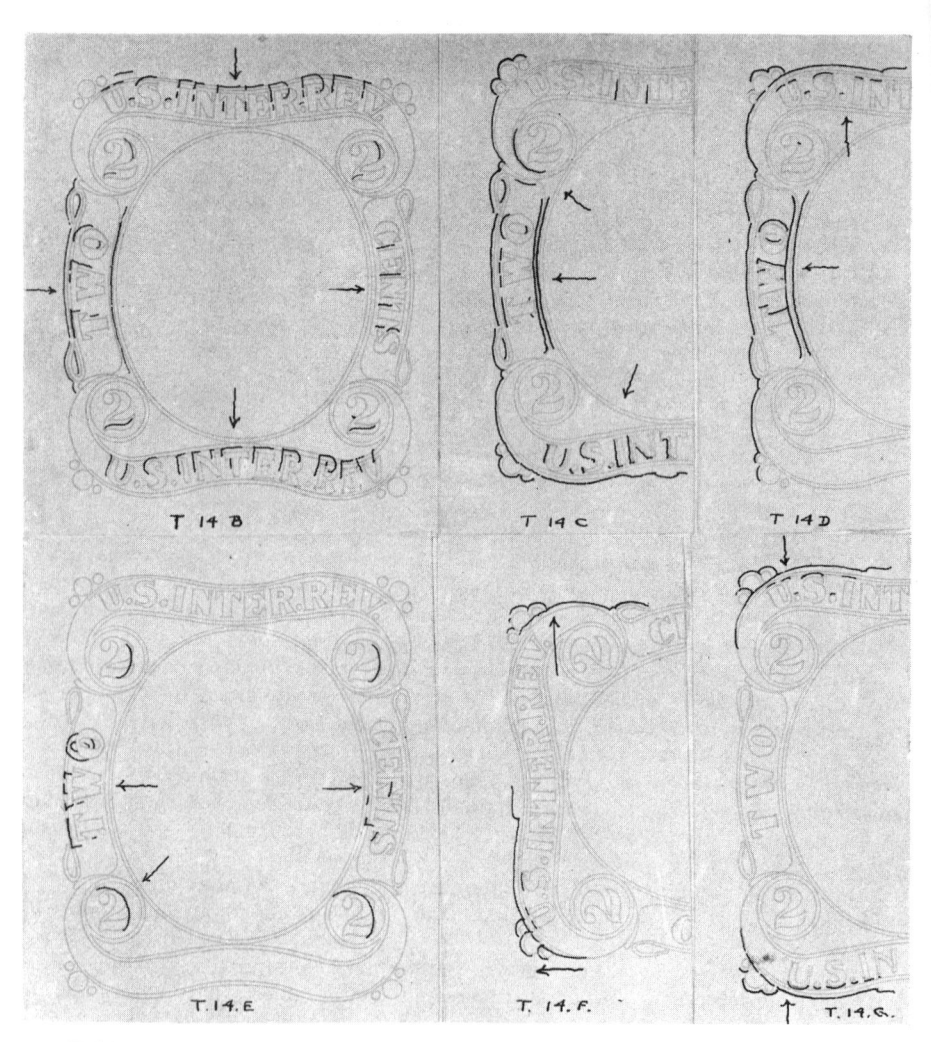

T-14-e (illustrated) is a S. W. shift showing slightly in the four numerals, in "TWO" and "CENTS" but not in the outer ribbons and balls at all. (Four found.)

T-14-f (illustrated) looks like a triple transfer. The shift shows both in the outer upper and lower border lines and balls at the left.

T-14-g (illustrated) might be termed a twisted transfer, the doubling is all outside of the frame lines and shows at the upper top left, top right, right bottom and bottom left.

Many minor varieties of this last noted D. T. were discovered. Sometimes the doubling shows in one corner only and in other specimens in two corners. (Fifty found.)

T-14-h Doublin of ribbon lines around "TWO." (Twenty found.)

There are numerous other minor varieties of several of the above noted shifts. These are I think due largely to the printing and show indistinctly on blurred and poorly wiped plate impressions.

58

There very likely are others that I have not happened to run across in my search and I would be interested in hearing from other members of the Unit who may have them in their collections.

* * * * *

The 5 Cent Inland Exchange.

Mr. Clayton W. Bedford, who is plating the 5 cent Inland Exchange, has discovered an interesting plate crack which is illustrated herewith.

He is getting along nicely with his task, but needs all the help that we can give him. The following letter was sent to the members of the Revenue Unit a few weeks ago:

"Dear Mr. Revenue Collector:—

The Revenue Unit of the American Philatelic Society are cooperating in an endeavor to replate the 5 cent Inland Exchange of the Civil War revenues, as announced in the American Philatelist on February 1, 1930.

The two plates from which this stamp was printed contain many shifts or double transfers and at least one major plate crack. It is desirable to know the plate positions and of some of the scarcer plate varieties.

Rather than wait over a period of many years for one collector to obtain this information, we have proposed cooperative action of all revenue collectors, irrespective of Society affiliation.

We have already received sixteen lots of Blocks, Strips and Pairs, including blocks of 30, 20, 15, 12, etc. With your cooperation we should be able to complete this work within the calendar year.

The Akron collectors have arranged an accurate registration and identification system and a fireproof safe for protection. Stamps not plateable will be returned at once with a receipt for those retained. All stamps received as a loan will be returned in December 1930, or at the request of the owner.

We know you will wish to assist in this work and you can do so by **sending in all blocks, strips or pairs and such singles as have margins attached.** Once every two or three months you will receive a circular letter telling of the progress of the work and in the end you will receive your stamps with an enhanced value attached to them.

Cordially yours,

C. W. BEDFORD."

If you can help us with this work will you kindly so so?

A 5 Cent Inland Shift

Mr. Howard Elliott has found a particularly fine double transfer on the 5 Cent Inland. It is illustrated herewith. Mr. Elliott's copy is one of a pair. It is so clear that a glass is quite unnecessary. We sent it down to Mr. Bedford, who is plating this stamp and he finds that it checks with a copy he has found. Not yet located on the plate, but it will be. The D. T. occurs in the entire upper part of the stamp in both lettering and numerals. It is a thing of beauty,—to those of us who like shifts.

* * * * *

An Interesting Catalogue.

Mr. Heyliger de Windt has sent us a very interesting old catalogue of "POSTAGE, AMERICAN & FOREIGN, AND U. S. REVENUE STAMPS" published by Sever & Francis at Cambridge, Mass., in 1863. It gives a partial list of our Revenue Stamps issued up to 1863. It omits many, such as the 6 Cent Proprietary, the $200 U. S. I. R., the 10 Cent Proprietary, etc. Curiously enough it has the $50 U. S. I. R. listed as a "Conveyance" stamps.

There is one note in the catalogue that is rather interesting. It is as follows:

"New Internal Revenue Stamps will be issued in place of those now in use. They will have a border around the vignette, on which will be printed, at the top, figures representing three or four years, as '63, '64, '65, and on the sides and bottom, the names of the months and figures for the days from 1 to 30. The method of cancellation will be to cut out with a knife, before affixing the stamp, the whole border, except the letters and figures representing the date required. This will render the second use of a stamp impossible. Stamps of a similar character have been suggested for postage."

The 4 Cent Proprietary.

Dr. Robert Chambers has uncovered several interesting shifts on the 4 Cent Proprietary,—one shows a doubling on the right side frame lines and at the top in "U. S." lines and corner balls; the second is a beautiful double of the upper part, lines and lettering; another has a decided shift to the right at the top; the fourth copy looks very much like a triple transfer, the upper part is strongly shifted, with a doub'e both upward and to the right in the right hand upper corner. A fifth copy has a strongly marked diagonal scratch at the right, through the "E" of "Cents " Mr. Phillip Little, Jr., tells me that there are some twenty-eight shifts on this stamp.

Another interesting item is a 1 Cent Telegraph with what looks like a marked shift in the lower left corner, in the numeral lines and "TEL" of "Telegraph." We want to see another copy of this before we pass final judgment.

Dr. Chambers also sends us three copies of the 2 Cent Express with a strongly marked irregular vertical line outside the left frame line. We have known of this stamp for some time and it looks somewhat like a cracked plate variety, tho we are inclined to think the stamp is from the outside left row and that the irregular line at the left is continuous up and down the sheet. Who knows?

* * * * *

Mr. W. W. Bradbury, of Santa Barbara, California, has favored the Unit with several interesting items,—a number of stamps showing the imprint of Butler and Carpenter and Joseph R. Carpenter,—several double perf varieties and a number of double transfers. He has several of the well known shifts on the 2 Cent Proprietary, 2 Cent Internal and 5 Cent Certificate, and about eight varieties of the double transfer on the 5 Cent Inland Exchange, the best example being the shift to the left which shows practically all over the stamp. This latter checks with a mint copy owned by your Secretary. He also has discovered that he has the centre stamp showing the diagonal crack on the 50 Cent Mortgage Mr. Bradbury, in joining the Revenue Unit, writes—"I am very much interested in Revenue Stamps and the many thousand copies that I have had for nearly forty years are unpicked. I shall be glad to study them as I have been saving them for my old age and hope to get a great deal of pleasure with them." It looks to us as though Mr. Bradbury was in for a real treat.

* * * * *

A New Stitch Watermark.

Dr. Homer Collins, of Duluth, Minnesota, advises us that he has discovered a copy of the 25 Cent Power of Attorney, perforated, with a stitch watermark. This is a new one to add to our list. We already have this noted in an imperforated item, but not as Dr. Collins has found it.

United States Revenue Society

H. S. ACKERMAN, Treasurer.

This might be called the swan song of the United States Revenue Society. For some years this Society has ceased to actively function. It accomplished much in its active years, and its handbooks and special articles are still standard.

It is my purpose at this time to give an accounting to its former members as to the cash balance left in my hands as treasurer. Your hold-over board have given earnest consideration to the question and have unanimously decided to pay the balance on hand over to the American Philatelic Society Revenue Unit as a fund to publish a handbook on revenues, such as the matter being published by that Unit in the American Philatelist. A free copy to go to the members of the Unit.

There was one unsettled claim on the Insurance Fund and that now has been finally adjusted. The balance of about $170.00 will be turned over the Unit as directed by the Board.

My suggestion to all revenue collectors is to join that Unit, the real successor of this Society. It is under the able management of Mr. Beverly S. King.

Our fellow member, Clayton W. Bedford, who is plating the 5 cent Inland Exchange stamps, is getting along famously with his work. He writes me as follows:

"There are two scratches and one plate flaw that are constant on Plate 5 F, which have been of great help in replating. From now on I will be able to give a collector plate positions on most of his stamps from the later plates, even though I return the stamps at once. I hope that some of our members may have some additional multiple copies or single copies showing the margin or imprint, that they will be willing to send on to me for inspection. I will be glad to return them promptly, if they so desire."

We would request that any of our members who have interesting copies of this 5 cent Inland Exchange send them on to Mr. Bedford, to help him in this good work. His address is 319 Vaniman St., Akron, Ohio.

Mr. George F. Kirschner has sent us about a dozen different Revenue stamps for inspection. Many of them are of varieties that you are familiar with. One is the 5 cent Inland Exchange with a clear doubling of the word "FIVE" and the ribbon lines at the left.

Another is the 25 cent Certificate, imperforated, with a twisted transfer, that is, the left line is doubled at the top, the top line is doubled at the right, the right at the bottom and the bottom line on the left side. This is an unusually clear copy of this stamp.

A minor shift on the $3.00 Charter Party is also worthy of note. This shows a slight upward double transfer in "THREE" and "CHARTER."

The most interesting one of the lot is a $1.00 Life Insurance showing an extra line on the right. We understand that these long stamps were "rolled in" on the plate sideways, which would account for many of the irregular extra lines at the sides.

We have received several inquiries about an apparent doubling of the word "FIVE" on the 5 cent Foreign Exchange. This is not a double transfer and it is constant on all of the Foreign Exchange stamps that we have seen.

Mr. Kirschner has also kindly submitted to the Unit an interesting copy of the 3 cent Bank Check, which shows a double transfer in the word "CENTS" and also in the word "CHECK" at the bottom of the stamp.

He has also sent us two copies of the 5 cent Inland Exchange, one showing some curious lines at the lower left and the other one of the well known shifts. I have asked him to forward these on to Mr. Bedford.

* * * * *

TWO MORE STITCH WATERMARKS.

Unit member Edwin Milliken, who is whiling away his time in Paris, writes me that he has acquired a stitch watermark on No. 3910, same being the 15 cent Blue and Black of the second issue. He says that it is a horizontal stitch and is quite clear. One of the first reported for this issue.

Mr. Don R. Bennett, one of our members from Detroit, has found a stitch watermark on the 10 cent Power of Attorney. This has not been listed before.

* * * * *

Mr. W. W. Bradbury, of Santa Barbara, California, one of the Revenue Unit's new members, has submitted a number of stamps showing constant plate flaws. Mr. Bradbury has discovered a copy of our old friend, the 25 cent Entry of Goods, with a double line at the top, but his copy happens to be on silk paper, the first one being reported in this way.

Mr. Victor Weiskopf has shown me a copy of the $1.00 Life Insurance on particularly thin paper. It is almost like light cardboard, and was cancelled July 3, 1869.

We have received from Mr. C. F. Hawley a mint strip of four of No. 3814, the 2 Cent U. S. I. R. One of the stamps shows a broad irregular line close to and cutting into the "S" in "CENTS." It was Mr. Hawley's thought that this might be a defect in the plate or an ink run. It looks to us more like some foreign substance on the plate during the printing.

Insurance Cancellations Found on United States Revenues of 1862-71

ROBERT F. HALE.

The following cancellations are those of Fire Insurance Companies only. No life or casualty companies are included, unless the particular company wrote fire or casualty business together. In some cases I have been able to identify the name of the company from the cancellation, as for instance, the "S. Ins. Co." The list is complete to March 3rd, 1930.

The following is far from complete and any further additions, or corrections, will be gladly accepted.

Company	Color	Type	Remarks
Adriatic Fire, N. Y.	black	circle	reported
Aetna, Hartford, Conn.	none	none	on policy
Aetna, N. Y.	black	oval	
Agricultural, Watertown, N. Y.	black	circle	on policy
Albany, Albany, N. Y.	blue	circle 2	on policy
Albany City, Albany	blue	oval 2	on policy
Albany City, Albany	black	circle 2	
American, N. Y.	black	circle 2	
A. M. Ins. Co.	blue	circle	
Buffalo-German, Buffalo, N. Y.	pen	——	on policy
Citizens, N. Y.	black	circle 2	
Commercial, Chicago	blue	oval 2	
China Mutual, Boston	black	oval	
Commerce, Albany	black	circle 2	
Continental, N. Y.	blue	circle 2.	
Croton, N. Y.	black	rectangle	
Dividend Mutual, Glens Falls, N. Y.	pen	——	on policy
Empire City Fire, New York	black	circle	
F. & T. Ins. Co.	green	circle	
Franklin County Mutual, Malone, N. Y.	pen	——	on policy
Globe Cire	?	?	reported
Great Western, N. Y.	black	circle	
Hampden, Springfield, Mass.	black	oval	
Home	?	?	reported

63

Indianapolis Fire, Indianapolis, Ind.	blue	oval 2	
Jersey City Fire, Jersey City	blue	oval 2	
	black	circle 2	
Lenox, N. Y.	blue	circle	
Liverpool & London Fire & Life	black	3 line	
Lorillard, N. Y.	black	rectangle	also agt. on policy
Manhattan, N. Y.	black	circle	may be life ins.
Market, N. Y.	black	circle 2	
Manufacturers, Boston	blue	circle 2	
	black	circle 2	
Merchants, N. Y.	none	———	on policy
Merchants Mutual, New York	?	?	reported
Miami Valley, Cincinnati	blue	oval 2	
	black	oval 2	
Montauk, N. Y.	black	circle	
Niagara, N. Y.	none	none	on policy
North British and Mercantile, Edinburgh...	black	oval 2	
New York Fire, N. Y.	black	circle	
New York Mutual, N. Y.	black	circle	
Queens, N. Y.	blue	oval 2	
Peoples Fire, Worcester, Mass.	pen	———	on policy
P. F. Ins. Co.	black	circle	Possibly Penn Fire
Phenix, Brooklyn	black	circle 2	
Phenix, Brooklyn	blue	oval 2	
Phoenix, Hartford	blue	circle 2	
Republic, New York	blue	circle	
S. Ins. Co.	blue	circle	
S. & L. D. Fire & Marine, Boston, Mass.	blue	oval 2	
	black	oval 2	
Union Mutual	black	oval 2	New York?
Vermont Mutual, Montpelier, Vt.	black	circle	
Washington, Boston, Mass.	black	circle 2	possibly a life Co.
Western Massachusetts Mutual, Pittsfield...	pen	———	on policy
American, Baltimore	pen	———	on policy
Providence Washington, Providence, R. I....	pen	———	on policy
Orient Mutual	black	circle	
Minn. Farmers Mutual	blue	oval 2	

Those companies listed as having a pen cancellation, or none, are for stamps on original policies only, as I expect that most of the companies employed rubber stamps for cancelling at some time and these should show up.

The figure 2 following the type of cancellation denotes a 2 line circle, or oval, enclosing the name of the company. Otherwise the cancellation is understood to have been one line surrounding it.

Many of the above cancellations appear on various values and varieties of the revenues of the civil war period. These are not listed here, as such a listing would be cumbersome, and ungainly to handle. I am very anxious to obtain, at at least list, cancellations on every stamp possible in this issue and will greatly appreciate receipt of specimens for purchase, or inspection, either off or on original policies.

(Mr. Hale's address is—Malone, N. Y.)

The Battleship Revenues

There are some interesting and very beautiful shifts to be found among the Battleship Revenue stamps of the 1898 series. Dr. E. Maclay Gearhart, one of our Unit members, has sent a nice one, on the 25 Cent Documentary, which may be new to you. The doubling occurs in connection with the lower and left outer frame lines,—also shows in the numerals at the top and in the letters, the circular vignette line and in other parts of the stamp (illustrated). The frame of this

series was designed by R. Ostrander Smith, formerly of the Bureau of Engraving and Printing. When the World War came along and private proprietary stamps were issued, this same frame was used in printing the stamps for several different companies.

Dr. Gearhart sends one of the ⅝ cent Red, Johnson & Johnson, which shows a double transfer to the left. This may be found in the lettering at the top and bottom of the inner line of the circular panel at the right, and the outer frame line at the upper left.

Dr. Gearhart also sends two minor transfers on Proprietary stamps issued by J. Elwood Lee Company. On a ⅛ cent blue the lower frame line is doubled to the right and on a 5 cent Brown the left frame line is doubled toward the bottom.

He has also discovered an interesting shift in the 2 Cent Liberty Head in the 1875 issue. This, though faint, is one of the best shifts that we have seen. The lower frame line is doubled and the vertical lines of shading in the ribbon on either side of the "2" and above and below the panelling containing the words TWO CENTS.

* * * * *

Mr. Robert F. Hale, of Malone, New York, has sent us an interesting copy of the $3.00 Manifest, showing two strong diagonal lines, each one about ½ inch long in the lower part of the stamp. These run over the margin and should show in the stamp below. Have any of you a duplicate? It is hard to tell whether these are scratches or cracks. We are anxious to see another copy.

* * * * *

Mr. Clayton W. Bedford was in New York the first week of June and spent an evening with the writer, showing him the results to date of his plating of the 5 Cent Inland Exchange. He has one plate practically complete, lacking but very few locations. It was particularly interesting going over his work. On Wednesday evening, June 4th, Mr. Bedford attended a meeting of the Collectors Club in New York and favored the members with a general talk on the subject of plating, showing them the result of his work. It is needless to say that his talk was very much appreciated.

A Two Cent Proprietary Double.

Dr. Robert F. Chambers, Chairman of the Revenue Unit, has uncovered a most interesting variety of the 2 Cent Proprietary, first issue. The entire stamp is either shifted all over to the left or else it is a peach of a double print. The only way, of course, to be sure, is to see another copy. We thought that we had a very wonderful upward double transfer of the 25 Cent Insurance last year,—another copy turned up which seemed to be an absolute duplicate of it, but by very careful examination of enlarged photographs under a glass a few points did not check and the stamp turned out to be a double or shifted print rather than a double transfer. Of course it makes almost equally as interesting a specimen but the double prints are not constant on the plate. It is the first time that we have seen the 2 Cent Proprietary in this condition and will be very much interested in hearing from any of the Unit members who may have a copy of it. The shift is to the left, as we said before, and shows practically all over the stamp, both in the lettering, numerals and ornamentation.

Dr. Chambers also sends for checking a copy of the 50 Cent Conveyance, with a diagonal scratch to the right in the lower part, thru the "E" of "CONVEYANCE." Mr. Sherman and Mr. Little both have copies of this specimen in their collections.

Dr. Chambers also sends a 2 Cent Bank Check, Orange,—2 Cent Proprietary and a 2 Cent Bank Check, Blue,—all three stamps showing strongly marked scratches. We think the plates of these stamps will turn out to have just as many scratches as were discovered by Mr. Train in his study of the 2 Cent U. S. I. R.

* * * * *

Double Perforations.

These double perforation stamps seem to be "coming back" into popular favor. We know of several collections now being formed. They used to be quite popular and commanded a premium over catalogue.

In a recent number of Mekeel's Mr. Poole commented on them as follows:

"These double perforations should be worthy of as much consideration as a double grill, for in one case the stamps were run through the grilling machine twice, and in the second case run through the perforating machine in a similar manner."

Our advice would be to save any that you may come across.

The $1.00 Mortgage.

Mr. G. Van de Kieft, of New York City, has sent us a very interesting copy of the $1.00 Mortgage, unperforated, showing a nice double transfer. This occurs

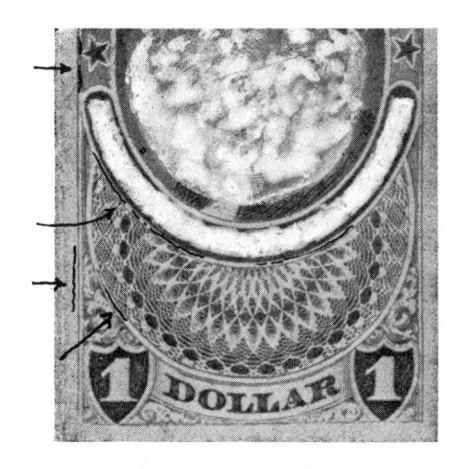

under a panel containing the word MORTGAGE where a second line shows broken in spots. It is very clear and does not require a glass to be seen. (Illustrated.)

* * * * *

Our old friend, Judge A. H. Benners, has sent us an original document bearing three copies of the 50 Cent Entry of Goods, plus a 5 Cent Certificate.

On one of the 50 Cent stamps something has happened to George Washington's right eye. Whether it is a constant plate flaw or simply some foreign substance on the plate we cannot tell, but in any event the eyeball is partially missing, making the Father of his country appear as though he was winking at you.

* * * * *

Our note regarding Mr. C. F. Hawley's strip of four of No. 3814, Two Cent U. S. I. R. one of the stamps of which showed a broad irregular line close to and cutting into the "S" of "CENTS", calls forth a comment from member Casper J. Dorer, who says that he has two copies of this stamp and that there is no question in his mind but what it is a damaged plate variety. His two copies came from different sources and were used a year apart almost to the day,—one in 1870 and the other in 1871. This is just the information that we were looking for and definitely places this particular copy.

* * * * *

Mr. Dorer also mentions the $1.00 Life Insurance sent us by Mr. Victor Weiskopf on particularly thick paper, being almost like cardboard, (this was printed "thin" instead of "thick" due to a typographical error.) Mr. Dorer says that he has several of the 2 Cent U. S. I. R. on particularly heavy paper, similar to very light cardboard. We know of a number of other varieties that come on this type of paper.

Revenue Bisects

The rates on photographs during our early Revenue period seem to have varied somewhat. On the backs of many old daguerreotypes and photos we find two one cent and a single two cent and on others a three cent Proprietary. On a few we may be fortunate enough to discover a two cent stamp together with half of another, making up a three cent rate. Proprietary stamps were supposed to be used on photographs up to April 1864. After that date any Revenue stamp was permissible.

Just a word about the original plates from which these stamps were printed. They measured 12½"x16" and plate numbers are found only at the bottom of the sheet below the imprint. Prior to April 30, 1864, and in all cases where the same plates were used subsequently as well as prior to that date, each title was given a distinctive control or index letter. This letter immediately follows the plate number itself and the number is invariably the same as the face value of the stamp. The control letter "A" was used for the Proprietary stamps.

Subsequent to April 30, 1864, after which date all titles or specific designations were abolished, and with the exception of the Proprietary stamps, all were lumped under the heading of "General Stamps,"—this system seems to have been allowed to fall into disuse and on the new plates transferred after that date no regular system seems to have been followed regarding these control letters. This is well illustrated in the Five Cent Proprietary which was first issued August 18, 1864. The only plate number known on this stamp is "5-O" the "O" being the Playing Card letter.

The One Cent Proprietary plate is also found with a second number which is immediately to the right of the control letter, and as ten plates are known to have been used for this value it is probable that this number refers to the number of the plate in the series. Curiously enough the Four Cent Proprietary is the only other plate known to bear this extra number and in this instance the order is reversed and this number is at the extreme left,—reading "1 Plate No. 4A." The number used on the plate of the Three Cent Proprietary was "3-A" and this stamp we usually find on the backs of photographs,—we can find no record as to the amount or amounts of the tax imposed. A letter dated September 8, 1864, from Commissioner J. J. Lewis to Butler & Carpenter, is rather interesting. It is as follows:

"* * * A desire has been expressed for some larger denomination of Proprietary stamp, to be used on photographs. I wish, therefore, to have a plate prepared for fifty cent Proprietary stamps, and would enquire whether one of the plates for general fifty cent stamps could not be so changed as to answer the purpose? If not, it will be necessary that a new plate should be engraved, but will be pleased first to hear from you."

Next, under date of September 22, 1864, is the following from E. A. Rollins, Commissioner, to Butler & Carpenter:

"* * * You need not do anything about the preparation of a plate for a 50c Proprietary stamp at present."

This is succeeded by the following, dated September 27, and addressed to J. J. Lewis, by Butler & Carpenter:

"Your favor of the 22nd inst. relinquishes your intention to have a fifty cent Proprietary—lest delay should occur when you needed it, we have engraved this plate; and it will be ready to print in a few days. Shall we print- and, if so how many sheets."

We have no record of any proofs from this plate. The stamp, of course, was never issued and the plate was evidently destroyed. Why this high tax?

All of which has nothing to do with Revenue Bisects, but is noted simply as a matter of interest, particularly the story of the fifty cent Proprietary. Regarding Bisects I have been fortunate in finding a number of them. Stamps used on the backs of photographs were usually pre-cancelled with pen marks or initials and are, therefore, seldom tied to the photograph. This makes it a very eask matter to "fake" such items and it behooves one running across such a find to make certain notes on the photograph, certifying its authenticity.

One of these Bisects was recently sent in by Mr. H. O. Roberts. He favored us with two photographs, one of which carried a three cent Proprietary on the back and the other a two cent Bank Check plus half of another, making the three cent rate. The letter came from the photographic establishment of Hatch & Rawson, of Main St., Milford, Mass. In my collection I find a similar photograph from the same concern, carrying a three cent Proprietary. Both the latter stamp and the two on Mr. Robert's photograph are pen cancelled in exactly the same way, with a capital letter "H". I have also a photograph from the establishment of E. L. Willis, from the same address in Milford, Mass., evidently the successor to Hatch & Rawson. The photograph from Willis' shop carries a pair of Bank Check stamps, one of them being bisected, again making the three cent rate. These two stamps are both cancelled by pen "E. L. W."

I have been talking to Mr. Hugh Clark for some time past about Revenue "bisects" and can now report that for the first time since the issuance of the Specialized Cataloge these stamps will be listed this year. It may pay you to look thru your old family album and old checks,—you may discover something interesting.

* * * * *

J.R.L
J.C.M
C. W.
Aug. 15
1864.

Mr. A. C. Bates of Chicago has been making a study of printed cancellations on our early Revenue stamps. He recently picked up in Chicago a copy of the $1.00 Passage Ticket No. 3873-C, bearing the initials J. R. L., J. C. M., C. W., with the date August 15, 1864.

Mr. Bates is interested in learning where this cancellation was used and just what the initials mean, as well as any other known dates of its use on the same or other stamps.

We are illustrating the cancellation herewith and if any of our members can answer Mr. Bates in any way, we would be very glad to hear from them.

PROPRIETARY SHIFTS.

While on the subject of Proprietary Stamps we might review them from the Double Transfer angle.

The two cent stamp has given us to date two good shifts, one to the right in the lower lettering and label and a second at the top in both lettering and label.

The three cent variety shows several,—a doubling of the top frame line and balls, additional lines at the left side, at top or bottom and another with the bottom lines and balls doubled.

The four cent stamp has numerous examples of shifts,—Philip Little claims at least twenty-eight,—they occur at the top, bottom and sides. Judge Emerson showed us a proof block of 72, a few months ago, in which a number showed shifted transfers at the lower right and side and several at the top. The most marked shift on this variety, however, is the one where the lower ornaments, lettering, balls and the word "CENTS" are doubled. Burger and Company sent us a part perf copy of this the other day for inspection and we are illustrating it herewith. The writer has this variety in proof form, it being one of a block of four. The cut has been made from this proof.

No shifts have as yet been found on Proprietary stamps of the one, five, six or ten cent denominations.

The 50 Cent Mortgage

A Stamp Replete With Interest.

By WARNER S. ROBISON.

As there appears an ever increasing demand on the part of U. S. Specialists for information on plate cracks, double transfers, etc., I have endeavored to describe the more interesting items of my U. S. Revenue 50c. Mortgage collection with the idea that any small contributions which I might make along this line would gladden the heart of one or more collectors, increase his desire to live, and incidentally make the world a happier place in which to live.

Some of the finest engraving work ever consummated is to be seen on the U. S. 19th Century Revenues. For sheer beauty of workmanship and artistic design they are unsurpassed. To the collector they are a source of joy and happiness.

The 50c first issue revenues are beautifully engraved in **taille douce** being printed from steel plates 12½ by 16 inches, in sheets of 85 in five vertical rows of seventeen stamps, with a uniform spacing of 3/32 of an inch between the rows. At the bottom of the plate was the Imprint "Engraved by Butler & Carpenter, Philadelphia" on a solid tablet with beaded edge, and directly beneath "Plate No. 50T". All varieties of the 50c first issue revenues bore the plate number "50"; the control letter "T" after the plate number, appearing on the Mortgage plates through the entire first issue.

Records show that the first delivery on this stamp was made by Butler & Carpenter Nov. 22nd, 1862, and that up to April 30th, 1864, 396,568 had been issued. These figures are not indicative of the total number printed, which must have exceeded these figures by several times, for the stamps were used well up into the seventies.

The perforating of these stamps was twelve to two centimeters, although copies are met with in imperforate and part perforate condition. The latter conditions being due to the fact that the printers were hard pressed for delivery and allowed sheets to pass from their hands without perforating or without completing the process of perforating.

The papers used were white wove of varying thicknesses and an experimental silk. A copy with stitch watermark, unlisted in Scott's Specialized, is herewith noted. A fine range of shades from dark to light blue are procurable with a little conscientious effort.

Two examples of cracked plates on the 50c Mortgage have been illustrated by Mr. King in The American Philatelist and have created considerable interest. Four examples of so-called major cracks in their entirety are herewith described and illustrated.

As these plate flaws in all cases have been found on two or more copies of the stamp, it is conclusive proof that they are constant.

Figs. 1   2   3   5

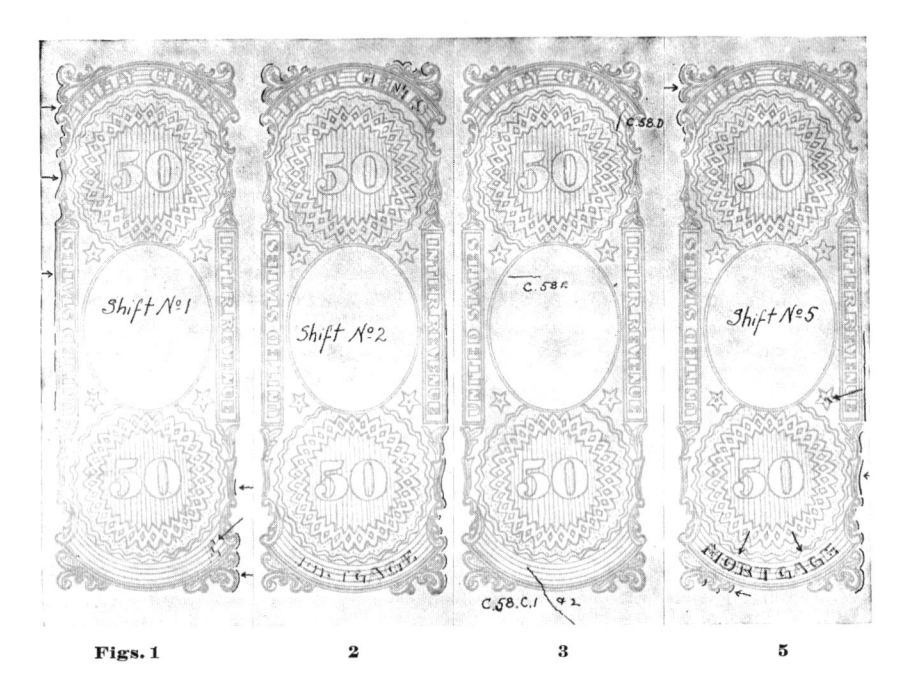

C58A1—C58A2 is the most prominent of the major cracks, beginning at the left of the lower numeral five and running downward between O and R and into T of fifty and the stamp below. In C58A the upper line entering the vignette is not a continuation of the main crack, but is a crack separate and distinct. (Illustrated in The American Philatelist Jan. 1929.)

C58B1—C58B2—C58B3 the second of the major cracks starts at the I of Inter. Revenue, runs north-eastward crossing the stamp to the right thru F of fifty and on into the stamp above, running thru the T of Mortgage and nearly to the E of revenue. (Illustrated in A. P. for June, 1929.)

C58C1—C58C2 begins at the O of Mortgage, runs south-eastward thru R and stops at the E of cents in the stamp below. (Illustrated lower Fig. 3.)

C58D starts just below and to the right of S of cents and runs easterly and slightly downward for about 3 mm. (Illustrated upper part Fig. 3.)

C58C1 and C58D1 occur in the top row.

It is also of note that the stamp with C58D occurs on the plate adjacent to and to the right of the stamp with C58C1.

C58E is a horizontal crack about two millimeters in length in the light area of the hair just above the forehead. From the wide right margins found on each of the stamps so far brought to light, it is fair to presume this stamp to be a right marginal copy. (Illustrated, center Fig. 3.)

Several additional minor or surface cracks occur, and should be of considerable value in plating.

Two of these which have been checked are as follows:

a. A short diagonal line about one mm. in length and running S. W. to N. E. thru three of the shading lines below the T in Mortgage.
b. Dot over the E of Mortgage.

DOUBLE TRANSFERS: These are created by a second impression of the transfer roller on the plate due to the first impression being out of register. As double transfers in common parlance are generally referred to as "Shifts", I will refer to them as such.

At least four shifts are known on the 50c Mortgage and are here described and two of which are illustrated in Figs. 1 and 2.

Shift No. (1): Counter clockwise; showing, (a) a doubling to the left frame line from top left following the contour of the design downward to a point about opposite the middle of the word United; (b) a doubling of the lower right side and (c) the "E" of Mortgage.

Shift No. (2): Also counter clockwise but much stronger than (1); showing, (a) a doubling of top left, (b) at top right, (c) at bottom right, and (d) in "G" and "E" of Mortgage.

Shift No. (3): Showing a doubling north of "FIFT" of fifty.

Shift No. (4): Showing a doubling (a) at the lower right and (b) in the "E" of Mortgage.

Mr. C. W. Bedford, A. P. S. Member 8144, informs me that he will shortly start plating the 50c Mortgage, and I shall therefore turn over to him everything that I have on this stamp, and earnestly request that all those who can aid in this grand work loan Mr. Bedford their data and material, specially pairs, strips and blocks.

In conclusion, I wish to state that I owe much of the inspiration that caused me to work many a night on the 50c Mortgage until the wee small hours of the morning, to Mr. John Nicklin, Mr. Beverly S. King, and the "Boston Revenue Book."

* * * * *

We are also illustrating an interesting shift sent us by Mr. Phillip Little,—this is similar to double No. 1 described above by Mr. Robison, but it appears on other portions of the stamp. We have called this shift No. 5. (Fig. 5.)

SOME FIFTY CENT STAMPS—1st ISSUE.

Mr. Theodore Behr, of Modesto, California, has forwarded a number of copies of the Fifty Cent stamps, first issue.

One copy of the Fifty Cent Lease appears to be on laid paper. Another shows a strong guide line across the top.

A pair of Original Process shows what looks like a roulette along one side, but we think this was caused by the stamps being torn apart by the aid of an indented ruler. Other copies of the Original Process stamp show a slight downward shift in the lettering in the lower label. This is not, however, the shift that has been illustrated or noted in the catalogue. Additional copies show plate flaws or slight scratches. A reconstructed horizontal pair of the Fifty Cent Passage Ticket show a strong scratch running from the "N" of "Revenue" into the "I" of "Unit" on the adjoining stamp.

Among a number of Fifty Cent Mortgage, part perf, we find one with a guide line on the left; another on laid paper; the centre stamp thru which our old friend, the diagonal crack, passes,—and a pair showing a light scratch starting on the "R" of "Mortgage" on the upper stamp to the "E" of "Cents" on the lower stamp. This lower stamp was reported by Mr. Dorer some time ago.

Plating the 5 Cent Inland Exchange

Revenue Men & Shift Hunters, Attention!

Clayton W. Bedford, our enthusiastic and hard working member, is doing a job! Locating the various positions on Plate 5 F of the 5 Cent Inland Exchange has been completed with but three positions still to be identified. This work has been made possible and has been done within a year, due to the hearty co-operation of our members in lending Mr. Bedford their strips and blocks of this stamp. These were all returned to the various members last December, as promised.

There seems to be a third, or mystery plate, that we have no record of. Mr. Bedford tells us that this contains many varieties and work on it should continue.

Plate 5 F has 8 major double transfers, 41 good double transfers and 85 minor ones. There are 36 normal positions, 26 scratches and plate flaws and 4 misplaced guide dots. On Plate 5 there are probably no more than 3 plate varieties,—1: The crack; 2: the big shift, and 3: a minor top shift.

The story and description of the plates will very probably be published in The American Philatelist, but Mr. Bedford is anxious to illustrate the result of his work by about sixty plate positions in rotaprint form. To do this it will be necessary to get one hundred subscribers at $3.00 each. To make our records complete we should stand behind the publishing of these important plate position reproductions. The work will, of course, be done at cost, and the reproductions will be similar to those now being used by the Shift Hunters and the B. I. A. It will only be by this further co-operation that we will be able to take full advantage of his research work. Mr. Bedford's address is 319 Vaniman St., Akron, Ohio. You may notify him direct or notify me that you will be one of the one hundred underwriters.

These illustrations will not be published in the American Philatelist and are for private distribution only.

* * * * *

PLATING THE 5 CENT CERTIFICATE.

Mr. Howard B. Beaumont, one of our members, is plating the 5 Cent Certificate, first issue, and has already definitely located sixty-three of the one hundred seventy stamps on the plate. He wants some help, and any of you who can send him blocks of four or larger or any stamps showing sheet margins will do a lot toward the general work of the Revenue Unit. Mr. Beaumont's address is Room 1105, B. & O. Building, Baltimore, Md.

NEW NARCOTIC.

Mr. Allan P. Vestal reports a new Narcotic stamp. It is of the 1 Cent denomination, size 3, imperforate, and is issued normally as a single.

* * * * *

AN INTERESTING BISECT.

Our little talk on bisects in the November issue seems to have excited a certain amount of interest. Mr. Carl W. Hurst, of Chillicothe, Ohio, sent us an original military exemption document that he has had in his collection for a long while, and which he found in the basement of the County Auditor's office at the Ross County, Ohio, Court House.

The document shows that having "carefully examined Geo. H. Thomas—he is disqualified for military duty"—signed by S. B. Anderson, M. D., and sworn before a notary public under date of August 13, 1864. The stamp consists of a vertical half of the 10 Cent Blue Inland Exchange, pen-cancelled by J. C. N., Notary, with an additional note alongside the stamp in the same handwriting reading

> "Have no 5 Cent
> None in town
> J. C. N.
> N. P." (illustrated)

There is no question in our mind but what this is a genuine bisect, and a very interesting copy.

A. S. Yount has discovered a red circular cancellation of the E. I. du Pont de Nemours Company on the 2 Cent Blue Express, Civil War Revenue. We did not realize that the du Pont Company was in operation as long ago as this. In looking it up Mr. Yount tells me that the company was organized in 1802 and supplied powder for the war of 1812.

* * * * *

P. R. Crooker of Canajoharie, N. Y., in going over a find of Revenues has discovered a part perf copy of the 50 Cent Mortgage which shows one half of the vertical crack as illustrated in the Specialized Catalogue.

* * * * *

Howard B. Beaumont of Baltimore has one of what looks like a perfectly sound copy of the 2 Cent Proprietary Blue, first issue, imperf. It has good, wide margins and looks all right but so far as I know no one has ever seen a pair of these, therefore we cannot list it.

* * * * *

O. H. Roberts of Hopedale, Mass., has discovered that he has a 5 Cent and about one third of another 5 Cent Proprietary, making a 6 Cent rate. He doesn't remember where he found this but he does remember removing it from the original paper which, of course, was a great mistake.

* * * * *

Joseph S. Grant of Mitchel Field, Long Island, has sent two ⅝ Cent Proprietary stamps, one showing a decidedly strong mark in the upper right corner which may be either a plate flaw or have occurred in the printing. We are on the lookout for another copy of this stamp. Another ⅝ Cent shows a slight shift to the left showing faintly over the entire stamp.

* * * * *

Casper J. Dorer has sent two copies of the 2 Cent U. S. I. R. with a strongly marked line about ⅛ of an inch long at the "S" of "CENTS" which runs into the medallion. This seems to be a constant plate flaw and one does not need a glass to see it. Mr. Dorer also submitted two copies of this interesting stamp each one with an imprint, the first showing "Butler & Carpenter" and the second "Joseph R. Carpenter."

* * * * *

Elliott R. Ryder of Troy, N. Y. has sent a copy of a ⅝ Cent Black Proprietary showing a very strong double impression. This has not as yet been noted.

In the November number we illustrated an initial cancellation on a copy of the $1.00 Passage Ticket submitted by A. C. Bates. We had no way of placing this and asked for information. Robert Weber, of Poland, N. Y. has very kindly sent us an original deed with stamps attached bearing the initials as illustrated. The initials "J. R. I.", "J. C. M." and "C. W." stand for J. R. Ingersoll, J. Craig Miller and Charles Willing, all being trustees of the Estate of William Bingham, and the deed is in reference to the sale of some property in Potter County, Pa. The stamp that Mr. Bates has must have, therefore, come from a similar deed.

WASHINGTON IN TROUBLE

This is not a Revenue note, but let us have a laugh now and then!

A block of eight of the current 2 cent Washington that had slipped on the printing press somehow and come up covered with streaks of red ink all over the design, called forth the following,—started, of course, by our Unit member Judge A. H. Benners of Alabama:

    1.—"Doctor Foster went to Glouster
        In a shower of rain;
    He stepped in a puddle up to his middle
    And never came back again.
    But see what Washington has done!
    He stepped in a puddle of paint;
    Some may think it caused by drink—
        His defenders'll say it ain't!"
                      A. H. B.

    2.—"And any philatelist seeing his plight
        Would chortle, and gurgle with glee,
    Regardless of what a ridiculous sight
        Has been made of our old father, G."
                      W. E.
            (Dr. William Evans)

    3.—" 'Tis bad enough, I really think,
        To prove George's feet were clay.
    After throwing mud they resorted to ink,—
        How do they get that way?"
                      Toasty.

    4.—"A hero, once red, had the blues,
    He was plattered with ink and with glues,
        "These splashes," he said,
        "On my face and my head
    No doubt you would call Rupert Hues!"
                      E. P. B.
            (Ellis Parker Butler)

    5.—"Father George is sweating blood
        Like in it he's been swimmin',
    I think the Ku-Klux did it for
        His running after wimmin'."
                      R. H.
       (Last signature probably a forgery.—Ed.)

The Plates of the 5c Inland Exchange

By C. W. BEDFORD.

A Cooperative Study by the Revenue Unit of the American Philatelic Society.

According to the Boston Revenue Book, this stamp was first printed on October 4th, 1862 and first delivered to the government on the 23d of the same month. Up to April 30th, 1864, when designated use was cancelled and any revenue stamp was permitted to be used on any document, there had been issued 7,809,722 stamps, 503,915 of which, according to records, had not been completely perforated. Subsequent to April 30th, 1864, the 5c Inland Exchange and 5c Certificate plates were continued in use for many years with the result that these plates became badly worn. A large percentage of otherwise good plating material, are such poor prints that they are worthless for that purpose. A clearly printed, nicely centered block is not at all common and even single copies, showing full details of the plate when viewed under a glass, are difficult to obtain.

The Plates.

There were probably at least three 5c Inland Exchange plates. The first was labeled "Plate No. 5", the second bore the marking "Plate No. 5F", and there are strong indications of a third, or unknown marking, that we will call the "Mystery Plate". The plates were of steel, 12½x16 inches in size and contained 10 horizontal rows of 17 subjects or 170 stamps in all. There were no centerlines or arrows and both the vertical and horizontal rows were spaced 3/32 of an inch apart. The letter "F" on the second plate was a control letter used on the Inland Exchange stamps of all denominations, the Plate number of the 10c Inland Exchange, for example, being Plate No. 10F. Plate No. 5 appears to have been made before this system was started and the control letter seems to have fallen into disuse after April 30th, 1864.

Plate No. 5.

All stamps issued during 1862 and most of those in 1863 were probably from plate No. 5, as all part perforate and imperforate stamps so far inspected seem to come from this plate. Most copies show the faded color of ink that seems to be characteristic of the early prints from this plate but perforated copies from plate 5 are also found with the bright red ink as chiefly used for the later plates.

There appears to be but very few varieties from plate 5, except for layout dots, layout lines and rocking-in dots. In a virgin lot of over 3000 plate No. 5 singles secured from the same Court House, only three varieties were found. They are as follows:

(1) The largest shift yet discovered on this stamp, however, comes from Plate No. 5. B. D. Forster has a horizontal block of six, perforated, with full left margin, showing that this outstanding variety is found in the second vertical row from the left. C. C. Damon has a vertical block of six with part of the top margin, showing that this shift is in the second horizontal row. Its plate position is, therefore, No. 19. All copies, so far reported, are perforated.

(2) The plate crack also comes from Plate No. 5. This was first observed in a horizontal block of ten, perforated, submitted by James H. Young, the crack showing in the upper right stamp. A vertical, imperf pair with the crack in the lower stamp shows that it starts at a dot just above the stamp and travels downward in a crooked, zig-zag line into the left eye (right on the stamp) of the portrait. One clearly printed copy shows the lower portion of the crack very faintly

and is evidently an early print after the crack started. O. H. Wolcott submitted a fine specimen showing unconnected small cracks in the cheek of the portrait below the main crack. This is probably a late state of this position and is the only copy reported that shows the crack extension.

(3) A small top shift, showing in and above the letters "U. S.", completes the list of varieties that have been identified with this plate.

Plate 5 material is usually identified by the light or faded shade of ink and by the vertical layout lines that so frequently cut the upper right ball. Multiple dots at the upper right corner are also quite common. Color alone is not a definite criteria as plate No. 5 items are found with the deep red shade of the later printings and later plate product is sometimes found with the faded shade of the early printings, but these reversed shades are not at all common. The poor ink used with plate No. 5 makes clear prints a rarity. This, together with but three plate varieties and a scarcity of material of any kind makes the plating of the first plate an improbability.

Plate No. 5, with its crack, after being in use only a little over a year, was probably discarded during September or October, 1863, being replaced by Plate No. 5F. As there is no trace of this crack or of the big shift on plate No. 5F, it is evident that plate No. 5 cannot be considered as the "early state" of plate No. 5F.

Plate No. 5F.

Stamps from the second plate on documents bearing the same data, show cancellations dated as early as November, 1863 and were in use as late as the early '70's. The great majority of all 5c Inland Exchange stamps were printed from this plate.

ENGRAVED BY Butler & Carpenter. PHILADELPHIA
Plate No. 5 F

Three marginal markings have been observed in the right, left and lower margins, respectively, but no marking has been observed in the upper margin. The imprint in the lower margin is centered under the three positions 161, 162 and 163, position 162 being the center stamp in the lower row. "Plate No. 5" is found under the imprint directly beneath position 162. The control letter "F" is usually separated from the "5" by the perforations and appears beneath the left side of position 163.

It has been quite surprising to locate two copies of stamp No. 86 and one copy of stamp No. 102, from the extreme ends of horizontal row No. 6, with margins attached, showing marginal markings that have not previously been reported. Position No. 86 with left margin, shows two letters or numerals "O O" of heavy Roman type, 3mm high and spaced 1½mm apart. Position No. 102 with right margin shows the same "O O" marking except that they are spaced only 1mm apart. Due to plate wear, which so frequently shows in excess on marginal stamps, these three copies are rather poor prints and also of faded color. Additional copies are needed, especially in block or strip in order to authenticate the positions. We have not been able to find the markings for positions 69 and 85, just above these two marginal markings but as the left "imprint" should read "up" and the right "imprint" should read "down" or vise versa, it appears that there are no other marginal markings immediately adjacent.

Many attempt have been made to distinguish the different reliefs on the transfer roll but all seem to be perfect and identical. Clear prints from all three plates show the same little slips of the engravers tool on the die for in many cases the horizontal shading lines of the medallion extend out unevenly into the margin and are identical for all plates. This indicates the use of only one die for all plates.

From the systematic layout of plate No. 5F we can form a rough idea as to the order of rocking-in and of the number of reliefs on the transfer roll. Heavy rocking-in dots at Top-center, are found above the stamps in rows 5 and 8. Just above these rows we find rocking-in dots at the lower right balls in rows 4 and 7. From this it is probable that rows 5, 6 and 7 were rocked-in at one setting of the roll and plate and that rows 8, 9 and 10 constituted another setting. This would indicate at least three reliefs on the roll. Rows 1, 2, 3 and 4 may have been transferred from the same three reliefs or there may have ben a fourth.

Considerable difficulty was encountered in transferring on the second plate. It is due to the many varieties thus produced, that replating has been possible. Only one single stamp has been found that shows evidence of recutting and this stamp has not yet been plated. The following items are found on plate No. 5F:

8 — Major shifts.   36 (?) Normal positions.
41 — Good shifts.   26 — Scratches, etc.
85 — Minor shifts.   4 — Exceptional guide dots.
Guide dots, in the upper right corner of nearly all positions.
Guide dots, center-top, in the 5th and 8th rows.
Guide dots, at the lower right corner of the 4th and 7th rows.

Plate No. 5F is easily replatable and sufficient material will be found so that many collectors may have the pleasure of reconstructing the plate. To make this work easier we have prepared an extensive and detailed report, comprizing tables showing the shift characteristics of 168 plate positions, a table showing the guide dot variations and 47 shifts as well as most of the scratches are illustrated in detail. This report has been reproduced by the Offset print process at a cost less than that required for making copper plates for publishing in the usual manner. This report may be obtained for $3.00 by addressing the author at 319 Vaniman St., Akron, Ohio. The reports are sold at cost and are of standard letter size, punched for filing in a standard three ring binder. A neat title page, printed in two colors, is provided showing the design of the 5c Inland Exchange taken from the large copper plate that was made in order to properly illustrate the plate varieties. The illustrations are taken from half-tone negatives. Binder covers are obtainable at any stationery supply house. For those who care to mount and illustrate their stamps a small half-tone copper plate has been made showing the design of the stamp and mats printed in tint or full black are available.

The Mystery Plate.

Many blocks have been found that do not plate-in to plate No. 5F and have little or none of the characteristics of plate No. 5. Their appearance with late dates of cancellation, early in 1868 and with a more brilliant shade of red ink, long after plate No. 5F was in use, seems to indicate a third plate. All Proofs, so far inspected, appear to be taken from this third or Mystery plate. At least six good shifts belong to this plate and there are many top shifts of an entirely different character than found on the first two plates. The replating of the Mystery plate is well started and will be continued. Further cooperation is requested in showing us all blocks or strips and especially all proofs. In returning such items we will endeavor to mark the plate positions and plate number on outstanding items but cannot offer to do this on singles. This service will be gratis for the privilege of seeing items new to us and only return postage is requested.

We have had the pleasure of checking the Certificates of Deposit from the Ulster County Bank of Kingston, N. Y. from January, 1863 to November, 1871. Stamps from plate No. 5F first appear in November, 1863 and the Mystery plate first shows up in March, 1868. Apparently plate No. 5F was discarded due to plate wear for on March 22d, 1867, Butler and Carpenter wrote to E. A. Rollins as follows: "The five cent Inland Exchange has not been in use for several months * * *." It therefore seems probable that the third or Mystery plate was made sometime in 1867 and that plate No. 5F was discarded late in 1866.

Cooperative Replating.

Following an announcement in the Revenue Unit column of the American Philatelist in January, 1930, that the Unit would attempt the replating of this stamp, the mailman started delivering packages at my address. Entire sections of many large collections were removed and unselfishly forwarded with many letters offering full cooperation. Even several dealers offered their entire stock for the work. As a result, Plate No. 5F was replated except for two positions, all within the year of 1930. We know of no greater tribute to cooperative philatelic endeavor than this accomplishment that would have taken many years for a single individual even with unlimited means. The following are worthy of mention as giving material assistance:

W. Y. Fillebrown	James H. Young	A. P. Vestal
Beverly S. King	J. Lehman	Benjamin Cadbury
C. C. Damon	W. S. Robison	Dr. S. Konwiser
Heyliger de Windt	Phillip Little, Jr.	E. R. Vanderhoof
W. W. Bradbury	O. S. Wolcott	E. M. Jones
F. W. Wright	H. B. Beaumont	Dr. R. F. Chambers
Geo. F. Kirshner	E. V. Pollock	L. J. Flerfage
W. G. Saxton	H. L. Knock	W. G. Windhurst
Dr. W. R. Bostwick	B. D. Forster	F. N. Hilliard
H. M. Jones	P. V. Hogan	P. M. Weiss
H. H. Elliott	J. G. Dorn	G. W. Corwin
Don R. Bennett	Alvin Good	Casper J. Dorer

There are several other revenue stamps on which sufficient variety is found to justify an attempt at replating. The $1.00 Power of Attorney was heavily recut and contains many shifted transfers. The 50c Mortgage shows many shifts and cracks. The 5c Certificate, 4c Proprietary and the 20c Foreign Exchange plates are full of double transfers. Arrangements have been made to start work on three of these items. H. B. Beaumont, 1105 B. & O. Bldg., Baltimore, Md., is working on the 5c Certificate. A. W. Carpenter, 56 Hamilton Ave., Akron, Ohio, has a fine start on the $1.00 Power of Attorney and C. W. Bedford, 319 Vaniman St., Akron, Ohio, is plating the 50c Mortgage. All of this work is sponsored by the Revenue Unit and you cooperation will be appreciated. Under the able leadership of Beverly S. King, Secretary of the Revenue Unit, an amazing amount of new information on revenues has been made available and acknowledgement is made of his continuous assistance and council.

Another Bisect.

George B. Graham, of Buffalo, writes that he has a copy of No. 3996, which is a regular postage stamp surcharged with the large initials "I. R." He says that this is a bisected copy of this stamp, being the lower left hand side, and is on the original document, which is a Pacific Mutual Accident policy and was issued December 24th, 1898. The stamp is tied to the document with a cancellation which looks like July 1898. Just why the policy is dated December and the stamp cancelled in July he is unable to explain unless these policies were sent out from the home office with the stamp affixed and cancelled and then left with the local agent to use.

We have seen several examples of these "I. R." stamps cut diagonally to make up odd rates, whether these were prepared philatelically or not is a question—possibly some of the Unit may have other examples.

* * * * *

W. R. Staplin, of Atlanta, Ga., is the owner of a nice looking block of four 50 Cent Conveyance, Imperf. They are on a piece of the original document but unfortunately whoever cut them out of the document made a bad slip and cut into the lower left hand stamp which ruins its otherwise almost perfect condition.

* * * * *

Eugene C. Wood, of Breckenridge, Mo., has submitted a number of interesting items, the best one being a twisted shift on the $1.00 Power of Attorney.

* * * * *

Jere Hess Barr has been sending our Cancellation Committee a lot of interesting data on pre-cancels of the early Revenues. We had the pleasure of having a chat with him at the Collectors Club at a meeting the other evening and had quite a pow wow on Revenues. He suggests that it would be interesting to start a collection of the various "cut" or scarifying cancellations on Revenue stamps. We don't know whether this has ever been done or not.

* * * * *

Plating The 5 Cent Certificate.

Howard B. Beaumont, Room 1105 B. & O. Bldg., Baltimore, Md., is still working on the plating of the 5 Cent Certificate and wants any help that members can give.

Insurance Cancellations.

Morton D. Joyce has been working with Robert W. Hale, in continuing check list of the insurance company cancellations and will have something to report very soon.

* * * * *

Pre-Cancel Committee.

Your Pre-Cancel Committee report progress in connection with the listing of the pre-cancel stamps of the Civil War and the 1898. This committee you may remember consists of the writer, Morton D. Joyce and Victor W. Rotnem. We have held many meetings together and have checked in repeatedly with Franklin

F. Smith and C. H. Chappell, who have given considerable assistance to us. Joyce and I are working on the Civil War issues and Rotnem and Joyce on the Spanish War Revenues. It is much more of a job than we anticipated and will take considerably longer to finish than we talked of when we were discussing the matter at the convention in Boston last year. Any communications relating to Proprietaries should be addressed to Mr. Rotnem at 121 Windermere Road, Grasmere, Staten Island, and all data relating to Playing Card, Civil War and '98 Documentaries to Morton D. Joyce, 1165 Fifth Ave., New York City. The list will run into the thousands before we get thru with it, particularly if we take up the hand-stamped copies.

THE STAMP ACT

By HARRY M. KONWISER.

When George Grenville became Prime Minister of Great Britain he moved, on March 10, 1764, an amendment to the Sugar Act reading: "It may be proper to charge stamp duties on the colonies and plantations."

The beginnings of Colonial taxation have been traced by William Cullen Bryant, to Governor Cosby, of New York, who in 1734 had proposed to the Assembly "a duty upon Paper to be used in Law, and in all conveyances and Deeds," but this proposition was not adopted. A year later Lieutenant-General Clarke, of New York, proposed that a tax should be imposed by Parliament but Governor Clinton wrote to the Duke of Newcastle offering his opinion that any scheme of taxation, without the Colonists' knowledge, might prove dangerous to His Majesty's interest.(1) The next reference to the project of taxing the American colonies is found among the English archives, under date of July 5, 1763, in a note by Hugh McCullon, a treasury clerk, in which he stated that a stamp duty on vellum and paper money in America would produce upwards of £60,000 a year.

When the news reached Boston that a Stamp Act was being proposed for the colonies, a meeting of protest was held at Faneuil Hall, in Boston, and other Colonies, no less alarmed, emphasized strong objections against the proposed tax. During October 1764, the General Assembly of New York addressed a memorial to the House of Commons, in protest; and, at the same time, appointed a Committee to correspond with the other colonies. Rhode Island, Virginia and Connecticut instructed their agents to ask for a Commons' hearing and Pennsylvania protested to Grenville through Benjamin Franklin.

On August 11, 1764, the Earl of Halifax sent instructions to all the colonies that they should transmit to him "a list of all instruments made use of in public transactions, law proceedings, grants, conveyances, securities of land or money within your government, with proper and sufficient descriptions of the same; in order that, if Parliament should think proper to pursue the intention of the aforesaid resolution, they may thereby be enabled to carry it into execution in the most effectual and least burdensome manner."

Massachusetts immediately objected, as did Virginia, the latter specifically stating their protest against "taxation without representation." When the Act was passed Richard Henry Lee of Virginia, in February 1766, said, "Every abandoned wretch who shall be so lost to virtue and public good as wickedly to con-

---
(1) Documents relating to Colonial History of New York.

Burn's Coffee House, Bowling Green, New York City, Headquarters for the "Sons of Liberty."

tribute to introduce the said act into this Colony, by using stamp paper or by other means, will with the utmost expedition be convinced that immediate danger and disgrace shall attend his prostitute purpose." Bancroft's History of the United States devotes considerable space to the manner of the resistance of the colonists to the Stamp Act, citing the various Colonial measures adopted in their general disapproval.

Under the impending operation of the Stamp Act delegates from nine Colonies met at New York October 1765, and in the language of the Massachusetts Circular, "to consult together on the present circumstance of the Colonies, and the difficulties to which they are and must be reduced by the operation of the acts of Parliament, for levying duties and taxes on the Colonies; and to consider of general and united, dutiful, loyal and humble representation of their condition to His Majesty and to the Parliament, and to implore relief." This convention was known as The Stamp Act Congress. Despite the obvious discontent of the colonists, Grenville introduced the famous Stamp Act, and it was passed on March 22, 1765, by a vote of 294 to 42 and became effective November 1, 1765. By this act every document was declared illegal and void unless written on paper bearing the government stamp. The cheapest stamp being one shilling, and for the more important documents the prices ranged upward from this sum.

Bryant's History of the United States says that following the adoption of the act, every colony spoke in reply, in no uncertain terms and the Virginia Legislature, which assembled in May 1765, adopted the Patrick Henry resolution, which became famous in the course of the debate on which Henry said, "If this be treason, make the most of it."

Opposition to the Stamp Act was voiced by the Virginia Assembly which met during May 1765, at which session Patrick Henry offered a series of resolutions, asserting that the colonists had brought with them full rights of British subjects at home; that the two royal charters of James the First had declared these rights; that taxation by the people themselves was the distinguishing characteristic of

British freedom; that usage had confirmed this right in the colony; and as a result the famous fifth resolution: "Resolved, therefore, that the general assembly of this colony have the sole right and power to lay taxes and imposts upon the inhabitants of this colony; and that every attempt to vest such power in any person or persons whatsoever, other than the general assembly, has a manifest tendency to destroy British as well as American Freedom." There was considerable oposition to the resolutions, much abuse was cast on Henry, and after a long contest the resolutions were adopted by a very small majority. The alarm spread throughout America with astonishing quickness and the ministerial party was overwhelmed. The public career of John Adams, our second President, began with his offering public resolutions at Braintree, and his maintaining an argument in behalf of the town of Boston, addressed to the Colonial government in oposition to the Stamp Act. All of the Colonies, in their assemblies, pronounced the Stamp Act illegal and on the first Tuesday of October 1765, a meeting of representatives of nine of the colonies was held in New York. This, the first Continental Congress, passed a resolution of protest.

The Colonists began their campaign against the British tax by binding themselves not to import English goods, and orders that had gone forward were countermanded. It was soon found that it would be impossible to enforce the use of stamped paper. Many of the government's agents resigned and others who did not had their homes attacked. The newspapers led public opinion in warm appeals to patriotism and in New York the "Sons of Liberty" took upon itself the general direction of the opposition. (Illustration.) When a vessel arrived in the Harbor of New York with stamps on board for use in Connecticut it was at once boarded, the packages seized, taken on shore and a bonfire was made of them. (The total revenue from the sale of these stamps is placed at £4,000.—Encyc. Brit.)

On February 17, 1766, following Parliamentary discussions in which William Pitt and Edmund Burke, as well as Grenville took part, the Stamp Act was repealed by a vote of 275 to 167. This repeal brought enthusiasm to the Colonies, and the Virginia Assembly voted to erect a statue of King George III. A similar honor was proposed to Pitt, in Maryland, but New York exceeded in enthusiasm, the Assembly decreeing the erection of statues of both the King and of Pitt; and on the King's birthday, shortly afterward, the people assembled in the Fields (now City Hall Park) and set up a Liberty Pole, at the foot of which the King's health was drunk in hogsheads of punch.

Lossing's History of the United States gives the full text of the British Stamp Act, the opening formula to each of the thirty-nine paragraphs being: "For every skin or piece of vellum or parchment, or sheet, or piece of paper, on which shall be engrossed, written or printed .. .. A stamp duty of" (here follows the amount of the tax.) Seventeen different amounts are named for the thirty-nine different taxes, as follows: 3d, 4d, 6d, 1 shilling, 1s6d, 2s, 2s3d, 2s6d, 3s, 4s, 5s, 10s, 20s, £2, £3, £4, £6. Stamps of these seventeen denominations were impressed in relief upon one of the lower corners of the parchment, after there had been affixed thereto, by a bit of tinfoil, a thin layer of paste board of the size of the die. Different colors appear to have been used on which to emboss the stamps, and (probably) each value had a different color.

Of the known existent stamps there is an olive green, value 2s6d. There is also some doubt as to whether the Lossing illustration correctly represents the shilling stamp sent to America in 1765. (The Lossing item is similar to the

The 2sh.6d. Stamp. From the Morton D. Joyce collection.

Bryant illustration of a "Royal Stamp"—Ed.) It might be well to record the fact that very few, if any of these stamps were actually used in America. At least part of the known shipments of these parchments returned to England, were reissued there after the American stamps had been clipped off and the ordinary British stamps had been impressed in place of them. Two bags full of these, according to the American Journal of Philately, chanced to be preserved in Somerset House and in 1846 George Bancroft saw them there, as noted in his History of the United States. The 40th section of the Stamp Act placed a duty of a shilling on every pack of playing cards and ten shillings on every pair of dice sold or used in the colonies. Section 41 of the Act, relating to the tax on newspapers, etc., in the colonies, placed duties, indicating eight values and these eight stamps named in Section 40-41 were all surface-printed and quite different from the seventeen embossed stamps named in the preceding sections.

Newspaper Stamp.

These stamps, according to the personal observation of the writer in the American Journal of Philately, who saw the Somerset House lot, were engraved on copper, each plate containing 25 stamps and two plates (50 stamps) being printed on each sheet. There were apparently eight plates, for each of the eight stamp values required—the plates seen numbering from one to eight, and the stamps being individually marked from one to two hundred—though the proof impressions, according to this writer, show only half as many in evidence at present (1876). Each plate measured 12½ by 7¼ inches, containing three rows of stamps, (9 in the top row, 8 in the others) and the size of the sheet is 15x22 inches. At the foot of each sheet is an inscription reading:

"Brought by Mr Thomas, Major Engraver, two Copper Plates for Penny Duty on Newspapers and Pamphlets, the one numbered from 51 to 75 and other from 76 to 100 inclusive. The impressions whereof are here on this sheet numbered. In Witness Whereof we have hereunto set our Hands the 18th April 1765. By order of the Commissioner.

"We do hereby acknowledge to have this day received back the above mentioned copper plates to be deposited among other plates and dies, used in the service of the Stamp Revenue, to be kept according to the Method and Usage of the office. Witness our Hands the 18th April 1765. J. B., G. C., W. J., W. A., F. M. I."

The initials represent the autograph signatures of the stamp officers, written with lead pencil, though the rest of the inscription is in ink. From the Book of Vouchers for 1765, in which were bound the proof sheets of all the stamps prepared for use in any part of the British Empire, the specimens for "America" seem to have been torn out in the Somerset House lot.

The newspaper stamps measure one inch by inch-and-one-half in size. A crown supported by a crossed sword and sceptre surrounded by the circular garter, "HONI-SOIT-QUI-MAL-Y PENSE" resting on scroll work, above which is the word "AMERICA" while below the central circle is a label inscribed "HALF PENNY", "ONE PENNY", or "TWO PENCE" as the case may be Stamps for almanacs were smaller, about ⅝ by ⅞ inches, the crossed sword and sceptre supporting a small circle containing a six pointed star in the centre of which is the cross of St. George. This circle is surmounted by a crown, above which appears the word "AMERICA", on the left side "DUTY", on the right side "PENCE" and below is "TWO", "FOUR", or "EIGHT", as the case may be. The six almanac stamps are all of the same color, reddish brown, and are numbered at the bottom. A writer in the American Journal of Philately, (name not recorded) says he was granted special permission to take photographs of the sheets he refers to, the original sheets designed for American use in 1765.

The Royal Stamp.   **Almanac Duty Stamp.**

At the William sale at the American-Anderson Galleries, December 2, 1929, a lot was sold for $41, described as "English Revenue stamps for use in the American Colonies, 2sh 6d on blue paper. The regular design of the revenue stamps of Great Britain with the word "AMERICA" above the crown." Another lot sold for $29, described as "1765 Revenue Proofs, ½d brown, 4d brown on heavy hand made paper. Proofs of the two values of revenue stamps which the British government made for use in America in 1765, of the greatest rarity, as but five or six copies are known." When investigating these stamps in London in 1876 Mr. Bagg received permission to make facsimiles of the original proof sheets on file in the Revenue office and received from an official of that office original proofs cut from the sheet made in 1765. (Illustrated from copies in the collection of Morton D. Joyce.)

The third lot, sold at $18, was described as "Early American Revenue stamps, 6d, embossed in Great Britain 2sh 6d. It is evident from this stamp, which the British government made for use in this country before 1776, it was reissued in Great Britain but remained 2sh 6d. The two embossings are quite distinct and the word "AMERICA" plainly legible."

The "Royal" stamp, herewith illustrated, is reproduced from Bryant's History and while it seems to agree with the general descriptions of the actually issued stamps the word "AMERICA" is conspicuous by its absence and the letter "B" (probably for "BRITISH") appears at the right above "1". (Possibly

Bryant's Illustration of the Royal Stamp.

this illustrates a "Royal" stamp without the word "AMERICA.") This item was drawn by Runge for Bryant's History and is from "a paper in the New York Historical Society's collection." The tax on documents chiefly affected more prosperous citizens but the tax on tea affected both rich and poor and though not exhorbitant its injustice was resented everywhere and at many seaports tea was destroyed or refused admission. The destruction of one cargo of tea at Boston became famous as "The Boston Tea Party " Although the tea tax was not paid by documentary stamps these latter are often referred to as "Tea Party Stamps."

Report of the Revenue Unit
For the Fiscal Year Ending August 31, 1931.

This is the fourth year of the A. P. S. Revenue Unit. We now have seventy (70) members, forty-three (43) have paid their dues for 1931.

Our members taken an active interest in the Unit and the Secretary is kept fairly busy answering letters and passing on various points in connection with Revenue stamps.

In addition to the regular Revenue notes, handled by Mr. King, and appearing in each number of The American Philatelist, the following special articles by members have been published:

    50 Cent Mortgage—by Warner S. Robinson
    5 Cent Inland Exchange—by Clayton W. Bedford
    An article on the Boston Tea Party Stamps—by Harry M. Konwiser

A Committee consisting of Messrs. King, Rotnem and Joyce are at work listing printed cancellations on the early Revenue stamps of this country.

Financial Statement

Cash on hand August 1, 1930	$ 7.46	
Dues received, year 1930-31	43.00	
Received from old U. S. Revenue Society	170.00	
Received from members for Cancellation Check List	110.00	$ 330.46
Expenses:		
Postage	$ 30.31	
Photographs for illustration purposes	8.50	$ 38.81
Balance on hand August 31, 1931		$ 291.65

Respectfully submitted,

ROBERT F. CHAMBERS, Chairman.

* * * * *

Replating the 5 Cent Certificate

"I have now located 153 of the 170 plate positions on the first plate and have a large amount of material assembled for the second plate including a reconstructed block of 70 vertically thru the center of the sheet.

My progress has been slow, being interrupted by frequent business trips. I have had to work alone and at times with a small amount of material. I have, however, received very fine assistance lately from Texas and a lot of material from Don Bennett. I believe I have now the material to complete the first plate as soon as I can find time to work on it.

(signed) HOWARD B. BEAUMONT."

* * * * *

Replating the 50 Cent Mortgage Cracks

"Following the completion of the replating of Plate 5F of the 5 Cent Inland Exchange by the Revenue Unit members during 1930 and after the hundreds of fine items had been returned to their owners, a call was issued for the loan of pairs, strips and blocks of the 50 Cent Mortgage in an attempt to determine the plate positions of the well known cracks on this stamp.

Again the Revenue Unit members and several others responded with a wealth of material with which to start work and a list of contributors would approximately duplicate the list of cooperators as previously published with the 5 Cent Inland Exchange data.

It sounds like a fairy tale but it is true that Don R. Bennett sent in such a large number of items that within a single evening the three cracks were completely listed.

The large vertical crack (C58A) extends from position 64 down into position 81 in the bottom row. This places the big crack at the bottom of the plate in the 5th vertical row from the right.

The large diagonal crack (C58B) extends from position 25, diagonally downward to the left thru position 43 and into position 42. Position 43 is the center stamp in the sheet, figuring both vertically and horizontally.

The small diagonal crack (C58C) starts in the top row in position 12 and extends downward, diagonally to the right, into position 29.

As far as we know, Plate No. 50V was the only 50 Cent Mortgage plate and comprised 5 horizontal rows of 17 stamps each or 85 stamps in the sheet. There are several Double Transfers on the 50 Cent Mortgage that have not as yet been plated. As most of the right half of the plate has been seen they are probably to be located in the left half, or perhaps there is an early and late state of the plate. The plating will therefore be continued and further assistance is requested.

The largest block we have seen is a block of 17 showing the large diagonal crack, complete. This fine block is owned by W. W. Bradbury. Data on the shifts has already been published in the Revenue Unit columns by W. S. Robinson who is still assisting in the intricate problem of completing the data on this plate.

(signed) C. W. BEDFORD."

* * * * *

Replating the $1.00 Power of Attorney

"This interesting stamp may be called the '3c-'51 of the revenues' and well does it deserve the name. So far we have not found a single stamp or proof that shows the stamp as it was engraved on the die, and a Die Proof is unknown. Nearly every position on the plate seems to have been RECUT. There are several fine shifts and many small ones like the plate layout lines and layout dots afford a profusion of 'landmarks' for replating.

With the large block of proofs in one of the Eastern collections and the many fine items at hand, we have a fairly complete representation of the entire plate, but the 'Rosetta Stone' that links them together has not yet been found. Over one-third of the plate has been definitely plated and you may have the pair, strip or block that ties the rest into the plating. Every little helps so send all the help you can.

(signed) A. W. CARPENTER."

* * * * *

Check List of Printed Revenues

"This has turned out to be a real job and altho considerable progress has been made by your committee the work is still far from completed. We hope in the next number to give a report from Mr. Joyce on the work that he has done on the Playing Card company cancellations.

(signed) BEVERLY S. KING."

The 50 Cent Conveyance

By W. W. BRADBURY,
64 Hermosillo Park, Santa Barbara, California.

As there appears to be a constant demand for information on plate varieties of the early revenue stamps of the U. S. this article is written with the hope that to will bring pleasure to those who enjoy hunting for these things.

Believing it is easier to visualize from an illustration than a mere description, a few of the most pronounced scratches occurring on this stamp are shown on the accompanying cut.

#1 was mentioned in the A. P. for Sept. 1930.

#2 is a continuation of #1.

#4-#5-#6-#7-#8, together with five minor scratches occur on one stamp, making it a very interesting plate variety—#4 was mentioned in the A. P. for February 1929, #8 is a continuation of this, #9-#10 occur on the same stamp with eight other consistent plate markings.

#12 is left of #9-#10.

#18 occurs on the same stamp that has the line in "C" that was mentioned in the A. P. for February 1930.

The other numbers occur each on a separate stamp and speak for themselves.

The writer has at least six copies of each example illustrated, which proves them to be constant, nearly all of these positions have several minor scratches that are also constant, and I will be pleased to illustrate to any one interested many other examples which are too numerous to include in this article.

The imprint has only been seen on the left hand side of this stamp reading down, "Engraved by Butler & Carpenter Philadelphia," it would be of great interest to learn if anyone has seen this imprint, or a similar one, in any other position.

Printed and Other Pre-Cancellations of Playing Card Manufacturers on Civil War Issue Revenue Stamps

By MORTON DEAN JOYCE.

Although collectors of United States Revenue stamps are familiar with the printed cancellations which occur on the Civil War issues and recognize them as the earliest extensive use of pre-cancellation in the United States, one finds the playing card varieties so infrequently that only a specialist with a large accumulation can attempt to allocate them. It is the purpose of this article to give a full and complete listing of the cancellations used by the several Playing Card Manufacturers who were so large that some of them are still in business today under their own name or who merged and are in business with a new corporate name.

Practically all the companies listed issued their own Private Die stamp later during the period when the Private Die Proprietaries, commonly called "Match and Medicine stamps," were issued. The over-prints serve as both cancellation and advertising medium and by some collectors are classed as provisionals used prior to the issuance of the corresponding private die stamps.

There are three sources of data: the Boston Revenue Book issued in 1899; Sterling's price list issued in 1888; and a small book on Revenue stamps by Julius Adenaw and published by the Scott Stamp & Coin Co. when they were located on East 23rd St. This book is still available while the other books occasionally are procurable at auctions. In this article the author has used these books and has listed as far as possible every item that could safely be identified. In the Sterling list there were four which are not included because there was no way to prove they were Playing Card Manufacturers. They are: Smith Baker Jr., New York #932 in the list; J. R. D. #944 who is believed to be John R. Durling of Brown and Durling, Wadsworth, Ohio, who used a Private Die Match Stamp; Grooms Bros. & Co. #930, and M. S. Mepham & Bro. St. Louis, #936. Each of these concerns has but one stamp listed by Sterling and all but the Grooms Bros. are on Playing Cards stamps of various values and, it is believed, were included by him for that reason. In order to include items which have not been seen by the author but which are listed in one or more of the three reference books the author has placed their respective numbers at the left of his numbers. The initials E. P. refer to items on a list sent in by Elliott Perry. All other items have been seen. The low numbers mentioned designate items taken from the Adenaw list; those in the nine hundreds come from Sterling's and the Boston Book's listings have numbers in the twenty-two hundreds.

The purpose of the check list which follow is to classify the varieties known to exist and the lists were prepared while arranging the personal collection of the author. New cancellations have come to his attention since the lists were started and many other varieties not included may be in the hands of collectors and dealers. It would be a pleasure to hear from those who have cancellations not included in the lists. Kindly address the author at 115 Broadway, New York City.

Most of the pre-cancellations mentioned in the lists are printed, but some of them should not properly be so called, although they may be similar. These are Type II of Andrew Dougherty, all of John J. Levy, Type V of Victor E. Mauger, and Type V of Lawrence Cohen & Co. They are included to complete the list of Playing Vard Manufacturers.

The author wishes to acknowledge the assistance of Elliott Perry in preparing the historical background and Beverly S. King for his aid in illustrating through drawings the various cancellations that appear throughout the article.

AMERICAN CARD CO.

There has been some doubt whether this concern was really a Playing Card manufacturer and evidence that it used the stamps attributed to it is not wholly conclusive. The first data on it is the listing by Sterling. Data gathered by Elliott Perry some years ago and recently confirmed by him shows that an American Card Co. was located at 14 Chambers St., New York City, from about 1863 to about 1867. Another reference giving the Chambers St. address and also 165 William St., both in 1862, states that "Union Playing Cards" were made by this company in that year. Possibly the cards were manufactured in Cincinnati and sold under the name "American Card Co." in New York. The name "American Card Company" was used in connection with cards of the Longley Card Company of Cincinnati stamped with a 5c value dated "1862" which is omitted from the lists because of insufficient data. At the same period there is evidence of a connection with the Paper Fabrique Company. As yet it is impossible to say whether the "American Card Co." was a manufacturer, or was a trade name used by one or more of the known manufacturers, and it may have been both. In view of the above it is felt that the company should be recognized as a Playing Card firm.

There is but one type: "Am C Co.—Aug. 1863" in two horizontal lines, similar to typewriter type measuring 17x3x2 and 18x3x2mm.

Am C Co..

Sept, 1863

	1	1c Playing Cards	Am C Co.	Aug.	1863
	2	1c Telegraph	Am C Co.	Sept.	1863
931	3	2c Bank Check, blue	Am C Co.	July,	1864

In the Ballard sale held in 1926 by J. C. Morgenthau & Co. a 2c Bank Check dated June, 1864 was in lot #1040. It is not included due to insufficient data.

CATERSON & BROTZ.

The initials C B to a playing card stamp collector mean only one concern, Caterson & Brotz. The stamps listed below cannot be definitely traced to Caterson & Brotz. They were originally listed under this firm by Sterling and later Adenaw included them in his book. Whoever "CB" may have been there is no doubt the initials are those of a manufacturer or distributor of playing cards. An original cover wrapping a pack of cards made by Samuel Hart & Co., and bearing one of the CB stamps is in the collection of the author and in addition, stamp #2 has a double cancellation, one "CB" and the other "S. H. & Co." which latter of course is the Hart firm. It would seem that there was some connection between the two, but what it was has not yet been discovered. As Caterson & Brotz apparently were not making playing cards before 1882 it is very doubtful if "CB" stands for Caterson & Brotz, but it is so listed until more data is available.

CB
Dec.
1868

There is but one Type. Three horizontal lines in script. CB joined, month and year in smaller type, measuring 8x5; 7x4x2; and 8½x3mm.

1		*1c Playing Cards Part Perf.	CB Dec. 1862. within 21mm circle
2		1c Playing Cards Part Perf.	CB Dec. 1862 and S. H. & Co. Jan'y. 1863.
3	911	1c Playing Cards	CB Jan'y. 1863.
4		1c Playing Cards	CB Nov. 1863
5		1c Playing Cards.	CB Dec. 1863
6	2	1c Proprietary	CB Dec. 1863
7	933	2c Playing Cards, blue	CB Dec. 1863
8	937	2c Proprietary, blue	CB Dec. 1865 red

*This is listed inasmuch as it appears on #2 and probably exists without the Hart cancellation.

In the Ballard sale held in 1926 by J. C. Morgenthau & Co., lot #1042 contained a 2c Proprietary, blue, "CB—April-1865" but is not included due to lack of sufficient proof.

COMIC PLAYING CARD CO.

No information is available regarding this concern. Only one stamp is listed. It is of the 1871-75 Proprietary issue and no mention is made whether the paper is violet or green. Sterling's book is the authority for its existence.

The cancellation reads "Comic Playing Cards, Nov. 18, 1876." Probably it is in two lines.

991   1   5c green and black.

ANDREW DOUGHERTY.

Before manufacturing Playing Cards in Brooklyn about 1848, Andrew Dougherty had been a New Bedford whaler. Around 1850 he had his factory in Cliff Street, New York; subsequently being located at Beekman St., and in 1872 erected a factory at 76-80 Center St. In 1896 he transferred his business to his sons. This firm is the only one which has operated under the same name from the Civil War period to the present time. It is, however, now owned by the United States Playing Card Co. In 1930 it was merged with the New York Consolidated Card Co., to form the Consolidated-Dougherty Card Co.

The cancellations on the Civil War stamps are divided into two major classes. The first being the initials A.D. in script, the "A" being the old-fashioned letter so often seen thirty or forty years ago while the "D" is similar to the one now used. Both letters have frills and it is due to them that the first major class is divided into four types by me. The second major class is in Roman capitals and is classified by me at Type V.

The Boston Book lists but two types, the difference being only in measurements. I have eliminated their second type which was probably caused by spacing and have sub-divided this cancellation into four styles of letters used.

TYPE I. "A. D.—Mar.—1863." in three horizontal lines measuring 11x4; 10x2½; and 8½x2½mm. The first line is in script and the balance in Roman Capitals. In this type A. has a loop on the right-hand side of the letter and shading on right stroke of letter, and in D., the line making the loop does not cross itself and the straight stroke is shaded.

TYPE II. This is similar to Type I but the lower two lines are in block letters and lines measure 12½x5½; 10½x4; and 10½x3mm. Only two stamps are listed under this type and the months are Jan. and Feb. of 1863. There are vertical lines at right and left. This cancellation is not a printed one but is probably a roller or handprinted one.

   TYPE III. This type differs from Type I in that neither letters A. nor D. are shaded and the line forming the loop in the D. crosses itself.

   TYPE IV. This has the same D. as in Type III and the loop on the A. is on the left hand side instead of the right.

3	1	1c Playing Cards	Type ?—A. D. 1862.
	2	1c Proprietary	Type I—A. D. Oct. 1862. no stop after D
E.P.	3	1c Proprietary (Imperf)	Type I—A. D. Nov. 1862.
913	4	1c Playing Cards	Type ?—A. D. Dec. 1862.
4	5	1c Playing Cards	Type ?—A. D. 1863.
	6	1c Playing Cards	Type II—A. D. Jan. 1863.
	7	1c Playing Cards	Type III—A. D. Mar. 1863.
	8	1c Playing Cards	Type IV—A. D. Mar. 1863. no stop after A
	9	1c Playing Cards	Type I—A. D. May. 1863. no stop after A
	10	1c Playing Cards	Type I—A. D. May. 1863. no stop after yr.
	11	1c Playing Cards	Type IV—A. D. May. 1863.
	12	1c Playing Cards	Type I—A. D. July 1863.
	13	1c Playing Cards	Type IV—A. D. July 1863.
	14	1c Playing Cards	Type IV—A. D. July 1863. double
	15	1c Playing Cards	Type I—A. D. Sept. 1863.
	16	1c Playing Cards	Type III—A. D. Sept. 1863.
	17	1c Playing Cards	Type IV—A. D. Sept. 1863.
	18	1c Playing Cards	Type I—A. D. Sept. 1863. red
	19	1c Playing Cards Imperf	Type I—A. D. Nov. 1863.
	20	1c Playing Cards	Type I—A. D. Nov. 1863.
	21	1c Playing Cards	Type I—A. D. Nov. 1863. colin after Nov.
	22	1c Playing Cards	Type III—A. D. Nov. 1863.
	23	1c Playing Cards	Type IV—A. D. Nov. 1863.
	24	1c Playing Cards	Type I—A. D. Nov. 1863. blue
	25	1c Playing Cards	Type III—A. D. Nov. 1863. blue
	26	1c Playing Cards	Type III—A. D. Nov. 1863. blue no stop after D
	27	1c Playing Cards	Type III & IV—A. D. Nov. 1863. double Type III no stop after D Type IV no stop after A and D
	28	1c Proprietary	Type I—A. D. Nov. 1863. no stop after A and D
	29	1c Proprietary	Type III—A. D. Nov. 1863.
	30	1c Express	Type I—A. D. Nov. 1863.
	31	1c Express	Type I—A. D. Nov. 1863. no stop after D
	32	1c Express	Type III—A. D. Nov. 1863.
	33	1c Express	Type IV—A. D. Nov. 1863.
	34	2c Proprietary orange	Type I—A. D. Oct. 1862.
	35	2c Playing Cards orange	Type II—A. D. Feb. 1863.
	36	2c Playing Cards orange	Type I—A. D. May. 1863.
	37	2c Playing Cards blue	Type III—A. D. Sept. 1863.
22	38	2c Playing Cards blue Imp.	Type ?—A. D. Nov. 1863.
	39	2c Playing Cards blue	Type I—A. D. Nov. 1863.

	40	2c Playing Cards blue	Type I—A. D. Nov. 1863. double
	41	2c Playing Cards blue	Type III—A. D. Nov. 1863.
	42	2c Playing Cards blue	Type IV—A. D. Nov. 1863. double
	43	2c Proprietary blue	Type I—A. D. Nov. 1863.
	44	3c Playing Cards	Type I—A. D. July. 1863.
	45	3c Playing Cards	Type I—A. D. July. 1863. no stop after A
	46	3c Playing Cards	Type I—A. D. July. 1863. double
	47	3c Playing Cards	Type III—A. D. July. 1863.
	48	4c Playing Cards	Type I—A. D. July. 1863.
E.P.	49	4c Playing Cards	Type III—A. D. July. 1863.
	50	4c Playing Cards	Type IV—A. D. July. 1863.
	51	5c Playing Cards	Type I—A. D. July. 1863.
	52	5c Playing Cards	Type I—A. D. July. 1863. no stop after A
2217	53	5c Proprietary	Type ?—A. D. Mar. 1863.
	54	10c Proprietary	Type I—A. D. July. 1863.
	55	10c Proprietary	Type I—A. D. July. 1863. no stop after A
	56	10c Proprietary	Type III—A. D. July. 1863.
952	57	10c Proprietary	Type ?—A. D. July. 1866. possibly error and is 1863.

No. 3 on the list has not sufficient margins to prove it was imperforate when issued.

Type V. ."A. D.—1864" in two horizontal lines of Roman capitals measuring 14x4½ and 9x3mm.

	58	3c Proprietary
34	59	3c Telegraph
	60	4c Proprietary
940	61	5c Express
	62	5c Foreign Exchange
43	63	5c Playing Cards
	64	10c Proprietary
	65	10c Power of Attorney

Lot 1053 of the Ballard Sale held in 1926 by J. C. Morgenthau & Co. had a 3c Playing Card which apparently is of Type V but without any further data it must be left unlisted.

DOUGHTY BROTHERS.

This firm is included in this article with considerable reluctance but many collectors in the past have beleived it had some connection with Andrew Dougherty and therefore the stamps are listed and the available data is given. It has been stated this firm was formed by the brothers of Andrew Doughterty and was enjoined from doing business. The author does not know that "A. D." had any brothers and according to "A History of Playing Cards And A Bibliography Of Cards And Gaming" written by Catherine Perry Hargrave and published by the Houghton Mifflin Company in 1930, (which truly wonderful book should be in the library of any one interested in Playing Cards and all lovers of fine printing,) the injunction probably referred to was granted against the Dorrity Playing Card Manufacturing Company for infringement on the Dougherty trade-marks and name.

While it is true that in 1865 and earlier the "Proprietary" stamps could legally be used on playing cards and the "Playing Cards" stamps on other merchandise subject to the proprietary tax, none of the Doughty Brothers stamps except the 2c value agree with the values required for the playing card tax schedule in effect in 1865. The 3c and 5c rates had been abolished in August 1864 and the 5c rate was not restored until August 1866. It seems quite likely the Doughty Brothers stamps were used on patent medicines, cosmetics, perfumery, or photographs ,rather than on playing cards.

DOUGHTY BROTHERS. 1865

DOUGHTY 1865

Type I. "DOUGHTY—1865" in two horizontal lines measuring 13x2 and 5x2mm; reads up; down.

Type II. "DOUGHTY—BROTHERS—1865" in three horizontal lines measuring 13x2; 15x2; and 5x2mm. Reads down.

1	2c Proprietary, orange	Type I	up
2	2c Proprietary, orange	Type I	down
3	2c Proprietary, blue	Type I	up
4	2c Proprietary, blue	Type I	down
5	5c Playing Cards	Type I	down
6	2c Proprietary, orange	Type II	
7	2c Proprietary, blue	Type II	
8	3c Proprietary	Type II	
9	5c Playing Cards	Type II	

(Continued in January Number.)

Printed and Other Pre-Cancellations of Playing Card Manufacturers of Civil War Issue Revenue Stamps

By MORTON DEAN JOYCE.

(Continued from December Number.)

SAMUEL HART & CO.

This concern was composed of Samuel Hart and Isaac Levy, both being cousins of Solomon L. Cohen of Lawrence, Cohen & Co. Offices were maintained in New York and Philadelphia and although the factory is supposed to have been in Philadelphia they may have made cards in New York also. The Hart firm, with John J. Levy, was joined with Lawrence & Cohen in 1871, forming the New York Consolidated Card Co.

Type I "S. H. & Co.—Dec.—1863." In three horizontal lines of script type measuring 13½x5x2; 4x2; and 8½x3mm.

	1	1c Playing Cards	Jan'y. 1863.	Assume this exists as appears on C B # 2.
	1	1c Playing Cards	Jan'y. 1863.	blue.
	2	1c Playing Cards	June, 1863.	
	3	1c Playing Cards	Dec. 1863.	
11	4	1c Playing Cards		

99

2223	5	1c Proprietary	Jan. 1863. Must be Jan'y but Boston book lists as Jan.
	6	1c Proprietary	Dec. 1863.
	7	2c Playing Cards, orange	Jan'y. 1863.
	8	2c Playing Cards, orange	Jan'y, 1863. blue.
	9	2c Playing Cards, blue	June, 1863.
	10	2c Playing Cards, blue	Nov. 1863.
26	11	2c Playing Cards, blue	Dec. 1863.
	11a	2c Playing Cards, blue	Dec. 1863. no S H & Co may be #11.
	12	3c Playing Cards	Jan'y, 1863.
	13	3c Playing Cards	Jan'y, 1863. blue.
	14	3c Playing Cards	Sept. 1863.
	15	3c Playing Cards	Oct. 1863.
	16	3c Playing Cards	Dec. 1863.
	17	4c Playing Cards	Jan'y, 1863.
2231	18	5c Proprietary	Jan. 1863. See note after #5.
2232	19	5c Playing Cards	Dec. 1863.

Adenaw lists under his #12 a 1c Proprietary cancelled in red "S. H. & Co." but no date. This may be in Type I or II. In the Ballard sale Lot 1065 had a 1c Proprietary cancelled "S. H. & Co." in Roman letters which is Type II. It may be that the Adenaw listing is this stamp. Neither is listed due to insufficient data.

Type II. Similar to Type I excepting that all but the month is in Roman Capitals. Measurements are 16x3x2; 9x4x2, and 8½x3mm.

2226	20	2c Proprietary, blue	Aug. 1865.
	21	2c Proprietary, blue	Dec. 1865. red.
2230	22	4c Playing Cards	Dec. 1865. Boston book Type 5 but feel it's almost my Type II.
	23	4c Proprietary	Dec. 1865.
2233	24	5c Proprietary	Aug. 1863.
945	25	5c Proprietary	April 1865.
	26	5c Proprietary	Dec. 1865.
2238	27	5c Proprietary	Aug. 1866.
45	28	5c Playing Cards	Aug. 1865. Assume it is this type.
46	29	5c Playing Cards	Sept. 1865. Assume it is this type.
	30	5c Playing Cards	Nov. 1865.
	31	5c Playing Cards	Dec. 1865.
	32	10c Proprietary	July, 1865.
955	33	10c Proprietary	Aug. 1865. Assume it is this type.
	34	10c Proprietary	Sept. 1865.
	35	10c Proprietary	Oct. 1865.
	36	10c Proprietary	Dec. 1865.
956	37	10c Proprietary	Aug. 1866. Assume it is this type.

Type III. Like Type II but all three lines in Roman Capitals measuring 16x 3½; 8x2; and 8x3mm.

2225	38	2c Playing Cards, blue	Nov. 1863. Boston Type III which is similar to my Type III.
	39	5c Playing Cards	August 1864.
	40	5c Playing Cards	April 1865.
	41	10c Proprietary	August 1864. Boston book type 6 but feel it is cloes to my Type III.

In the Ballard sale lot 1059 had a 4c Playing Cards dated Nov. 1864, but while it was listed under Hart no initials weer given and so is not listed here. The same applies to a 5c Playing ards dated Dec. 1863 in lot 1061.

LAWRENCE, COHEN & CO.
LAWRENCE & COHEN.

Lewis I. Cohen first began to manufacture playing cards in New York during the year 1832. He retired in 1854 and left the business in the hands of his son Solomon L. Cohen and his nephew John M. Lawrence under the firm name of Lawrence, Cohen & Co. In 1864 the name was changed to Lawrence & Cohen. It was under this name that they issued their private die stamps and hence it may be but little known that the original firm was Lawrence, Cohen & Co.

L.C.&Co. MAR. 1864.   **L.C. 1864.**   **L.&C. 1864.**

Cancellations Used by Lawrence, Cohen & Co.

Type I. "L. C. & Co.—NOV.—1862." in three horizontal lines of Roman capitals measuring 15x3½x2½; 9x2½; and 8½x2½ mm.

	1	1c Playing Cards	Nov. 1862.
923	2	1c Playing Cards	1863. no month.
2242	3	1c Playing Cards (Imperf)	Jan. 1863.
	4	1c Playing Cards (p. perf)	Jan. 1863.
	5	1c Playing Cards	Jan. 1863.
	6	1c Playing Cards	May. 1863.
	7	1c Playing Cards	July. 1863.
	8	1c Playing Cards	Sept. 1863.
	9	1c Playing Cards	Nov. 1863.
E.P.	10	1c Playing Cards	Jan. 1864.
	11	1c Playing Cards	Mar. 1864.
	11a	1c Playing Cards	Mar. 1864. period after Mar. dropped down.
	11b	1c Playing Cards	Mar. 1864. period after Mar. has only top half.
	12	1c Playing Cards	Mar. 1864. double.
	13	1c Playing Cards	May. 1864.
2245	14	1c Proprietary	May, 1863.
2246	15	1c Proprietary	July. 1863.
19	16	1c Proprietary	1864. no month.
E.P.	17	2c Playing Cards, orange	Nov. 1862.
	18	2c Playing Cards, orange	Jan. 1863.
	19	2c Playing Cards, blue	Sept. 1863.
935	20	2c Playing Cards, blue	Jan. 1864.
	21	2c Playing Cards, blue	Jan. 1864. red cancellation.
	22	2c Playing Cards, blue	Mar. 1864.
31	23	2c Playing Cards, blue	May. 1864.

Type II—"L. C. & Co.—Mar. 1, 1864.' in three horizontal line of Roman upper and lower case letters.

Mar. 1, 1864.   2249   24   2c Playing Cards, blue

Cancellations Used by Lawrence & Cohen.

TYPE III. "L. C.—1864." in two horizontal lines of Roman capitals measuring 6½x4, and 8½x3mm.

2248	25	1c Proprietary	1864.
934	26	2c Playing Cards, blue	1861. red. must be error and is 1864.
	27	2c Playing Cards, blue	1864

TYPE IV. "L. & C.—1864." in two horizontal lines of Roman capitals measuring 16x4, and 8x2½ mm.

36	28	3c Proprietary
939	29	4c Proprietary
	30	4c Playing Cards
	31	5c Playing Cards
	32	10c Proprietary
	33	10c Certificate

In the Ballard sale held in 1926 by J. C. Morgenthau & Co. lot 1079 contained a 3c Playing Cards with date 1864. This item is not listed due to lack of data, but it possibly is Type IV and should be mentioned.

TYPE V. A single line circle 20mm. in diameter inscribed "L. & C.—Aug. 2—1864' in Roman capitals.

35	34	3c Playing Cards	Aug. 2, 1864
36	35	3c Proprietary	Feb. 20, 1869
37	36	3c Proprietary	June 15, 1871
38	37	3c Proprietary	Aug. 22, 1872
	38	4c Playing Cards	Aug. 2, 1864
	39	5c Playing Cards	Aug. 2, 1864
2254	40	5c Proprietary	Aug. 2, 1864
954	41	10c Proprietary	Aug. 2, 1864

The Boston Revenue Book lists seven types of Lawrence & Cohen cancellations and this article follows somewhat their numberings. However, the initials "H. C." listed in the Boston Book as Types V and VII do not represent any one known by the name of Cohen in the playing card business at that time and therefore their types V and VII are not accepted. According to Elliott Perry there was a Henry Cohen in the perfumery business in 1867-68, but even he might not be the party as the stamps referred to are dated 1864 and 1865.

Under #923 Sterling lists a 1c Playing Cards dated July 1863, and assigns it to Cohen & Co. The remarks about Henry Cohen apply to this stamp and for that reason the cancellation should not be listed.

In the writer's collection is a 1c Playing Cards Boston Book Type V dated Jan. 1864 and a 4c Playing Cards Type VII dated Nov. 1864. The Boston Book also lists Type V, 5c Playing Cards dated Mar. 19, 1865 and Type VII on a 4c Playing Cards, dated 1864. This could easily be an error for their Type IV or #29 of this article.

Under Adenaw #50 is listed a 5c Inland Exchange cancelled "L & Co. 1864." It is doubtful if this is a Lawrence & Cohen cancellation and is therefore omitted from the present listing.

It should also be noted that while Types I, II, III and IV are evidently printed from type set up in forms, Type V is from a handstamp probably applied to each stamp separately. Further, the 3c rate on Playing Cards was abolished in August 1864 and never restored, while the 5c rate was abolished at the same time and not restored until August 1866.

JOHN J. LEVY.

Mr. Levy learned the playing card business in the factory of his uncle, Lewis I. Cohen, whose firm became Lawrence, Cohen & Co., and later Lawrence & Cohen. About 1853 Levy founded his own firm under the name of John J. Levy, which about 1868 became John J. Levy & Co.

J.J.L.
DEC.
1862.

The cancellations found are of one type, "J. J. L.—Dec.—1862." in three horizontal lines measuring 14x4; 10x3, and 11x3mm. The first line is in script capitals; the others in sans serif.

		1	1c Playing Cards	blue.
		2	1c Playing Cards	inverted blue.
		3	3c Proprietary	black
		4	3c Proprietary	inverted black.
		5	4c Proprietary	blue.
		6	4c Proprietary	inverted black
		7	5c Proprietary	blue
J.H.				
Barr		8	5c Proprietary	black
2258		9	10c Proprietary	color?

There is listed by Sterling and by Adenaw one stamp each which they allocate to John Levy. The writer has not seen either of the stamps, but lists them below. Number One could easily be number I as a 3 often looks like a 2. Number Two could, and probably is, number 7 or 8. Both gentlemen listed the stamp with two intials J. L. The stamps listed above have another L. which could have been so faint on the stamps seen as to account for the two initials.

| 929 | One | 1c Playing Cards | J.L. Dec. 1863. |
| 51 | Two | 5c Proprietary | J.L. Dec. 1862. |

In Sterling's there is listed under his number 948 a 5c Proprietary with the cancellation "L. & B.—Sept.—1864" which is credited by him to Levy and Brother. John J. Levy is well known as a playing card manufacturer, but Isaac Levy who was in Samuel Hart & Co., and later became secretary of the New York Consolidated Card Co., is perhaps little known to collectors. As both Isaac and John J. Levy were nephews of Lewis I. Cohen, the two Levys may have been brothers, but there is no information available to show that there was a firm of Levy & Brother. Therefore the listing made by Sterling is not accepted. In the writer's collection are a 2c Playing Cards, blue, 3c Proprietary, 4c Proprietary and 5c Proprietary cancelled "L. & Br.—Aug.—1865." in three horizontal lines measuring 14½x2½; 9x2½; and 13½x2½ mm. The month on the 2c is Aug.; 3c is June; 4c is June inverted; and the 5c is May. Also there is a 1c Proprietary cancelled "L. & B.—October—1866." These may be similar to the listing of Sterling and are mentioned for reference only.

VICTOR E. MAUGER.

Mauger was for several years the New York agent for Chas. Goodall & Son of London. A private die stamp made for Victor E. Mauger and Petrie was issued in 1877 and used for about three years. As some of the dates of the cancellations listed below fall within these years, it is difficult to understand why the name Petrie was not included in the cancellation.

TYPE I. "V. E. M.—Oct.—1870." in three horizontal lines of Roman Capitals measuring 11x2; 5x2x1; and 6½x1½ mm.

949	1	5c Proprietary	Dec. '67
53	2	5c Proprietary	Feb. '69
2259	3	5c Proprietary	Oct. 1870.
2260	4	5c Proprietary	Nov. 1870.

Number 3 and 4 of the above are taken from the Boston Book whose description is used. It is assumed that the other two are similar. Sterling lists 3 and 4 and Adenaw lists 1 and 3 so it is likely they are the same.

In the Ballard sale held in 1926 by J. C. Morgenthau & Co., lot 1084 contained a 5c Proprietary dated May 1870. This stamp is not listed as the data is insufficient.

TYPES II, III and IV which follow are on stamps of the 1875-81 Proprietary issue on watermarked paper.

TYPE II. An inverted Ace of Spades containing, in a colorless centre, the monogram "V. E. M." below in two lines of Roman type, measuring 8½x2x1½; and 3x2mm, "Dec. 18—'78."

5   5c black

TYPE III. A small Ace of Spades without initials, but dated like Type II, with two horizontal lines at top and bottom 8mm. long and 13mm. apart.

6   5c black.

TYPE IV. A green handstamp in three horizontal lines "Mauger—May 29—1879" measuring about 13½x2½; 13½x2½; and 7x3mm.

    7   1c green.

From August 1866 the only tax on playing cards was 5c per pack. It seems extremely unlikely that any manufacturer or dealer would have used five 1c stamps on each pack. For many years Mauger had a store at 110 Reade Street, New York City, and about 1881 Mary A. Mauger sold sauce at that address. About 1878 or 1879 Victor E. Mauger and Petrie also sold perfumery. Mauger was an importer and merchant and there is no evidence to show he manufactured any playing cards. Probably Type IV was used on perfumery or cosmetics.

"The Three Plates of the 5c-Inland Exchange"

The cooperative replating of the three plates of the 5c-Inland Exchange, by the Revenue Unit of the American Philatelic Society, continues with unabated interest. New material is continually being found and slowly the work is progressing. Plate 5F has been completed and enough material is at hand to cover the major portion of Plate 5 and of the Mystery Plate, but a large part of this material is still "wild" and awaits the finding of "key blocks" to tie it into these plates in the proper positions.

The Big Shift in Plate 5 was long ago plated from the following data. B. D. Forster has a mint block of six with left margin attached showing that this shift is in the second vertical row from the left. C. C. Damon has a used block of six with upper margin attached, showing this shift in the second horizontal row from the top. Its position is therefore No. 19 on the plate as there are seventeen stamps in each horizontal row. Many copies of positions 19 and 20 have been studied.

The corresponding positions from Plate 5F, positions 19 and 20, are in the possession of many collectors. Philip Little, Jr. has an exceptional block of 54 from the upper left corner of the plate. In none of these duplicate items is there the slightest trace of the big shift.

Now there comes to hand a block of proofs showing 42 positions from the upper left portion of the Mystery Plate. The upper and left sheet margins are intact and many interesting plate varieties are in evidence. Positions 19 and 20, however, are outstanding in that they are two of the rarest double transfers on this stamp and No. 19 is in the same location as the Big Shift of Plate 5 but shifted in a different direction. Only two stamps showing this Mystery Shift have so far been submitted and no stamp showing position 20 has yet been reported.

In order to show the difference between the three plates we here illustrate positions 19 and 20 for each. Having no data as to the plate number nor any record of its existence elsewhere, there is no better name for it than the Mystery Plate. Items from this unknown plate are far more rare than from plates 5 or 5F but they do exist in a number of collections, usually in a brighter shade of red than the common color for plate 5F.

Those who are working on the reconstruction of these plates and others who have copies of the seventeen page report on plate 5F will now note that we apparently have proofs from both plate 5 and from the Mystery plate, but that no proofs have yet been found from Plate 5F. This special report illustrated the shifts on 47 plate 5F positions, shows 24 plate scratches and contains replating charts for the entire plate. Copies are still available at $3.00.

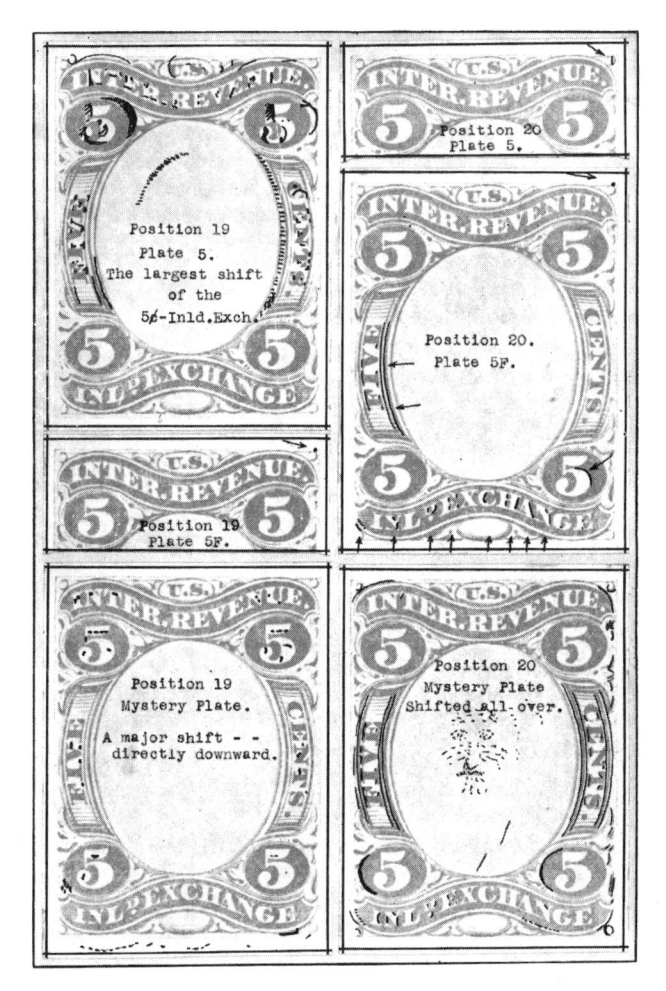

We are often asked what the charge is for giving plate positions on specimens submitted. While the replating work continues as a function of the Revenue Unit there will be no charge. We are desirous of seeing as many pairs, strips or blocks as possible and will be glad to mark the plate positions on the reverse side of all items that are clear prints and on which the position is known. However, we must decline to give positions for single stamps for the present.

C. W. BEDFORD, 19 Vaniman Street, Akron, Ohio.

REPLATING THE 2 CENT U. S. I. R.

Philip E. Hamilton, of Beaver Falls, Pa., is about to attempt to plate that interesting stamp of many shifts, the 2 Cent U. S. Internal Revenue, first issue.

As we know, there are many double transfers on this stamp, the writer knows of some eight or ten, and there must be many others.

Mr. Hamilton's idea is to replate the stamps from the second U. S. I. R. plate. Any of you who have blocks of four or more or any stamps showing marginal markings will be of substantial aid in this quest if you forward this material to Philip E. Hamilton, Attorney at Law, Beaver Falls, Pa. Mr. Hamilton says he will take good care of them and return them as promptly as possible.

You may recall that in the American Philatelist for April 1930 we had a very interesting article on this stamp by Unit member John H. Train, illustrated with six different examples of double transfers.

LeRoy E. Shaw has a full sheet of these stamps, original gum, and with full margins. Many of the known shifts do not show on this sheet, which as Mr. Shaw says, is proof positive that other plates were made. His description of his sheet follows, and is most interesting:

"Double Transfers on a Full Sheet of 2c U. S. I. R.

LeRoy E. Shaw

"A full sheet of Civil War revenues, original gum and with full margins, should be of interest to the revenue specialists and the data available is therefore presented at the request of the officers of the Revenue Unit.

"This sheet is comprised of 15 horizontal rows of 14 stamps each, making a total of 210 positions on the plate. The Boston Revenue Book states that the 2c-revenues contained 210 stamps per sheet comprising 10 rows of 21 stamps. This appears to be incorrect as to the number of stamps in a row for plate proofs have been observed on the 1c Express, 2c Express and 2c Proprietary wherein there are 14 stamps in a horizontal row as in the sheet which is being described.

"There are no marginal markings except the imprint which is centered at the bottom of the sheet with the usual inscription 'PRINTED BY (BUTLER & CARPENTER) PHILADELPHIA.' The words 'Plate No.' and the plate number itself are entirely missing. The Boston Revenue Book also omits the plate number for this stamp.

"The two shifts, T14 and T14a, as listed in Scott's S. U. S. catalogue, are not found on this sheet. This is direct indication that there was more than one plate and this is even more probable from the enormous number of stamps issued. Quoting from the Boston Revenue Book: 'After Sept. 30, 1867, this stamp was, with the exception of the 2c Proprietary whose use was restricted to proprietary articles and Playing cards, the only 2c stamp issued. It was printed only in orange and was last issued in October 1871. The total number issued was 456,724,925.' There were probably several plates, judging from the large number of plate varieties that are known in addition to those listed by Scott's, and which do not appear on this sheet.

"The 'usual' shift on the 2c U. S. I. R. is quite common. It is best located by looking for a doubling of the left side of the left scroll surrounding the word 'TWO.' It may be found in a multitude of minor variations of Degree of Shift, Angle of Shift and Extent of Shift. On this sheet alone there are at least 91 positions that show this shift under a good glass while 37 of these are easily seen and three or four are fairly good examples of a double transfer.

"Position No. 130, the fourth stamp from the left in the tenth horizontal row, is here illustrated. It is quite similar to T14 but the degree of shift is not so great and the doubling does not show in the upper label except under a glass. Position 116, just above 130 is a similar tho smaller shift, in fact all of the shifts on this sheet from the most minute up to position 130 are similar in position of shift, differing mostly in degree and extent. It is useless to further illustrate or describe the shifts as found on this plate."

NEW REVENUE STAMP FOR CIGARS.

Allan P. Vestal advises us that the Revenue office showed him the other day the new Revenue stamp for Cigars, which is the same as the old except for an imprint in red, series 102.

Italian Revenues

George D. Cabot, a new member of the Revenue Unit, called at my office the other day and showed me some very interesting Italian Revenue stamps, among which were the following:

A complete set of "Pesi e Misuri"—these run from 1 Centime to 30 Lire. The interesting part of these Revenue stamps is that they come in pairs, the left hand stamp showing the numerals of value in the center and the right a portrait of the King. In using these the stamp bearing numerals of value was placed on the Inspector's record and that bearing the portrait was placed on the certificate. These particular stamps were used in connection with weights and measures. One interesting pair of the 2.50 Lire was imperforate between, which I am told is quite a rarity.

Mr. Cabot also had a complete set of "Consolari," these stamps were issued for a special act which was cancelled within a year, and the stamps were in use only about nine months. The set is very rare, the 50 Lire value being especially scarce, less than one hundred copies being known. The design is similar to the "Pesi e Misuri," but they come in singles only and bear a portrait of the King. He also showed me a set of "Egeo," used by Italy for their colonists in the Aegean Sea, these are all surcharged in Piasters. He also has two interesting inverted specimens which are scarce, and an uncatalogued pair. Also has one inverted 5 Lire "Lusso e Scambi" pair—also an inverted surcharged 4 Lire Tassa di Bollo and a block of imperforate 20 Centime "Scambi Commerciali." He secured these stamps on a recent trip to Italy and they are certainly interesting specimens. Mr. Cabot is interested in knowing what other members of the Revenue Unit collect foreign Revenues, especially Italy and South America, and will appreciate hearing from any who do collect these stamps. His address is Room 3010, 22 East 40th St , New York City.

* * * * *

$1 FOREIGN EXCHANGE.

Our old friend Philip E. Hamilton has a copy of the $1.00 Foreign Exchange showing part of an imprint at the left side, the interesting thing about this stamp is that the imprint shows a double transfer. According to Mr. Bedford's records these shifted "imprints" are exceedingly scarce. Have any of you similar examples or perchance a vertical pair of this $1. value showing the entire imprint?

* * * * *

A SHIFT.

W. T. Kiepura, of Sioux City, Iowa, has sent in two copies of the $2.00 Green overprint with the large black "2." Both of these show double transfers in the upper part of the stamp. The shift is to the southeast, and it is about ½ mm, shows in the "U" of "US," "RE" of "REVENUE," upper left numeral and slightly at other points. The second copy shows some lines in the "RN" and "A" of "INTERNAL," "RNU" of "REVENUE," as well as in the left upper numeral. Shifts vary and are evidently not in the same position on the plate.

* * * *

HELP!

In checking over the printed and handstamped cancellations on Twentieth Century Revenues, Morton D. Joyce, of the Revenue Unit Committee, has uncovered a copy of the 1 Cent Trans-Mississippi that is surcharged in red "I. R." and under it the initials "L. H. C." Our guess is that this is L. H. Chapman, but we are not sure. He also has one surcharged with "I. R." with the initials "P. I. D. & Son" directly under it. This we know nothing about. Can any of you enlighten us? Another one that is baffling Mr. Joyce is a 2 Cent Battleship Documentary with the initials "E. D. S. & Co. 1901"—does anyone known what this is?

* * * * *

STITCH WATERMARK.

We are reporting a stitch watermark on the 2 Cent Lake Playing Card of the 1904 issue, #3992, in Scott's Monthly for March. This was uncovered by Mr. Joyce.

* * * *

ANOTHER BISECT.

Another bisect has turned up, this time Heyliger de Windt has discovered such a copy on an old photograph, together with a 2 Cent U. S. I. R. The bisect is a vertical half and was used to make up the 3 Cent rate.

A Reworked Plate for the 1c Express

C. W. BEDFORD.

For some unknown reason, a plate entirely entered by use of the 2c-Express relief was resurfaced or otherwise reconditioned and then entirely reentered by use of the 1c-Express relief. Remnants of the original 2c-Express entries appear scattered, here and there, over one of the 1c-Exprss plates. The fact data is as follows:

The 1c-Express plate, referred to, contains 210 plate positions or 15 horizontal rows of 14 stamps each. Over 135 positions out of the 210 have been replated, tying in to all of the four margins. The major portion of this replating comprises two enormous blocks of card proofs with many pairs, strips and blocks of stamps duplicating the proofs. There are said to be two plates carrying numbers 1D and 1E. We do not know to which of these two plates we refer but they are easily differentiated. The plate in question has many guide dots at the lower right corner while on the other plate the usual guide dot position is at the upper right corner.

In the lower margin of this plate, under the last stamp in the lower right corner (position No. 210 as illustrated), the entire top of a 2c first issue revenue appears clearly printed in the same color of ink as the 1c-Express stamp just above it.

Both proofs and stamps from position No. 210 show an apparent double transfer with a downward displacement but careful checking by the aid of overlapping photographic prints shows that the extra lines in this position are not from the 1c-Express relief but from a 2c revenue relief.

Illustrations A, B and C show three other similar but different stamps showing portions of this 2c revenue relief on the 1c-Express. These three stamps are as yet unplated as to position.

Position No. 66, as illustrated, definitely shows that this 2c revenue relief is the relief of the 2c-Express. In the lower margin of this stamp and just above position No. 80 remnants of the letters "SS" of "EXPRESS" are clearly visible. Photographic enlargements of No. 66 have been made and transparent tracings of the extra lines have been laid over an enlarged photograph of the 2c-Express. Every little extra dot, dash or line from the 1c falls accurately into its proper place on the 2c-Express design. This is accurately illustrated in the 2c-Express illustration.

Position No. 108 as illustrated, also shows parts of the top of the 2c-Express, the "E" of "REV." showing quite clearly. Positions 64, 100, 141 and 150 also show the same type of extra lines, being quite similar to No. 108.

It is important to note that all ten of the positions above described show exactly the same degree of downward displacement of the 2c relief on the 1c stamp and that these positions are widely scattered over the 1c-Express plate.

Incidentally and for completion of the data so far obtained, we illustrate the Double Transfer from the 1c-relief as found in position No. 138. Seven other positions are also doubled similarly in both lower numerals. They are positions 52, 56, 89, 131, 132, 172 and 176. The 1c relief also doubled in eight other positions, showing only in the lower right numeral. 89, 92, 98, 130, 136, 137, 177 and 178. Position 166 shows a heavy plate scratch starting heavily in the "P" of "EXPRESS" and running down into the lower margin. There is a small line in the second "E" of "EXPRESS" for position No. 181. This data will be of assistance to those who seek to replate the stamps from this plate.

* * * * *

Let us now turn from fact to speculation. We have no plausible explanation for this 2c plate reworked over into a 1c plate. Perhaps government orders were rushed, deliveries of the 1c express stamps were urgent and there was not enough time to bring in new blank plates so the work of entering an extra 2c plate was sacrificed to meet deliveries. Perhaps there was a 2c plate that was rejected due to unsatisfactory entering and economy caused the reuse of the plate. This is possible as the entire entering of the 1c was done considerably higher on the plate as compared with the first 2c entering. The low or "off center" characteristics of the 2c plate, as a whole plate, might have prevented the proper feeding of the paper into the press.

This surprising contribution comes as another example of the cooperative reconstruction of revenue plates by the members of the Revenue Unit of the American Philatelic Society. In this case there are three contributing members: A. C. Lane, Don R. Bennett and O. H. Wolcott. Mr. Lane furnished the proofs, Don Bennett sent a large perforated block from the upper right conrer of the sheet which definitely plated position No. 66 and Ollie Wolcott furnished the irregular block of five from the lower right corner which shows the top of the 2c relief in the lower margin.

The upper left and lower left corners with adjacent positions are still unplated and your continued cooperation is still needed. All data obtained will be published for the benefit of all collectors with full credit to all contributors. While this work is in progress Mr. Bedford will be glad to plate your strips or blocks of the 1c-Express without charge except for return postage. In return for this service, you may be the source of new data on this stamp.

There is at least one other, perhaps three more, cases of a revenue plate reconditioned and made over for a stamp of another denomination. There is one plate that was extensively RECUT and for which there is an EARLY STATE and a LATE STATE of the plate. This plate is easily replatable. There is one plate with a long row of TRIPLE TRANSFERS. There are many magnificent DOUBLE TRANSFERS scattetred here and there that have never been described and on several plates these doubles concentrat in one section of th plate. There is much interesting research still to be accomplished and your cooperation is needed by sending in pairs, strips and blocks of the following to C. W. Bedford, 319 Vaniman St., Akron, Ohio:

    1c Express, 5c Inland Exchange, 15c Foreign Exchange, 20c Foreign Exchange, $1.00 Power of Attorney, 60c 2d and 3d Issue, 1c Proprietary, Green and Black, 1871-75.

A Counterfeit Invert

Every so often we run across Revenue stamps with counterfeit perforations, clipped perfs. or fake cancellations, and very occasionally a counterfeit inverted head of the second or third issue turns up. An interesting copy of the latter has been uncovered by Carl Percy, of New York. This is a $2.50 second issue, on which the center medallion has been carefully erased and then by means of a photographic process the head of Washington has been replaced on the stamp in an inverted position. It is rather crudely done and would not fool anyone who is at all familiar with Revenue stamps or engraving.

* * * * *

15 CENT DOUBLE.

E. P. Nickinson, of Florida, has a very interesting copy of the 15 Cent Inland Exchange, first issue, perforated, with a beautiful double transfer to the right, showing practically all over the stamp. This is very similar to the 5 Cent Inland and 10 Cent Contract, both of which have been illustrated in The American Philatelist. There is a similar double on the 5 Cent Certificate. They are very clear cut and distinct and are really very beautiful items.

He also sent us a 2 Cent Proprietary showing a thin crack just outside the frame line on the right. This starts at the top of the stamp and runs down to the bottom of the lower perfs. and should evidently show on the stamp below.

* * * *

SOME QUESTIONS TO BE ANSWERED.

Fellow member Frank L. Applegate writes us as follows:

"Medford, Oregon, April 11, 1932.

"Mr. Beverly S. King,
  Secretary Revenue Unit, A. P. S.,
    New York.

Dear Sir:

I wonder if you could and would care to get the following queries printed in the A. P. They would seem to me to be of general interest to all collectors and students of our revenue stamps. Any answers or corrections to the following questions will be welcomed by the readers of this Department. Who can fill in the exact dates?

1. The Civil War Revenue Act was repealed all except the taxes on matches, medicines, playing cards, perfumery and bank checks .... 1872. The remaining schedules .... 1883.

2. The Documentary and Proprietary schedules of the Spanish American Revenue Act were repealed .... 1902.

3. The Proprietary Schedule of the Act of 1914 was repealed .... Presumably the Documentary Schedule has been in force ever since, though amended from time to time.

4. When was the Proprietary Act of 1919 repealed?

5. Was the Wine Act of 1916 ever repealed or amended so as to limit the denominations of stamps required, and when?

6. Which denominations of wine stamps are still in use? It is known that some of the values of the 1914 series were still in use supplementing the 1916 series long after the 18th amendment was passed in 1920, but are they still in use?

7. It is also apparent from reports of the Bureau that some of the Beer stamps were being prepared after 1920. Can any one report what values, if any, are still in use, and if not when their use ceased?

8. What Documentaries are still in use, and if not all denominations of Documentaries, Stock Transfer, and Future Delivery, when did the use of the various denominations cease and under what act?

9. Narcotics. Are they all still in use, and if not when did the use of the various denominations cease?

Respectfully submitted by"

* * * * *

G. N. Usticke of New York has submitted an exceptional piece of the 1 Cent Telegraph showing what is apparently a very unusual form of stitch watermark. This is an irregular block eight stamps wide by four high and the "stitch" lines show about twice the length of the ordinary watermark, and is in the form of an irregular continuous line right straight across the block. The Captain says that he only recalls seeing one other example of this kind of watermark which he found sometime ago on one of the higher values, and which he is at a loss to explain.

* * * * *

NEW REVENUE STAMPS?

It looks as though we might be in for some new Revenue Stamps if some of the proposed tax laws go through. If any do come out my advice to all you members is to secure them promptly and in the event of any oddities being discovered let us know so that we may note them in the Revenue Unit column.

A New Double on the 5 Cent Agreement

Don Bennett sends a copy of the 5 Cent Agreement, first issue, showing Double Transfer to the right. This is clearly indicated all over the entire stamp in a similar way to the 10 Cent Contract and the 5 Cent Certificate. He also sends a $1.00 Foreign Exchange, imperf, with the well-known extra frame line at the left. This may be new to some of you; three copies of the $1.00 Inland Exchange, first issue, each one showing break in the lower frame line in the lower left corner, and a dash in the upper left in the white border of the shield; a block of 50 Cent Conveyance, showing Double Transfer to the right on the lower right stamp, this is a good double and shows in the lower ornamental foliage as well as alongside the panel containing the words "INTER REVENUE."

* * * * *

NEW STITCH WATERMARKS.

The following have recently come to life:

10 Cent Documentary Battleship, showing horizontal stitch watermark.
3 Cent Playing Card, first issue, horizontal stitch watermark.
1 cent Blue Documentary Battleship, horizontal stitch watermark.

* * * * *

BATTLESHIP REVENUES.

W. T. Kiepura, of Sioux City, Ia., has been hunting for shifts and doubles on the Documentary Battleship stamps. Most of those he found are what we now call "Shifted Transfers" which occurred during the rocking-in process from the transfer roll to the plate, these always show on the narrow end of the stamp. There were five examples of these, all different, and all showing on the left hand side.

He also has uncovered a couple of good double transfers which show additional lines upward. One of these is particularly good, showing practically over the entire design. A pair of the 3 Cent Blue Documentary show a series of scratches in the upper border, and a 4 Cent Rose has a short transfer at the upper right.

* * * * *

Carl Percy, of New York City, sent in what looked at first glance to be a very interesting copy of the $2.50 Second issue Revenue, with the inverted center. On examination it turned out to be a fake and not a particularly good one at that. The original printed portrait had been removed, very likely by thinning the stamp, and a new one had been put on, evidently by some photographic process. It was rather crudely done but at first glance looked like the real article.

* * * * *

A couple of months ago, in a paragraph on Revenues, we spoke of Trans-Mississippi stamps pre-cancelled with the letters "L. H. C." and "P. I. D. & Sons," these being postage stamps properly surcharged and used for Revenues. Mr. Harrington has sent the following interesting story regarding the company who used these stamps:

POSTAGE USED FOR REVENUES.

By F. HARRINGTON.

"In 1894 L. H. Chapman started the operation of a packet boat between Utica and Little Falls, N. Y. The boat was named the "W. G. NIXDORF" after a Mr. Nixdorf, a member of Odd Fellows and a wholesale liquor dealer in Oneida. Mr. Chapman, also being a member of the same organization, placed before and after the name "W. G. NIXDORF" on each side of the boat the three links of the Odd Fellows.

This boat ran on the Erie Canal under the above name until the spring of 1900, when it was changed to "VICTOR ADAMS." At the time of the change Victor Adams owned and operated a knitting mill in Little Falls and a paper box factory in Utica. This boat ran under the latter name until 1917 when Mr. Chapman sold it. The boat was 92 feet long, and 16 feet wide, with a freight capacity of about 70 tons.

When this boat was making trips to Little Falls it was in the good old days of beer and the cargo ran 200 to 400 barrels each trip. The freight on the beer was used to pay the expense of operation, all other freight being profit.

Four men operated this boat other than Mr. Chapman, who himself was a pilot and engineer. After having headquarters in Little Falls for a period of 12 years he moved to Utica and the balance of his life as a boatman was spent in Utica, where he now lives.

At the outbreak of the Spanish-American War a tax of 1 cent was imposed on each bill of lading and Mr. Chapman, wanting to comply with the law, came to Utica to the Revenue Office to get the stamps but as no supply had been received up to that time he at once went to the Post Office and purchased 500 1 Cent stamps of the Trans-Mississippi issue and then made a bargain with the P. I. Daprix & Co., who operated a packet boat between Utica and Rome, N. Y., to stand one-half the expense of having these stamps surcharged "I. R." After this deal was made he took the stamps to a printer in Utica by the name of Purvis, who surcharged 250 "L. H. C." and 250 "P. I. D. & Son," and all of them "I. R." at a cost of $2.50.

In the printing one sheet was damaged and the balance was delivered to Mr. Chapman and Daprix & Son. As the supply of these stamps was very small and they were in use only a few days, and even before this small supply was used the Revenue stamps arrived in Utica and the use of the private surcharged stamps was discontinued. As near as I can learn only about 50 copies were not used. Counting the 50 unused copies and the sheet destroyed in printing would leave a total of 400 used of the "L. H. C." and "P. I. D. & Son" combined."

The 50 Cent Conveyance

We wonder whether any of our Revenue Unit members are willing to complete the task of plating the 50 Cent Conveyance of the first issue. Some little while ago C. W. Bedford was fortunate enough to get about two-thirds of a full sheet consisting of fifty-three stamps with parts of the top and right margins attached. Only a few plate varieties have been observed on this stamp, and they are all comparatively small in both extent and degree. They may be listed as follows:

1. Small shift in upper label.
2. Small shift at top-center and in upper right corner ornaments.
3. Two small shifts at lower right corner.
4. Diagonal scratch to the right thru the "E" of "Conveyance."
5. Heavy dot just before the "C" of "Conveyance."

In talking the matter over with Mr. Bedford he says: "With so little plate variety there is usually great difficulty in determining plate positions and even tho possible, the results would not justify the necessary work. The case of the 50 Cent Conveyance appears to be an exception due to the preservation of a large unsevered block of 53 stamps with parts of the top and right margins attached, as illustrated. This leaves only 32 plate positions to be determined for the location of six or more varieties, a comparatively small undertaking with a complete knowledge of the entire plate as the reward.

"Every position in this big, irregular block shows the diagonal dash in the flag of the "5" and a dot in the "0" of the lower numeral "50." This seems to be a die variety as there were surely more than one relief. This variety is easily observed on almost any single copy but has not been found on any other 50 cent denomination. None of the above listed varieties are found in this block so they are sure to be found in marginal pairs, strips or blocks which represent the blank spaces in the illustration. The margins should also be searched for a complete description of the imprint and plate number characteristics which may or may not be normal."

This block owned by Mr. Bedford is available for plating as well as his singles and pairs showing the plate varieties. I have a few blocks and strips which I will be glad to lend in connection with this work and I am sure that a great many of our other members will be willing to help.

The accompanying illustration shows the block of fifty-three stamps owned by Mr. Bedford, and it should be a simple matter to complete the plating and give position numbers of the few plate varieties.

			Top Sheet Margin.					
4	5	6	7	8	9	10	11	12	13	14
21	22	23	24	25	26	27	28	29	30	31
	Irregular block of None of the known in these positions			53 -- plate	50¢-Conveyance. varieties appear			
	39	40	41	42	43	44	45	46	47	48
	56	57	58	59	60	61	62	63	64	65
	73	74	75	76	77	78		81	82	83	84	85

Warner Robison recently sent me about fifteen copies of this stamp showing various plate scratches, and Revenue Unit readers may recall that in the American Philatelist for October 1931 our fellow member, W. W. Bradbury, had an interesting araicle on the plate varieties of this stamp. Who will volunteer to do the work?

* * * * *

THE 25 CENT POWER OF ATTORNEY.

At various times in the past a number of Unit members, including Kirshner, Sherman and Bedford, have showed me copies of the 25 Cent Power of Attorney with a slight doubling of the lower frame line. The clearest copy of this item, however, was sent to me just the other day by L. I. Newton, of Atlanta, Ga. Many of these shifted transfers on the Revenues are very blurred but Mr. Newton's copy seems to be a good clear print.

Mr. Newton also sent a beautiful copy of the 2 Cent U. S. I. R. Double Transfer T-14. He also has a good clean copy of the 2 Cent Orange and Black, second issue, with what looks to me very much like a vertical crack through the vignette head of George Washington. Of course we must find another copy of this to check with it before we can decide just exactly what it is.

Mr. Newton has also found copies of the diagonal and vertical cracks on the 50 Cent Mortgage.

MORE STITCH WATERMARKS.

Stitch watermarks, of course, may be found on any of our Revenue stamps if we look hard enough and long enough. Our old friend, Don Bennett, comes thru with the following, which of course we will be glad to see are listed in the next Specialized:

> 10 Cent Contract, old paper, perforated, horizontal stitch watermark.
> 10 Cent Inland Exchange, old paper, perforated, horizontal stitch watermark.
> 20 Cent Inland, medium paper, perforated, horizontal stitch watermark.
> 50 Cent Mortgage, medium paper, perforated, horizontal stitch watermark.
> Pair of $1.00 Foreign Exchange, old paper, perforated, horizontal stitch watermark.

Mr. Bennett also sent two copies of the 40 Cent Inland Exchange, perforated, showing a short scratch below the "L" of "INL." These check, which proves it to be a constant plate flaw. He also sent a beautiful copy of the $10. Conveyance showing a light outer line all the way down the right side of the stamp. This has every appearance of being a guide or position line.

Plating the 50 Cent Conveyance

In the September number of The American Philatelist we asked for a volunteer to plate the 50 Cent Conveyance, first issue, U. S. Revenue.

Justin L. Bacharach, of 1809 West Erie Ave., Philadelphia, Pa., has offered to do this work. Mr. Bacharach has been making a study of this stamp for some time and is therefore particularly interested in it.

Will any of you who have blocks or strips kindly forward them to Mr. Bacharach at the above address? He will take good care of them and see that they are returned to you just as soon as he is finished with them.

* * * * *

SHIFTED TRANSFERS ON THE MATCH AND MEDICINE STAMPS

C. H. Chappell has forwarded the following interesting list of Shifted Transfers on United States Match and Medicine Stamps. It is the first comprehensive list that has been attempted and should be added to. Very likely some of us have Double or Shifted Transfers on these stamps—if so, won't you send them in to me for examination?

U. S. Revenues, Shifted Transfers, Private Dies.

1c Black; Wm. Gates; Die II; Perf.; 1862; Silk; Position of Shift, Word "Matches"; Scott #5186.
1c Black; Bent & Lea; Perf.; 1862; Ex. Silk; Position of Shift, Left side; #5128.
1c Black; D. M. Richardson; Perf.; 1862; Silk; Position of Shift, Words "Inter. Revenue"; #5252.

1c Green; E. R. Tyler; Perf.; 1862; Paper, ?; Position of Shift, Circle; #5274.
4c Black, Hostetter & Smith; Imperf.; 1862; Silk; Position of Shift, Outer lines at right end of stamp; #5407.
2c Black; Dr. D. Jayne & Son; Uncut; 1862; Wmk.; Position of Shift, "Figures" in center and words "Two Cents"; #5420.
2c Black; Dr. D. Jayne & Son; Die Cut; 1862; Old; Position of Shift, "Figures" in center and words "Two Cents"; #5423.
2c Black; Dr. D. Jayne & Son; Die Cut; 1862; Silk; Position of Shift, "Figures" in center and words "Two Cents"; #5423.
2c Black; Dr. D. Jayne & Son; Die Cut; 1862; Pink; Position of Shift, "Figures" in center and words "Two Cents"; #5423.
2c Black; Dr. D. Jayne & Son; Die Cut; 1862; Wmk.; Position of Shift, "Figures" in center and words "Two Cents"; #5423.
1c Vermillion; I. S. Johnson & Co.; Perf.; 1862; Wmk.; Position of Shift, Words "U. S. Internal Revenue"; #5427.
1c Black; J. H. McLean; Perf.; 1862; Silk; Position of Shift, Words "Inter. Rev." at top; #5445.
2c Black; J. B. Rose & Co.; Perf.; 1862; Silk; Position of Shift, Words "Two Cents" at top; #5479.
2c Black; J. B. Rose & Co.; Perf.; 1862; Pink; Position of Shift, Words "Two Cents" at top; #5479.
6c Brown; H. H. Warner & Co.; Perf.; 1862; Wmk.; Position of Shift, Words "Remedies" in center; #5532.
1c Black; Byam, Carlton & Co., (wrapper); Imperf.; 1862.

* * * * *

POSTAGE STAMPS USED AS REVENUES.

Howard B. Beaumont has asked whether any list has been compiled of postage stamps used for Revenue purposes during the Civil War period. He has a few, including #68, #76 and #113, all on documents, of course. I have perhaps half a dozen in my own collection. Will be glad to hear from any of the Revenue Unit readers who have items of this sort.

* * * * *

MORTON JOYCE TAKES THE GRAND PRIZE.

Stephen Rich has just advised me that at the Pre-Cancel Exhibition recently completed in California, Morton Joyce, of the Revenue Unit, took the grand prize for the best exhibit with his pre-cancelled Playing Card Revenues on original wrappers.

Mr. Joyce, you may recall, is one of our committee on compiling a check list of the pre-cancelled Revenues of the various issues and it was in connection with his work on this committee that he rounded out his collection of pre-cancelled Playing Card stamps.

The Unit extends its congratulations to him.

In the October number of The American Philatelist we made note that Howard Beaumont had asked a question concerning the use of postage stamps used as Revenues. This brought responses from George R. Cooley, of Albany, who has seven such examples in his collection used on bank checks from 1863 to 1875. His items consist of Scott's Nos. 65, 73, 145, 146, 147, 158 and 178.

Robert F. Hale, of Malone, N. Y., writes that in his collection he has No. 73 on check, pen cancelled; No. 188 on check, pen and punch cancellation; No. 178 tied to check with rubber hand stamp cancellation; No. 253, Dr. K. & Co. Binghamton proprietary cancellation, and a copy of No. 338 hand stamped in blue with a United States Internal Revenue cancellation, the latter being off the document.

Dr. Lawrence L. Howe, of Clearfield, Pa., has sent me an old affidavit dated December 12, 1864, carrying a 3 Cent Rose, of the 1861 issue, and a 2 Cent Black Jack, pen cancelled.

In my own collection I have No. 63, 1 Cent Blue 1861, on a check, pen cancelled; No. 65, 3 Cent Rose, 1861, on check, pen cancelled; No. 67, 5 Cent Brown 1861, hand stamped, off cover; No. 73, 2 Cent Black, 1862, on a check, pen cancelled; No. 113, 2 Cent Brown, 1869, on a sight draft, pen cancelled; No. 157, 2 Cent Brown, 1873, on a check, pen cancelled; and No. 183, 2 Cent Vermillion, 1875, on a sight draft, pen cancelled.

Mr. Beaumont has written the following notes regarding these items, and to his list we have added the foregoing stamps:

* * * * *

Postage Stamps Used as Revenues and Revenue Stamps Used for Postage

By HOWARD B. BEAUMONT.

At various times, while looking over old papers for postage stamps, the writer has found instances where postage stamps have been used on checks and other documents in lieu of the requisite Revenue stamps. The same think has been observed by other collectors and at various times the items have been commented upon in The American Philatelist. In addition to the use of postage stamps for fiscal purposes there are cases where Revenue stamps have been used for postage.

Under what circumstances postage stamps were used for Revenue purposes will never definitely be known, but their use probably arose from a lack of Revenue stamps on hand at the time the documents were signed. How many different postage stamps were so used is still conjectural. The check list below has been made up from various articles in the Society's magazine supplemented by items in the writer's collection. It is likely that the list is far from complete but it is hoped that it can be made so with the help of the members of this organization. Items marked with on asterisk are in the writer's collection. Those with a double asterisk have not previously been noted in the Revenue Unit column.

Check List of Postage Stamps Used as Revenues.

\# 28—5c, 1847, used on a note in 1866.
   63—1 Cent, Blue, 1861, used on check, pen cancelled.
*65—3 Cent, Rose, 1861, used on check, pen cancelled.
**67—5 Cent, Brown, 1861, hand stamped, off cover.
**68—10 Cent, 1861, on an order to take depositions.
   71—30 Cent, 1861, on a check.
*73—2 Cent, 1862, used on a check, pen cancelled.
*76—5 Cent, 1863.
   87—2 Cent, 1867, 11x13 grill.
   88—3 Cent, 1867, 11x13 grill.
   92—1 Cent, 1867, 9x13 grill, pair on a note.
**93—2 Cent, 1867, 9x13 grill, on a receipt.
*113—2 Cent, Brown, 1869, on a sight draft, pen cancelled.
  113a—2 Cent, 1869.
  114—3 Cent, 1869.
**145—1 Cent, 1870, used on check.
  146—2 Cent, 1870, used on check.
**147—3 Cent, 1870, used on check.
  157—2 Centfi 1873, used on a check, pen cancelled.
*158—3 Cent, 1873, on a check.
  178—2 Cent, 1875, tied to check with rubber hand stamped cancellation.
  182b—1 Cent, 1879.
**183—2 Cent, 1875, on a sight draft, pen cancelled.
  184—3 Cent, 1879.
  188—10 Cent, 1879, used on checks, with pen and punch cancellation.
**253—3 Cent, 1894, Dr. K. & Co., Binghampton proprietary cancellation.
**285—1 Cent, Trans-Miss. pair on check.
  286—2 Cent, Trans-Miss.
  290—10 Cent, Trans-Miss., three on a certificate of deposit.
  338—10 Cent, 1908, with U. S. Internal Revenue blue handstamped cancellation off document.

The finest item on the list is, of course, the 5 Cent 1847, on a note dated in 1866 and now owned by Mr. H. H. Elliott, Treasurer of the A. P. S. The next best is the 30 Cent 1861 on a check dated May 29, 1863, issued by Rawson and Whipple at the Shetucket Bank of Norwich, Conn.

The use of the 2 Cent Black Jackson and of the 3 Cent 1861 must have been greater than that of the other postage stamps.

In addition to the stamps listed above we have seen a 6 Cent Treasury used on a check but we are not adding it to the list until we have examined it and determined which issue it is. We have in our collection an uncancelled copy of No. 75, the five cent red-brown of 1862, which we know was originally upon a check. It is also our understanding that there has recently been found a check bearing six uncancelled copies of this stamp.

The use of Revenue stamps for postage appears to be much less common than the reverse. The short check list below has been compiled from articles in the Magazine. We hope the members of the Society will be able to expand it.

Check List of Revenue Stamps Used for Postage.

#3814—2 Cent U. S. I. R. used with 1 Cent, 1869.
3818—3 Cent Telegraph.
3826—5 Cent Inland Exchange.
3997—2 Cent surcharged I. R.
4028—2 Cent Documentary of 1898.
4226—2 Cent Documentary of 1917.

At the present writing the only one of the items on the list that we have been able to find is a poor copy of No. 4226.

* * * * *

5 CENT AGREEMENT D. T.

The usual double transfer on this stamp shows in an extra line in the stem of the four numerals. Mr. Olaf Nagel, of Chicago, called at my office the other day and showed me a new example of a transfer in this stamp, which showed a doubling in the word "Five" and also slightly in the lower lettering.

He also had a nice copy of the $1.00 Power of Attorney, perforated, on medium paper, with a well defined horizontal stitch watermark.

* * * * *

CRACKED PLATES.

C. W. Yarrington, Jr., of Gary, Ind., sent us an interesting copy of the 50 Cent Brown Stock Transfer Revenue of Massachusetts. This shows a series of horizontal surface cracks starting at about midway up and extending all the way to the top and into the gutter of the stamp.

Mr. Yarrington says that this is constant on fourteen copies that he has been able to locate, it is a very interesting specimen.

* * * * *

PUERTO RICO PROVISIONALS.

Col. Hamilton's remarks in the November "Journal" relative to the ¼ Cent Battleship stamp surcharged "Guam" has produced a letter from R. B. Preston, of Schenectady, N. Y. He says:

"In regard to Colonel Hamilton's statement that he had not known of the 1898 Revenues overprinted, I wonder if he referred to overprints for GUAM only.

"I am enclosing a pair of the 1c Documentary that was made to do duty in Puerto Rico, although probably a bit differently than the GUAM as this seems to have been used for a Puerto Rican Excise Tax. Possibly these stamps were made to do duty throughout the territory annexed after the war with Spain."

Mr. Preston enclosed a vertical pair of the 1 Cent Blue Documentary, overprinted "PORTO RICO, I. C. EXCISE REVENUE" in three lines, he says that he bought this in an assortment of stamps from a native in Puerto Rico in 1914.

The Low Value Proprietary Stamps of 1871-1875.
Plate Varieties.

C. W. BEDFORD.

Through the cooperation of Arthur C. Lane we have been able to examine an almost complete set of plate proofs of the Proprietary stamps of 1871-1875, from the 1c to the 10c inclusive and take pleasure in presenting an almost complete record of the plate varieties on these interesting stamps. Since examining these proofs we have been able to find several of the same varieties on the stamps so this issue should take on a new and added interest to revenue collectors.

The plate number imprint on these plates reads as follows:

B7   Engraved by JOS. R. CARPENTER Philadelphia   7B

T. Patent July 13th 1869.

The black number of the vignette plates always show the letter BEFORE the numeral while the colored number of the border plate always shows the numeral first. In the above illustration the extra letter and period before "Patent" represents an indistinct letter and strong period that appears only on plate 7B of the 10c stamp. This is of the nature of a double transfer but it in no way seems to double any part of the imprint so that its origin is unknown.

On the opposite side of the plate from the plate number imprint there is found what we might term a "Patent Imprint" as follows:

WILCOX'S CHAMELEON PAPER, PATENTED MAY 16th 1871.
GEORGE T. JONES' PATENT.

The above is as the patent imprint appears on plate 18 of the 3c stamp, and on plate 14 of the 5c stamp. On plate number 4 of the 10c stamp an extra date was added as an afterthought for the alignment is not accurate and the result is a nonsymmetrical imprint. It appears as follows:

WILCOX'S CHAMELEON PAPER, PATENTED MAY 16th 1871.
GEORGE T. JONES' PATENT. 1 MARCH 22d 1870.

Here again there is an error for the extra numeral (1) that appears just before "March" but in line with "Patent" seems to have no connection with the imprint nor does it appear on other plates to which the same second date was added.

There were two plates for the 4c Proprietary stamp having the numbers 7A and 7B for the border plates and A7 and B7 for the center plates. On plate 7A the Patent Imprint has the second date but evidently a new imprint roller had been made for the new imprint is both symmetrical and properly aligned as follows:

WILCOX'S CHAMELEON PAPER, PATENTED MAY 16th 1871.
GEORGE T. JONES' PATENT. MARCH 22d 1870.

1c-Proprietary. Plates A1 and 1A. 15 horizontal rows of 14 stamps or 210 stamps per sheet. The two imprints are centered in the left and right margins opposite the eighth horizontal row. The plate number imprint is at the left and the patent imprint, with added date, is at the right.

Every position on both plates have been examined except a vertical block of 2x5 adjacent the left imprint. There are no plate varieties of importance in either plate A1 or 1A.

Plates B1 and 1B. These plates have no been examined.

2c-Proprietary. Plates A3 and 3A. Plate layout the same as for the one cent stamp. Every position on these plates have been examined except a vertical block of 2x5 adjacent the right imprint. There are no varieties on the center plate, A3.

On the border plate, 3A, we find seven as attractive double transfers as are to be found on any of the revenues. All of these varieties are somewhat similar and yet they are so individually different that any one may be easily recognized from the illustrations. No. 8 is the largest double for degree of misplacement and No. 5 is the next in degree but the strongest for visibility. Nos. 3 and 28 are similar but the latter does not show the double in the upper right shield. Nos. 27, 108 and 134 show the doubling in the upper label. Due to lack of space the upper portion of 27 is not shown. It is perhaps the weakest double of the group but taken alone it would be considered as a fine variety.

Just how rare these varieties are as stamps, we are unable to say. We have been able to find but one stamp, that being from position 5, for though these stamps are not high priced in the catalogue we see comparatively few of them offered. Proofs are about as rare as stamps but a plate variety shows up so beautifully on a proof that from this standpoint they are more desirable. The chameleon paper on which these stamps were printed detracts greatly from their appearance.

3c-Proprietary. Plates 18 (center) and 18 (border). Ten horizontal rows of 17 stamps or 170 stamps per sheet. The two imprints are centered in the upper and lower margins above and below the ninth vertical row. The plate number imprint is in the lower margin and the patent imprint, without the added date, is inverted in the upper margin.

Every position in these two plates have been examined except for five positions in the next to the lower rows (143, 144, 145, 146 & 147). There are no plate varieties of merit in the border plate.

There are three very fine double transfers of the entire portrait on the center plate in positions 53, 73 and 89. All of these three doubles occur in a block of 4x3 and as one glances at the block these three positions show the face of Washington very much darker than on the surrounding stamps. Under a glass almost

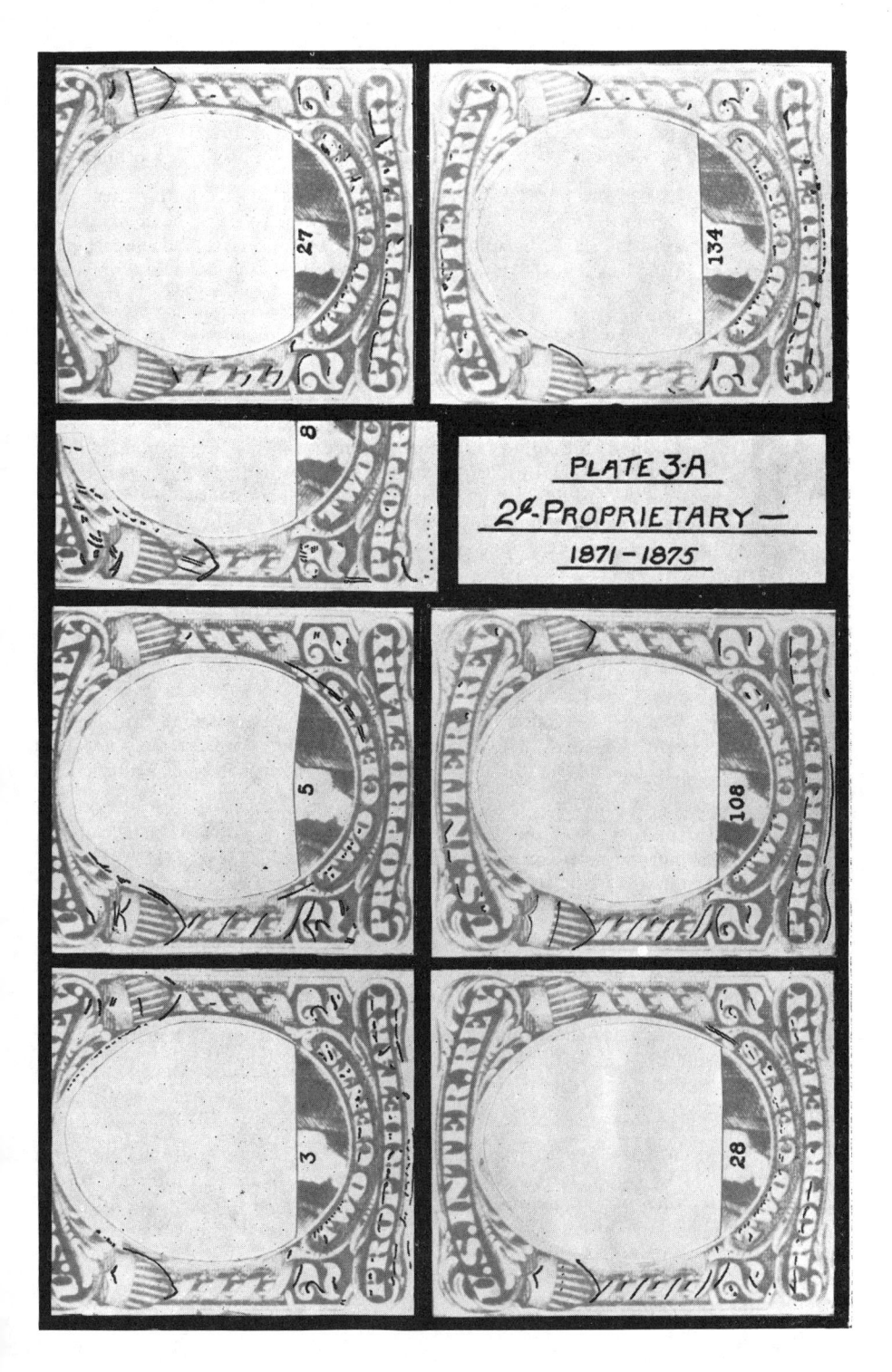

PLATE 3·A
2¢-PROPRIETARY —
1871-1875

every fine horizontal line is seen to be clearly doubled. Double transfers in the center of a bicolored stamp are a rarity and are seldom seen. When found on this three cent stamp they are items of exceptional interest. Not only are we not allowed to illustrate these varieties but in this case the doubling is so fine and so extensive that it would not easily show satisfactorily unless highly magnified.

4c-Proprietary. Plates A7 and 7A. Plate layout the same as for the three cent stamp. Only 123 positions out of the 170 have been examined. The positions unexamined are the upper left corner of the plate, 6x5, and the imprint blocks of ten at top and bottom. We will be glad to see blocks from these missing positions.

On the border plate, 7A, there is a very small double showing in "V. REV." of the top label. No varieties have been observed on the center plate, A7. The patent imprint is described above.

Plates B7 and 7B. All but thirteen positions on these two plates have been examined for plate varieties. There is one exceptional double transfer of the vignette in position 166 of the center plate, B7. The eyes, bridge of the nose, the coat lapel and collar are strongly doubled to the right. As most of the lines in the design are horizontal, the double fails to show in a misplacement to the right, except as described. There are no varieties in the border plate, 7B. The imprint is described above.

5c-Proprietary. Plates 14 (center) and 14 (border). Plate layout the same as for the three cent stamp. The patent imprint does not have the added date. There are no plate varieties on either plate. All positions have been examined.

6c-Proprietary. Plates 12 (center) and 12 (border). Plate layout the same as for the three cent stamps. The patent imprint and adjacent block, 5x2, with positions 143, 144, 145, 146 and 147 have not been examined on either plate.

There is no plate variety on the center plate. There are four small double transfers on the border plates in positions 17, 34, 81 and 83. All four show the doubling in the upper label with No. 34 as the best, also showing in "SIX CENTS" and in the numeral.

10c-Proprietary. Plates 4 (center) and 4 (border). Plate layout the same as for the three cent stamp. The plate number imprint and 14 positions have not been examined. The patent imprint was described above.

There are no plate varieties on the center plate. Position 114 in the border plate shows a small but clear double transfer in the upper label.

* * * * *

The above data is so nearly complete that every effort should be made to finish the work and close the book on these stamps with all the information on record. The balance of the material needed is known to exist and yet its location is unknown. We are especially interested in seeing the missing blocks of proofs with the imprints in the margins. The missing positions from the interior of the plates will also be found in imprint blocks.

REVENUES USED FOR POSTAGE.

In the December number of The American Philatelist we gave a list of postage used for Revenues—Jere Hess Barr, of Reading, Pa., has sent three other examples, one is a 2 Cent '69 used on a receipt dated February 16, 1870, pen cancelled; a second is Scott's #76, 5 Cent Brown, on a legal paper, dated January 7, 1862, which seems rather curious as this stamp was not issued until March 1862. The answer is found, however, on examination of the pen cancellation of the stamp which reads "September." Undoubtedly the stamp was applied sometime after the document was drawn.

Mr. Barr's third item is a beautiful copy of Scott's #78, 24 Cent Lilac, used on a check roll of labor performed in making repairs on the Third Division, Susquehanna Canal, during the month of October 1867. This 24 Cent stamp is used in connection with a 2 Cent U. S. I. R., and is tied to the document with a hand stamped cancellation reading "SUSQUEHANNA CANAL CO. SEPT. 1867."

These all have the appearance of being genuine and Mr. Barr states that he secured them from sources which he believes to be absolutely reliable.

He suggests that it might be interesting and desirable to list the 2 Cent #3805 and #3814, printed on checks, in exactly the same design as the adhesive Revenues, as a variety of the Revenues in the Specialized Catalogue. Of course you are all familiar with the latter item.

I have also received a letter from Harold C. Brooks, of Marshall, Mich., enclosing an envelope bearing two 1 Cent Green Proprietary stamps of the 1875 issue, Scott's #3983. These are tied on to the envelope with the cancellation of Mount Pleasant, Ohio. Mr. Brooks says that this was sent to him by a person answering one of his stamp ads in The Christian Herald in 1926. Not having been used contemporaneously it is, as Mr. Brooks suggests, only of passing interest. The stamps were evidently placed on the envelope in good faith and I would hardly call it a philatelic cover.

Mr. H. S. Riederer, of New Rochelle, N. Y., states that he has fine copies on original covers of the 2 Cent Proprietary and the 2 Cent Documentary of the 1898 issue, Scott's #4008 and #4028. Mr. Riederer says, "The #4008 has apparently not been reported as yet and it seems that Mr. Beaumont has not seen an authentic copy of #4028 used for postage. I must acknowledge that the #4008 is not actually tied to the cover, having been postmarked at a rural office with the office and date stamp on the cover and the target on the stamp, but I can vouch for the authenticity of the piece for I personally knew the person who sent it (the letter) to my father and I have possessed the cover ever since. The copy of #4028 is fully tied to the cover by the flag of the cancellation New York, N. Y. consisting of parallel vertical lines."

Sam Zander, of Galveston, Texas, has written that he owns a cover carrying a 2 Cent Proprietary, Blue, of the 1862 issue, #3812, duly cancelled and postmarked. "Unfortunately," says Mr. Zander, "the postmark is illegible, but the letter comes a long distance as the cover bears the inscription 'via Independence, Mo.'— the destination having been La Grange, Texas. The cover has been in my possession upward of forty years, and came to me out of the correspondence of a La Grange resident."

Frank D. Halsey, of Princeton, N. J., has in his collection a cover postmarked "New York, January 2, 1905" carrying a 4 Cent Proprietary #4011.

Dr. Robert E. Chambers comes through with the following additional covers from his collection. These are all of the 1898 issue, with the exception of one, which is a combination cover, 2 Cent Violet Brown Proprietary #4008; 2½ Cent Lake, Proprietary, #4009; 2 Cent Carmine Rose, Documentary, #4028; 1 Cent Pale Blue, Documentary, #4027, used in conjunction with the 1 Cent Columbian postage stamp #230.

The way these items are coming in we may get a real check list before long. Then the question will arise as to whether they should be listed in the Specialized Catalogue. BEVERLY S. KING.

Financial Statement—Revenue Unit A. P. S.

For Fiscal Year Ending Aug. 31, 1932.

GENERAL ACCOUNT.

Cash on hand August 31, 1931	$ 11.65	
Dues received, 1931-32	47.00	$ 58.65
Postage	$ 19.42	
Photographs for illustration purposes	4.90	$ 24.32
Cash on hand August 31, 1932		$ 34.33

SPECIAL ACCOUNT.

Cash received from old Revenue Society	$ 170.00
Cash received from members for work on Cancellation Check List, 1931	110.00
	$ 280.00
Expended for work on Check List during 1932	$ 25.00
Cash on hand August 31, 1932	$ 255.00

You will see from the above that the Revenue Unit is in pretty good financial condition at the present time. Our expenses for postage and photographic work for the past year amounted to only $24.32, which leaves us a balance in the General Account of $34.33, which should be ample to carry the Unit for the present year up to August 31, 1933.

In view of this balance on hand, and bearing in mind that these are depression days it has been decided to waive or remit all dues for the current year 1932-33. We presume that all of you members of the Revenue Unit, upon reading this notice, will give a loud cheer, at least we hope you will. We trust that the above will meet with your approval.

* * * *

PLATING THE 50 CENT CONVEYANCE.

J. L. Bacharach, of 1809 Erie Ave., Philadelphia, Pa., who has been plating the 50 Cent Conveyance, first issue, wishes to express his thanks and appreciation to all of the Revenue Unit members who have been kind enough to lend him material for this work. This material I understand has all been returned.

Mr. Bacharach is now anxious to purchase blocks of this stamp in units of any size larger than strips of three, as he would like to have a complete plate consisting entirely of his own material. Those of you who have duplicate blocks of this stamp I am sure will be glad to oblige him.

* * * * *

ODD NOTES.

Olaf Nagel, of Chicago, has submitted four copies of the 50 Cent Original Process, first issue, perforated, each stamp showing a slight shifted transfer at top. The outer frame line is doubled and there is a spot above the "E" of "CENTS."

Mr. Nagel asks whether this is the double transfer listed in Scott's Specialized—it is not—the one noted in the Catalogue consists of a strong double transfer along the left side of the stamp with a continuous line thru the words "UNITED STATES." This was illustrated in the Revenue Unit column of The American Philatelist for September, 1929.

The item submitted by Mr. Nagel I have seen before, Dr. Chambers and Dr. Gearhart both have copies in their collections, as I believe many of the rest of you have.

* * * * *

In the same letter Mr. Nagel enclosed copy of the $5. Conveyance, first issue, perforated, with a white or unprinted triangle section about ¼" high in the lower right corner. This doesn't look as tho it was caused by a fold in the paper but rather by an extra scrap of some sort that had adhered to the sheet during the printing process. He also sends an irregular block of three of the 10 Cent Power of Attorney, the two bottom stamps forming a pair being incomplete in the printing, but in this case after leaving the press had become damaged and a strip torn off, the sheet was then brought back to shape by pasting a strip of blank paper where the tear had occurred and the stamps were then perforated. This is quite an interesting curiosity.

* * * * *

Mr. Nagel also submitted a copy of the 10 Cent Certificate showing horizontal stitch watermark. A former copy of this was sent to us some little time ago by Mr. Brookman, and noted in the December number of the Journal.

* * * * *

POSTAGE STAMPS USED AS REVENUES.

Two other items have been called to our attention by Mr. Nagel, of Chicago, one being #95, 5 Cent Brown, 1867 issue, grilled, used on a note dated August 23, 1870, and #113, 2 Cent Brown, 1869, used with six 1 Cent Proprietary Revenues, and dated January 26, 1871.

A. B. Casey, of Erie, Pa., has produced a copy of the 4 Cent Orange Trans-Mississippi #287, used as a Revenue stamp. Mr. Casey states that this stamp was used as a Revenue on a New York Central Bill of Lading in 1908. It is surcharged with a large "R" in black, and shows part of a rubber stamp cancellation "JUL SYRACU"—the "R" is also a rubber stamp.

H. T. Browning, of Bay City, Mich., writes me as follows:

"A friend recently gave me an accumulation of some of the older U. S. postage issues. In this I found a number of stamps which I believe were used for Revenue purposes. These included a pair of Scott's #258, three copies (one straight edged) of #273, and one straight edged #274. I enclose one of the copies of #273; the cancellation on each of the other items mentioned is almost identical. Unfortunately these stamps reached me 'off the paper,' but the individual who gave me the stamps was at one time in the banking business, and his opinion is that these stamps were used as Revenues. I will be glad to have you retain the copy of #273 for your collection, if you so desire."

R. J. Mechen, of Edwards, N. Y., sends me a 2 Cent Brown #146, used on a check on The Central National Bank of Rome, dated February 18, 1872, signed by A. J. Carmichael. With this he sends three similar checks signed by the same party, two of them carrying the customary 2 Cent U. S. I. R. and the third a 2 Cent second issue. Mr. Mechin found these in an antique shop in Ogdensburg some time last summer while looking for some old trotting horse prints.

Revenues Used As Postage

R. C. Fisher, of Nashville, Tenn. has a straight edge copy of the $2. Rose 1917 issue, Scott #4238, used as postage. Mr. Fisher advises me that it was used on a tag of registered bank mail sent from the Federal Reserve Bank of Atlanta to the Cumberland Valley National Bank, at Nashville, Tenn., March 1, 1918.

Milton R. Miller, of Batavia, N. Y. writes me as follows:

"In my collection there is a cover with a 2c black jack and a 1c express, part perforate, used to prepay the 3c rate. The cover is addressed to the "Clerk or Deacon of the Baptist church, West Bethany, Genesee county, N. Y." The cover was in a find I made three or four years ago, being in the possession of, I imagine, a son of the said clerk or deacon.

"The letter inside is dated Feb. 1, 1864, Stockton, Chautauqua county, N. Y. The Rev. Jesse Elliot was the writer. In his communication the reverend gentleman notes that the West Bethany church is without a pastor, outlines his forty years experience in the ministry, frankly states that at present he finds it "too hard to ride and preach as much as I have done for some years, and at the same time support my family" and suggests he would like to settle down in a nice place like West Bethany.

"The Rev. Mr. Elliot was evidently hard put to it for a 3c stamp, and after scurrying around located the above combination. The stamps are tied by a black grid, but the post office of origin is not mentioned on the face of the letter by either written or printed postmark."

R. J. Mechin, of Edwards, N. Y. advises me he has a cover from Marshall, Mich., carrying a 2 Cent Orange, U. S. I. R. overlapped with a 3 Cent 1869, tied together with a cancellation, on an advertising cover. Mr. Mechin also has a 3 Cent '69 used on a check, pen cancelled.

Dr. Samuel Konwiser, of Newark N. J. submits the following used for postage:

#3802—1 Cent Proprietary pair on cover from West Redding, Ct. (Jan. 9, 1884)

#3997—2 Cent surcharged I. R. with 1c green #279 from Newark, N. J. July 2, 1898

2 Cent Documentary from Newark, N. J. February 26, 1902 (Battleship).

Postage Used As Revenue.

Harry E. Gray, of Oakland, California, owns a copy of the 1 Cent 1869 on a piece of a receipt. It has a circular cancellation struck in green, reading "Madison & Burk" with their address and date Oct. 1, 1869. Madison and Burk were and still are Realty operators in San Francisco.

One of the most interesting items submitted so far comes from John Cabot, Jr., of New York. This consists of a strip of three 10 Cent 1861, used on a Promissory note for $300 dated April 1, 1868, pen cancelled.

Jere Hess Barr, of Reading, Pa., has sent three additional items from his collection, the first being a check on the Farmers Bank of Reading, dated May 25, 1863, carrying a 1 Cent Blue 1861, the second a check on the National Union Bank of Reading, dated May 19, 1876, carrying a 2 Cent Vermillion, and the third a check on the same bank dated January 1, 1867, carrying a 2 Cent Black Jack.

These are all pen cancelled. The last named check, in addition to the 2 Cent Black Jack, carries a 2 Cent U. S. I. R. uncancelled. Mr. Barr, in commenting on this, thinks that "it is altogether probable in the case of the 2 Cent Black Jack, that the bank may have refused to accept this and made Mr. Potteiger who signed the check add a 2 Cent Revenue stamp. It looks as if Mr. Potteiger was rather careless and took the first thing at hand in stamping his checks." All three are drawn by the same person.

* * * * *

1 Cent Documentary Stamps.

Some of you may have noticed colored dots in the periods before and after "Cents" on the 1 Cent Documentary stamps of the 1917 issue. Some plates carry these dots, others do not. Clayton W. Bedford took this up with the Bureau of Engraving and Printing, and A. W. Hall, the Director, writes as follows:

"The making of the offset plates for the initial printing of the issue of 1917 documentary stamps and the printing therefrom were done by commercial companies. Thereafter the making of the offset plates and the printing were done by this bureau. All certified impressions of the 1-cent documentary stamps, series of 1917, from plates made by this bureau, have been examined and it is found that a dot appears in the periods on all of them.

"We have no certified impressions of the printings by the commercial lithograph company which printed the initial stamps of the issue. Possibly these stamps did not contain the dots referred to."

This may be the answer.

* * * * *

50 Cent Life Insurance.

George F. Kirshner, of Kansas City, Mo., has submitted copy of the 50 Cent Life Insurance, first issue, perforated, with a horizontal scratch in the right side, opposite the top numeral "50." Also a copy of the $1. Inland Exchange with a double in the upper part, showing in the word "DOLLAR", top lines of shield and top frame line. There is a somewhat similar copy to this that has been noted, where the tops of the shields are so strongly doubled that they extend above the frame line.

More Revenues—Postage

We are gradually increasing our check list in connection with Revenues used for postage and Postage for Revenue.

Henry W. Holcombe of New York submits a copy of #147, 3 Cent Green, 1870-71 issue, used on a check drawn on Tallant & Co., Bankers, by the firm of M. M. Cook & Son, Leather Hose & Belting, 201 Battery St., dated San Francisco Sept. 2, 1870. The stamp is cancelled by two short pen lines diagonally across the southeast corner and tied to the check by the embossed name and address of the drawee.

Mr. Holcombe also submits a copy of #73, 2 Cent Black Jackson, 1862-66 issue, used on a Bill of Lading, of the Worcester Railroad Corporation, dated Boston Sept. 14, 1864. The stamp is cancelled in manuscript on the same date.

Charles E. Phillips, of New York, has unearthed two interesting postage used for revenue—these are a piece of original document, tied on with hand stamped cancellations.

One piece carries a 2 Cent Bank Check, 10 Cent Certificate and 24 Cent Grey Lilac, Scott's No. 78A. The other strip carries a pair of the 4 Cent Inland Exchange, one copy of the 10 Cent Bill of Lading and one copy of the 24 Cent Grey Lilac, 1862-66 issue, Scott's No. 78A.

The nice part about both these copies is that they are tied on with hand stamp reading "Susquehanna Canal Co. July 1867."

* * * * *

PLATING EARLY REVENUES.

Lieutenant-Commander E. P. Nickinson, Box 425, Pensacola, Florida, has assumed the task of plating the $1 Inland Exchange. I sent him what I had a short time ago, the largest being a block of twelve, and from that running down to blocks and strips of three or four. The Commander also secured material from various other members of the Unit, but he has not enough on hand yet to complete his work on the plate. He has tried to get material from dealers, but they do not seem to have any.

If any of you fellow members have blocks or strips of this stamp won't you please send them ont to Commander Nickinson, so he may complete the job? He is willing to buy certain blocks and strips if any of you care to sell them. He tells me that "apparently there are two states of the plate, the principal distinction being in color, all bright red copies are late state and all of the dull red copies the early state. There was an intermediate shade that was used in 1869, which may be either early or late."

He is preparing a series of notes on this plate which will be published a little later. Please give him what help you can.

* * * * *

2 CENT PROPRIETARY.

In going over his Revenue stamps looking for plate flaws, Commander Nickinson discovered and sent me three strips of the 2 Cent Proprietary, first issue. One of these showed a light and a heavy line in the margin at the top of the stamp. Another showed a very heavy line, as tho the space between the two first mentioned had been filled up. The third stamp showed a single line only. Took this up with C. W. Bedford and found that he called them "gutter marks." He says that the gutters became worn by constant plate wiping, and held the ink, the early printings showing a very faint line and the later printings showing a broader, more blurry line.

Mr. Nickinson also calls our attention to a nice double on this stamp that shows in "U", "R", and "V" of "U S INTER REV," in the ribbon of the right upper numeral, in the word "CENTS" and in the word "TWO." This is the first one that we have seen of this transfer.

Warner S. Robison, of Mentor, Ohio, sends a 2 Cent Proprietary with what looks like a crack on the face of the vignette. This runs from the forehead over the left eye, down across the nose to the right cheek.

* * * * *

PLAYING CARDS STAMP—PERF. 11.

From Billy Whittemore of Larchmont, N. Y. comes a copy of the Playing Cards stamp, Scott's Type PC 2, listed by Scott as perf 10, yet this copy is Perf 11, and is cancelled with date 1931. It also bears the initials "C P C" in very small type. Doubtless the initials of the company which used the stamp. This is an uncatalogued variety and one that should be well worth looking for. (Linn's Weekly Stamp News)

* * * * *

Olaf Nagel, of The Nabi Stamp Co., Chicago, has sent us some interesting double transfers on Revenues. Most of them have been noted. He has an interesting block of seventeen U. S. I. R. three stamps of which show interesting and clear double transfers, one of them is very close to 14A, illustrated in the Specialized. The other two are different, and I imagine check with some of those found by Train and illustrated in The American Philatelist a couple of years ago.

He also sends two copies of the 5 Cent Express that check regarding double in "U S" at the top of the stamp, not very many shifts have been found of this variety. R. B. Sherman some little ago submitted one with a double in the word "EXPRESS" showing in the "E" "X" and "R". These are the only two I know of.

Victor W. Weiskopf not very long ago showed me a crack on this stamp running from the "R" of "INTER" down into the left eye of the vignette. This was quite pronounced, he had two copies of it.

* * * * *

STITCH WATERMARKS.

We have always claimed that stitch watermarks could be found on any of the issues, but it is very seldom that we find them in the second or third issues. Mr. Nagel submits a block of four of the 2 Cent Orange and Black showing a good example of this stitch watermark.

* * * * *

CRACKED PLATES.

C. W. Bedford recently brought up the question as to whether the well known "lines" that appear on the 50 Cent Mortgage were really cracks or scratches. Nobody has answered this question satisfactorily as yet, but we are more inclined to the belief that they are strong scratches rather than cracks, due to the clearness and straightness of the lines. The more we study cracks the more we seem to find that they are very irregular in form and that they appear in both early and late states. The more the plate was used the more pronounced and wider the crack becomes, in fact it is sometimes quite blurry in effect.

There is such a crack on the 25 Cent Insurance, first issue, that we have known of for some time. Mr. Nagel calls our attention to it in a recent letter. This starts at the bottom of the stamp, in the letter "E" of "INTER" and runs in an irregular line upward thru the "I" of "INSURANCE" and into the star above. On one copy dated August 21, 1864, this is quite pronounced, in another copy dated 1867 it is very ragged and blurry. The latter stamp, however, is poorly printed which may account in general for the appearance of the crack.

Perhaps some of you may be able to check this from stamps in your own collection.

* * * * *

10 CENT CERTIFICATE.

The best known plate flaw on this stamp is the crack or scratch from the bottom of the "T" of "CERTIFICATE" running downward diagonally across the margin. This should show in the stamp below.

We have known a double on this stamp, tho not a very pronounced one. This occurs on both sides, in the word "TEN" and in "CENTS" and can be seen readily with the aid of a glass. Dr. E. M. Gearhart, of Erie, Pa. called our attention to this about a year and a half ago, but I don't recall whether we noted it or not, I don't think we did. Mr. Nagel recently sent me two duplicates of this which checked with Dr. Gearhart's copy. We have listed this in the Specialized Catalogue.

More Revenues Used for Postage

In time we will get quite a list of these stamps, and I also hope in time that we may be able to establish a value for them and have them properly listed. Items keep coming in from time to time. Many of them are duplications of those already noted, but only serve to prove that lots of postage stamps were used in this way, and also that in certain cases revenue stamps were used in lieu of postage stamps.

Since the publication of our last list in the April American Philatelist the following items have been sent in. We list them all, even though they may be in some cases duplications of what we have listed before.

We have received from Stephen D. Rich a cover carrying two 1 Cent Green, surcharged "I R"; another cover with a 2 Cent Black Jack plus a 1 Cent Telegraph, making a customary 3 Cent rate, and a third cover with a 2 Cent Documentary Battleship.

E. S. Betts, of Saginaw, Mich., sends us an envelope from Prescott, Mich., with a cancellation date of February 22, 1927. It is addressed to H. T. Bryant, Sales Agent of the National Cash Register Co., and carries a 2 Cent Carmine Rose Documentary stamp of the 1917 issue, #4226.

Robert F. Hale, of Malone, N. Y., submits the following: 2 Cent Proprietary, Blue, #3812c, used on cover and postmarked Logansport, Ind., April 1st. The postmark is not dated but a memorandum of receipt is dated 1873. The cover was mailed to a local address, and has the stamp well tied on with a rather heavy killer.

Henry W. Holcombe, of New York City, reports the following in his collection: #147, 3 Cent Green, 1870-71 issue, used on a check drawn on Tallant & Co., Bankers by the firm of M. M. Cook & Son, Leather Hose & Belting, 201 Battery St., dated San Francisco, Sept. 2d, 1870. The stamp is cancelled by two short pen lines diagonally across the SE corner and tied to the check by the embossed name and address of the drawee. Also #73, 2 Cent black Jackson, 1862-66, issue, used on Bill of Lading of the Worcester Railroad Corporation, dated Boston Sept. 14, 1864. The stamp is cancelled in manuscript on the same date.

Mr. Holcombe also reports that he has a fine copy of #3804c, 2 Cent Bank Check, blue, fully tied to a fine cover and postmarked New York, Jan. 25, 1898.

* * * * *

POSTAGE USED FOR REVENUE.

Olaf Nagel, of Chicago, submits a 5 Cent Brown, Type II, 1857-60 issue, that has been used as a Revenue on a marriage license issued by Gallatin County,

Ill., in 1864. The license is signed and the stamp is initialled and dated by J. Onjett, Minister performing the ceremony.

J. Delano Bartlett, of El Paso, Texas, reports a check dated Dec. 15, 1873 for $4.95 with a 1 Cent blue 1870, Scott's #134. This is a single stamp tied to check with check protector puncher. (The tax was 2 cents, but this paid only 1 cent.) He also reports a check dated November 9, 1875, for $35.77, with a 2 cent Brown, Scott's #157, and a check dated August 10, 1898, for $5.00, with a 2 Cent Omaha, Scott's #286.

* * * * *

ANOTHER REVENUE BISECT.

F. W. Curtis, of Clearfield, Pa. submits a small promissory note dated April 1, 1867 carrying one 10 Cent Power of Attorney and the upper diagonal half of another copy. This note was not paid until April 9, 1869, and the two stamps are dated April 8, 1869, evidently put on at the time the note was paid.

This stamp is already listed in the Specialized, and this is the second copy that has come to light.

* * * * *

DATES OF REPEAL OF REVENUE ACTS.

In the July 1932 number of The American Philatelist, Frank L. Applegate asked a series of questions regarding the date of repeal of various War Acts and Schedules.

We asked for information on this subject, and Henry W. Holcombe, of New York City, has been able to answer all of the questions. His report is as follows: * * *

"In the July 1932 issue of The American Philatelist my friend Frank L. Applegate posed a number of questions which seemingly should be of general interest to collectors and students of our revenue stamps.

Mr. Applegate tells me in a recent letter that not a single reply to any of the questions has been received to date. I hoped that other members would take their pens in hand—but rather than let the questions go unanswered for a longer time, I give the data herewith.

Question No. 1 reads "The Civil War Revenue Act was repealed all except the taxes on matches, medicines, playing cards, perfumery and bank checks ....1872. The remaining schedules............1883.

The second part of the question being the easier, I will answer it first. The 47th Congress by the Act of March 3rd, 1883, abolished the above taxes as well as those on savings bank deposits, on the capital and deposits of banks and reduced the duties on tobacco by one-half. The tax on bank checks was declared to be irritating and hampering in its nature; the tax on matches was on a household article of hourly and necessary consumption by all classes; the tax on savings bank deposits was a tax on thrift; the tax on patent medicines and perfumeries was vexatious because levied on innumerable articles; and the taxes on the capital and deposits of banks were not needed. The loss in the total revenue was not as great as anticipated, as there was a constant gain from the duties on spirits and fermented liquors.

The answer to the first part of the question cannot be so readily stated. However, the sequence of the most important Internal Revenue acts were as follows—the Act of July 13, 1866, repealed the tax on coal and pig iron, and lowered the duties on manufactures, products, and gross receipts of corporations, etc., taking off at one blow $45,000,000. The Act of March 2, 1867, reduced the rate on cotton, and repealed duties on a considerable number of manufactured products, exempted incomes up to $1,000, and repealed the gross receipts tax on advertisements and toll roads. The Act of February 3, 1868, repealed the tax on cotton; the Act of March 31, 1868, finally removed all taxes upon goods, wares, and manufactures except those on gas, illuminating oils, tobacco, liquors, banks, and articles upon which the tax was collected by means of stamps; the Act of July 30, 1868, reduced the tax upon distilled spirits from $2.00 to 50 cents per gallon; and the Act of July 14, 1870, brought the system of internal revenue taxation down to the level at which it was maintained until 1883. The taxes left were those on spirits, tobacco, fermented liquor, adhesive stamps, banks and bankers, and a small amount on manufactures and products.

In general, "all taxes which discriminated against prudence and economy, as the taxes upon repairs; against knowledge, as the taxes upon books, paper and printing; against capital and thrift, as the differential income tax; against the transportation of freight by boat or vehicles, and against the great leading raw materials, as coal and pig iron, cotton, sugar, and petroleum," were quickly swept away, leaving taxes which might be regarded in the light of luxuries, "involving an entirely voluntary assessment on the part of the consumer." The special licenses, stamp, corporation, and income taxes were continued, but later in 1870, when the debt had been largely funded, and the receipts from customs, and distilled and malt liquors and tobacco showed a large increase, nearly all the license taxes except those on brewers, distillers, and dealers in liquors and tobacco, were repealed. The income tax was continued until 1872, with the rate reduced to 2½% upon incomes in excess of $2,000.

Question No. 2 reads "The Documentary and Proprietary schedules of the Spanish American Revenue Act were repealed............1902." These taxes were repealed by the Act of April 12, 1902, except the tax on mixed flour.

Question No. 3 reads "The Proprietary Schedule of the Act of 1914 was repealed............" The Revenue Act of 1914 was superseded by the Revenue Act of 1916 and later by the Revenue Act October 3, 1917.

Question No. 4 reads "When was the Proprietary Act of 1919 repealed." Certain excise taxes in the Revenue Act of 1919 were repealed in the Revenue Act of November 23, 1921.

Question No. 5 reads, "Was the Wine Act of 1916 ever repealed or amended so as to limit the denominations of stamps required, and when?" Sec. 3328, Revised Statutes; Sec. 2, Act of October 22, 1914, and very probably others, pertained to the taxing of wines in bottles, altho the latter Act provided for a tax on still wines, not otherwise specifically provided for, at the rate of 8 cents per gallon. Sec. 402, Revenue Act of 1916; Sec. 611, Revenue Act of 1918 and Sec. 451, Revenue Act of 1928, did not mention wine in bottles, but specified the amount of tax payable per gallon according to the alcoholic percentage reckoned by volume and not by weight, the stamp (or stamps) to be affixed to the packages or cases of wine. It is possible, and probable, that under the various Acts and considering the different containers in use, some denominations of wine stamps may not have been required.

Question No. 6 reads, "Which denominations of wine stamps are still in use? It is known that some of the values of the 1914 series were still in use supplementing the 1916 series long after the 18th amendment was passed in 1920, but are they still in use?" Regulations No. 71, relative to the production, fortification, tax payment, etc., of wine show the wine stamps still in use. Article

XXX—Stamps, Par. 172 reads "Wine stamps for the tax payment of wines will be provided in denominations of 1 cent, 3 cents, 4 cents, 6 cents, 7½ cents, 10 cents, 12 cents, 15 cents, 18 cents, 20 cents, 24 cents, 30 cents, 36 cents, 50 cents, 60 cents, 72 cents, 80 cents, $1.20, $1.44, $1.60, $2, $4, $4.80, $9.60, $20, $40, $50, and $100.

Question No. 7 reads, "It is also apparent from reports of the Bureau that some of the Beer stamps were being prepared after 1920. Can any one report what values, if any, are still in use and if not when their use ceased?" Some special tax stamps for brewers and dealers were printed after January 16, 1920. However, the manufacture of beer being illegal, beer stamps were not in use after that date. They will, of course, be issued as soon as the Act permitting beer is effective!

Question No. 8 reads, "What documentaries are still in use, and if not all denominations of Documentaries, Stock Transfer and Future Delivery, when did the use of the various denominations cease and under what act?" Documentary stamps are still in use. Regulations No. 71, referred to in Question No. 6, under the heading of "Denominations of Documentary Stamps," Art. 129, Documentary stamps issued.—reads "Under authority conferred upon the Commissioner of Internal Revenue in section 805 (a) of the Act, the following adhesive stamps have been prepared; Documentary stamps, Schedule A; 1 cent, 2 cents, 3 cents, 4 cents, 5 cents, 8 cents, 10 cents, 25 cents, 40 cents, 50 cents, 80 cents, $1, $2, $3, $4, $5, $10, $30, $60, $100, $500, $1,000."

Question No. 9 reads, "Narcotics. Are they still in use, and if not when did the use of the various denominations cease?" Yes, they are still in use. The denominations in use, of course, depends on the packages used by the different manufacturers. As recent cancellations have been noted on several values, it is known that many values, particularly the strip stamps, are still being used.

As stated in the answer to Question No. 1, the stamp taxes on Match & Medicine, as well as on bank checks, etcetra, were abolished by an Act of Congress on March 3rd, 1883. In the Boston Revenue Book various last dated of issue are given for the different M. & M. stamps. My recollection is that in at least one instance the last issue date is given as August or September, 1883. This is believed to be in error. The effective date under the above mentioned Act was July 1, 1883, and it is not believed that any manufacturer had private die stamps as such printed after that date, altho it is barely possible the Bureau printed a few stamps after the die had been changed eliminating the "U. S. Inter. Rev." from the original—thereby converting the stamps into what we know as "labels." There seems to be no evidence that the Bureau ever printed any labels.

I trust the answers to Mr. Applegate's questions will be of general interest to all collectors and students of our revenune stamps.

            Cordially yours,

            HENRY W. HOLCOMBE."

Metallic Tax Stamps for Cotton

By CLARENDON BANGS.

In the study and classification of United States Revenue Stamps there has remained one section or division which has heretofore received only scant notice. I refer to the Metallic Tax Stamps used during and after the Civil War, and which were issued for use upon raw cotton as a war tax measure.

The first tax on cotton was enacted by the Thirty-Seventh Congress in its second session, and was approved July 1st, 1862. By this Act a tax of one-half cent per pound was levied upon raw cotton.

The tax of one-half cent per pound was in force less than two years, for, by an Act of the Thirty-Eighth Congress, approved March 7th, 1864, the tax was raised to two cents per pound; and, by an Act of the same Congress, approved June 20, it was provided, among other things, that "Every collector to whom any duty upon cotton shall have been paid shall mark the bale, or other packages, upon which the tax shall have been paid, in such manner as shall clearly indicate the payment thereof, etc."

The method of marking to show that the tax had been paid was usually by paint. Some months later the idea of having a tag to be attached to the package was evolved.

In July, 1866, the tax was raised to three cents; and again reduced by an Act of the Thirty-Ninth Congress in 1867. The tax was wholly repealed by an Act of the Fortieth Congress, approved February 3rd, 1868.

There are no other laws upon the subject; however, from time to time circulars were issued by the Department which were designed to instruct both officials and the general shipping public.

The Commissioner of Internal Revenue was authorized by Congressional enactment to make rules and regulations for the proper collection of the tax. The office of Commissioner was a new one, created as a war contingency. The incumbent had no precedents to guide him. Congress was enacting war tax measures almost daily. The office was overburdened with work. The thousands of collectors and assessors appointed to collect internal revenue taxes were largely men of no previous experience in this particular field.

The tax was to be paid upon the raw cotton by the producer before removal from the place of production.

The first tag was printed on a piece of canvas attached to a wire, with a barb on the outer end. The barb was inserted into the bale. There is but one known copy of this tag in existence. The wording on the tag was, "United States Internal Revenue, Cotton," with the emblem of an eagle with arrows held in its talons. The next one was of parchment, similar to the canvas tags. Then an oval brass tag, to be attached by a wire, and to be punched to indicate the collection district.

Later, a brass tag about twelve inches in length, with a barb, was authorized and issued by the Government. There was a variety of designs of this type of stamp. All letters of the alphabet were used and they were also numbered serially. These metallic stamps are very scarce, and in a used condition almost unknown, because of the intrinsic value they were carefully removed from the bales and sold as brass.

(Editors Note: We found it impossible to illustrate the brass stamp Mr. Bangs supplied with this interesting revenue item, and in view of this Mr. Bangs has generously offered to supply a tag to the first five A. P. S. collectors living outside of Georgia who will write him direct at 1219 Albemarle Ave. N. E., Atlanta, Georgia. Should more than five requests be received there will be a drawing of names held by the Atlanta Stamp Society to determine the five winners. Distribution will be made after August tenth to give all a chance.)

The Boston Revenue Book

For over two years a group of about ten revenue collectors have been gathering data on the first issue revenue plates as a side issue to their first interest in plate reconstruction. Thirty states of fourteen plates can now be displayed jointly, and we hope this will be possible at the next large philatelic exhibition.

There have been several suggestions that the Revenue Unit rewrite the old "Boston Revenue Book." The large accumulation of data above mentioned seems to make it possible to do this with respect to the first revenue issue, with the rest of the issues held in abeyance for future consideration.

There have been over sixty cooperating revenue collectors who are responsible for our present information. It is now time to seek wider assistance and to rapidly consumate the correlation of the first issue data into a Revenue Unit publication.

We ask that the following data from collectors be sent to the Secretary. (No stamps unless requested.)

1. List of all large revenue blocks, 1st issue only.
2. List of Imprints, Plate Numbers and Marginal Markings. This is important.
3. Data, ideas and suggestions that our members feel will be useful. We wish to make this section of the "Unit Revenue Book" as complete and as valuable as possible.

* * * * *

REVENUE STAMPS USED FOR POSTAGE.

By HOWARD B. BEAUMONT.

Many of the covers listed below as belonging to Mr. F. H. Barrows were sent to Clark & Co., of Providence, R. I. This firm conducted a mail order business in cheap jewelry and advertised extensively in rural papers and farm journals. To the people who purchased from this firm apparently anything with gum on it was a postage stamp, a fact which explains the late use of No. 3814.

No. 3800, 1c Express. Mr. Barrows has a small business cover used from Plimpton, Mass., to Pawtucket, R. I., March, 1863, on which is a single 1c Express used for postage. The stamp is pen cancelled but not tied.

Mr. Milton R. Miller, of Batavia, N. Y., reports the use of this stamp, partly perforated, together with a two cent "black Jack" to form the three cent rate. They are tied to the cover with a black grid. The letter was written Feb. 1, 1864, from Stockton, Chatauqua County, N. Y., to the clerk or deacon of the Baptist Church, West Bethany, Genesee County, N. Y.

No. 3802, 1c Proprietary. Another cover owned by Mr. Barrows was franked with a single copy of this stamp for use locally in New Bedford, Mass. The Revenue did not pass for postage as the cover is marked "Held for Postage" and a 2c Jackson has been added.

Dr. Samuel Konwiser, Newark, N. J., has a cover from West Redding, Conn., postmarked Jan. 9, 1884, on which are a pair of this stamp.

Mr. Philip Straus, of Baltimore, has a patriotic cover on which, in addition to a three cent No. 65, are seven copies of No. 3802, a single on the face and a strip of six on the back. There is nothing to indicate why the revenues were added.

No. 3804, 2c Bank Check, blue. Mr. Heyliger de Windt, of Great Barraington, Mass., has a cover used locally in New York City on which is an uncancelled pair of this stamp. The cover is marked "Due 4".

No. 3812, 2c Proprietary, blue. Mr. Sam Zander, of Galveston, has a cover on which this stamp has been postally used. The postmark is illegible but the cover was sent to LaGrange, Texas, while the stamps were current.

Mr. R. F. Hale, of Malone, N. Y., also has a copy of this stamp postally used on a cover postmarked Logansport, Ind., April 1, (1873). The stamp is tied with a heavy killer.

Mr. de Windt sent for examination a very interesting cover on which this stamp had been unsuccessfully used for postage. Over the revenue and completely covering it was pasted a 3c 1861, an unusually wide copy with the gutter margin on the right. Unlike other revenues which did not pass for postage this cover is not marked as held for postage.

No. 3813, 2c Proprietary, orange. Another interesting cover owned by Mr. de Windt bears an uncancelled copy of No. 3813. This cover, from Dubuque, Iowa, to Fort Atkinson, Iowa, (forwarded to Waucoma, Iowa) is stamped "Held for Postage" and has a single No. 65 tied with blue concentric circles.

No. 3814, U. S. I. R. Mr. H. H. Elliott has a cover mailed from Subletts Tavern, Va., to Petersburg, Va., June 29, 1870, bearing a copy of this stamp with a one cent 1869 to form the three cent rate. This cover is not marked due.

Mr. Barrows has two covers on which this stamp has been used for postage. One is tied with "Hobson, Mo., July 26, 1898," and came from the Clark correspondence. The other was used from Webster, Mass., to Owls Head, Maine, Sept. 14, 1898. In spite of the late use of these stamps there is no question but they are genuine.

Mr. R. J. Mechin, of Edwards, N. Y., reports an advertising cover bearing this stamp overlapped by a 3c 1869.

No. 3818, 3c Telegraph. Mr. Beverly S. King has a cover in his collection with a copy of the 3c Telegraph used for postage. He also has a single off cover cancelled Ellenville, Nov. 5, 1863.

No. 3824, 5c Express. Another cover owned by Mr. de Windt has a single No. 3824 tied with a black waffle iron killer. It was used while the stamp was current and there are no markings on the cover to indicate that the postal use of the revenue was question.

No. 3826, 5c Inland Exchange. The postal use of this stamp has been reported by two collectors. That owned by Mr. Delf Norona was used from St. Louis to Wheeling and is marked "Due 6." The copy owned by Mr. de Windt has a fine double transfer. It was used in March, 1868, from New York to Windham, Conn., and is not marked due.

No. 3843, 25c Certificate. Mr. E. Girod, of Sumas, Wash., reports a single copy of this off cover with the postmark at Kissam, N. Y., Oct. 28, 1868.

No. 3945, 2c Second Issue. Mr. Norona has a single of this on a Spanish American War patriotic cancelled at Hoboken, N. J., June 20, 1899. While it may have been made to order it was accepted for postage.

No. 3967b, 2c Fifth Issue. Mr. Barrows reports a copy of this used in 1899. It did not pass for postage and was marked "Held for Postage." A two cent No. 279b was added and both it and the revenue are tied to the cover with the flag cancellation of the National Export Exposition of 1899.

No. 3983b, 1c Proprietary. A pair of these were used on a cover from Cornwall Bridge, Conn., to Great Barrington, Mass., in 1932. They were not accepted for postage. Mr. de Windt, who now owns this cover, investigated and found that the cover was not made to order.

No. 3995, 1c Surcharged I. R. Mr. de Windt submitted a part of a cover bearing this stamp and a single No. 279 tied with the flag cancellation. Postmarked Syracuse, Dec. 26, 1899.

No. 3996, 1c Surcharged I. R. A registered letter, legal size, owned by Mr. Barrows, carries a pair of these stamps together with a single of No. 319 and a pair of No. 281. This cover, used in 1905 from Lorraine, Va., to South Creek, N. C., had previously been used to carry an advertisement from Chicago to Lorraine and its use for registry was a second use. The same collector has a single copy of this stamp on a wrapper postmarked Madison, N. Y., Oct. 30, 1903.

No. 3997, 2c Surcharged I. R. The same collector has a copy of this stamp used in Boston on March 24, 1913. Both Mr. Barrows and Dr. Konwiser report covers used locally in Newark, N. J., in 1898 bearing a single of No. 3997 and a single of No. 279. The similarity of these covers suggests that they may have been made to order.

No. 4008, 2c Proprietary. Another copy from the Clark correspondence and now in the collection of Mr. Barrows carries a copy of this stamp nicely tied to a cover used from Savannah to Providence, March 31, 1899.
The postal use of this stamp is also reported by Mr. H. S. Riederer, of New Rochelle. This cover was used in a rural office and the stamp is not tied.

No. 4009, 2½c Proprietary. Mr. Robert E. Chambers has a cover with a copy of this stamp used for postage.

No. 4011, 4c Proprietary. Mr. Frank D. Halsey, of Princeton, N. J., has a cover postmarked in New York on January 2, 1905, on which this stamp was used for postage.

No. 4027, 1c Documentary. Mr. Barrows has four covers each bearing a pair of this stamp. One, from Bellton, Ga., passed without question, but two did not and these have regular two cent stamp pasted over the revenues. The fourth cover is a patriotic with two singles used in Huntingdon, Pa., Jan. 17, 1899.

Mr. Chambers reports a cover with a single No. 4027 in combination with a one cent Columbian to form the two cent rate.

No. 4028, 2c Documentary. Mr. de Windt has a fine copy of this stamp with a double transfer tied to a business letter used in Boston on January 1, 1902.

Mr. Barrows has twenty-one covers franked with this stamp, of which seven, used in 1898 and 1899, are marked "Held for Postage," and the balance used from 1900 to 1927 passed for postage.

A copy of this stamp on a Civil War Patriotic is owned by Mr. W. P. Clark, of Bridgeport.

No. 4076, 1c Documentary. Used on a business letter May 14, 1916, from Burlington, Wis., to Sheboygan, Wis., and now owned by the writer. Formerly owned by Mr. W. W. Free.

No. 4226, 2c Documentary. The writer has a cover on which this stamp was used for postage from Honolulu to Baltimore in 1921.

Mr. Barrows has two covers on which this stamp was used for postage. The first, used in 1923, passed without question; the other, used on March 11, 1929, to Washington, was held for postage.

No. 4238, $2.00 Documentary. Mr. R. C. Fisher, of Nashville, has a copy of this stamp used on a tag attached to registered mail sent from the Federal Reserve Bank of Atlanta, to the Cumberland Valley National Bank of Nashville, March 1, 1919.

* * * * *

SALE OF REVENUE STAMPS TO COLLECTORS.

Have just received word from Hon. C. B. Eilenberger that postmasters of all first and second class offices and that post offices of the third and fourth classes located in county seats now required by law to sell documentary internal revenue stamps, shall accept and fill any order received by mail for the purchase of such stamps from stamp collectors, providing such order is accompanied by a remittance to cover the value of the stamps desired, plue return postage and registry fee.

The denominations of the documentary internal revenue stamps that may be thus purchased are as follows: 1c, 2c, 3c, 4c, 5c, 8c, 10c, 20c, 25c, 50c, $1, $2, $3, $5, $10, $30, $60, $100, $500, $1,000.

Imitation Sparkling Wine

By ROSCOE L. WICKES.

The facts that led up to the issuance of this unique stamp are these:

In 1910 there was a firm on West Chicago Avenue in Chicago making a beverage they advertised as "Sparkling Burgundy, Reisling," etc. As this was a Snythetic product and not fermented grape wine, the Pure Food Government Authorities got after them, and in the course of their investigation found that they were fortifying their different brands with quite a percentage of alcohol. The case was then turned over to the Internal Revenue Department and after a long controversy, (about two years, if I remember correctly), the Government finally issued this stamp for them, and also compelled them to change their labels and advertising matter to read "Imitation Sparkling Wine."

It is needless to say that with the word "Imitation" so prominent on both label and stamp, the public would not buy their product and they soon after went out of business.

These facts were given me in 1915 by the Revenue Agent who had charge of this case for the Government, and it was through him that I obtained all the remainders in the Chicago Internal Revenue Office. I do not remember just how many I obtained, but it was less than one hundred of each denomination, Pints and Quarts. The Government sold these stamps, if my memory serves me correctly, at two and one half cents for pints and five cents for quarts. As near as I have been able to learn the Government never issued any more of these stamps, and probably never will have any more calls for such a stamp, and the lot I had was all that ever were passed on to the collector. If this was a regular revenue, instead of a tax paid, and catalogued by Scott, it surely would today be one of the rarities and command a high price. I have only a plate number block of each left.

There were two stamps, 1 Quart, blue, Plate No. 37788, and 1 Pint, red, Plate No. 37744. Size 0.62"x6.13" (Illustrated.)

They were printed on double line watermarked paper, U. S. I. R. and were rouletted. Legend: "Act of June 6, 1872. Imitation Sparkling Wine, Series of 1912."

REVENUE FRAUD.

Philip E. Haminlton writes:

"In a find of old legal documents I found on one of them two strips of five of the 5 Cent Certificate stamp, one strip pasted neatly over the other strip so that only the lower one third of the under strip was showing. On soaking them off, to my surprise, I found that the lower strip was bisected horizontally and only the lower half of the strip was present.

At once I replaced the stamps on the piece of document and they are still in my collection. Evidently, for a tax of 50 cents, the user of these stamps saved 12½ cents and used the upper half of the bisected strip on some other document, but I have never been able to find it."

* * * * *

CUSTOMS BANDS FOR CIGARS.

If you will refer back to the re-engraved Bank Note Postage Stamps of 1882, Scott's Nos. 206 and 207, you will find the (b) variety listed as "Punched with eight small holes in a circle." This was one of several patented (?) devices which the Government experimented with for the purpose of preventing fraud by reuse of stamps. The perforated circle in the stamps was supposed to tear easily and thereby prevent erasure of the cancellation.

This device of punched holes is quite rare on postage stamps, but was widely used in Tax Paid Revenues and Customs Labels as illustrated above on a Custom's Cigar Band, printed by the "Bureau" in 1871. In some cases this method was combined with double paper, the holes being only in the upper or thin layer.

An interesting "Fraud" but "Within the law" for these days is known on this Customs Cigar Band. It is said to have been engraved by employees of the Bureau who were thrown out of work by modern machinery installed at the Bureau of Engraving and Printing. It is the exact replica of the above illustration but reads:

"U. S. CUSTOMERS"

instead of "U. S. Customs." This data was submitted by L. O. Cameron.

* * * * *

"SHINPLASTER" USED AS REVENUE.

John S. Campbell writes the Unit:

"While searching through the old documents belonging to my grandfather, (I was quite a novice in 1929,) I found a superb copy of the 50 Cent postal currency showing the likeness of five 10 Cent 1861 U. S. stamps, pasted on the document, being used as a rveenue. It was cancelled with a pen, "April 8, 1863, S. M. C.," corresponding with the signatures in the document. Foolishly I soaked it off and sold it to a coin collector for 75 cents. He still has it."

* * * * *

10 CENT BILL OF LADING.

Philip E. Hamilton, of Beaver Falls, Pa., is plating the 10 Cent Bill of Lading, first issue. He lacks but twenty positions, and has not as yet located the double transfer noted in Scott's Specialized Catalogue. Mr. Hamilton writes me asking whether it is possible to obtain a copy of this double transfer for examination and location purposes.

I have never seen this particular double and so far as I have been able to discover no one else seems to have a copy of it. If any of you revenue collectors have a double transfer of this stamp will you kindly lend it to Mr. Hamilton, so that he may complete his work on this plate? Address him as above.

* * * * *

MORE BISECTS.

Mr. Hamilton adds to our list as follows:

A strip of four 5 Cent Agreement tied to a vertical half of a 5 Cent Certificate; a 2 Cent U. S. I. R. and a 2 Cent Bank Check, both vertical bisects, tied to the document.

Mr. Hamilton is rather puzzled about the 5 Cent Certificate bisect used in connection with the strip of four of the 5 Cent Agreement. This makes up a rate of 22½ Cents which, so far as I know, was not legal.

He also has some interesting specimens of attempts to use the 2 Cent Black Jack as revenues. He says he has a number of Black Jacks so used, two of which he considers unique, as the postage stamp was put on and cancelled and when it did not pass muster revenue stamps were placed directly over the Black Jack so that the receipt shows both stamps. I have a similar example of this in my own collection, a revenue over a 3 Cent '61. Mr. Hamilton's stamps are pen cancelled with initials and date by the same person who signed the receipts.

John Paalzow, of South Orange, N. J., submits the upper and lower half of the 10 Cent Bill of Lading used on certificates, hand stamped, tied on by the National Savings Bank of Wheeling and dated July 1866.

* * * * *

STITCH WATERMARK.

Eugene Costales has uncovered a copy of the $2. Blue and Black, second issue, with a horizontal stitch watermark.

Postage Stamps Used For Revenues
CHECK LIST.

No. 28, 5c, 1847. Mr. Howard H. Elliott, Treasurer of the A. P. S., has a check used in 1866 on which a single 5c 1847 has been fiscally used.

No. 48a, 5c, 1857, type II. Mr. Olaf Nagel, of Chicago, has a marriage license issued by Gallitin County, Illinois, in 1864 on which is a copy of the five cent, brown, type II, of the 1857-60 issue. The license is signed and the stamp initialed by J. Onjett the minister who performed the ceremony.

No. 63, 1c, 1861. Mr. Beverly S. King has two checks issued by Smith and Rice, of New York, in February, 1863, on each of which a single No. 63 had been used as a revenue. One of these checks has been acquired by the writer.

A single on check is reported by Mr. Barr.

No. 65, 3c, 1861. This stamp is more frequently found fiscally used than any other postage stamp. It has been reported by a number of collectors as used on checks and notes. We have a copy used with a 2c Express, partly-perforated, to form the 5c rate.

Mr. Lawrence L. Howe, of Clearfield, Pa., has had a number of affidavits on which the five cent rate was formed by a combination of this stamp and a two cent Jackson. One of the affidavits is now in the writer's collection.

No. 67, 5c, 1861. A copy of this stamp with a fiscal cancellation, off the check, is reported by Mr. King.

No. 68, 10c, 1861. Mr. Philip Straus, of Baltimore, recently secured a number of notes on which this stamp was used for revenue purposes. One, dated March 1, 1862, used a copy of No. 68 and a single 10c Inland Exchange, partly-perforated; another dated March 9, 1867, has a 50c Life Insurance with No. 68; a third, dated Feb. 17, 1864, carries three uncancelled copies of No. 68 and a 50c Original Process; a fourth has a strip of five of No. 68 and a pair of No. 76.

A strip of three on a promissory note dated April 1, 1865, is owned by Mr. John Cabot, Jr., of New York.

In our own collection we have a single on a court order to take depositions.

No. 71, 30c, 1861. A copy of this stamp is known on a check dated May 29, 1863, and issued by Rawson & Whipple on the Shetucket Bank of Norwich, Conn. Originally reported by Mr. G. A. Doyle of Bridgeport, Conn., it is now owned by Mr. W. P. Clark of the same city.

No. 73, 2c, 1862. This stamp was frequently used for fiscal purposes and has been reported by a number of collectors. We have seen a number of copies, both singly and in combination with other stamps.

Mr. LeRoy E. Shaw, of Pittsfield, Mass., has a fine copy used with a 2c Bank Check. Mr. Barr has a copy used with a 2c U. S. I. R.

Mr. W. A. Edgar, of Baltimore, had several checks on which this stamp had been unsuccessfully used as a revenue stamp and had been covered with a 2c U. S. I. R. Unfortunately all but one of the checks were ruined by soaking off the stamps before the unusual condition was noted.

Our copy is on a receipt for cord wood issued Sept. 6, 1866.

No. 75, 5c, 1862. This stamp is known to have been used fiscally but whether any still exist on original documents is unknown. A New York collector had a strip of six, uncancelled, on a check but the present location of both the check and the collector is not known. A number of checks were found in Baltimore each bearing an uncancelled copy of this stamp but they were all soaked off before their peculiar use was recognized.

No. 76, 5c, 1862. We have a copy of this stamp fiscally used on a part of a release. A single on a part of a legal document is owned by Mr. Jere Hess Barr, of Reading.

A pair, together with a strip of five of No. 68, is on a note now owned by Mr. Straus. The same collector has a note with three singles of this stamp and a 50c Original Process.

No. 78, 24c, 1862. At least five documents are known bearing copies of this stamp used for revenue purposes. Four are from the same source-payrolls of labor on the third division of the Susquehanna Canal Co. in 1867.

The canal company prepared monthly payrolls of labor which were signed by each employee when he received his wages. As the signatures constituted receipts it was necessary to pay a tax of five cents per hundred dollars. On the four payrolls known to the writer (there may be more in existence) the tax was paid with 24c stamps of 1862 together with low denomination revenues. Two of the rolls are owned by Mr. Barr, one having a single and the other a pair of 2c U. S. I. R. in addition to the postage stamp. The other two rolls are owned by Mr. Charles Phillips, the well known New York dealer. One of the rolls has a 10c Certificate and a 2c Bank Check, the other has a 10c Bill of Lading and a pair of 4c Inland Exchange used with the postage stamp. All stamps on all the rolls are cancelled with the hand stamp of the canal company.

The fifth document is a bill of sale owned by Mr. Herbert Atherton for "7 Milchs Cows and 1 Sorrel Horse, between 7 and 8 years old". On this document there is a strip of four of No. 78 and a pair of the two cent Jackson.

No. 87, 2c, 1867, 11x13 grill. Mr. Elliott reports the fiscal use of this stamp but gives no details.

No. 88, 3c, 1867, 11x13 grill. The fiscal use of this stamp is reported by Mr. Elliott.

No. 92, 1c, 1867, 9x13 grill. A pair of this stamp used as revenues on a note is reported by Mr. Elliott.

No. 93, 2c, 1867, 9x13 grill. We have a receipt dated March 27, 1869, on which is a single No. 93, pencancelled.

No. 94, 3c, 1867, 9x13 grill. Mr. Edgar has an uncancelled copy on a check of the First National Bank of Harrisonburg dated Jan. 12, 1869.

No. 95, 5c, 1867, 9x13. Mr. Nagel reports a copy of this on a note dated August 23, 1870.

No. 12, 1c, 1869. Mr. Harry A. Gray, of Oakland, Cal., has a piece of a receipt bearing a copy of this stamp with a circular green cancellation "Madison & Burke, Oct. 1, 1869". This firm is still in business in San Francisco.

No. 113, 2c, 1869. Mr. Jere Hess Barr has an interesting receipt book kept by Mrs. Hannah Huyette, of Birdsboro, Pa., during the period 1865 to 1875. On nearly all the receipts a 2c U. S. I. R. was placed but on Feb. 16, 1870. Mrs. Huyette used a two cent Horseman. An amusing feature of the book is the fact that in it Mrs. Huyette's name is spelled in thirteen different ways.

Mr. Nagel reports a note dated Jan. 26, 1871, bearing a single No. 113 and six one cent Proprietary stamps.

In our collection we have a single on a note. The fiscal use of this stamp is also reported by Mr. King, Mr. Elliott and several other collectors. Mr. Elliott also reports the fiscal use of No. 113a.

No. 114, 3c, 1869. The fiscal use of this stamp has been reported by a number of collectors and its use in this manner is probably as common as that of the various three cent Bank Note issues. In our collection it is represented by a single and on a check dated Feb. 21, 1870.

No. 135, 2c, 1870, grilled. Mr. Fred H. Barrows, of Providence, has a check dated August 13, 1873, on which a fine copy of this stamp is fiscally used.

No. 145, 1c, 1870. Mr. George R. Cooley, of Albany, reports a check on which this stamp was used for revenue purposes.

A certificate of indebtedness owned by Mr. Philip Straus has a pair and a strip of three No. 145, a single 10c Certificate and three 5c Certificates.

No. 146, 2c, 1870. Mr. W. A. Edgar has twelve checks issued in Harrisonburg, Virginia, in 1871 to 1873, on all of which a single of this stamp was used as a revenue.

The fiscal use of this stamp has also been reported by Mr. King, Mr. Mechin, and Mr. Barr. Based on the number of copies we have seen it is one of the postal issue most commonly used for fiscal purposes.

No. 147, 3c, 1870. Mr. Cooley has a check with a copy of this stamp on it. A note owned by Mr. Straus has a single No. 147 and a 2c U. S. I. R. to make the five cent rate. The same collector has a single No. 147 on a note.

No. 152, 15c, 1871. Mr. Edgar has a check of the First National Bank of Harrisonburg dated May 20, 1871, on which a single 15c of 1871 has been fiscally used. The stamp is tied to the check with a manuscript cancellation. As the check is only for forty dollars there was, of course, no necessity for using more than a two cent stamp and the fiscal use of this stamp must be ascribed to a lack of revenue stamps by the drawer.

No. 156, 1c, 1873. Another check from Harrisonburg now owned by Mr. Edgar has a superb uncancelled single of No. 156.

No. 157, 2c, 1873. Mr. King has a check issued Oct. 10, 1874, at Troy, New York, which has a single, pencancelled copy of this stamp on the reverse, tied with a stamped cashier's endorsement.

No. 158, 3c, 1873. This we have on a check dated Oct. 5, 1878. It has also been reported by Mr. Elliott and Mr. Cooley. Mr. Edgar has three copies on as many checks from Harrisonburg, Virginia.

No. 178, 2c, 1875. Mr. King has a copy on a draft issued in New York March 10, 1876, pencancelled but not tied. Reported on a check by Mr. Cooley and also by Mr. R. F. Hale, of Malone, N. Y., the latter having a check with the stamp tied with a hand stamp. Mr. Barr reports one copy on check while Mr. Edgar reports four checks, each with a single of this stamp.

No. 182b, 1c, 1879. The fiscal use of this stamp is reported by Mr. Elliott.

No. 183, 2c, 1878. The fiscal use of this stamp has not been fully verified.

No. 184, 3c, 1879. The fiscal use of this stamp has been reported by Mr. Elliott.

No. 188, 10c, 1879. Mr. Robert F. Hale has a check bearing a copy of No. 188 with both pen and punch cancellation.

No. 253, 3c, 1874. Mr. Hale has a copy of this with the proprietary cancellation of "Dr. K & Co." of Binghamton. It was also reported by Mr. Barrows.

No. 273, 10c, 1895. Mr. King has a copy of this stamp, off document, pencencelled "I. R., O. Bus. Aug. 26, 1898". Undoubtedly this is a fiscal cancellation. Another fiscally used copy, also off document, is reported by Mr. H. T. Browning, of Bay City, Mich.

No. 274, 15c, 1895. A copy, off document. but fiscally used is reported by Mr. Browning.

No. 279, 1c, 1898. The fiscal use of this stamp by Kilmer and Company is reported by Mr. Barrows.

No. 279b, 2c, 1898. Mr. Barrows also reports the fiscal use of this stamp by Kilmer and Company.

No. 285, 1c, Trans-Mississippi. We have a check issued in Detroit on July 12, 1898 with a pair of this stamp fiscally used.

No. 286, 2c, Trans-Mississippi. Mr. R. S. Nelson, of Selme, Ala., reports a check with a copy of this stamp used as a revenue.

No. 290, 10c, Trans-Mississippi. Three copies of this stamp are on a certificate of deposit owned by Mr. Don R. Bennett.

No. 287, 4c, Trans-Mississippi. Mr. A. B. Casey, of Erie, Pa., has a copy of this stamp which had been used on a New York Central R. R. bill of lading in 1908. The stamp is surcharged with a large "R" and has part of a rubber stamp cancellation.

No. 258, 10c, 1894. A pair fiscally used but off document is reported by Mr. Browning.

No. 338, 10c, 1908. A copy, off document, with a U. S. Internal Revenue, blue hand stamped cancellation is reported by Mr. Hale.

No. 1514, 2c, Interior Department, 1873. Mr. Heyliger de Windt has shown us a check issued in Great Barrington, Mass., on which is a single uncancelled copy of No. 1515. As this was an original find the fiscal use of this cannot be doubted in spite of its lack of cancellation.

No. 1573, 3c, Treasury Department, 1873. Mr. W. A. Edgar has a check drawn on the First National Bank of Harrisonburg, Virginia, Sept. 15, 1873, on which is a copy of this stamp used for fiscal purposes. The stamp is not cancelled but there is no question of authenticity involved as this check, like the others reported by Mr. Edgar, was purchased directly from the bank.

2 Cent U. S. I. R.

Our fellow member, Philip E. Hamilton, of Beaver Falls, Pa., has been doing some intensive work replating the 2 Cent U. S. I. R. and has made some very interesting discoveries. We hope that we will have a full report from him with illustrations very shortly. He writes us as follows regarding this stamp:

"With exception of imprint, have now completed the big re-entered plate of the 2 Cent U. S. I. R. from which your block having crack comes. Thought you would be interested to know that this is an accomplished fact. Am sorry to state that I have not as yet located for my plate the rest of the crack, nor part of the crack as contained in your block. The crack must have developed just before the use of the plate was discontinued. I have part of same used in 1870. There is not a position on the plate that is not shifted, due to re-entry, and I feel perfectly sure that there is not a plate in existence showing such wonderful plate varieties. The fourth vertical row is a sight in itself, but there are many very large transfers, all due to re-entry of the plate, in my opinion. It is quite possible that the plate is the result of a double re-entry because it has a number of triple transfers on it. All positions are tied in by overlapping blocks, making the plating accurate. All but twelve or fifteen positions have distinct guide dots. Perforations mar these few, but do not seriously affect the transfers on same. T14a and T14 do not come from this plate, but from another late re-entered plate, half of which is now completed, including imprint."

* * * * *

10C BILL OF LADING.

Mr. Hamilton is also plating the 10 Cent Bill of Lading. If any of you can help him in connection with this stamp it will be appreciated. He writes us as follows regarding it:

"The 10 Cent Bill of Lading plate is complete with the exception of part of imprint. Have located the one missing position and hope to acquire it this week. Due to scarcity of blocks this has been an exceedingly difficult plate to reconstruct, but all positions on the plate are tied in. There are several transfers on the plate, one nice plate flaw, and several other nice plate varieties, all of which I shall shortly announce. Strange as it may seem to you this is one plate which can be reconstructed from single copies, provided it is possible for me to so illustrate the top marginal line of each row of stamps of the full pane, and in my judgment after two years effort it is probable that future panes will only be reconstructed by the use of single copies. I have found it the scarcest of all revenue stamps in blocks."

* * * * *

REVENUES USED FOR POSTAGE.

Col. Albert W. Draves, of Milwaukee, Wis., sends us a copy of the 2 Cent Battleship roulette used as a 2 Cent stamp on a letter from Boston to Sing Sing

Prison, New York dated September 9, 1898. It is a nice clean copy cancelled with a flag cancellation.

* * * * *

POSTAGE USED FOR REVENUE.

John S. Campbell, Jr., of Cadiz, Ohio, has submitted an unusual cover from Almena, Kansas, February 1, 1888, mailed to Tiffin, Ohio. It was originally franked with a 2 Cent Blue, fifth issue Revenune, rubber stamped "Due 2 ct." and a vertical bisect of the 3 Cent Postage Due stamp was attached. Both the revenue and the bisected due stamp are firmly tied on the cover with the same killer cancellation probably used at Tiffin.

* * * * *

THE EXTENSIVE LIST of Postage stamps used for Revenues which appeared in the October issue under the Revennue Unit Column was written by Member Howard B. Beaumont of Baltimore, Md. No credit was given him at time of publication and in view of the excellence of the list we offer our apologies for the inadvertent oversight.

JUSTIN L. BACHARACH, 4115 46th St., Sunnyside, L. I., New York.

Shall We Carry On?

By BEVERLY S. KING.

About a year ago, practically at the start of the National Recovery Administration, the Secretary of the Revenue Unit was called to Washington to take part in the recovery work. Being a practicing architect in New York, he was perhaps qualified to meet representative Committees of various manufacturing and building industries who were journeying to the Capitol to work out codes of fair competition for their industries.

The work was confining and the hours were long, it was quite usual to work every night, Sundays included, until eleven, twelve or even as late as two o'clock in the morning. It was also customary to meet a Committee in the morning, hold a public hearing in the afternoon and confer with one or two other Committees during the evening. It was anticipated at the start that possibly a hundred industry Codes might be presented, and no one dreamed that the retail trade alone would split itself up and present more than a hundred codes. Much less did they think that the metal working and machinery business would suddenly discover itself to be, not one industry, but more than three hundred separate industries. More than four thousand proposed codes were finally, after strenuous efforts, reduced to about fifteen hundred of sufficient major importance to consider making into law. Fortunately, later, by agreement with industry groups his number was further reduced to less than a thousand.

That work, the most interesting I ever got into, is now completed, and we are now classifying industries, coordinating and further combining Codes, and assisting Code Authorities in administering them.

I am what is termed Deputy Administrator, and at the present time my office has jurisdiction over sixty five industries, consisting of 17,000 factories or plants, 450,000 workers, and having an invested capital of over $3,000,000,000.00.

All of which has nothing to do with stamps, except that being so busy, I offer it as my alibi for neglecting the Revenue Unit, as well as my Specialized U. S. columns in both **Scotts Monthly** and **Stamps**.

Work down here is now easing up a bit and I want to get back in the game with you men who have kept up Philatelic research. I had hoped to attend the American Philatelic Convention at Atlantic City this summer, but work prevented it. A few weeks ago I received a fine letter from George T. Turner telling me in substance what occured at the Convention, where our Revenue Unit had a meeting with a few members present.

155

Our old and valued friend and former Chairman, Clayton W. Bedford, as you may recall passed on some time ago and since then no new Chairman has been elected, nor has anyone volunteered to carry on the wonderful work he was doing in connection with shifts, transfers, and re-plating of Revenue Stamps. Clayton's "Revenue" records were to have been turned over to me for the benefit of the Unit, but I was too busy to take them on at that time. His "Shift Hunter" postage stamp records were turned over to Lee M. Ryer of Seattle, Washington, who is also back in the game after a lapse of six or seven months. Ryer is very likely the one student best equipped to carry on my old friend Bedford's research work on postal issues. He is receiving help from such U. S. specialists as Frank L. Owen, Don Lyburger, Max Johl, Chas. Meservey, W. M. Miller, Dr. G. C. Fritchel, George Sloane, Frank Halsey, W. T. Kiepura, Walter Stevens, J. A. Ross and numberless other well known Philatelists who are specializing in the postage stamps of our country.

A short time ago we had just as many or more, all well known in the revenue game. Are you still there men?

Shall we carry on?

Justin Bacharach, who has collected revenues for years and has done some plating has offered to act as temporary Chairman. I will be glad to continue as Secretary, and between us with the help of you revenue collectors we will put the Revenue Unit back on the map. That is, if you want it.

* * * * *

George T. Turner has now reconstructed a plate of the 10 cent Certificate that he has been working on, and mighty good work it is.

Turner asked me what stamp he should start on next. My suggestion to him was to tackle the forty cent Inland Exchange, this stamp has never been re-plated, the only difficulty being that they are hard to secure in pairs, blocks, strips or larger multiples. But I feel sure that many of you have them and will be glad to lend them to Turner for research work. I think that Morton Joyce and Dr. Gerhardt, for instance, have such material.

These are at least two fine transfers that I know of, and somewhere I have records of others. The two most familiar ones are illustrated herewith. Unfortunately, my New York home is closed and most of my stamps and records are inaccessable just now. If any of you know of other shifts or transfers on this stamp and will send them on I'll be glad to prepare drawings for illustration purposes, and if you have any pairs or larger, or single marginal copies send them to George T. Turner, 424 N. Duke Street, Lancaster, Pa., who will take good care of them and return as soon as he is through.

AN UNUSUAL USE OF PRIVATE DIE MATCH STAMPS.

The receipt for money paid on a land contract (illustrated above) was found in July 1934 in the State of Ohio. It was in an old envelope among a lot of miscellaneous stamps and papers purchased from a non-collector.

It is stamped with two private die match stamps—D. M. Richardson No. 5252a and Griggs & Scott No. 5203—both pen cancelled with initials and the date September 7th, 1866 corresponding with the date on the instrument.

Seemingly the use of Match Stamps in this manner does not appear to be altogether legitimate. Presumably the regular documentary stamps were not available at the moment, so these Match Stamps were carefully removed from boxes of matches and used in their stead.

—Henry W. Holcombe.

IN MEMORIAM

BEVERLY S. KING
A. P. S. 7292

Last month our dear old friend sent us the good news that he was again ready to renew his labors as Secretary and Editor of the Revenue Unit column. Last month we published his first article with the now poignant heading "Shall We Carry On?" And now, two letters before us, one, his last contribution to the American Philatelist, the other, the numbing, shocking news of his tragic death. Stricken in the prime of life by an automobile driven by a nineteen year old boy. "Bev" we know would have us write lightly, even cheerfully of this nasty quirk of Fate—but we cannot write at all, cannot even think of his being with us no longer.

Beverly S. King, born 56 years ago, was a noted architect of New York City, having his offices at 18 E. 41st St., and his home in White Plains, N. Y. A Life Member of The American Philatelic Society, and one of the keenest collectors of U. S. issues we have ever had. In collaboration with Max G. Johl he prepared the now widely known books on "The U. S. Stamps of the Twentieth Century" which are regarded as companions to Luff's work on the U. S. Stamps of the 19th Century. Mr. King owned one of the finest collections of 20 Century U. S. in the country, most unusual by reason of the original drawings and essays it contained of the recent stamps. Two years ago he accepted a position as Deputy Administrator of the N. R. A. and made his headquarters in Washington, D. C., having in charge the supervision of the codes relating to the plant equipment section of the N. R. A. Mr. King was former President of The Collectors Club of New York City and the Westchester County A. P. S. Chapter, and contributed to all the stamp magazines on his favorite studies on U. S. 20th Century and Civil War Revenues. He is survived by his wife and two daughters. No collector has ever been more beloved of his associates than Beverly King. He was all that one could hope for in any man, a prince among men, a scholar and a gentleman. No tribute of ours can equal the memory that his friends will ever carry with them. He still lives in our hearts as always.

* * * * * *

The Two Cent Liberty
Last Philatelic Writings of BEVERLY S. KING.

Lawrence L. Howe has found some interesting items of No. 3967, the two cent blue profile of Liberty, 1875 Issue. One specimen shows a slight shifted transfer to the West or left, another a transfer to the South, the latter very slight, but it seems to be there. One unused copy shows a well defined vertical scratch from the I of

"Internal" downward to the W of "Two." Still another copy is on very thick soft paper, or perhaps it is double paper, one cannot be sure, this particular copy at least is separated about half way down and it looks as tho it might be double paper. It is entirely possible to "split" most any soft paper stamp with a safety razor blade and make what looks like a "double paper" specimen, but this doesn't seem to have been done with this particular stamp. Personally, I'v never seen a double paper variety of this item, have you?

The Scott Catalog lists this 2c Liberty as coming part perf and imperf. I may have been responsible for this, I don't remember, as most of my notes are in New York. Mr. Howe found two of these on old checks, with straight edges top and bottom. They may be good, I cannot tell, but I always want to see a pair! Of course, this is asking a lot on my part, but I am convinced that a P. P. or Imperf. of this stamp is a scarce animal, if at all.

* * * * * *

THE TWO CENT BANK CHECK

Mr. Howe also has run across the 2c orange bank check, 3805—1st issue, with the well known downward shifted transfer, showing in "Bank Check" and the lower lines of the ribbon, two varieties of this shift in fact. There are many more on this stamp to the West, North and South, and some nice ones have been illustrated in the American Philatelist in years past by the Revenue Unit.

Speaking of part-perf. stamps, I received a letter from E. V. Pollock not long ago calling my attention to three copies of the 2c orange bank check that looked as though they might have come from a part-perforated sheet. These were all singles, however, two of them perforated vertically and the other one horizontally. One of the vertically perforated copies had very good margins.

I have found a number of these myself, and, as a matter of fact, have several stamps on the original checks, but this does not prove anything to my mind as I have never yet seen a pair or strip of these stamps part-perf. There is no reason at all why they should not exist and if any of you at any time come across such an item I will appreciate receiving information about it.

The particular lot noted by Mr. Pollock was purchased some six years ago from a non-collector who was local Deputy County Clerk at the time, and on the face of it it does not look as though these particular stamps had been tampered with. The first issue stamps, as you know, were very hurriedly perforated and the demand being so great many sheets of certain varieties were sold without being perforated at all, and others being perforated in only one direction.

* * * * * *

FIVE CENT CERTIFICATE IMPERFORATE

Mr. Pollock also calls my attention to a block of ten imperforate 5c Certificates, No. 3823. This block is two stamps high by five stamps wide and comes from the lower left corner of the sheet. It is certainly a rare baby. A pair of these stamps catalog at $3.50, a block of four being listed at $60.00. This block of ten should be worth somewhere between $150.00 and $200.00.

Some of you may recall that when Phil Ward was disposing of a well known revenue collection sometime ago he mentioned a block of eight 5c Certificates imperforate. The chances are that both Judge Emerson of Providence and Morton Joyce of New York have larger pieces than this. I know that these two gentlemen secured the cream of the White Collection a few months ago, but I am not certain as to the size strips or blocks of this particular stamp that either the Judge or Joyce may have in their collections.

* * * * * *

FIFTY CENT ORIGINAL PROCESS

There are many interesting plate flaws on the 50c Original Process, No. 3859—First Issue. Many of you are familiar with the shifted transfer to the west extending vertically thru the lettering. This is a scarce bird but well worthy of a hunt. The other day I saw one to the East or right, an easily discernible extra line along the frame outside the word "Revenue" and continuing downward outside the first two leaves of the foliated ornament, (illustrated). Another amusing item carries a well defined crack or scratch across the top right ornament, (illustrated). There are many more scratches on this stamp and one can only surmise that the plate must have been tossed about quite a lot, resulting in lots of blemishes.

Back in the active field of revenue collecting again. We have been fortunate in securing the material accumulated by Bedford and King and we will attempt to go ahead from where their work ended.

At present we plan to publish a list of date cancellations on revenues, revenues used for postage (revised and brought up to date). We will also attempt to bring the list of stitch watermarks up to date and list both insurance company and railroad cancellations on revenues.

Started work on the material so kindly sent us by Russel King, brother of "Bev" and find that it will take quite a bit of time to get the material in shape. Have found a set of cards which appear to be a list of major varieties of the first issue revenues. Will check them and illustrate all those not before illustrated as soon as possible.

We have an almost complete set of revenue unit notes. We need page 322 of the February 1929 issue, pages 386, 87 and 88 of the April 1930 and pages 291 and 92 of the March issue of 1931. These will give us a complete set of notes from February 1928 to September 1933.

Have a list at hand of many collectors who are supposedly plating various first issue stamps. Would like to correct it and bring it to date. Any collectors working on this material please advise.

At the present time there is no financial subsidy, so please include return postage on all mail.

Also anxious to record all big pieces together with owner and to trace their history as far as possible. If you have any larger than 25 pieces of any of the first issue revenues please advise. Photos would be appreciated if available. We plan to make a fairly complete library of these items.

Notes on the 50c Mortgage

By Justin L. Bacharach.

In going over the Bedford-King material the first thing that struck us as being unusually interesting was the material in relation to the fifty cent mortgage. The major crack illustrated in the Scott catalogue is position 64. The crack continues through the margin of the stamp and shows slightly at the top of position 81. Remember, the sheet is made up of five rows of 17 stamps each—total 85 stamps. The plate imprint and number occurs at the bottom of the sheet. It reads engraved by Butler & Carpenter .... (our piece stops at this point).

Plate No. 50 (if there is an initial I would like to know, our piece does not show that far). There are also several other interesting markings. The diagonal crack again illustrated (I believe that it was illustrated in 1930) shows the crack in the latter stages of use of the plate. It occurs in position 26, 42 and 43. There is also a tool gash that occurs on late printings of position 63.

There are many other varieties. I quote from the letter of Charles W. McLellan sent me in 1932:

Position 2—Two guide dots in lower left corner
36 similar to position 2.
12 & 29—Small diagonal crack through "R" of Mortgage into "e" of Cents
13—Small crack in foliage and right margin opposite "cents"

Would like to hear from any collectors working on the plating of this stamp so that we can get more data.

Have more notes on the 50c conveyance and most of the plate varieties of the 50c conveyance. This is all the material that is in any position to write up at present. Are there any collectors that are working on these or other revenues. Please advise at once with material as well as photographs. We need the material.

Since our first article have received several letters. Will answer them as rapidly as possible. In the same mail the Cunard-White Star Line tells us all about the Queen Mary. If there is a special cover we'll let you know in the next issue.

George McNabb: Sorry, but the King material had no copies of the plating of the 5c inland exchange. Has any member one for sale. If so, advise George McNabb, 229 W. Seymour Street, Philadelphia, Pa.

W. R. Shepherd: Please photograph the cracked plates and I'll try to find their plate position. We have the 5c Inland, 50c Conveyance plated. Trying to get the rest of the 50c Mortgage. There are many types of stamps imprinted on bank checks. Nassau Stamp Co. has a specialized collection. First Issue stamps exist on many types of paper, but according to Scott Stamp & Coin Co. these types of paper are not definite enough as to either use or texture to list.

The following is the list of stitch watermarks on the first issue. Unfortunately the records do not indicate whether the stamps seen were imperf., part perf. or perf.

3802	1c Proprietary	3831	10c Bill of Lading	3858	50c Mortgage
3804	2c Bank Check	3832	10c Certificate	3859	50c Orig. Process
3805	2c Bank Check	3834	10c Foreign Exch.	3860	50c Pass. Ticket
3808	2c Express	3836	10c Power of At.	3862	50c Surety Bond
3809	2c Express, orange	3842	25c Bond	3863	60c Inland Exch.
3812	2c Proprietary	3843	25c Certificate	3864	70c Foreign Exch.
3814	2c U. S. I. R.	3844	25c Entry of Goods	3866	$1 Entry of Goods
3815	3c Foreign Exch.	3845	25c Insurance	3868	$1 Inland Exch.
3818	3c Telegraph	3846	25c Life Insur.	3869	$1 Lease
3819	4c Inland Exch.	3847	25c Power of At.	3874	$1 Power of Atty.
3821	4c Proprietary	3848	25c Protest	3883	$2.50 Inland Exch.
3822	5c Agreement	3849	25c Warehouse Rec.	3884	$3 Charter Party
3823	5c Certificate	3851	30c Inland Ex.	3885	$3 Manifest
3824	5c Express	3852	40c Inland Ex.	3888	$5 Conveyance
3825	5c Foreign Exch.	3853	50c Convey., blue	3895	$10 Prob. of Will
3826	5c Inland Exch.	3854	50c Entry of Goods	3897	$20 Conveyance
3829	6c Inland Exch.	3857	50c Life Insur.		

We have added a few, noting their type to this list. Will all members who have these items please send lists and denote which type of stamps. If the stamps are not listed in the catalogue we will try to have them added, but must have the stamps themselves to show to the cataloguers.

Preliminary Data of Plating the 10c Certificate

GEORGE E. TURNER, 1015 N. Lathrop Ave., River Forest, Ill.

The plating of the 10c Certificate being practically completed, the writer is submitting some of the major data at this time, in the hope that some material can be located which will prove some of the points still in doubt.

Anyone wishing to reconstruct this plate with single stamps will have little difficulty in doing so, with the forthcoming data. The guide dots are very characteristic and make the work relatively easy; besides the stamp is reasonably priced and there is no great scarcity.

There was only one plate made of this stamp, however, it exists in two states, an early and late, or first and second, as you prefer to designate them. The original is Plate No. 10 A, shown by a full margin copy of the lower left corner stamp (#154) in the accompanying illustration. This is the first instance of the existence of a corner plate number, known to the writer. This corner number does not take the place of the usual plate number found under the imprint. Whether plate numbers occur in the other three corner margins is unknown, unless some one possesses such marginal items.

The late state came into existence in the latter part of 1869 or very early in 1870, prior to March first which is the earliest date noted thus far. To date the plate number has not been seen for this state; the Boston Revenue Book gives it as "10 C", can someone prove it?

Stamps from the late state can be fairly easily separated due to the characteristic brilliant, light blue color and the very clear impression of the design. A great aid is the extensive re-entry of this late state, which produced some 70 "re-entered double transfers", a very expressive terminology that comes as a suggstion from Philip E. Hamilton. These re-entered double transfers have the appearance of being a twisting of the design, particularly noticeable in the upper right and/or the lower left corner of the design. The re-entry was so extensive that it may be logical to assume that all positions were re-entered, as the clear cut designs of this state tend to bear out. The most markd, or strongest, re-entered double transfer is position #17, the upper right corner stamp. Practically the whole of the left side is doubled.

One very fine double transfer is found on this plate as illustrated here. It is strongly double to the right, and shows the upper left ball clearly doubled, the left lef of the "N" of CENTS is crossed, at its middle, by the serif of the first entry, a portion of the scroll of CENTS shows in the right margin, the period after CENTS is also doubled, and the bottom lines of the TEN scroll show faintly in the white medallion circle. On clear early impressions there can be noted a guide line at the top of the design which should not be mistaken as a part of the double transfer. No re-entered doubling shows on the late state of this position, yet the double transfer remains clear, without apparent change. Its position is #93, which is perhaps odd, since being near the center of the plate. It may be that, when the siderographer renewed his work, the following day, at this point he found the press improperly lined up at the start, due perchance to the usual lag of the screw threads.

The major crack, as illustrated, is the second stamp in the bottom row, #155. The crack starting under the second "T" of CERTIFICATE, without a doubt runs to the edge of the plate, although, no full margin has been seen under this stamp. Does any one have such an item? The crack remains on the late state and the position is one that shows a slight re-entered double transfer.

Other flaws, as well as some scratches exist on the plate and in most cases show on both states. More scratches however appear on the late state, and they have the peculiarity of being two parallel lines, very close together, of which the left line is generally a bit stronger than the right line.

The plate is one of 170 subjects: arranged 17 positions horizontally and 10 positions vertically. The imprint is centered in the lower margin and reads,

"Engraved by—Butler & Carpenter—Philadelphia" Who owns a complete one?

Some very general remarks regarding the note worthy arrangement of the guide dots is presented at this time.

1. The left marginal stamps have no guide dots at either the upper or lower left corners. The writer prefers to call the dot, which is ½ mm. from the lower left corner of the first stamp in the sixth row (#86) a lay-out dot.
2. In most lower right corners there appears an elongated protrusion of the frame lines, which may be classed as a dot. There are numerous instances where a dot is clearly defined here, and 28 where two dots are noted.
3. With but a single exception, none of the positions in the upper six horizontal rows have guide dots at either of the upper corners. At the upper left corner #78 has a dot, but more than likely it was for lay-out purposes.
4. The most characteristic dot or dots, on the stamps of the first six rows is to be found at the lower left corner, (except as noted in #1 above).
5. The lower four (7th to 10th) horizontal rows have the characteristis guide dots at both upper corners, (except as in #1 above).
6. No stamp in the last mentioned four rows has a guide dot at the lower left corner.
7. A faint guide line shows in the bottom of the design and crossing the margins between the stamps of the fifth row, except in four stamps.
8. Another guide line crosses the plate above the stamps of the 8th row. There are at least twelve other positions showing such a guide line.

9. A faint guide line runs vertically along the right frame lines of the stamps of the 9th vertical row. In some positions it is coincident with the frame line, however, positions 43, 77, 145, and 162 show it clearly separated.

After laying out the guide lines and dots diagramatically it was apparent, that for a general statement, to say first that the stamps on the first six rows are without guide dots at the upper corners and that the principle dots are those appearing at the lower left corner. Secondly, that for the lower four rows the significant dots are those at both upper corners. Also in these last rows no dots are at the lower left corner.

The possible explanation of why the guide dots changed from the lower left corner in the first six rows to the upper corners in the last four rows became apparent upon studying the diagram. The belief is that the siderographer after laying out the dots for the two center horizontal rows (5th & 6th) continued to work upwards. Having completed the top row, he then inverted the plate and continued to work upwards, this was done to have sufficient support under his hands and so as not to be working "over-the-edge" of the plate. Thereby the dot which appears in the lower left changed to the upper right. In other words, he worked both ways from the sixth horizontal row, and always upwards; and to do this necessitated the turning of the plate.

Assistance and suggestions, with the loan of any material, will be greatly appreciated, so this plating maybe completed and written up.

We have seen the new Cigarette Tube Tax stamps, Series of 1933. Bought some tubes recently and got the stamps. Any collectors that want them, send 10c. Will reply as long as the supply lasts. Also bought 12 packs of the old style. Will send them with the tube package at the same figure as long as they last.

During a recent meeting of the Collector's Club in New York, spent quite a bit of time discussing the revenue stamps with several prominent collectors. Plan to get out a list of some of the material soon.

Since the last issue we have received the Government announcement of the tobacco stamp sale. We reprint herewith the story that appeared in the New York American Stamp Review:

Washington, March 12.—The Bureau of Internal Revenue stated today that due to numerous requests of stamp collectors they will resume the sale of tobacco stamps at their face value, solely for philatelic purposes, until July 1, 1936, unless supply is exhausted prior to that date.

The bureau cannot assume the responsibility for selling so-called "well centered" types of stamps. No order for stamps will be filled in excess of one sheet (50 stamps) of each denomination to any one person.

Stamps are flat plate printed as follows: ¾c, 1½c, 2¼c, 3c, 3¾c, 7½c, 11¼c, 18¾c, 37½c, 75c, 93¾c, $1.12½, $1.50.

The total price for a set of one stamp of each denomination is $5.18.

Requests should be directed to the Collector of Internal Revenue, Room 1002A, Internal Revenue Building, Washington, D. C., and should be accompanied by cash, certified check or post-office money order in an amount equal to the face value of the stamps, plus postage. Remittances should be made payable to "Collector of Internal Revenue, Maryland District." In the even the purchaser does not include the necessary registration fee, the stamps will be sent by ordinary mail at the purchaser's risk.

Commenting editorially on the sale of these stamps the Philadelphia Ledger says:

Collectors of stamps must sometimes be tempted to mourn that there are too many worlds to conquer. Of the making of postage stamps there is no end, and the complete and perfect collection is an impossibility. Only by specialization within narrow limits can the real and earnest philatelist achieve his heart's desire.

Revenue stamps offer a limited and legitimate field for some serious stamp collectors. Even of these there may be too many. It is the hobby of a lifetime to collect all the little scraps of paper which the Government has issued as receipt for taxes paid.

But foresighted philatelists are now offered a unique opportunity. They may begin at once, if they will, to collect potato stamps and can purchase a complete and unused set at par from the Bureau of Internal Revenue. Perhaps there will be other issues of revenue stamps which will be declared unconstitutional, superfluous or inadvisable before they can be used. For the trifling sum of $5.18 the collection can be begun. And if enough collectors want potato stamps, and others like them, the problem of a substitute for the processing tax may be settled.

We have also received notices from several collectors in which they state that the stamps that they are receiving are in many instances straight edged and oftimes off center.

Revenue Unit

GEORGE T. TURNER, *Chairman*, No. 12327.
Box 461, Newark, N. J.

"We Shall Carry On"

As your newly appointed chairman, I send you greetings, and wish you to know that I feel **our** answer to King's challenge (Amer. Phil. p. 325, March '35) is "we will carry on."

The Unit activities are not solely limited to revenue specialists. Our purpose will be to present authoritative information of interest to all collectors. Certainly, among the Society's 4400 members there are a greater number of collectors who possess fine and valuable revenue material than those 55 indicated in the roster as particularly interested in various phases of the revenue field.

Within your pages doubtless, a revenue item resides which when recorded and illustrated will further the constructive work to be undertaken.

Various suggestions have been received and our intention is to proceed with a program somewhat as outlined below:

A. To illustrate all existing major varieties, double transfers, cracked plates, etc. that are catalogued. This will be a lasting record regarding these items. The exact plate position will be determined, if possible. Reports will take up one denomination at a time.

B. Report and record all data pertaining to Imprints, Plate Numbers, including corner numbers and stitch watermarks.

C. Proceed with the work relating to Postage issues used as revenue and Revenue stamps used for postage.

D. Continue the study on the subject of bisects.

E. Assist in every way possible those plating revenues.

F. Maintain a permanent record of the existing full sheets and large blocks as a kind of "pedigree" list.

You probably realize that the Chairman can not possibly collect sufficient material or possess all the items on a given subject. The mass of material is in your hands. Everyone's cooperation is earnestly desired to carry forward this constructive work. As in the past, the chairman will act primarily as the "recording or clearing agent" for your discoveries, interests and articles. When you have an interesting item please submit it for recording. You may be assured of a prompt return. Have no hesitation about writing me your criticism or suggestions. To the best of my ability I shall assist you with your problems.

It is my intention to start the major variety illustrations (A above) as soon as possible, so send in immediately the material on the denominations 1c through 4c of the first issue. Don't leave it for the other fellow, remember yours may be the only existing copy, and the duplication of items gives the soundest proof of an actual variety. Through this "centralized" clearing process there is no telling what interesting new discoveries will be forthcoming. The best of the loaned copies will be used for illustration and credit goes to the owner.

Articles on revenue subjects will always be welcome and shall receive precedence over the current listings. We want to give all the support possible to you students, research enthusiasts, and those plating.

The fine response accorded the "re-birth" of this Unit is indeed heartening. The numerous letters received evince an extensive interest in the U. S. Revenues and the desire on the part of the collectors to cooperate in doing constructive work. To rewrite and enlarge the Boston Revenue Book was an oftexpressed desire of C. D. Bedford. Likewise, Beverly S. King had hoped to devote his philatelic resources to the same end. Now, it becomes the task of this Unit and all the collectors to carry on.

You enthusiasts will find much by way of an historical interest in the first of Mr. Joe L. Bopeley's articles, p. 358, April American Philatelist.

The cataloguers are to be congratulated on the improved and enlarged Revenue Section. The inclusion of pertinent data is excellent. However, on two points that appear in the prefaced notes, p. 155, 1937 U. S. Specialized Catalogue, we take exception:

1) Imprints are not limited in placement to the bottom of a plate. Numerous examples are known of imprints at the left and one at the right side. Further, two are known reading "Jos. R. Carpenter." This indicates that new plates were possibly made after the death of Mr. Butler, Oct., 1868, or the addition of the succeeding partner's imprint was made at the time of re-entry, late in 1869, to plates originally made without imprints. It seems doubtful that all imprints were changed when the reworking was performed. Perhaps, some one can show examples of an early and late state imprint of an individual plate with such change?

2) April 30, 1864, is questioned as the lawful date permitting the indiscriminate use of the stamps. The second paragraph, p. 25, Boston Revenue Book, gives this date but, no doubt it merely indicates a change in the accounting system of the engravers, whereby they grouped all stamps by denomination rather than by designation and denomination. For example, after Apr. 30, 1864, the separate stocks, previously recorded specifically as 3c Foreign Exchange, 3c Playing Card, 3c Proprietary and 3c Telegraph were combined in the single entry "The 3c General" and referred to as the "general Stamps."

The above interpretation is suggested in view of the exact statute, the particular section being quoted in full:

Vol. 12 U. S. Stat. at Large, p. 632, Act of December 25, 1862, 3rd Session, 37th Congress. An Act to amend—Internal Revenue Act—approved July 1, 1862.

"**Sec. 3. And be it further enacted,** that no instrument, document, writing, or paper of any description required by law to be stamped, shall be deemed or held invalid and of no effect for want of the particular kind or description of stamp designated for and denoting the duty charged on any such instrument, document, writing, or paper, provided a legal stamp or stamps denoting a duty of equal amount shall have been duly affixed and used thereon: **Provided,** that the provisions of this section shall not apply to any stamp appropriated to denote the duty charged on proprietary articles."

From this evidence, the whole original scheme of a specific stamp for denoting a particular document's type of transactions was eliminated, after approximately two and three-quarter months. Thus, there occur many seemingly misused stamps for the greater part of the period this act was in force. Such apparently absurd uses as having a 5c Express stamp on a Marriage certificate are found.

The most obvious reasons for the change to permit the indiscriminate use are:

Delays in the delivery of stamps at the beginning.
B—Lack of sufficient quantities for wide distribution.
C—Objections of users to the necessity of having on hand so many different kinds, which would require a large amount of money tied up in stamp stocks.
D—Perhaps, the general confusion surrounding the interpretation of the law in regard to the specific or appropriate stamp to affix.

Some of you historians may be able to show conclusive evidence in this direction. A study of the incorrect usage of particular stamps on very early documents should prove interesting to the collector of revenues on paper.

You are invited to attend the Convention. Plan to be on hand for the Revenue Unit meeting. Try and make your 1937 vacation include a trip to Detroit August 31. We look forward to the pleasure to becoming acquainted with the collectors interested in Revenues. One of the active members has promised to bring his entire collection for review at the Unit's meeting. You will find it very attractive and instructive.

Work has been begun on a bibliography of all published items on the U. S. Revenues. This has been a great need for some time; not only in this phase of philately, but for the whole subject. Do not expect this listing in the near future, it is a real task that will require considerable time.

Items are coming in for the proposed schedule of records we are attempting to work up, send in yours, it will not be too late, The job must be as complete as possible in order that any value can be derived from its use. Write a letter telling what you have, if you hesitate to send it, then if necessary we can ask that you submit it later, for comparison.

Revenue Used For Postage.

Among a lot of recent covers acquired by the chairman, one was found which is stamped with No. 4091, well tied to the cover with Ind. & Peo. / R. P. O. handstamp having an R. M. S. killer. Dated Mar. 30, 1917, from LeRoy, Ill. to Chicago.

Mr. E. V. Pollock, Ottumwa, Iowa, has submitted a Medicine stamp, No. 5382a showing a stitch watermark. The great interest in the Match and Medicine stamps will, I believe, warrent work to bring the listing of such items into the catalogue. Only a very few of the many varieties that occur on these stamps are listed at present.

The Unit will gladly sponsor this listing of major varieties. So send along your notes on the same.

Be sure to attend the Unit's meeting at the Convention. A good attendance is hoped for, which will afford the opportunity to meet you Revenue collectors. Time and place will be announced at the first Convention session.

A real research contribution from the pen of Mr. David O. True appeared in the July issue, page 538, dealing with the present data on marginal markings found on the first issue of the revenue plates. The excellence of this study warrants the assistance of others. Why not look over your marginal copies, plate number items, imprints, etc., and send the notes directly to Mr. True.

Mr. Phillip Little, Jr. writes that the two cent express (both orange and blue) has a number and control letter "2E" in the margin at the lower left corner. Further, that his corner marginal item of the ten cent proprietary is without a similar designation. For the purpose of checking and record, it will be wise to advise us of both (1) those you have with corner markings and (2) those you have without such.

The chairman some time ago saw a ten cent Inland Exchange showing the upper right corner stamp (position #17) with sufficient margin to show the existence of an inverted "10." It is not recalled if this is accompanied with a control letter. Possibly an illustration can be arranged for, thus affording a permanent record.

Possibly the Commissioner of Internal Revenue could be persuaded to illustrate the revenue stamps in a booklet as has just been done so excellently by the Post Office Department. It would be a particular aid to Revenue collectors and philately in general. The Fiscal Stamps of the United States by L. W. Crouch (#2 of the Stamp Lover Booklets—Edited by Fred J. Melville) only covers the period to 1902 and lacks in completeness by not illustrating each denomination. The Post Office Department has set the precedent, let us as a Unit press for a similar work showing the Revenues. May I have your comments?

We agree wholeheartedly with the July Editorial comment, page 547, relative to the illustration bill. By all means revenue stamps should be included and it would be wise to have such specifically designated. It would be well to write the committee on Post Offices and Post Roads or your Senators regarding this matter. Be sure to refer to Senate Bill 2550 (Hayden-Duffy Bill).

REVENUE FOR POSTAGE.

From Mr. Charles L. Hoffman comes the record of his cover with a pair of #3995 (one cent postage stamp of 1895 Surcharged I. R.) used to pay postage, cancelled in Austin, Texas, July 1, 1898, and backstamped Waco, Texas, July 2, 1898. Further interest is found in the contents of the letter itself, the whole of which is quoted:

    Mr. Ray B. B............
        Waco, Texas

    Dear Sir:
        Two pair of U. S. provisional 1 cent revenue stamps, (similar to those enclosed,) have reached me on letters bearing no other stamps, through the U. S. mails, and they have therefore been postally used. So I experiment further by using two on the cover to this letter, which I wish you to keep if it goes through, and in acknowledging the receipt of this, please use the enclosed stamps on the cover addressed to me.

               Yours very truly,
                    H. G. A..............

Doubtless the parties were collectors, but certainly the novelty of the mis-use intrigued the one sufficiently to try it himself. While it might be possible today we would not recommend such experimentation. Let us hol to the proper use of the stamps as there is enough "racketeering" in some phases of philately without introducing another.

The Unit's annual meeting will be held during the Convention at 3:30 P. M., Thursday, September 2nd. Come and enjoy an interesting session.

Another stitch watermark is reported on a private proprietary, the 4c **J. I. Brown & Son**, #5318b in the collection of Mr. H. C. Hopkins, of California.

New Amendment to Bottling-in-Bond Act.

From the **Congressional Record—Senate,** July 2, 1937, page 8749, sent the Editor by Frank Rossi of Chicago is noted the passage of this change in the above Bill. It will be of interest to those of you who collect "liquor" stamps of various kinds.

As an explanation of this Bill we feel that quoting Mr. Harrison's reply to Mr. Borah's query for an explanation will suffice as giving you the full act itself.

". . . The Bottling in Bond Act of 1897 provided for placing green strip stamps on bonded liquor bottles. Those stamps had to be printed in the Bureau of Engraving and Printing, and it was necessary that much identifying data be overprinted on such stamps. The procedure has proved to be most cumbersome. It was necessary to perform a separate printing job to overprint these stamps in each instance. In the liquor Taxing Act of 1934 we provided for placing red stamps on bottles containing unbonded liquor, and provided also that commercial interests might, under departmental regulations, handle the overprinting of identifying data. The Treasury Dept. has recommended that practically the same procedure be followed in the case of the green stamps, and they claim that we will get a little more revenue from it and that it will materially expedite the production and distribution of these stamps. The interests that are concerned do not object to the bill, but have approved it. . . ."

House bill 6737, which reads as follows:

Be it enacted, etc., That the first and fourth paragraphs of section 1 of the act entitled "An act to allow the bottling of distilled spirits in bond", approved March 3, 1897, as amended (U. S. C., 1934 ed., Supp. II, title 26, sec. 1276), are designated "(1)" and "(6)", respectively, and the second and third paragraphs of said section are amended to read as follows:

"(2) Every bottle when filled shall have affixed thereto and passing over the mouth of the same a stamp denoting the quantity of distilled spirits contained therein and evidencing the bottling in bond of such spirits under the provisions of this act, and of regulations prescribed hereunder.

"(3) The Commissioner of Internal Revenue, with the approval of the Secretary of the Treasury, shall prescribe (a) regulations with respect to the time and manner of applying for, issuing, affixing, and destroying stamps required by this section, the form and denominations of such stamps, applications for purchase of the stamps, proof that applicants are entitled to such stamps, and the method of accounting for receipts from the sale of such stamps, and (b) such other regulations as the Commissioner shall deem necessary for the enforcement of this act.

"(4) Such stamps shall be issued by the Commissioner of Internal Revenue to each collector of internal revenue, upon his requisition in such numbers as may be necessary in his district, and, upon compliance with the provisions of this act and regulations issued hereunder shall be sold by collectors to persons entitled thereto, at a price of 1 cent for each stamp, except that in the case of stamps for containers of less than one-half pint, the price shall be one-quarter of 1 cent for each stamp.

"(5) And there shall be plainly burned, embossed, or printed on the side of each case, to be known as the Government side, such marks, brands, and stamps to denote the bottling in bond of the whisky packed therein as the Commissioner may by regulations prescribe."

The Annual Meeting of the Unit was held during the Convention and conducted as an informal gathering. The following Revenue enthusiasts were present, Messrs. P. G. Andres, D. R. Bennett, H. Boies, J. L. Bopeley, H. H. Elliott, and the chairman. Mr. Bopeley very kindly brought his remarkable assemblage of Revenue Stamped Documents in which the members evinced considerable interest. A portion of this vast collection was a prize winning feature of the Detroit Exhibition. Mr. Bennett captured the Detroit Club's Brisley Cup with his extensive showing of Revenue varieties and blocks. The Unit can justly be proud of the honors accorded these two men.

The 10c Certificate plating was displayed to those present by the chairman.

Discussion centered mainly upon the work the Unit might do in compiling the data necessary for the eventual rewriting of the Boston Revenue Book. It was suggested that each one plating should be assisted by the Unit members in first compiling pamphlets upon the individual stamps, as they are plated. Thus the person most familiar with the specific stamp and its varities, etc. would prepare the authorative data.

The members are urged to earnestly cooperate in this undertaking. You can assist by submitting a record from your collecting listing the following points:

1. All pieces larger than blocks of four, noting whether margins are attached, and any other marginal markings.
2. Marginal markings: Imprints, Plate Numbers, etc. on any items you have.
3. Bisect items.
4. Revenues used for postage, etc.
5. Major varieties that occur on the above items should be indicated.

To date very little has been sent in in answer to an earlier request. We know of a great number of Revenue collectors from whom we have had no word. Let's all get in some notes and carry on the Unit's work.

* * * * *

Below is the listing of large blocks and other pieces that have been brought to our attention, principally by Mr. Beaumont and from "Dean's List."

In order to make his listing complete we should like to have much more data, and want the owners to write in, giving the following points:

1—Present owner.
2—Number of stamps in piece; denomination; imperf., part perf. or perf.; any margins attached.
3—Arrangement of stamps in block, thus for example Block of 18 (in an irregular shape):

```
    2— 3— 4— 5            Method: Number all the positions to give
    8— 9—10—11—12         a complete rectangular piece, show only such
13—14—15—16—17—18         positions as exist.
19—20—21—
```

Of course if plate positions are known these should be used in place of the above description.
4—Full sheets should be so reported with the number of stamps. If reconstruced it should be so indicated.
5—It would be of interest to state the cancellation data, giving the penned initials, or firm's name if handstamped, the date, etc.

First Listing of Revenue Sheets or Large Blocks.

1c Express, part perf., block 79.
1c Playing Card, imperf., block 50 later reduced to 30.
1c Proprietary, imperf., block 4. Perf., block 35.
2c Bank Check, imperf., block 12. Perf., block 24 (orange); Beaumont owner
2c Playing Card, part perf., vert. strip 4.
2c U. S. I. R., several sheets known.
2c Proprietary, sheet 210; Kahn owner.

3c Playing Card, perf. strip 10 and blocks.
3c Telegraph, imperf., blocks 6, 12, 15. Perf., block 12; Beaumont owner.
5c Agreement, perf., silver paper, mint block 30; Beaumont owner.
5c Certificate, perf., block 90, 40, 60, known to Beaumont.
5c Playing Card, perf., block 10; Beaumont owner.
10c Certificate, imperf., one block exists. Perf., blocks 14, 13; Turner owner.
10c Inland Exch., imperf., one block exists.
10c Bill of Lading, perf., block 69 (?); Hamilton owner.
25c Power Atty., perf., mint sheet; True owner.
50c Conveyance, perf., block 53; Bedford was owner.
50c Mortgage, perf., block 17; shows complete diagonal crack.
50c Probate Will, imperf., block 32; Seebohm's sale Dec. 1932.
50c Original Process, block 39; Ward owner.
40c Inland Exch., part perf., block 4, vert. strip 3; Turner; perf., block 10; True owner.
$1 Conveyance, part perf., a block exists.
$1 Life Ins., imperf., blocks 6 and 8.
$1 Passage Ticket, imperf., a block exists.
$1 Inland Exch., block 12; King was owner.
$1 Probate Will, imperf., horiz. strip 6.
$5 Charter Party, imperf., block 7 (has disappeared).
$5 Probate Will, imperf., blocks 21, 18.
$10 Charter Party, imperf., block 4 and 6.
$10 Mortgage, imperf., block 9.
$20 Probate Will, perf., blocks 4 and 6.
$25 Mortgage, imperf., block 4.
$50 U. S. I. R., imperf., block 14, horiz. strip 4.
$200 U. S. I. R., imperf., sheets are known, 8 per sheet. Perf., sheets are known.

We shall look forward to having many additions to this. Please, everyone, cooperate, also the dealers that hold any of this material.

Mr. Dave True dropped in for the Third Congress and it was a pleasure to meet him and see some of his fine items. The chairman had the privilege of reading a paper before this gathering, entitled "Some Notes on Revenue Plating." You may be interested in what was said about the method of plating stamps, and the general facts about the revenue plates.

A few collectors have sent in the data on the sheets and large blocks that they own. Have you checked and reported yours? Please do so and cooperate in this listing. The Unit is anxious to have this as complete as possible, for it will be of lasting value to you collectors. Send along your list of pieces, even if written in pencil. Look again at last month's column and note the suggestions on recording.

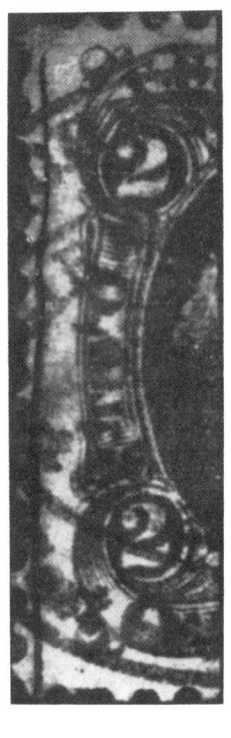

Fig. II.
4c Proprietary
#3821-c

Fig. I.
2c Express
#3808-c

Dr. E. M. Gearhart has submitted an interesting 2c Express item. It is illustrated here (Fig. I) and shows what looks like a crack running thru the vertical margin. Some time ago Mr. E. V. Pollock mentioned a similar item, but since we do not have them together for comparison, they cannot be checked. Perhaps someone else has this item. If so, we suggest that it be sent to Dr. Gearhart so that he can make the comparison, thus establishing if this is truly a major variety.

Mr. J. L. Bopeley owns the 4c Proprietary, of which the upper right corner is illustrated (Fig. II). A plate flaw or more likely a gouge is clearly evident, running downward from the margin thru the N of Revenue and just to the figure 4. Has anyone a similar item that will afford proof of this fine plate variety? Perhaps this runs up into the next stamp above or the top margin.

More Postage Used For Revenue.

No. 68—Two singles on a $1,000 note with three pairs of the 5c proprietary. This remarkable item with these two 10c stamps of 1861 is the property of Mr. F. N. Newton Jr.

No. 76—A block of three of this 5c stamp of '62-'66 on a $500 note with a 10c Bill of Lading is another item from Mr. Newton. Both show 1866 as the dates of use.

Revenue Mats.

From time to time inquiries have been made relative to the mats for revenue stamps. These mats were prepared under the direction of the late C. W. Bedford and are still on sale. For those unfamiliar with what a mat is, it can best be described as an enlarged outline drawing of the stamp design. They can be used to mount your specific varieties upon, thus making a very neat and convenient arrangement on your album pages. They also permit you to sketch in the detail of a variety, such as double transfer lines. The location of cracks or flaws, dots and other markings may likewise be shown in their relation to the design.

The chairman has had these on hand for the Unit's use but does not stock them. The bulk of this mat material upon Mr. Bedford's death went with the other **Shift Hunter** material to Mr. L. M. Ryer, 1521 17th Ave., Seattle, Washington. His letter dated August 1937 states the following are available:

No.	Description
1	Universal for 2c Civil War Revenues, First Issue.
2	Universal for 3, 4, 5, 6, 10, 15, 20c Revenues, First Issue.
3	25c Civil War Revenues, First Issue.
4	50c Civil War Revenues, First Issue
5	$1.00 Civil War Revenues, First Issue.
6	5c Inland Exchange.
6a	5c Inland Exchange 6"x8" (Priced higher).
7a	$1.00 Power of Attorney 8½"x11" (Priced higher).
11	Universal for Span. War DOCUMENTARY.
12	Universal for Span. War PROPRIETARY.

(Note: Other postage issue mat designs also on hand).

Further, Mr. D. Blake Battles informs me he also has a small supply of some of these. His address is 259 So. Balch St., Akron, Ohio. These mats can be had in assorted lots or by the 100 of the same kind.

Large Block Listing.

It is a real pleasure to report that a great many letters have been received giving the data on large pieces. However, in order to have this compilation as complete as possible there are still many gaps and numerous denominations without any posting of even a block of four. We shall wait for more of you to report and check up during these Winter months, "stampic-months." Don't forget your strips, as well. The data on Imperforates and Part Perforates is greatly needed, list even strips of 3, and pairs of the rarer items. Perforated items need only listings of those over blocks of 4, save on the higher values. The list shown in the December column was only to get this started. Where are the owners of those sheets that were noted?

We need the cooperation of ALL collectors, non-A. P. S. as well, so pass the word around, to your friends, fellow collectors, and at the club meetings. Everyone's help is solicited. Do not hesitate to report even that one multiple piece you may come across. We shall endeavor to acknowledge all the letters; as yet we have not required the services of a secretary.

Be sure to note: 1—Whether Imperf., Part Perf. or Perf. 2—The color where there is a difference. 3—The size (a) total stamps in the piece and (b) their arrangement, as (7x3) for a block of total 21. Always give the number horizontally first and the vertical number of stamps in the piece second.

REVENUE PLATERS

We have not heard from you men. What is the status of your work, and what items are you specializing upon? C. W. Bedford published a fine write-up on the 5c Inland Exchange, except for what he termed the "mystery plate." P. E. Hamilton has the 10c Bill of Lading finished. G. T. Turner has the 10c Certificate and the 50c Conveyance has been done by J. L. Bacharach. Certain others are well along, if not now completed, but as yet we have no definite record on file of your efforts. We shall endeavor to assist in every possible way. Possibly help can be given those needing to complete one of the states of certain plates. Many characteristics carry over one plate to another and by a little cooperation among ourselves similar points from the various platings should prove of value.

Stich Watermark

From Mr. H. C. Hopkins of Pasadena, Calif., comes a 10c Documentary (Battleship), #4032, with a faint stitch watermark. He has reported two such new items thus far. Have you looked your revenues over for this variety?

Marginal Markings

In looking through Dr. J. R. Hawkin's, of Oak Park, Ill., collection we spotted a nice single of the $1.90 perf. first issue with a part of the imprint showing on the left.
Many of these items are being designated in the large block compilation, from the reports thus far received. One or two of these are mentioned here:

> 5c Inland Exchange—Pair position 86 & 87 with left margin in which appears the plate number "00", in the collection of Mr. F. W. Curtis. In the same collection is a block of six position numbers 145 to 147; 162 to 164 with imprint and "5F", this is the bottom margin at the center of the sheet.
> 20c Inland Exchange—Block of four perf., with bottom margin showing the portion of the imprint that reads, "Engraved by—", recently acquired by the chairman.

Should you have any of these drop your notes to Mr. David O. True at Miami, Florida, Box 1574, whose article on the subject appeared in last July's American Philatelist, page 538.

Plating

Do you have any strips or blocks of the 40c Inland Exchange? This material is greatly needed by the Chairman in order to complete the plating of this very interesting denomination. If you will be kind enough to loan your items, send them in now and they will be returned within a reasonable time. Any assistance in this work will be greatly appreciated.

We hope to hear from the other platers on how they are progressing. In the past quite a few were working on this specialized phase of revenues but lately little has come from these enthusiasts. Are you still carrying on?

Next Month

A tabulation of interest to match and medicine collectors will be published next month; it deals principally with new varieties.

THE UNIT IS TEN YEARS OLD

Back in February of 1928, the first Revenue Unit Column appeared in this Journal, under the able pen of Beverly S. King. As our Secretary and Editor he served until his tragic accidental death in March of 1935. His excellent work remains deeply engraved on the pages of philatelic history. A total of 63 Unit Columns appeared during this span. This current number, the second in our 11th year, is No. 79. A great wealth of information has been presented for collectors and it will ever remain valuable. We hope the present membership will support us in the future.

MATCH AND MEDICINE VARIETIES

Howard H. Elliott has given us a very extensive list of many varieties in his collection. The last major listing on this subject appeared back in the column of Oct. 1932, but was limited to shifted transfers. Mr. Elliott reports the following:

Experimental Silk Paper.

1864-83 Match Stamps

#5116 Barber Match Co.
5122 A. Beecher & Son
5128 Bent & Lea
5134 Bousfield & Poole
5145 D. Burhans & Co.
5157 F. E. Clark
5166 W. D. Curtis
5171 James Eaton
5175 P. Eichele & Co.
5186 Wm. Gates
5203 Griggs & Scott
5211 L. G. Hunt
5221 Lacour's Matches
5230 Matches
5236 N. Y. Match Co.
5237 N. Y. Match Co.
5252 D. M. Richardson
5254 D. M. Richardson
5260 E. T. Russell
5391 John F. Henry
5392 Herrick's Pills
5423 Dr. D. Jayne & Son

5269 Star Match Co.
5270 Swift & Courtney
5274 E. R. Tyler
5277 Universal Safety Mach Co.
5279 Wilmington Parlor Match Co.

1862-83 Medicine Stamps

#5311 Brandreth
5315 F. Brown
5308 D. M. Bennett
5303 Demas Barnes & Co.
5317 John I. Brown & Son
5319 Dr. John Bull
5320 Dr. John Bull
5342 Oliver Crook & Co.
5351 Perry Davis & Son
5370 Hall & Ruckel
5372 Dr. Harter & Co.
5384 Helmbold
5389 John F. Henry
5518 U. S. Proprietary Med. Co.
5527 Dr. J. Walker
5541 Edward Wilder

5439 Alvah Littlefield
5445 Dr. J. H. McLean
5453 Merchants Gargling Oil
5470 D. Ransom & Co.
5477 Schenck's Pulmonic Syrup
5483 A. B. & D. Sands
5477 Ring's Vegetable Ambrosia
5495 A. L. Scoville & Co.
5496 A. L. Scoville & Co.

1864-81 Perfumery Stamps

#5570 R. & G. A. Wright

1864-83 Playing Card Stamps

#5589 Chas. Goodall
5593 J. J. Levy

STITCH WATERMARKS

#5269 Star Match Co. wmk. paper
#5426 Johnson, Holloway & Co. silk paper

DOUBLE TRANSFERS

Match Stamps

#5116 Barber Match Co.—silk paper
5116 Barber Match Co.—wmk. paper
5128 Bent & Lea—silk (Exper. Silk)
5134 Bousfield & Poole—old paper
5147 Byam, Carleton & Co.—wmk.
5160 James L. Clark—wmk.
5186 Wm. Gates—silk
5202 Griggs & Goodwill—silk
5213 Ives Matches—old
5252 D. M. Richardson—silk
5257 H. & W. Roeber—old
5269 Star Match Co.—wmk.
5270 Swift & Courtney—silk
5271 Swift, Courtney & Beecher Co.—wmk.

Medicine Stamps

#5307 Barry's Proprietary—silk
5317 John I. Brown & Sons—silk

5344 Jeremiah Curtis & Son—silk
5381 Heldmbold—old
5383 Helmbold—old
5423 Dr. D. Jayne & Son—pink
5423 Dr. D. Jayne & Son—wmk.
5427 I. S. Johnson & Co.—silk
5441 Prof. Lowe—silk
5441 Prof. Lowe—wmk.
5445 Dr. J. H. McLean—silk
5445 Dr. J. H. McLean—wmk.
5468 Radway & Co.—seilk
5473 Reddings Russian Salve—silk
5487 Schenck's Mandrake Pills—silk
5488 Schenck's Mandrake Pills—silk
5517 John L. Thompson—old
5527 Dr. J. Walker—silk
5548 Wright's Indian Vegetable Pills—wmk.

Perfumery Stamps

#5564 Lanman & Kemp—silk

From F. W. Curtis comes the use of a Match stamp on a document. This is, or rather was, an illegal use of such stamps as the law specifically states the private issues were not for such usage. Mr. Curtis writes:

"A note for $25.00 stamped with two 2c Bank Checks, orange, and a 1c black Match stamp, #5255." This is of Richardson Match Co.

Plate Numbers and Marginal Markings

The 3c Foreign Exchange (#3815c) has been shown us with an inverted "3 I," number and control letter in the upper margin. This is over the left stamp of a block of 8 (2 horiz. x 4 vert.), perforated. We are wondering if this block is from the upper corner of the plate? This would then made another corner plate number item. Who has an item with both top and side margins?

One of our New York members has material which is being assembled to form a complete sheet of the 10c Proprietary (#3837c) and this shows on an imprint at the bottom, without a Plate No. The Boston Revenue Book states this plate bears the number "10 A." If some one can show us this then it will be proof of more than one plate existing for this denomination.

Several copies of the 25c Power of Attorney (#3847) with plate numbers have been called to our attention, by Phillip Little, Jr., David O. True and Morton D. Joyce, where the control letter really is an inverted "A," rather than a "V." You need not use a glass to see the A's "cross-bar." Evidently the engraver got hold of the wrong letter when applying his die. Does a true "V" exist on someones copy, we should like to hear of it?

Who has a 50c Life Insurance (#3857) showing the "50G^2" number, as listed in the Boston Book? We have seen a perforated single with enough of the margin to show "Plate No." but no numeral and control letter.

Dr. Clifford D. Harvey reports having a $10.00 Mortgage, imperforatd (#3894a) with large margins at the bottom showing part of the imprint, which reads, "—RAVED BY Butler & C—," and pen cancelled Aug. 25, 1863.

Mr. True informed me sometime ago that in the "JOS. R. CARPENTER" imprints the letters are all capitals, while in the "Butler & Carpenter" imprints only the first letters are capitalized. This is an interesting observation and difference of note, how many of you had discovered this fact? For further information on this subject refer to Mr. True's excellent article in last July's issue.

Unit Announcements.

Your chairman has tried to create interest in and dig up data on Revenue stamps during the year just past. Considerable work is in progress, the two major items being: First, to list all the large pieces of each denomination, and secondly, the preparation of a check list of the varieties that exist on each denomination, which possibly can be fully illustrated. It is hope dthat you have found interest in some of the notes in this column. Please drop us a line if you have any suggestions or criticisms.

We need your assistance, many of you have some phase of revenue collecting in which you specialize; why not write us about it and send in an article? We have an article on the Florida State Revenues to appear soon, and the promise of a listing of the Railroad cancels on revenues, which is still in preparation. What can you contribute? To carry on your Unit, the assistance and cooperation of every revenue collector is needed.

New York City Tax Stamps

Effective May 1, 1938, two stamps were issued by the City of New York, to be affixed to packs, tins, and cartons of cigarettes sold in the City. This tax is to provide for the city's "Emergency Relief." This new tax stamp might be classed as a "city fiscal" issue, and so far as we know is the first of its kind, since we are unaware of any other city collecting a tax by the use of a stamp.

The stamps are ½ x ⅝ inch, with the letters **N. Y. C.** in an arc near the top, the value shown in the center, and the word **RELIEF** across the lower portion. The two values are:

    1c—white lettering on a deep green background—for affixing to packs of 20 cigarettes.
    3c—white lettering on a red background for affixing to tins of 50 cigarettes.

On the reverse side—viewed thru the cellophane wrapper—appear repeated horizontal lines (about 9 per stamp) reading "City of New York."

These stamps are of the decalcomania type—like the children's colored transfer pictures—are easily applied, and cannot be removed without being destroyed. This type of stamp has bee nfound to be the simplest and most effective in its adhesion to cellophone. The City's contract is with the Rayner-Consolidated Decalcomania Corp. of Jamaica, N. Y.

There are rumors of a new design on the next order as the present quantities have been practically used up. For those who have asked about the number cancellations, we are informed these numbers are the jobbers' license numbrs.

Meters have also been employed. Th one type seen is a 1c purple ink, serrated border line measuring 32 mm. horizontally by 16 mm. vertically; "N. Y. C. RELIEF" at top in letters of varying height, figure 1 in center over the word "CENT," a three-leaf foliage on each side of the figure; the word "METER" in the lower left corner, number (of 5 figures) in the lower right corner, with a line extending between these.

Our attention has been called to other cities that have used stamps to collect an excise:

Kansas City, Mo. (Cigarette Tax)
City of Bend, Oregon (Beer)
City of Klamath Falls, Oregon (Beer, Liquor, Wine)
City of Marshfield, Oregon (Wine)
City of St. Angel, Ore. (Malt Liquor)
City of No. Bend, Ore. (Beverage Tax)
City of Salem, Oregon (Beverage Tax)
City of Bellingham, Wassh (Beverage License Fee)
City of Seattle, Wash. (Beverage License Fee)
City of Tacoma, Wash. (Beverage License Fee)
City of Toppenish, Wash. (Revenue)

Doubtless there are others and we shall be very pleased to learn of them. We want, for the Unit's file, a record of all fiscal stamps, whether Federal, State, or City, issued in the U. S. Drop us a line about what you can report.

Future Delivery Stamps At An End

Mr. Morton D. Joyce has shown us the Statute which repeals the tax on all transactions in produce, stocks, etc. for future delivery, effective June 30, 1938. Thus the use of the documentary stamps, overprinted "Future Delivery," will be terminated.

Match & Medicine

A few more experimental silk papers are reported by Mr. W. T. Kiepura, of Sioux City, Iowa:

#5220—1c W. S. Kyle	#5407—4c Hostetter & Smith
5235—1c N. Y. Match	5469—1c D. Ranson & Co.
5336—1c Collins Bros.	5572—3c R. & G. A. Wright
5366—4c Seth Fowle	5573—4c R. & G. A. Wright
5385—6c Helmbold	5585—5c A. Dougherty

He also has a Stitch Watermark on #5345-a, 1c Curtis & Brown.

It is with a great deal of pleasure that we publish the list of noteworthy varieties, so far unrecorded, sent us by Mr. Henry W. Holcombe, a true M. & M. enthusiast and authority. He has described the location of the shifts in detail, thus enabling you to check your copies. Maybe you have a different variety. If so, let us hear about it, or submit it for comparison.

Shifted Transfers

#5195–a T. Gorman & Bro.; 1c black; old paper; position of shift, left frame line.
5274–b E. R. Tyler; 1c green; silk paper; position of shift, lettering at top and in circle.
5317–a John I. Brown & Son; 2c green; old paper; position of shift, frame line at lower left.
5403–d Home Bitters Co.; 2c blue; watermarked paper; position of shift, ornament to right of center design and adjacent lettering.
5420–d Dr. D. Jayne & Son; 2c black; uncut; watermarked paper; position of shift, figures in center and words "TWO CENTS."
5423–a Dr. D. Jayne & Son; 2c black; die cut; old paper; position of shift, figures in center and words "TWO CENTS."
5424–b Dr. D. Jayne & Son; 4c green; die cut; silk paper; position of shift, "FOUR CENTS," right "IV" and doubling of inner oval frame line under "TERNA."
5439–a Alvah Littlefield; 1c black; old paper; position of shift, to right in "ON" of ONE.
5445–c Dr. J. M. McLean; 1c black; pink paper; position of shift, "PRIETA" of PROPRIETARY.
5487–d Schenck's Mandrake Pills; 1c green; imperforate; watermarked paper; position of shift, frame line at upper right.
5495–a A. L. Scovill & Co.; 1c black; old paper; position of shift, (a) upper circles and adjacent shade lines; (b) "NE of ONE; (c) "NATI" of CINCINNATI.
5585–b A. Dougherty; 5c blue; silk paper; position of shift, upper 5's and in center lettering.

Experimental Silk Papers

#5127 H. & M. Bentz, 1c blue.
5358 P. H. Drake & Co., 4c black.

Stitch Watermarks

#5154 Byam, Carlton & Co.; 1c black; old paper; vert. at right.
5209 B. & H. D. Howard; 1c lake; old paper; vert. at right.
5427 I. S. Johnson & Co.; 1c vermilion; watermarked paper; horizontal.

We have another collectors' list which we are working over and hope to be able to illustrate some of the varieties.

"Embossed Revenue Stamped Paper News"

The above is to be the title for a new paper devoted to the interests of collectors who specialize in this phase of revenues. The announcement received promises eight issues a year dealing with information on stamped paper, data on new discoveries (pictures where possible) and advertisements of material for sale.

Mr. James F. Magee, Jr., of Hamilton Court, 39th and Chesnut Sts., Philadelphia, Pa., is acting as editor, and you collectors should benefit greatly from this specialized publication, so we are passing the word along to you with the hope that you will get behind Mr. Magee. Write to him for further details.

Another item for all revenue collectors that have Embossed Stamped Paper items in their collection is a blank check-list which will be forwarded you upon request from either Mr. Colin MacR. Makepeace, #12999, or Mr. Morton D. Joyce, #4426. You are asked to cooperate in compiling a complete list which will be of value in the revision of the catalogue. All you need do is fill in the blank properly and return it; the assistance will be very much appreciated.

Plating Notes

10c Proprietary—#3837. Only three positions in the top row of the plate are needed to complete the sheet owned by Morton D. Joyce. If you have anything, single or multiple, with the top margin showing, he would appreciate the loan of the items for a short time, so as to verify and determine the plate characteristics of these missing positions.

40c Inland Exchange—#3852. The chairman wishes to report very slow progress on this work. But a single reply was received from the request for material issued back in March. However, a very remarkable find was sent us by Mrs. Charles W. Kern. She has kindly loaned me her four full vertical strips of six in part perforated condition. One stamp in the second horizontal row shows the major double transfer, which partially locates this outstanding variety. We have the privilege of holding this some time longer and now want you other collectors to loan your blocks and strips. They will all be acknowledged upon receipt and held in safe keeping and returned to you, either immediately upon request at any time, or by the end of this year. Please act now so that this second "cooperative" plating endeavor can be made a success. In a similar fashion, it was excellently done by the Unit members for the 5c Inland Exchange under the able hand of the late C. W. Bedford. We shall do our best in so far as the plating work goes and full credit will be given all who assist with their material.

It is our hope that one complete plating can be accomplished each year by some individual or through the combined efforts of the Unit members, and be published for the benefit of philately.

We start this month the fine check-list prepared by Mr. True on the Florida State Revenue Stamps. It is our hope that one of the revenue enthusiasts in each state will write-up the Revenue Stamps of his state. This will be an excellent contribution to the field of revenues as it has been quite some years since any listings of these State Issues have appeared. In recent years there has been a considerable increase in this form of taxation. We have just received another state, Utah, which we hope to publish later. Now let us hear from the others. We shall be pleased to act as a clearing point, so that if more than one compiler is working on a state, they can be advised and thus work in cooperation, which will avoid duplication of effort. What is your State?

Florida State Revenue Stamps

By DAVID O. TRUE, No. 13488, Box 1574, Miami, Fla.

In compiling this check list the assistance of various State Officials and Revenue dealers is acknowledged. The list is corrected to June 1, 1938.

The first stamps of the State of Florida were issued by the Department of Agriculture in 1889, for Fertilizer Inspection. There were three stamps, no denominations, colors black, green and brown on white paper and a sea horse design on the side.

These were followed by successive issues of feed and fertilizer stamps by this department, three issues, all without designation of purpose, but with the number of pounds shown. Then have followed three issues each of the feed and fertilizer stamps with values expressed in the corners, instead of in large figures across the face, and with the purpose of issue stated.

Under the same department, an issue of Fruit Inspection stamps were put out in 1925, but the complete values are not known to date. Four other issues have followed, with values to $9.00.

An issue of Oil Inspection stamps was issued, of which five denominations are known, up to $1.25. There were probably others. They resemble in color and make-up the South Carolina stamps for the same purpose. The former are no longer in use.

The first Egg Inspection stamp was issued July 1, 1931 and alone comprises the first issue. In 1933 a set of three stamps supplanted it, with separate classifications on the stamp. The third issue is now in use, and in these stamps and labels are combined and called "Labels".

Under the Department of Comptroller, there were two issues of Documentary stamps, the first having "Documentary" at the top, and the second has "Florida" at the top. Both were issued in denominations up to $100.00.

The same department has issued Orange Advertising stamps in three issues with denominations up to $4.00; Grapefruit Advertising in three similar sets up to $12.00; Tangerine Advertising in three sets also, up to $20.00.

Under the State Beverage Department, the first Alcoholic Tax stamps were issued in 1935, circular top, with palm tree design. The second issue was a map stamp, with values in a label. The third set had the numerals of value in a circle, and had an added 1¼c value. The values of these stamps ran to 20c. A new issue brought out this year has values 50% in excess of the old sets, to reflect additional revenue taxes.

In addition to the four issues enumerated above, there was an issue of Alcoholic Inspection stamps, small ones of ½c, 1c, and 2c; larger ones of 6c and 12c values.

The check list that follows of the Florida Tax Stamps, is grouped for reference purposes.

(Editor's note—Mr. True has mimeographed copies of this list which he will send any one interested in having a copy. It has the items designated which constitute his want list.)

A—Issues of the Department of Agriculture.

A- I—Citrus Fruit Maturity (grade) "Inspection" Stamps.

    (a)—First Issue, 1925. Perf. 14; 1½c and 15c both Orange and blue. $5.40 Orange and green. (Incomplete listing, other values are known).

    (b)—Second Issue, 1927. Perf. 12; Small shield (9½x11mm.) and thin line of printing. Nathan Mayo, Commissioner, on this and all later issues. 1c Orange and blue on green paper, overprinted "Special" in red; 2½c orange and blue; 25c orange and brown; $2.50 orange and purple; $7.50 orange and red; $9.00 orange and green.

    (c)—Third Issue, 1932. Perf. 12; larger shields (10½x13mm.) and thick lines of printing. Same colors. 2½c; 25c; $1.25; $2.50; $7.50; $9.00.

    (d)—Fourth Issue, 1935; Oranges in corner, large stamp, 75mm. wide, and denominations of same design and colors, orange and green; 1c; 5c; 10c; 50c; $1.00; $2.50; $4.00.

    (e)—Fifth (present) Issue. Same design and color as 1935 issue, but only 50mm. wide; 1c; 5c; 10c; $1.00; $4.00; the use of the $2.50 old type has been continued, and no stamp of this denomination has been issued in this last issue tho it was probably prepared, and its later use may be anticipated.

A- II—Egg Classification Stamps. All issues signed Nathan Mayo, Commissioner.

    (a)—First Issue, 2c denomination only, which was the charge per case of 30 dozen eggs, stamps 95mm. wide; 2c black on yellow.

    (b)—Second Issue, same design but stamps 110mm. wide; 2c black on yellow; 2c red on white; 2c blue on white.

    (c)—Third (present) Issue. Name changed to Inspection Fee labels, rate changed to 4c per case of 30 doz. eggs.

        a') Florida Egg labels—4c; 2c and for 1 doz. carton.
        b') Shipped Egg labels—4c; 2c and for 1 doz. carton.
        c') Cold Storage labels—4c; 2c and for 1 doz. carton.
        d') Processed Egg labels—4c.
        e') Unclassified Egg labels—4c.

A-III—Oil Inspection Stamps.

    (a)—First Issue, (not now in use). Nathan Mayo, Commissioner. Tax rate 1c on 8 gallons. Larger denominations were—larger stamps: ¼c—2 gal. gray; 1¼c—10 gal. red; 6¼c—50 gal. green; 62½c—500 gal. light green; $1.25—1000 gal. brown; (Incomplete values.)

Florida State Revenue Stamps

By DAVID O. TRUE, No. 13488, Box 1574, Miami, Fla.

A-IV—Inspection Tax Stamps.

    (a)—First Issue, Sea Horse at side. No denominations. Engraved "Inspection Tag—Paid". L. B. Wombwell, Commissioner. 1889. Fertilizer; Colors, Black on white; Green on white; Brown on white.
    (b)—Second Issue. Same as the first issue, but printed in black. B. E. McLin, Commissioner, 1902—Fertilizer, for—100, 125, 200, 250 pounds.
    (c)—Third Issue. Frame and size rather similar to first issue. All denominations red on white. B. E. McLin, Commissioner, 1905—Feed. for—50, 100, 125, 175, 200 pounds.
    (d)—Fourth Issue. Same as second issue in frame and size. W. A. McRae, Commissioner.

        a')—Feed—50 pounds, brown; 100 pounds—red; 175 pounds—orange.
        b')—Fertilizer—100 pounds—green; 200 pounds—blue.

A-V—Feed Inspection Stamps.

    (a)—First Issue. Red on White. W. A. McRae, Commissioner. 1914. Values in all four corners: 100 pounds.
    (b)—Second Issue. Perf. 14½. Nathan Mayo, Commissioner. 50 pounds —gray; 100 pounds—red.
    (c)—Third (present) Issue. Perf. 12. Nathan Mayo, Commissioner. All denominations above 10 lbs. have been discontinued for tags. 5 lb. —purple; 8⅓ lb.—green; 10 lb.—red; 25 lb.—lilac; 50 lb.—brown; 100 lb.—red.

A-VI—Fertilizer Inspection Stamps.

    (a) —First Issue. Perf. 14. W. A. McRae, Commissioner. 1914. Values in all four corners: 100 lb.—green; 200 lb.—blue.
    (b)—Second Issue. Perf. 12; 50 & 100 lbs. also perf. 14½. Nathan Mayo, Commissioner. 5 lb.—black on salmon; 8⅓ lb.—black on yellow; 10 lb.—black on blue; 25 lb.—yellow on white; 100 lb.—green on white; 200 lb.—blue on white; 1 ton—black on orange; 5 ton—black on green.
    (c)—Third Issue. Wholesale (phosphate(fertilizer, Tax rate 20% of retail: 50 lb.; 1 ton; 5 ton: only 3 denominations issued.

B—Issues of the Department of Comptroller.

B- I—Documentary Stamps.

(a)—First Issue. "Documentary" at top. Ernest Amos, Comptroller. In use Sept. 24, 1931 to Jan. 3, 1933: 10c red; 30c purple; 50c blue; $1.00 green; $3.00 black; $5.00; $10.00; $25.00; $100.00.

(b)—Second (present) Issue. "Florida" at top. J. M. Lee, Comptroller. Issued Jan. 3, 1933. 10c—blue; 30c—yellow; 50c—green; $1.00—red; $3.00—dark green; $5.00—black; $10.00—blue; $25.00—light blue; $100.00—brown.

B- II—Orange Advertising Stamps.

(a)—First Issue. Orange on white, large size, 72mm. wide. J. M. Lee, Comptroller. In use Sept. 1935 to Sept. 1936. 1c; 5c; 10c; 50c; $1.00; $4.00.

(b)—Second Issue. Stamps were issued in red on white. Size only 42mm. wide. J. M. Lee, Comptroller. 1c; 5c; 10c; 50c; $1.00; $4.00.

(c)—Third Issue. Same size and design as second issue, and both the second and third issue now in use. 1c; 5c; 10c; 50c; $1.00; $4.00.

B-III—Grapefruit Advertising Stamps.

(a)—First Issue. Orange on white, 72 mm. wide. J. M. Lee, Comptroller. In use Sept. 1935 to Sept. 1936. 3c; 15c; 30c; $1.50; $3.00; $12.00.

(b)—Second Issue. 42 mm. wide, blue on white. J. M. Lee, Comptroller. 3c; 15c; 30c; $1.50; $3.00; $12.00.

(c)—Third Issue. Same as second, but in green on white. 3c; 15c; 30c; $1.50; $3.00; $12.00.

B-IV—Tangerine Advertising Stamps.

(a)—First Issue. Sept. 1935 until Sept. 1936. Orange on white, 72 mm. wide. J. M. Lee, Comptroller. 5c; 25c; 50c; $2.50; $5.00; $20.00.

(b)—Second Issue. Same values, 42 mm. wide, color black on white.

(c)—Third Issue. Same values and size as second, but light blue on white.

C—State Beverage Department.

C- I—Alcoholic Excise Stamps.

(a)—First Issue. Circular top, palm tree design. Printed by American Decalcomania Co. June 1935. 1c, 5c, 8c, 10c, 16c, 20c.

(b)—Second Issue. State map. Figures in labels. Large and small size labels and maps. Printed by Meyercord Decalcomania Co. Issued Dec. 1925. 1c, 1¼, 5c, 8c, 10c, 16c, 20c.

(c)—Third Issue. Numbers of value in circles. Printed by Consolidated Lithographing Co. June, 1936. Each value was issued with state map in yellow on red background, but each was also printed with the map i nother colors. For several months the tax rate of 30c per quart was met by use of the 20c stamp for which an overcharge of 50% was made, as with each other denomination of this series:— 1c, 1¼c, 5c, 8c, 10c, 16c, 20c.

(d)—Fourth Issue (present). Similar to Third Issue except for denominations. Jan. 1938. 1½c, 1⅞c, 7½c, 12c, 15c, 24c, 30c.

C- II—Alcoholic Inspection Stamps.

These stamps were issued on liquor "not for consumption in Florida." The rate was ½c per pint, or 24c per case. Discontinued June 5, 1937. Small oval stamps—½c blue and black; 1c green and black; 2c purple and black; large rectangular stamps—6c blue and red; 12c green and red.

"Civil War Revenue Provisionals"

Mr. Eugene Klein has written in **Stamps** p. 9 vol. 25, No. 1, Oct. 1, 1938, of material from the old Philadelphia Custom House. Several documents were found with a handstamp upon the affixed stamps reading **"Used for 50-cent Stamp"** in two lines with a small fleur-de-lys design preceding the word "Used" and following the word "Stamp".

It is stated that these were used over an extended period "1865 to 1868", also, that certain bisects of the 50c were similarly handstamped.

Some question has been raised regarding these items. It seems rather absurd that a 25c stamp should be surcharged when all that was necessary would have been to utilize two of the 25c stamps for the multiple rate.

It would seem hardly justifiable to prepare a handstamp for so few items, and above all it appears quite unlikely that a clerk would run out of stamps so many times on such an extended period as is stated.

If this surcharge was applied by the user then who received the additional amount collected, or how was it paid to the Internal Revenue Collector?

If the collector ran short of stamps and applied the surcharge then it would seem possible that similar documents of other parties should turn up from within his district.

It cannot be explained because of a revision or change in the rate charged for **Entry of Goods** at Custom Houses. The rate enacted July 1, 1862, is shown below, which was maintained unchanged by the Act of June 30, 1864, and was in force until repealed June 6, 1872.

Entry of Goods at Custom Houses—

```
Value up to $100 . . . . . . . . . . . . . . . . . . . . . . . . . 25c
Value up to $100-$500 . . . . . . . . . . . . . . . . . . . 50c
Over $500 . . . . . . . . . . . . . . . . . . . . . . . . . . . . $1.00
```

Entry for withdrawal from warehouse 50c.

It is our opinion that further study and a fuller explanation be given before these items receive an appropriate listing.

Revenue Unit Note

2c PLAYING CARDS

What appears to be a crack on this stamp (#3810c) has been shown us by Mr. Frank M. Morgan. The crack starts in the lower right "2" and runs downward between the "DS" of CARDS and on possibly into the next position below. It is a right marginal stamp as the copy seen has a portion of the right margin attached. Has anyone else seen this same crack on his stamps?

Revenue Large Blocks & Multiple Pieces

Since the first listing a year ago, Amer. Phil. p. 268, Dec. 1937, and the request for cooperation in preparing this present record, twenty-eight collectors have supplied us with lists of the pieces in their holdings. We wish to thank each one for their part in making this list what it is. Truly it shows what can be accomplished if we all work together. There is certainly a tremendous wealth of material recorded and much of interest to all collectors will be derived from this compilation.

We know that this is not complete and that it does not represent all the known items. You would do a great favor to the Revenue enthusiasts if you would check your collection items with this list and report anything that you have. It is hoped that we can revise or supplement this list as you inform us of items you possess in your collection.

Most of the abbreviations used are familiar to you all, and for ready reference we list certain designations here:

H—horizontal; V—vertical; size expressed (H x V); Blk—block; Stp —strip; Pr—pair; T—top; B—bottom; L—left; R—right; marg.— margin; Impt—imprint.

The list gives the Catalog Number, Denomination, character of perforation, size, description and Owner. This is followed by a simpler listing of other large pieces reported. A bracketed number following an item indicates the number of such reported.

Cat. No.   Denom., Perf., Size, Description and Owner.
3800   1c Expr.; Imp.; Blk 9 (3x3) R marg Ward; Blks 5, 4 (2); H Stps 5, 4 (2) V Stps 4, 3 (2)
       P. P.; Blk 8 (4x2) (2) Emerson; Blks 6, 4; H Stp 4; V Stps 7, 5 (2)
       Perf.; Sheet 210 (Reconstructed) Joyce; Blk 50 (5x10) R marg. Bennett; Blks 40, 8, 4; H Stp 5
3801   1c Ply. Cds.; Imp.; V Pr Clapp; V Pr Ward; H Pr Emerson
       P. P.; V Pr Clapp; V Pr Ward; V Pr Joyce; V Pr Emerson
       Perf.; Blk 30 (6x5) Ward; Blk 4; H Pr.
3802   1c Prop.; Imp.; V Pr Clapp; V Pr Joyce; H Pr Ward
       P. P.; H Stp 5 (2) form blk 10 Joyce; V Prs (3)
       Perf.; Blk 116 (irreg.) Joyce; Blks 70, 50, 35 (3), 28, 25, 21, 20 (2), 15, 12, 10 (2)
3803   1c Tel.; Imp.; H Stp 4 Emerson; H Pr (2); V Pr (3)
       Perf.; Blk 4 True; H Pr Clapp
3804   2c Bk. Ck. BLUE; Imp.; Blk 21 (3x7) True; Blks 12, 8, 6 (2), 5, 4 (2)
       P. P.; Blk 30 (10x3) T & L marg. Emerson; Blks 16, 10, 8, 6 (2), 4
       Perf.; Blk 25 (5x5) uncanc Bennett; Blks 24, 19, 18, 10 (3), 9, 8
3805   2c Bk. Ck. ORANGE; P. P.; —— unreported
       Perf.; Sheet 210 (Reconstructed) Joyce; Blk 111, 72, 25, 21, 9
3806   2c Cert.; Imp.; Blk 4 Saxton, Blk 4 Joyce, Blk 4 Emerson H Pr (2)
       Perf.; Blk 56 (7x8) B marg Emerson; Blks 28, 21
3807   2c Cert. ORANGE; Perf.; H Pr Clapp
3808   2c Expr. BLUE; Imp.; Blk 18 (3x6) Joyce; Blks 18, 17 (4), 12 (3), 11 (2), 9, 8, 6 (4)
       P. P.; H Stp 4 L marg Emerson; V Stps 3 (4); H Pr (3)
       Perf.; Blk 25 (5x5) Joyce; Blks 8, 6; H Stp 3

3809　2c Expr. ORANGE; Perf.; Sheet 210 (less 4) Little; Sheet 210 (reconstructed) Joyce; Blk 28, 15, 4
3810　2c Ply. Cds. BLUE; Imp.; —— unreported
　　　P. P.; V Stp 4 Emerson; V Pr Clapp
　　　Perf.; Blk 32 (8x4) R marg Joyce; Blks 25, 21, 9, 8
3811　2c Ply. Cds. ORANGE; Perf.; Blk 3 (2&1) Clapp
3812　2c Prop. BLUE; P. P.; Blk 12 (3x4) (2) ??; V Stp 4; V Pr (2)
　　　Perf.; Blk 45 (9x5) Joyce; Blks 18, 15, 14, 12 (2), 10, 9, 8, 4 (2)
3812e 2c Prop. ULTRAM.; Perf.; Blk 10 (5x2) Joyce; Blk 4; V Pr.
3813　2c Prop. ORANGE; Perf.; —— unreported
3814　2c USIR; Perf.; Sheet 210 (14x15) (2) True; Blks 60, 45, 44, 35, 28, 25, 24 (3), 23, 16, 8
3815　3c F. Ex.; P. P.; H Pr Clapp, H Pr Emerson; H Pr Ward
　　　Perf.; Blk 8 (4x2) Hale; Blk 6, 4; H Stp 9
3816　3c Ply. Cds.; Imp.; V Pr (2) Clapp; V Pr Emerson.
　　　Perf.; Blk 7 (4&3) Ward
3817　3c Prop.; P. P.; V Stp 4 Clapp; V Stp 3, V Pr.
　　　Perf.; Blk 32 (8x4) Little; Blks 18, 15, 14, 12 (2), 8, 6 (2), 5
3818　3c Tel.; Imp.; Blk 15 (3x5) Emerson; Blks 12, 6, 4 (2)
　　　P. P.; Blk 40 (5x8) Joyce; Blks 11, 6, 4. V St 4, 3 (2)
　　　Perf.; Blk 35 (5x7) Ward; Blks 32, 12, 9 (2), 4 (3)
3819　4c I. Ex.; Perf.; Blk 32 (8x4) Bennett; Blks 6 (3), 4 (2)
3820　4c Ply. Cds.; Perf.; Blk 9 (3x3) Ward; V Pr Clapp
3821　4c Prop.; P. P.; V Stp 3 (2) Emerson; V Pr (7)
　　　Perf.; Blk 20 (5x4) Joyce; Blks 6, 4; H Stp 3 (2); V Stp 3
3822　5c Agree.; Perf.; Blk 48 (6x8) B marg Impt Fitts; Blks 40, 30, 16, 12, 10, 9, 8
3823　5c Cert.; Imp.; Blk 10 (5x2) Emerson; Blk 4 (2); H Stp 4 (2), H Stp 3; V Stp 4
　　　P. P.; Blk 12 (irreg.) Joyce; Blk 4 (2); V Stp 4 (2), 3
　　　Perf.; Sheet 170 (reconstructed) (2) Joyce; Blks 90, 60 (2), 40, 27, 20, 16, 15, 14, 10; H Stp 10
3824　5c Expr.; Imp.; Blk 72 (9x8) Ward; Blks 70, 49, 24
　　　P. P.; Blk 10 (5x2) Boies; Blks 9, 8 (2), 4 (2)
　　　Perf.; Blk 30 (6x5) unused Vanderhoof; Blks 20, 9, 8, 6, 4 (4)
3825　5c F. Ex.; P. P.; H Stp 5 on docum. Ward
　　　Perf.; Blk 52 (irreg. reconstructed) Bennett; blks 30, 15, 10 (2), 9 (2)
3826　5c I. Ex.; Imp.; Blk 8 (4x2) True; Blks 8 (2), 6, 4
　　　P. P.; Blk 12 (6x2) Emerson; Blks 10, 8 (2), 6, 4 (2), V Stp 6; V Pr (4).
　　　Perf.; Blk 63 (7x9) Ward; Blks 56, 54, 30, 20, 12, 9, 8. H Stp 10
3827　5c Ply. Cds.; Perf.; Sheet 170 (reconstructed) oyce; Blks 40, 20, 16, 10 (3), 6
3828　5c Prop.; Perf.; Blk 16 (4x4) Joyce; Blks 14, 7, 6, 4
3829　6c I. Ex.; Perf.; Blk 16 (4x4) Bennett; Blk 16 (8x2) Joyce, Blk 8, 4 (2)
3830　6c Prop.; Perf.; —— unreported
3831　10c B. L.; Imp.; Blk 5 (3&2) Slevin; Blk 5 (2&3) Koester; Blk 4 (3); H Stp 5 (2); H Pr (3)
　　　P. P.; V Stp 5 Joyce; H Pr; V Pr (4)
　　　Perf.; Blk 140 (?) Hamilton; Blks 32, 21, 12, 10, 8 (2), 4 (3); H Stp 4
3832　10c Cert.; Imp.; Blk 5 (3&2) Ward; Blk 4; H Stp 3 (2); H Pr (2); V Pr (2)
　　　P. P.; V Stp 5 Saxton; V Stp 5 (3) Blk 4; V Stp 3 (2); V Pr (3); H Pr.
　　　Perf.; Blk 21 (7x3) Turner; Blks 20 (2), 14, 13, 10 (2), 9, 8, 6 (3)
3833　10c Cont. BLUE; P. P.; V Stp 5 Joyce; Blk 4; V Pr (4); H Pr.
　　　Perf.; Sheet 170 (reconstructed) Joyce; Blks 25, 16, 15, 10 (3), 9
3833e 10c Cont. ULTRAM.; P. P.; —— unreported
　　　Perf.; Blk 27 (9x3 Joyce; Blks 20, 6, 5, 4
3834　10c F. Ex. BLUE; Perf.; Sheet 170 (reconstructed) Joyse; Blks 6 (2), V Stp 5, 3
3834e 10c F. Ex. ULTRAM; Perf.; H Stp 5 Ward, H Pr.

List of Handbooks and Catalogues Pertaining to Revenue Stamps

For those desiring a bibliography or list of reference books dealing with revenues we have compiled the following list. Many of these are in the library at the Collectors Club, New York, and their assistance in making this list as complete as possible is duly appreciated; some items are in the Unit's reference file which your chairman has at hand. These last have all been marked with an asterisk, and the others constitute a want list as it has been our intention to make the Unit's file complete, and it would be greatly appreciated if you are willing to supply any of the missing books, or numbers.

HANDBOOKS:

Bartlett, J. D. & Prevost, J. W., 1909, 64 pages, U. S. Private Tobacco Proprietary Stamps. (*)
Bedford, C. W., 1930, 15 pages, Replating the 5c INLAND EXCHANGE Civil War Revenue Stamp. (*)
Boston Philatelic Society, 1899, 423 pages, Historical Reference List of the REVENUE STAMPS of the U. S. (compiled by Toppan, Deats, Holland—commonly known as "The Boston Revenue Book"). (*)
Crouch, L. W. (19??), 15 pages, The FISCAL STAMPS of the U. S. (Stamp Lover Booklets, No. 2, Edited by F. J. Melville, London.) (*)
Eagle, C. H., 1899, 8 pages, Lecture delivered before the Section on Philately of the Brooklyn Institute of Arts & Sciences, Dec. 15, 1899.
Holcombe, H. W., 1935, 32 pages, Check List—License & Royalty Stamps—Used in the U. S. 1860-85.
Sterling, E. B., 1882, 2 pages, Reference List—Old Stamped Paper of U. S. 1755-1845. (*)
Scarlett, O., 1880, 14 pages, A Complete Cyclopaedia of All Revenue Stamps of U. S.
Scarlett, O., 1884, 10 pages, Reference List of U. S. Proprietary Match, Medicine & Playing Card Stamps.
Scarlett, O., 1893, A Complete Cyclopaedia of All the U. S. Revenue Stamps. (Issued in five separate pamphlets—Part I pages 1-32, Part II pages 33-48, Part III p. 49-64, Part IV p. 65-80, Part V, p. 81-98.)
Trifet, F., 1879, 4 pages, Reference List of Private Proprietary Stamps of U. S. (*)
West, C., 1918, 52 pages, U. S. Revenue Stamps.
U. S. Revenue Society Annual Publication,
    1st, 1907, 35 pages; 2nd, 1908, 36 pages; 3rd, 1909, 24 pages; 4th, 1910, 27 pages; 5th, 1911, 18 pages; 6th, 1912, 42 pages; 7th, 1913, 31 pages; 8th, 1914, 29 pages; 9th, 1915, 28 pages; 10th, 1916, 35 pages. (The Unit needs 1913 and 1916).
    Supplements 1910, 32 pages, Handbook & Check List U. S. STATE REVENUE STAMPS, by J. D. Bartlett. (*)
    1912, 76 pages, U. S. Internal Revenue Stamps.
    Hydrometers, Lock Seals, by J. D. Bartlett & W. W. Norton. (*)

———?, 1883, 16 pages, Collector's Handbook of the Private Proprietary Stamps of the Tobacco Manufacturers of the U. S.—Printed on Tin Foil by the J. J. Cooke Co.—Printed on Paper by the Graphic Co.—(Levick, J. N. T., advertisement appears on back).

CATALOGUES:

Adenaw, Julius, (19??), 75 pages. A Complete Catalogue of the Revenue Stamps of the U. S.; Including all Private and State Issues. (Scott Stamp & Coin Co.) (*)
Albrecht, R. F., 1894, Revs. pages 48-62, Our Catalogue; The Standard Amer. Cat. (a)
Applegate, F. L., 1936, 56 pages, Catalogue State & City Tax Stamps. (*)
— 1937, 16 pages, 1937 Supl. to above. (*)
Bartels, J. M. & Co., 1899, Revs. pages 31-36, Stand. Price Cat. & Ref. List of the Plate Numbers of the U. S. Adhesive Postage Stamps—4th Edition.
— 1902, Revs. page 28, Second supl. to above 4th Ed.
Berlepsch, M. C., 1899, 32 pages, U. S. Private Proprietary Stamps Check & Price List No. 5. (*)
Bogert & Durbin Co., 1893, Revs. pages 37-43, Cat. of Postage Stamps.
Brown, Wm. P., 1887, Revs. page 3, Price Cat. of U. S. & Foreign Postage Stamps No. 7, (b).
Durbin & Hanes—1889, Revs. pages 20-22, Stand. Cat. of Postage Stamps, 17th Edition.
— 1891, Revs. pages 20-22, same as above, 18th Edition.
Durbin & Hanes—(—??), 8 pages, Price Cat. Match & Medicine Playing Card Stamps.
Gibbons, Stanley, Inc.—1939, Revs. pages 82-100, Illustrated & Priced U. S. Cat. (loose leaf). (*)
GREEN, D., & Rordame, A., 1937, 27 pages, A Cat. of UTAH STATE Revenue Stamps. (*)
Gremmel, Henry—1893, Revs. pages 22-25, Stamp Cat. of Postage Stamps of the Western Hemisphere.
— 1896, Revs. pages 66-74, Comprehensive Cat. of U. S. Postage Stamps.
— 1894, Revs. pages 38-49, The Stand. Postage Stamp Cat. (c)
———??, Revs. pages 10-11, Prices Paid for all Postage Stamps and U. S. Revenues.
Henry, John F., Jr.—1887, Revs. page 3, Price Cat. of U. S. & Foreign Postage Stamps No. 7. (b)
Holton, E. A.—1889, Revs. pages 14-20, Stand. Cat. of Postage & Revenue Stamps 19th Edition. (d)
— 1890-91, Revs. pages 28-34, Stand. Cat. of Postage & Revenue Stamps, 20th Ed. (e)
— 1892, Revs. pages 37-43, Stand. Cat. of Postage & Revenue Stamps, 22nd Ed. (f)
Krassa, 1894, Revs. pages 38-49, Stand. Postage Stamp Cat. (c)
Mekeel's, C. H.—1889, Revs. pages 8-17, Priced Cat. of Amer. Postage Stamps, 1st Edition. (*)
— 1894, Complete Stand. Cat. of Postage Stamps of World. Revenue Sections by Sterling, E. B. pages 467-483. (*)
— 1897, Revs. pages 16-19, The International Postage Stamp Cat. (h)
Moreau, C. L.—1897, Revs. pages 16-19, Free Cat. of Postage Stamps. (h)
Scott, J. W., & Co.—1874, Revs. pages 3-7, The Revenue Stamp Cat.
— 1894, Revs. pages 48-62, Our Cat., The Stand. Amer. Cat. (a)
Scott & Company, Standard Cat. of Postage & Revenues.
1883, 43rd Ed. Revs. pages 62-65; 1884, 44th Ed. Revs. pages 63-66; 1885, 45th Ed. Revs. pages 67-70; 1886, 46th Ed. Revs. pages 67-70.
Scott Stamp & Coin Co., Ltd., Standard Cat. Postage & Revenue Stamps.
1886, 47th Ed. Revs. for Doc. page 8, supl. Priv. Prop. pages 73-75; 1887, 48th Ed. Revs. pages 13-18; 1888, 49th Ed. Revs. pages 14-19; 1889, 50th Ed. Revs. pages 14-19, (d); 1890-91, 51st Ed. Revs. pages 28-34, (e); 1891-92, 52nd Ed. Revs. pages 37-43, (f); 1892-93, 53rd Ed. Revs. pages 37-43; 1894, 54th Ed. Revs. pages 38-49, (c).

The Stand. Postage Stamp Cat.
1895, 55th Ed., Revs. pages 40-52; 1896, 56th Ed., Revs. pages 43-55; 1897, 57th Ed., Revs. pages 45-57; 1897-98, 58th Ed., Revs. pages 47-59, & Supl. to 58th Ed., Revs. page 4 (1898); 1900, 59th Ed., Revs. pages 48-61; 1901, 60th Ed., Revs. pages 50-64; 1902, 61st Ed., Revs. pages 50-64; 1903, 62nd Ed., Revs. pages 50-64; 1904, 63rd Ed., Revs. pages 51-65; 1905, 64th Ed., Revs. pages 53-67; 1906, 64th Ed., Revs. pages 53-67; 1907, 66th Ed., Revs. pages 51-66; 1908, 67th Ed., Revs. pages 51-67; 1909, 68th Ed., Revs. pages 29-45; 1910, 69th Ed., Revs. pages 30-46; 1911, 70th Ed., Revs. pages 30-46; 1912, 71st Ed., Revs. pages 31-47; 1914, 72nd Ed., Revs. pages 32-48; 1915, 73rd Ed., Revs. pages 33-49; 1916, 74th Ed., Revs. pages 33-51; 1917, 75th Ed., p. 36-52; 1919, 76th Ed., p. 37-53; 1920, 77th Ed., p. 38-56; 1922, 78th Ed., p. 32-50; 1923, 79th Ed., p. 32-51; 1924, 80th Ed., p. 53-78, (partial illustr. begun); 1925, 81st Ed., p. 54-80; 1926, 82nd Ed., p. 55-81; 1927, 83rd Ed., p. 57-84; 1928, 84th Ed., p. 59-85; 1929, 85th Ed., p. 60-86; 1930, 86th Ed., p. 61-87; 1931, 87th Ed., p. 64-90; 1932, 88th Ed., p. 65-91; 1933, 89th Ed., p. 34-41, (large size vol., no Private Prop. in following Ed.). Supl. Cat. of Misc. U. S. 1933 Ed. Private Prop. Revs. pages 24-29; 1934, 90th Ed., p. 34-42; 1935, 91st Ed., p. 35-43; 1936, 92nd Ed., p. 37-46; 1937, 93rd Ed., p. 42-53; 1938, 94th Ed., p. 46-55.

Scott Publications Inc.—The Stand. Postage Stamp Cat., 1939, 95th Ed., Revs. pages 49-59. (*)

Scott Stamp & Coin Co., Ltd.—The International Stamp Cat., 1897, Revs. pages 16-19, (h).

Scott Stamp & Coin Co., Ltd.—Specialized U. S. (first issued 1923—but no revenues listed until 1928). 1928, p. 176-186; 1929, p. 188-205; 1930, p. 201-218; 1931, p. 201-220; 1932, p. 210-228; 1933, p. 219-237; 1934, p. 234-253.

— U. S. Stamp Cat. (Specialized). 1935, p. 108-125; 1936, p. 123-147; 1936 —Exhibition Ed., p. 143-169; 1937, p. 155-187; 1938, p. 183-221.

Scott Publications, Inc.—U. S. Stamp Cat. (Specialized). 1939, Revs. pages 225-266. (*)

Sterling, E. B.—1877, Revs. pages 16, 34, Descriptive Cat. of U. S. Stamps, 1st Ed. —1882, Descriptive Price Cat. of Revenue Stamps U. S. (issued separately). 2nd Ed., 1882, 22 pages; 3rd Ed., 1883-84, 22 pages; 4th Ed., 1886, 75 pages; 5th Ed., 1888, 167 pages. Note in 1888 Sterling publ. Biographical Sketches, Testimonials, and Press Notices about his work and works.) (The Unit needs 1st & 4th to complete.)

Various—1920—U. S. State Revenues, 108 pages (loose leaf). Compiled by Adinaw, Bartlett, Henyon, Vanderhoof, Grout, & Applegate. (*)

Notes: All the U. S. catalogues have been checked for Revenue listings and only those Editions appearing above contain same on the pages indicated. We shall be very pleased to learn of any omissions.

    (a) Albrecht, Scott—same but for cover.
    (b) Brown, Henry—same but for cover.
    (c) Gremmel, Krassa, Scott—same but for cover.
    (d) Holton, Scott—same but for cover.
    (e) Holton, Scott—same but for cover.
    (f) Holton, Scott—same but for cover.
    (h) Mekeel's, Moreau, Scott—same but for cover.

If you know of other literature—other than periodicals—we shall be very glad to present additions to this listing.

Revenue Large Blocks & Multiple Pieces

(Continued from page 360.)

A few additional collectors have written in, sending their lists, have you? We should like you to check thru your items and report anything that you have in multiple. It need not be the largest piece known. If you feel this should be continued drop us a card, as we are wondering if you collectors deam this survey interesting enough to have the balance published in this column.

Cat. No. Denom., Perf., Size—Description—Owner.
3835 10c I. Ex.; Imp.; Blk 10 (2x5) (seen by Joyce); Blk 4 (2); H. Pr. (3) V. Pr.
      P. P.; Blk 5 True; V. Stp 5 (3); H. Stp 5; Blk 4 (2); V. Stp 4 (3); V. Stp 3 (3); V. Pr. (3).
      Perf.; Sheet 170 (reconstr.) Joyce; Blk 84, 34, 15, 10 (6); 9, 8, 4, H. Stp 8, 5.
3836 10c P. Atty.; Imp.; Blk 6 (3x2) Joyce; Blk 4, H. Stp 3; H. Pr. (3); V. Pr. (2).
      P+P.; V. Stp 10 B. marg. Impt. Joyce; Blk 9, 8, 4; V. Stp 5, 4, 3; H. Stp 3; V. Pr. (3).
      Perf.; Sheet 170 (reconstr.) Joyce; Blk 158, 30, 16, 6 (2), 4 (5); H. Stp 5 (2).
3837 10c Prop.; Perf.; Sheet 170 (—1 reconstr.) Joyce; Blk 12, 10, 9, 6, 4 (3), H. Stp 5, 3.
3838 15c F. Ex.; Perf.; Blk 4 Emerson; V. Stp 3; H. Pr.
3839 15c I. Ex.; Imp.; Blk 6 (3x2) Little; Blk 6 (3x2) Joyce; Blk 4 (2); H. Stp 3; V. Stp 3 (2); H. Pr.; V. Pr. (4).
      P. P.; Blk 12 (2x6) Ward; Blk 6; V. Pr. (5).
      Perf.; Blk 9 (3x3) o. g. Little; Blk 9, 6, 4 (2); H. Pr.
3840 20c F. Ex.; Imp.; Blk 4 Emerson; H. Stp 4; H. Pr. (3), V. Pr.
      Perf.; Blk 4 Emerson; H. Pr.
3841 20c I. Ex.; Imperf.; Blk 10 (2x5) (seen by Joyce); Blk 6 (2), 4 (3), H. Stp 3, H. Pr. (2), V. Pr.
      P. P.; V. Stp 5 Emerson; V. Stp 4, 3; V. Pr. (4).
      Perf.; Blk 28 (7x4) L. marg. Bennett; Blk 20, 12, 4, H. Pr. (2).
3842 25c Bond; Imp.; H. Pr. Clapp; H. Pr. Joyce; H. Pr. Emerson.
      P. P.; Blk 6 (3x2) Joyce; Blk 4 (3); V. Pr. (4).
      Perf.; H. Stp 7 Joyce; Blk 4 (3).
3843 25c Cert.; Imp.; Blk 20 (5x4) ? (Howe sold); H. Pr. (2).
      P. P.; Blk 8 (2x4) T. marg. Joyce; Blk 4 (4); V. Pr. (3).
      Perf.; Sheet 102 (reconstr.) Joyce; Blk 32, 30, 12 (2), 8, 4 (4), H. Stp 11, 7, 6, 4.
3844 25c E. Gds.; Imp.; Blk 4 Saxton, Blk 4 Swan, Blk 4 Emerson, Blk 4 Joyce; H. Pr.; V. Pr.
      P. P.; V. Pr. Clapp, V. Pr. Emerson, H. Pr. Ward.
      Perf.; Blk 4 Emerson; H. Stp 4 (2), H. Pr.
3845 25c Ins.; Imp.; Blk 12 (4x3) Swan; Blk 4; H. Pr. (2).
      P. P.; Blk 9 (3x3) Joyce; Blk 4 (3); V. Pr. (3).
      Perf.; Blk 12 (4x3) Boies; Blk 12 (4x3) Bennett; Blk 12 (6x2) Joyce; Blk 8, 6 (2), 4; S. Stp 4, 3.

3846 25c L. Ins.; Imp.; Blk 4 Beaumont; H. Stp 4; H. Pr. (2); V. Pr.
P. P.; V. Pr. Clapp; V. Pr. Emerson.
Perf.; Blk 4 Emerson; H. Pr.
3847 25c P. Atty.; Imp.; Blk 12 (3x4) L & T marg. Impt. Emerson; Blk 4 (2); H. Pr. (2); V. Pr.
P. P.; Blk 6 (2x3) Emerson; V. Pr. (3).
Perf.; Sheet 102 True; Sheet 102 Joyce; Blk 14, 10, 9, 8, 6, 4; H. Stp 3 (2), H. Pr.
3848 25c Prot.; Imp.; Blk 4 True; Blk 4 Joyce; Blk 4 Emerson; H. Pr. (3), V. Pr.
P. P.; V. Pr. Emerson; V. Pr. Clapp.
Perf.; Blk 4 Emerson; H. Pr.
3849 25c W. Rec.; Imp.; Blk 4 Emerson; Blk 4 Swan; H. Pr. (4); V. Pr.
P. P.; V. Pr. Clapp; H. Pr. Emerson.
Perf.; Blk 4 Emerson; H. Pr.
3850 30c F. Ex.; Imp.; H. Stp 12 Ward; H. Stp 5, 3 (2), Blk 4; H. Pr. (3), V. Pr.
P. P.; H. Pr. (2) Emerson.
Perf.; Blk 6 (3x2) Emerson; H. Pr. (2).
3851 30c I. Ex.; Imp.; H. Stp 3 Emerson; H. Stp 3 Joyce; H. Pr. (3).
P. P.; V. Stp 3 (2) Emerson; V. Pr. (3).
Perf.; Blk 14 (5+5+4) Bennett; Blk 4; H. Stp 3; H. Pr. (3).
3852 40c I. Ex.; Imp.; V. Pr. Clapp; V. Pr. Joyce.
P. P.; Blk 24 (4x6) reconstr. Kern; Blk 9, 4 (4); V. Stp 3 (5); V. Pr. (3).
Perf.; Blk 10 (5x2) True; Blk 5, H. Pr. (4), V. Pr. (3).
3853 50c Conv. BLUE; Imp.; Blk 32 (8x4) Emerson; Blk 20 (2), 12, 8, 4 (3); H. Stp 9; H. Pr. (3).
P. P.; Blk 10 (2x5) R. marg. Joyce; Blk 9, 4 (2); V. Stp 4, V. Pr. (3), H. Pr.
Perf.; Blk 53 (irreg.) Bacharach; Blk 25, 16, 12, 8, 6, 4 (3); H. Stp 7, 3; V. Pr.
3854 50c Conv. ULTRA.; Perf.; Blk 14 (7x2) Emerson; Blk 12, 8.
3855 50c E. Gds.; P. P.; Blk 6 (2x3) Joyce; Blk 6 (2x3) Emerson; V. Pr. (33).
Perf.; Blk 12 (3x4) Koester; Blk 11, 10 (2), 9 (2), 8 (2), 6 (2), 4 (2); H. Stp 7.
3856 50c F. Ex.; Imp.; H. Stp 3 Watson; H. Pr. (3).
P. P.; V Stp 4 Watson; V. Pr. (2); H. Pr. (2).
Perf.; Blk 4 Emerson; H. Pr.
3857 50c Lease; Imp.; Blk 6 (2x3) Joyce; Blk 4 (2); H. Stp 6; H. Pr. (3).
P. P.; Blk 6 (2x3) Emerson; Blk 4; V. Stp 3; V. Pr. (2).
Perf.; Blk 18 (6x3) B. marg. Impt. Joyce; H. Pr.
3857 50c L. Ins.; Imp.; Blk 12 (4x3) Emerson; Blk 12 (6x2) (seen by Joyce); Blk 4 (2); H. Stp 6, 3; V. Pr.; H. Pr. (4).
P. P.; H. Stp 3 Clapp.
Perf.; Blk 4 Emerson; H. Stp 4 (2); V. Stp 3; H. Pr.
3858 50c Mort.; Imp.; Blk 20 (5x4) Alexander; Blk 10, 4 (2); H. Stp 4, 3; H. Pr.
P. P.; Blk 15 (5x3) Joyce; Blk 4; V. Stp 3; V. Pr. (3).
Perf.; Blk 40 (8x5) True; Blk 17, 10, 6 (2), 4.
3859 50c Org. Pro.; Imp.; Blk 10 (4+4+2) Joyce; H. Stp 8, 6, 4 (2); Blk 4 (2); H. Pr. (5).
Perf.; Blk 39 (irreg.) Ward; Blk 28, 27, 18, 16, 4; H. Stp 10, 4.
3860 50c Pas. Tik.; Imp.; Blk 4 (reconstr.) Joyce; H. Pr. (2), V. Pr.
P. P.; V. Pr. Clapp; V. Pr. Emerson; H. Pr. Ward; H. r. Emerson.
Perf.; Blk 11 (2+5+4) B. marg. Impt. Joyce; Blk 6, H. Pr.
3861 50c P. Will; Imp.; Blk 32 (?) ??; Blk 4, H. Stp 4 (2), 3, H. Pr. (2), V. Pr.
P. P.; Blk 4 Emerson, Blk 4 Joyce; V. Pr.
Perf.; Blk 6 (3x2) Ward; H. Stp 6, H. Pr. (2).
3862 50c S. Bond BLUE; Imp.; H. Stp 4 (2) Joyce; H. Pr. (5).
P. P.; Blk 18 (6x3) B. marg. Joyce; Blk 6, 4 (3); V. Stp 3 (2), V. Pr. (3).
Perf.; Blk 47 (9x5+2) T marg. Joyce; Blk 40, 36, 32, 12 (2), 10, 6 (2), 4.

3862e 50c S. Bond ULTRA.; P. P.; unreported.
      Perf.; Blk 6 (3x2) B. marg. Koester; Blk 4; H. Stp 4; H. Pr. (2).
3863 60c I. Ex.; Imp.; Blk 10 (5x2) Joyce; H. Stp 8, Blk 4; H. Pr. (3).
      P. P.; Blk 12 (4x3) Joyce; Blk 10; 4; V. Stp 4; V. Pr. (5).
      Perf.; Blk 12 (4x3) Emerson; Blk 4; H. Pr. (2); V. Pr.
3864 70c F. Ex.; Imp.; H. Pr. Clapp; H. Pr. Joyce.
      P. P.; Blk 4 Joyce; V. Pr. (2); H. Pr.
      Perf.; Blk 8 (4x2) Ward; Blk 7, 6; H. Stp 3; H. Pr. (2).
3865 $1 Conv.; Imp.; Blk 24 (4x6) Emerson; Blk 10 (2), 9, 8, 6, 4 (3); V. Stp 5 (2); H. Stp 3.
      P. P.; Blk 4 ??; V. Pr. (3).
      Perf.; Blk 48 (8x6) Joyce; Blk 18; H. Stp 3 (2).
3866 $1 E. Gds.; Imp.; H. Stp 7 Swan; H. Stp 5, V. Stp 5; Blk 4, H. Stp 3 (2).
      Perf.; Blk 9 (3x3) Emerson; Blk 6 (2), 4 (2); H. Stp 6.
3867 $1 F. Ex.; Imp.; H. Stp 5 Emerson; H. Stp 3 (2); H. Pr. (2); V. Pr. (2).
      Perf.; Blk 18 (irreg.) Turnbull; Blk 12, 10, 6, 4 (4); H. Stp 8 (2), 5 (3), 4 (5); 3; V. Stp 4.
3868 $1 I. Ex.; Imp.; Blk 18 (6x3) Little; Blk 6, 5, 4 (2); H. Stp 4 (2).
      P. P.; H. Pr. Clapp.
      Perf.; Blk 35 (7x5) L & B marg. Impt. Hamilton; Blk 12, 10 (2), 8, 7 (2), 6 (2), 5, 4 (5); H. Stp 5 (3); 4 (4), 3 (14).
3869 $1 Lease; Imp.; Blk 6 (3x2) Swan; Blk 4 (2); H. Stp 3 (2).
      Perf.; Blk 40 (8x5) Watson; H. Stp 7; Blk 6 (2), 4 (3).
3870 $1 L. Ins.; Imp.; Blk 6 (3x2) Emerson; Blk 4 (2); V. Pr.
      Perf.; Blk 6 (3x2) Kern; H. Stp 5 (2); Blk 4; H. Pr.
3871 $1 Manifest; Imp.; Blk 5 (irreg.) Hamilton; H. Stp 5 (2); Blk 4 (5); H. Stp 4, 3.
      Perf.; H. Stp 5 Nicodemus; Blk 4; H. Pr. (2).
3872 $1 Mort.; Imp.; Blk 6 (2x3) T. marg. Joyce; Blk 6, 4 (6); V. Stp 4.
      Perf.; Blk 4 Clapp; Blk 4 Emerson; Blk 4 Joyce; Blk 4 Ward.

REVENUES ON DOCUMENT TO BE GIVEN AWAY

Through the kindness and generosity of Mr. Morton D. Joyce, the Unit has been given several hundred pieces of Revenue on Documents. It is Mr. Joyce's wish that they be sent to those interested. Therefore, we have made them into lots of about 38 items. Five lots have only one of each document, no duplicates. These will go to the first five persons sending a quarter, 25 cents, (stamps satisfactory), to defray cost of mailing. Your requests will be supplied in the order received.

REVENUE NIGHT AT THE COLLECTORS CLUB

Mr. J. B. Kremer was awarded first honors for his showing of Match and Medicine Stamps. Mr. M. D. Joyce received second, with his fine collection of Revenues in pairs, blocks and large multiples. Competition being limited to but 60 pages, greatly handicapped the exhibitors and hardly did justice to those outstanding collections, as well as causing the judges considerable difficulty.

Mr. Howard Drummond was third, for a display of Match and Medicine Stamps. Mr. George Cabot showed Potatoe Tax, Tobacco Sales Tax and various State Revenues, including the recently discovered Delaware issue. Your Chairman exhibited his plating of the 10 cent Certificate.

DATA WANTED ON IMPRINTS AND PLATE NUMBERS

If you will take an hour or so and check your collection for this information it will be highly appreciated. Our desire is to compile a listing of the known plate numbers and imprints.

Please indicate the stamp it is on; if a single, whether only a portion shows, or has full margin; if on a block, indicate if complete imprint and number show. Also, designate bottom or left, as the case may be.

Try and distinguish clearly if imprint reads "Butler & Carpenter" (lower case letters), or "JOS. R. CARPENTER" (capital letters).

Do not omit your singles or proofs, as they are vaulable for this research. Any other marginal markings should be indicated as well.

Let us know your 1st, 2nd, 3rd, issues, also Match and Medicine, and Propriatory issues, first; then the 1898 series down to date.

Revenue Large Blocks & Multiple Pieces

Cat. No. Denom., Perf., Size—Description—Owner.
3873 $1 Pas. Tik. Imp. H. Stp 5 Ward; Blk 4; H. Stp. 3 (4); V. Stp. 3; H+Pr. (3).
   Perf. Blk 4 Emerson; H. Pr (2).
3874 $1 P. Atty. Imp. Blk 10 (5x2) Emerson; Blk 4 (2); H. Pr.; V. Pr.
   Perf. Blk 40 (8x5) Watson; Blks. 22, 20, 10 (3); 9, 7 (2), 6, 4 (2); H. Stp. 4 (2); V. Stp. 3 (3).
3875 $1 P. Will Imp. Blk. 9 (3x3) R marg. Emerson; H. Stp 6; 5, 3 (3); Blk 4; H. Pr. (2).
   Perf. Blk 4 Saxton; H. Stp 4; H. Pr.
3876 $1.30 F. E. Imp. unreported
   Perf. Blk 4 Emerson; H. Stp 4 (2); H. Pr. (2).
3877 $1.50 I. E. Imp. Blk 24 (8x3) Ward; Blks. 12 (2), 6; H. Stp 6; H. Pr. (3).
   Perf. Blk 4 Emerson; H. Stp 4, 3; H. Pr.
3878 $1.60 F. E. Imp. H. Stp 3 Watson; H. Pr. (2).
   Perf. (?) Pr. (2) Emerson.
3879 $1.90 F. E. Imp. unreported
   Perf. Blk 4 Joyce, Blk 4 Emerson; H. Pr. Clapp.
3880 $2 Conv. Imp. Blk 5 (2+2+1) Emerson; H. Stp 5 (2); V. Stp 5; Blk 4; H. Stp 4, 3; H. Pr. (2); V. Pr.
   P. P. V. P. Clapp.
   Perf. Blk 35 (7x5) Joyce; Blks. 12 (2), 6; H. Stp 5, 3 (2); H. Pr.
3881 $2 Mort. Imp. Blk 6 (2x3) Swan; Blk 4, H. Stp 4, 3 (2); H. Pr. (4).
   Perf. Blk 18 (4+4+5+5) Turner, N. B.; Blks 9, 4 (2); H. Stp 4, 3 (2); H. Pr. (2); V. Pr.
3882 $2 P. Will Imp. H. Pr. Clapp; H. Pr. Emerson.
   Perf. Blk 18 (6x3) Emerson; H. Pr. (2).
3883 $2.50 I. Ex. Imp. H. Pr. Clapp; 2-H. Pr. Emerson.
   Perf. Blk 7 (2x3+1) Bursley; Blk 6 (2), 4 (2); H. Stp 3, V. Pr. H. Pr.
3884 $3 Chart. P. Imp. Blk 6 (3x2) Emerson; H. Stp 3; V. Pr. (2).
   Perf. H. Stp 5 Joyce; H. Stp 5 Emerson; Blk 4, (3), H. Pr. (2).
3885 $3 Manif. Imp. H. Stp 3 Watson; H. Stp 3, Emerson; H. Pr.; V. Pr. (3).
   Perf. Blk 4 Emerson; H. Pr. (2); V. Pr.
3886 $3.50 I. Ex. Imp. H. Pr. Watson; V. Pr. Clapp.
   Perf. Blk 4 Watson; Blk 4 Joyce; H. Pr. (4); V. Pr.
3887 $5 Chart. P. Imp. Blk 7 (?); H. Stp 4 (2); H. Pr. (2).
   Perf. Blk 6 (3x2) Emerson; H. Pr. (2).
3888 $5 Conv. Imp. H. Stp 8 Joyce; Blk 4; H. Stp 4 (3); H. Pr. (6).
   Perf. Blk 10 (5x2) Bennett; Blk 10 (5x2) Emerson; Blk 9; H. Stp 8 (2), 4; H. Pr.
3889 $5 Manif. Imp. Blk 6 (2x3) Joyce; H. Stp 5; Blk 4; H. Stp 4; H. Pr. (2).
   Perf. Blk 10 (5x2) Emerson; H. Stp 5, H. Pr.
3890 $5 Mort. Imp. H. Stp 3 Joyce; H. Stp # Emerson; H. Pr. (3).
   Perf. H. Stp 3 Joyce; H. Stp 3 Emerson; H. Pr. (3).

3891 $5 P. Will Imp. Blk 18 (9x2) Ward; H. Stp 3; H. Pr. (2); V. Pr.
Perf. Blk 18 (6x3) Joyce; H. Stp 3, H. Pr.
3892 $10 Chart. P. Imp. Blk 4 Joyce; H. Pr. (2); V. Pr.
Perf. Blk 4 L. Marg. Emerson; H. Stp 3; H. Pr. (2).
3893 $10 Conv. Imp. Blk 8 (4x2) L. marg. Joyce; Blk 4 (4); H. Pr. (4).
Perf. Blk 6 (3x2) Joyce; H. Stp 4 (2); H. Pr.
3894 $10 Mort. Imp. Blk 6 (3x2) L marg. Emerson; H. Pr. (2).
Perf. H. Stp 4 Emerson; H. Pr. (2).
3895 $10 P. Will Imp. H. Pr. Clapp; V. Pr. Emerson.
Perf. H. Stp 8 Alexander; Blk 6, 4; H. Stp 5 (2), 3; H. Pr.
3896 $15.00 Mort. Blue Imp. Blk 4 Joyce, Blk 4 Ward; H. Stp 3; V. Pr. (4).
Perf. H. Stp 3 Emerson; H. Pr. (4).
3896e $15.00 Mort. Ultram. Perf. H. Pr. Clapp, H. Pr. Emerson.
3897 $20.00 Conv. Imp. Blk 12 (6x2) Emerson; H. Stp 5 (2); Blk 4 (3); H. Stp 4 (2); V. Pr. (3); H. Pr.
Perf. Blk 14 (7x2) Emerson; Blk 4, H. Stp 5; H. Pr. (2).
3898 $20.00 P. Will Imp. V. Stp 3 Ellington; V. Pr. (5); H. Pr.
Perf. Blk 6 (3x2) Emerson; Blk 4; H. Pr. (2).
3899 $25.00 Mort. Imp. Blk 4 Joyce; H. Stp 4 (3); H. Pr. (4).
P. Perf. H. Pr. Joyce; H. Pr. Clapp.
Perf. H. Stp 4 Emerson; H. P. (3) V. Pr.
3900 $50.00 U S I R Imp. H. Stp 6 Emerson; H. Stp 5 (2); Blk 4 (4); H. Stp 4 (2); H. Pr. (2); V. Pr. (2).
Perf. Blk 9 (3x3) B marg. Impt. Joyce; Blk 9 (2); Blk 4; H. Pr. (3).
3901 $200.00 U S I R Imp. Sheet 8 (2x4) Joyce; Blk. 6; V. Stp 3; V. Pr. (4).
Perf. Sheet 8 (2x4) Ward; Blk 6 (2); V. Stp 4 (3); V. Pr.

This completes the tabulation of the First Issue. The others will appear shortly. We wish to express our thanks to all those who have cooperated and sent in the lists of their collections. The Emerson list, as well as the Ward items were obtained from a record made of the material they exhibited at TIPEX.

A supplement and correction list will next appear. So those who wish to have their material included should write immediately.

Plating the 5c Certificate—First Issue

Over a period of several years Mr. Howard B. Beaumont (A. P. S. No. 9513) has been working out the plating of the 5c Certificate, Scott No. 3823. As a result of his study and effort, the data is now available on the Early State of this plate. To aid those desiring to reconstruct a sheet, he has prepared a plating chart 18x15, on which stamps can be mounted. The plate arrangement is shown and the upper right corner of each of the 170 positions is drawn diagramatically with the characteristic guide dot indicated.

This is the first attempt to supply you enthusiasts with "charts" in such form. Mr. Beaumont has done a creditable bit of research and deserves considerable praise for his presentation. Such knowledge as can be gained from these plating studies will be presented by the Unit. Several of these are in preparation and it is hoped other collectors will find interest in plating revenues.

Accompanying the chart are three pages of text, which furnish the "Plating Key", marginal marking data, location of the transfers and some general facts. The guide dots are classified into four types to make reconstruction simple and rapid.

Several controversial points are mentioned and further proof is necessary to clear these up or solve the questions. Perhaps your block of 4 may hold the answer. If you will kindly forward your **blocks of 4** (or larger) to Mr. Beaumont, they will be indexed and returned.

The chart and text can be purchased for $1.00 by writing direct to Mr. H. B. Beaumont, c/o Hillen Station, Western Maryland Railroad Co., Baltimore, Maryland.

NEW YORK CITY TAX STAMPS—ADDITIONAL ISSUES.

Two issues have come and gone, and a fourth is now current, since our first report on this local tax stamp in last June's column. So far, there has been but one issue of a three cent stamp. The new items are only the one-cent denomination.

2nd Issue: Black with rose background—approximately ½" square with serrated edge. The label at the top reads "CITY OF NEW YORK". The word "Relief", in a slight arc above the city's seal appears centered below the label. The denomination figures, 1c, are on both sides of the seal.

3rd Issue: Black, on orange background—11/16"x⅜" in size, the initials N. Y. C. in a diagonally ruled label at the top left, the city seal in a circle in the upper right corner. "Relief" is centered in a lower label, between quadrants in the two lower corners that enclose the denomination figures, 1c. In the center panel on a dot background the serial number is printed in **black**.

4th Issue: Black on a green background—11/16" long by ⅜" high in size. This is similar to the last above (3rd) except the seal is "behind" the center panel and thus only the upper two-thirds shows. The serial number in the center panel is printed in **red** and the numerals are smaller type.

These are all decalcomanias and all have City of New York on the reverse side. Both serial numbers are in addition to the jobber's number stamped on each as a cancellation.

There has been no change in the meter design. To date, we have collected 9 different meter numbers, as follows: 20101, 20102, 20104, 20107, 20108, 20112, 20115 and 20116. Shall be pleased to learn of other numbers you may find.

This city tax is for Relief purposes and each package of 20 cigarettes bears a 1c tax stamp.

Large Blocks and Multiple Pieces

CORRECTIONS AND ADDITIONS

A few errors occurred in the listings that appeared in the previous columns, page 359 Jan., page 531 Mar., and page 723 May of Vol. 52, 1939. The following corrections should be made.

3827—Perf.—the name should read Joyce.
3831—Perf.—Blk 130 (irreg.) and not 140.
3834—Perf.—correct spelling to Joyce.
3845—Imp.—blk 12 size is (4+8).
3855—P.P.—V. Pr. only 3, not 33.
3869—Perf.—delete blk 40, listed by error.
3890—Imp.—Emerson's is an H. Stp. 3.

Some other material has been reported. Therefore to the listings as published the items below should be added. The owner's name is shown only where it becomes the largest piece, or in cases of equal size.

ADDITIONS

3800a—blk 4; b—blk 9 (3x3) Swan; c—blk 30, 28; H Stp 5;
3801a—blk 4 Watson; b—V. Pr (2) Watson;
3802b—V. Pr.; c—blk 36, 12;
3803c—blk 4 Watson;
3804a—V. Stp 3 Phillips;
3805c—blk 49; d—blk 6 (2x3) silk, Nicodemus.
3806a—blk 6 (3x2) Swan; blk 4; H. Stp 4;
3808b—blk 15 (7+8) Joyce; V. Stp 5;
3814c—blk 70, 16, 8; H. Stp 8;
3815c—blk 16 (1 7 8) Andres.
3817b—V. Pr.
3819c—blk 12, 10;
3821b—V. Pr (2); c—blk 15;
3822c—blk 8, 6 (2);
3823c—blk 30, 6;
3824a—blk 10; b—V. Stp 3 (2); c—blk 4; V. Stp 4; H. Stp 3 (2);
3826a—blk 10 (5x2) Swan; V. Stp 4, 3; H. Stp 3; b—blk 8; V. Stp 4, 3; c—blk 40, 16, 14, 10, 9, 8 (2).
3828c—blk 4.
3829c—V. Stp 4.
3831a—blk 24 (reconstr.) Phillips; c—blk 46, 41, 15, 14, 10 (2), 9, 8, 7, 6 (2), 5 (2), 4 (9); H. Stp 9, 7, 5(5), 4 (4).
3832c—blk 45 (9x5) Phillips.
3833b—V. Stp 5 Bursley, V. Pr.; c—blk 10.
3834e—blk 6 (3x2) Purcell, blk 6 (3x2) Watson.
3835b—blk 20 (5x4) Bursley, blk 12; V. Stp 6, 5, 4 (2). c—blk 10.
3836b—V. Stp 5.
3840a—H. Pr.; V. Pr.
3841a—H. Pr.; b—V. Stp 5 T. marg. Phillips, V. Stp 3 (2).
3842a—V. Pr. (6); b—blk 4; V Pr. (8).
3847a—blk 6, 4; c—blk 33, V. Stp 3, H. Stp 4.
3851b—V. Pr. (2).
3852c—blk 4.
3853a—H. Pr.
3858a—H. Pr.; b—V. Pr.
3859a—H. Pr.; c—blk 14.
3860a—H. Pr.
3861a—H. Stp 4, H. Pr.
3862b—V. Stp 3, V. Pr.; H. Pr. (3).
3866a—H. Stp 3.
3868c—blk 4 (2).
3869c—H. Stp 3.
3888a—blk 4.
3889a—blk 4.
3891a—H. Stp 4.

If you have not sent in a list of the multiple items in your collection, it would be much appreciated if you would cooperate by doing so, in order that this record may be as complete as possible.

We have greeted two revenue collectors who come to visit the New York Fair. Mr. Joe L. Bopeley of London, Ohio, accompanied by his family were in the city about a week. His collection of on-document-revenue proved highly interesting and was enjoyed by Mr. Joyce and myself, on the several occasions we got together.

Again we two spent a very pleasant evening with Mr. Wm. Swan, of Detroit, Mich., who was accompanied by his son and daughter. Cancellations was the topic and those of the Railroads in particular received attention.

MULTIPLE PIECES OF 2ND ISSUE.

Cat. No.   Denom.   Size—Description—Owner.
3903   1c Blk 6 (3x2) L & B margs. (mint) Emerson; Bk 6 (2x3) Joyce; H Pr.
3904   2c 2 Blk 6 (3x2) Joyce; Blk 4 (2); H Pr.
3905   3c Blk 4 Emerson; H Pr (3).
3906   4c H Pr. Clapp; H Pr (2) Emerson.
3907   5c Blk 18 (6x3) Joyce; Blk 10, 8 (2), 6, 4; H Pr.; V Pr.
3908   6c Blk 4 Emerson; H Pr.
3909   10c Blk 20 (5x4) B marg, Impt. Emerson; Blk 10, 8, 4 (4); H Pr.
3910   15c Blk 12 (3x4) mint Emerson; H Pr.
3911   20c Blk 20 (5x4) mint Emerson; Blk 8; H Pr.
3912   25c Blk 24 (8x3) mint Emerson; Blk 14, 6 (2), 4; H Stp 6 (2), 4.
3912a   25c Sewing Mach. Perf. H Stp 6 Joyce; Blk 4 (3).
3913   30c H Stp 3 Emerson; H Pr.
3914   40c Blk 8 (2x4) on doc. Phillip; H Pr (3).
3915   50c Blk 12 (4x3) Bennett, Blk 12 (6x2) True, Blk 12 (4x3) Emerson; Blk 11, 6, 4 (2), H Stp 7, 5, 4, 3 (2).
3915a   50c Sewing mach. Perf. H Stp 7 Joyce; Blk 4.
3916   60c H Stp 4 mint Emerson.
3917   70c H Stp 5 mint Emerson; H Stp 4; H Pr.
3918 $1 Blk 18 (6x3) Emerson; Blk 13, 10, 8 H Stp 4; V. Pr., H Pr.
3919 $1.30 H Pr. Emerson.
3920 $1.50 H Stp 3 Clapp, H Stp 3 Emerson.
3921 $1.60 H Stp 3 Emerson.
3922 $1.90 H Pr mint Emerson.
3923 $2 Blk 21 (7x3) Ward; Blk 4 (2); H Pr.
3924 $2.50 Blk 8 (4x2) Saxton; Blk 4 (2) H Stp 3.
3925 $3 Blk 4 (2) mint Emerson; H Pr (2).
3926 $3.50 H Pr (2) Emerson, V. Pr (2) Emerson.
3927 $5 Blk 12 (6x2) L marg. Joyce; Blk 6; H Pr.
3928 $10 H Stp 7 Joyce, H Stp 7 Emerson; H Pr.
3929 $20 H Stp 4 Bursley; H Pr (3).
3930 $25 Blk 4 Ward; H Stp 3, H Pr. (2).
3931 $50 Blk 4 Emerson, H Pr (3).
3932 $200 None.
3933 $500 None.

MULTIPLE PIECES OF 3RD ISSUE.

3944 1c Blk 4 Emerson; H Pr. (2).
3945 2c Blk 27 (9x3) Joyce; Blk 21, 15, 8 (2), 6, 4.
3946 4c V Pr. Clapp; V Pr. Emerson; H Pr (2) Emerson.
3947 5c Blk 14 (7x2) Jyoce; Blk 12, 8, 4 (2); H Pr. V Pr. (2).
3948 6c Blk 4 (2) Emerson; H Pr (2).
3949 15c Blk 6 (3x2) Emerson; V Ctp 3; H Pr (2).
3950 30c Blk 4 Emerson; H Stp 3; H Pr.
3951 40c Blk 10 (5x2) mint, Emerson; H Pr.
3952 60c Blk 9 (3x3) mint Emerson; H Pr.
3953 70c none reported.
3954 $1 Blk 20 (7+7+6) Kern; Blk 12, 10, 9; H Stp 3 (2) H Pr (2).
3955 $2 Blk 8 (4x2) [reconstr.] Bennett; Blk 4 (2); H Stp 4; H Pr (3).
3956 $2.50 Blk 6 (3x2) Emerson; H Pr (2).
3957 $3 Blk 4 (2) Emerson; H Stp 3 (2); H Pr (3).
3958 $5 Blk 18 (9x2) L marg, Impt. Emerson; H Stp 8; H Pr (2).
3959 $10 Blk 4 (2) Emerson; H Stp 4, 3; H Pr.
3960 $20 Blk 4 Emerson; H Pr (4).

The multiple pieces of the **INVERTED CENTERS** are very rare and those known are as follows:

3934 1c Tnd V Pr. Joyce.
3935 2c 2nd H Pr. Joyce. ⎤
3936 5c 2nd H Pr. Joyce. ⎦ Note correction below
3940 50c 2nd H Stp 5 Joyce; H Pr (2).
3961 2c 3rd Blk 32 (4x8) mint Ward; Blk 24, 6, 4.

It appears that there are fewer pieces of the Second and Third Issues in blocks than of the First Issue. Perhaps you collectors have not reported on these two issues. If you have not done so, please report what items you own. Shall we take up the Proprietaries next or jump to the 1898 Issues?

DUES: No attempt has been made to collect dues since taking over the Unit, and no records of Unit members or dues paid were turned over to me. In looking thru the former columns, I find that the annual dues were $1 and that there were 34 members at one time. Are you men still interested in supporting the Unit? It is run for those interested in Revenues in all their phases. I have born the expense thus far and it has not been burdensome. However, there are plans that call for some funds and since you are all to benefit it would be well to cooperate in sending in your dues to support this undertaking.

STATE REVENUE CATALOG: If you have not seen this fine work by Mr. Geo. D. Cabot, we wish to say that it is the last word in the field of State Revenues. Get your copy now, and learn of a side-line that will furnish many hours of enjoyment. The book is complete in every detail, illustrations of all types with prices. There have been a great many new items in the recent years—numerous cigarette taxes, as well as liquor taxes, to say nothing of other miscellaneous local taxes.

LARGE BLOCK CORRECTIONS: A major error was made in the list of inverts in multiple. Delete No. 3935 H. Pr. and No. 3936 H. Pr. While Mr. Joyce would like to own such items if they existed, he has only singles of these two.

NEW DISCOVERIES: From the Unit's first Chairman Mr. H. S. Ackerman, comes information that he has found a stitch watermarked copy of (Scott No. R-152) the Liberty Head. We were greatly surprised to see that stitch watermarks have been removed from the catalog listing. It seems unfortunate that such distinct paper varieties are omitted. Perhaps the explanation will be forthcoming soon. The other item found by Mr. Ackerman, is the overprint STOCK TRANSFER—serif type—on the 20c documentary of 1929-30 perforated 11x10. This should follow RD-41 in the numbering. Perhaps others of this compound perforation can be found among your copies. It might be worthwhile to check them over.

2c EXPRESS IMPERF. WANTED: Only two positions are needed by Mr. Joyce to complete this plate in the Imperforate state. They are No. 209 and 210, the two stamps from the bottom row in the lower right corner. If those members who have not sent in their pieces of this stamp will cooperate by sending them in to Mr. Morton D. Joyce, 60 Wall St., New York, N. Y. he will check them and return within ten days. Our guess is that the two positions needed may be found in a block of nine which came from the same source and was sold separately. Check your material and let him know, as it would be a fine thing to have a reconstruction in the imperforate condition. There are some interesting facts and discoveries about this plate and it is being written up now, but the work will lack completeness unless some one can produce these two positions.

The SIXTY Cent Stamp of the SECOND & THIRD Revenue ISSUES

By George T. Turner.

Interest in the 60c denomination of these two issues has been aroused, because of the controversial interpretation regarding the cause which produced the foreign relief found on certain positions of the 60c plate.

So far as is known, nothing has appeared in periodical literature prior to George B. Sloane's report on the variety in his column, U. S. Varieties, STAMPS, p. 121, Vol. 24, #4, July 23, 1938. He attributes the doubling of the design to an error which occurred at the time of rocking in the reliefs, and identifies the foreign relief as that of the 70c denomination of the same issue. To explain this variety his theory is that the two reliefs were on the one transfer roll. Briefly, when the 60c design was transferred to the plate, the roll was rocked too far and the 70c design was thus partially transferred to the plate in certain instances. This solution was corroborated by collaboration with Elliott Perry and conclusively stated in a later column, STAMPS, p. 337, Vol. 24, #10, Sept. 3, 1938.

Some twenty or more years ago, Messrs. Nast and Vanderhoof were aware of this variety but no explanation was published. Messrs. Bedford and King also knew of it, for there is, in the Unit's file of 1931, correspondence between them, which also includes a drawing.

George C. Black presented in Weekly Philatelic Gossip, p. 688, Vol. 27, #25, Mar. 4, 1939, the C. W. Bedford theory, which concludes that a discarded plate of the 70c stamp was resurfaced and then entered for a plate of the 60c denomination. He believed that when resurfaced the plate was not thoroughly cleaned, that is, the 70c designs were not completely removed. Therefore, when the 60c design was entered, the old design "shows-through" in certain positions. While such an interpretation is a possibility, it is extremely remote. The facts, upon diligent examination and study, definitely do not prove the Bedford theory. It is fully believed that were Mr. Bedford alive he would be among the first to concur in the more positive and factual interpretation.

A full proof sheet, on cardboard, of the 60c plate is in Morton D. Joyce's collection. It is in the Third Issue colors, orange and black. No proofs are known of the 60c in the Second Issue colors, blue and black. Through Mr. Joyce's courtesy the sheet was made available for study. With this complete sheet it has been possible to thoroughly examine and check every position.

Both Messrs. Sloan and Bedford failed to report all of the positions of the foreign

203

relief. There are **ELEVEN** different positions on the plate which show the 70c relief. The complete list is as follows:
    Nos. 18, 19, 21, 22, 24, 31, 34, 51, 69, 75, & 85.

To enable any one to identfy the positions specifically an illustration of each is shown. A 70c design is included for reference and those lines that appear in the 60c have been made to stand out. The salient features of each position are briefly described in the accompanying table, which will facilitate identification of a particular stamp.

Position   Description
18   Lines in upper label at both ends—those on right hardly visible.
Two lines under SIXTY—upper one broken beneath "I" & "X".
Diagonal mark shows in white border above "T" of INTER.
70c entry relatively "high" on 60.
Layout dot to right of point of left halberd.

19   No lines show at ends of upper label. Strong line crosses above center cylinder of right halberd.
One line under letters "XTY" of SIXTY—another faint line between "X & T" above bottom serif of "T".
No marks visible in white border above INTER.
70c entry quite "high" on 60.

21   Lines in upper label at both ends—only very short and extremely faint line at right. Strong line crosses ⅔ way up on center cylinder of left halberd.
One line under SIXTY from "S" to just under "Y"—breaks under "I".
Marks in white border above INTER. over "N" and "T".
70c entry relatively "high" on 60.
Two guide dots at upper right corner—outer one very faint.

22   Line only in upper label at right end—breaks at edge of halberd and continues slightly above.
One line under letters "X & T" of SIXTY, also "X & T" connected by line at foot.
No marks visible in white border above INTER.
70c entry quite "high" on 60.
Two guide dots at upper right corner—outer one very faint. Stronger one nearest design has vertical line below it.

204

24	Line only in upper label at right end, which is very, very faint, if visible at all. One short line under SIXTY, which appears to connect bottom serifs of "X & T". (This is about the sole characteristic.) No marks visible in white border above INTER. 70c entry quite "high" on 60. Perhaps the most difficult one to identify.
31	Lines in upper label at both ends, lines at right run beneath "Y". One line under "SIX" and halfway under "T" of SIXTY, appears unbroken. Numerous portions of the letters of SEVENTY show in white border above U. S. INTER. marks above "—S. INTE—"; also strong marks in "I" and "N", and fine horizontal line crosses bottom of "I". 70c entry placed medially on 60. Guide dot at upper right corner in line with right prong of halberd. One of clearest and strongest.
34	Two sets of curved lines at both ends of upper label. One line under SIXTY for its whole length. Portions of the letters of SEVENTY show in the white border above U. S. INTER.—above "—NT—"; also strong marks in "N", "T" and faint vertical line in "E". 70c entry placed medially on 60. Guide dot at upper right corner far from point, in line with outer edge of halberd. One of the strongest.
51	Lines in upper label at both ends—two sets curved lines at right. No line under SIXTY. Portions of letters of SEVENTY show in white border above U. S. INTER., particularly above "S, N, & T"; also marks in "N & T". Curved line in white border above "NTE". 70c entry somewhat "low" on 60. Some copies show faint guide line at top of design. One of the strongest.
69	Line only at right end of upper label, not very strong, does not run far into halberd. Line crosses ¾ way up center cylinder of left halberd. No line under SIXTY. No marks in white border above, or letters of INTER. 70c entry "low" on 60. Some copies show very faint guide line at top of design. Two guide dots at upper right corner—outer one faint—inner dot has vertical line below which looks like a "tail". Also lay-out dot on point of left halberd.
75	No lines at ends of upper label. Center cylinder of right halberd has curved line across center. No line under SIXTY. Portion of one letter shows in white border above INTER. just above "IN"; also diagonal line in upper right serif of "N". 70c entry "low" on 60. Flaw, strong spot of color (blue or orange) halfway from "Y" to right edge of upper label. (This is the most marked characteristic.)
85	Lines only at right end of upper label—meet design midway from "Y" to edge. One line crosses ⅔ way up on center cylinder of left halberd. No line under SIXTY. None of SEVENTY letters show in white border above INTER.; however there is curved line above "NT". Also diagonal line in upper right serif of "N". 70c entry "low" on 60.

You have observed that the **doubled portion** is confined to the upper portion only of the 60c design. Further, that essentially the same lines of the 70c are repeated each time.

Each double entry position follows a previously rocked complete 60c design. By actual measurement on the proof sheet, with a magnified 100th inch scale, the distance between the top of any 70c design and the bottom of the 60c design in the adjacent position above is .175 inch, or 4½ mm. This distance is exactly the same in each instance.

The 70c designs, where they occur, are not in identical location on the 60c design. This is due to the slight difference that exists in the spacing between 60c entries. Measurements, to the 100th of an inch, are given below for the spacing between the 60c designs of the first two horizontal rows, and for those other positions where a foreign relief appears. Brackets indicate the foreign relief positions.

Position	Spacing	Position	Spacing	Position	Spacing
1-(18)	10	8- 25	9 ½	15- 32	9
2-(19)	10 ½	9- 26	9 ½	16- 33	9 ½
3- 20	11	10- 27	9 ½	17-(34)	9 ½
4-(21)	10	11- 28	9	34-(51)	8
5-(22)	10	12- 29	9 ½	52-(69)	8
6- 23	10	13- 30	9	58-(75)	8 ½
7- 24	10 ½	14-(31)	9	68-(85)	8

Only a few hundredths of an inch difference in the vertical spacing exists. This slight variation effects the relationship of the 70c design to its 60c design. While in approximately the same location the 70c design appears either high or low on the overlaid 60c. Since the vertical spacing varies slightly, the 70c, where it shows, will be higher or lower on the 60c, because there is a constant distance between the 70c design and the adjacent 60c design above. The 70c is "high" on positions 18, 19, 21, 22 and 24; while "low" on positions 51, 69 and 85.

There appears to be no "hit-or-miss" arrangement in the plate location of these double entries, in fact, it is rather logical and quite uniform. The strongest double entries and the greatest number to be found in any vertical row, occur in the initially entered row. Such is as might be expected, because the siderographer at the beginning had to "feel-his-way" and determine to what extent the transfer roll could be swung when rocking in the 60c design. All the double entries occuring thereafter, with but one exception (#31), are not nearly so pronounced, as those in the first vertical row. This would indicate that he had got "into the swing" of rocking as the transferring progressed.

All the above facts lead to the conclusion, that the double entry variety—a 70c design on the 60c design—resulted from the use of a multiple design transfer roll. It is not a variety that occurred while rocking in the position in which it "shows", but resulted when the **adjacent position above** was entered. The 70c designs shows only when the roll was rocked or swung too far in transferring. The writer is not alone in this conclusion, both Messrs. Elliott Perry and Norbert J. Eich have substantiated the opinion after an examination of the proof sheet.

Doubtless it may be wrong to term the variety an error. It was unintentional and purely coincidental, that the 70c should appear on the 60c, as the working distance on the transfer roll between the two reliefs was so small. It perhaps would be more appropriate to attribute the variety's occurrance to the technic of the siderographer or his lack of skill in handling the two design roll, rather than a mistake on his part.

No 70c design appears in row one, positions 1 to 17, and the reason is somewhat obvious. Since the 70c relief followed below the 60c relief on the roll, it would not be in a position for transferring until a 60c design was completed. However, with two reliefs on the same roll, it would have been possible to begin a vertical row with the wrong relief. Such an error did not occur, as the 60c was correctly used each time to begin a row. One might expect to find the 70c design in the sheet margin below the positions of the fifth horizontal row. While this is a definite possibility, a close examination of the bottom margin on the proof sheet yields no evidence of a 70c design. Had one occurred, it would have been the conclusive evidence required by the multiple relief theory. Yet it might have happened and been removed by the clean-up usually given the margins of a plate.

Some persons may have the idea that a similar double entry could be expected on the 70c denomination. The 60c design might appear on the 70c design, since both reliefs were on the same transfer roll. Such a condition would show the top of the 60c design in the bottom of the 70c design. Unfortunately, for collectors, no such variety exists. No doubling of any of the 70c positions was found on the proof sheet of this denomination (green and black of the Third Issue) in Mr. Joyce's collection. The spacing between the bottom of the 70c relief and the top of the 60c must have been much wider than the 4½ mm. existing in the previous case.

Comment on the Resurfacing Theory.

Mere coincidence has to be relied upon to prove that a resurfaced plate was employed. If a 70c plate had been resurfaced, other lines or parts of such a large design, which are fully as strong, would surely have remained. It is certainly beyond all laws of probability that in eleven cases the identical portion, and only that portion, would have been left to show through. Again it is beyond all probability that the new design, when being rocked in, should be placed in juxtaposition to measure exactly 4½ mm. each time. Such accuracy is not even borne out by the spacing measurements given above.

At the time the Second Issue plates were ordered the War was over, and thus there was no rush to prepare a new issue, as there had been for the preceding first issue. For an engraving concern as large as Jos. R. Carpenter, and doing other engraving work besides the government revenue stamps, to run short of plates is indeed doubtful. Hammering and burnishing operations required to resurface a plate are slow processes and considerable time would be necessary to resurface a whole plate. Remember that the metal working equipment was not what it is today. Some small firms may resurface spoiled plates occasionally, but today this is even a greater expense than the price of a new metal plate. An engraver's time is too valuable and the cost to resurface would undoubtedly be prohibitive to any efficiently operated firm. Thus it is unlikely there was any reason to resurface a plate, and certainly it was not resorted to in this case.

Description and Additional Plate Data.

To present the complete data, characteristics and other varieties of the plate, the following information will be of interest.

A diagrammatic plate layout is illustrated. There are 17 stamps in each of five horizontal rows, making an 85 subject plate. The imprint reads "Engraved by (JOS. R. CARPENTER) Philadelphia", and below in a second line "Patent July 13th, 1869". It is centered in the lower sheet margin under positions #76-77-78. The plate numbers appear at each end of the engraver's imprint. "22" in orange, for the design, is to the right, located directly below the lower left corner of position #79, and "22" in black, for the vignette, is on the opposite end, located directly under the lower right corner of #75. The same plates, numbered "22-22", were used in printing both the Second and Third Issues, in the colors blue and black and orange and black respectively.

The paper imprint appears centered in the top margin above positions Nos. 8-9-10, and reads "Willcox's Chameleon Paper, Patented May 16th, 1871", with "George T. Jones' Patent" above in a second line. This paper imprint "reads out", that is the letters are upside down when the stamp is held normally.

Register marks exist on both right and left sides, in the margins adjacent to positions #35 and #51. They are composed of two crosses, one overlaying the other. On the proof sheet the black crosses are both a trifle inside the orange ones. These marks are employed to assure the alignment of the vignette with the design when the printing is being done, since the sheet is required to be put through the press twice, once for each color. Register marks can only be found on stamps from said two positions when a goodly portion of the sheet margin is still attached.

A guide dot is found for each position, which substantiates the fact that a single relief was used for the 60c in all its plate positions. These dots are located at the upper right corner of the design. Two dots are found on the positions in the top row, indicating the transferring was started each time in this row. The right or outer dot on positions #1 to 17 is slightly higher and much fainter than the inner one. These dots are about ½ mm. apart. The one dot on #17 is very small and extremely faint. The space horizontally between the guide dots throughout the plate is 22½ mm. with the exception of the space between the 16th and 17th vertical rows, where the following distances prevail:

#16-17 and 84-85 is 23 mm.; #33-34, 50-51 and 67-68 is 23½ mm.

This is noticeable in the alignment and #51 is slightly out of line, being further to the right. Both #67 and 68 are toward the right and markedly so. There is .135 inch between #66 and #67 while most of the horizontal spacing is .110 inch, with a few approaching .120 inch. Any blocks or pairs of stamps from this section of the plate would be termed wide spacing.

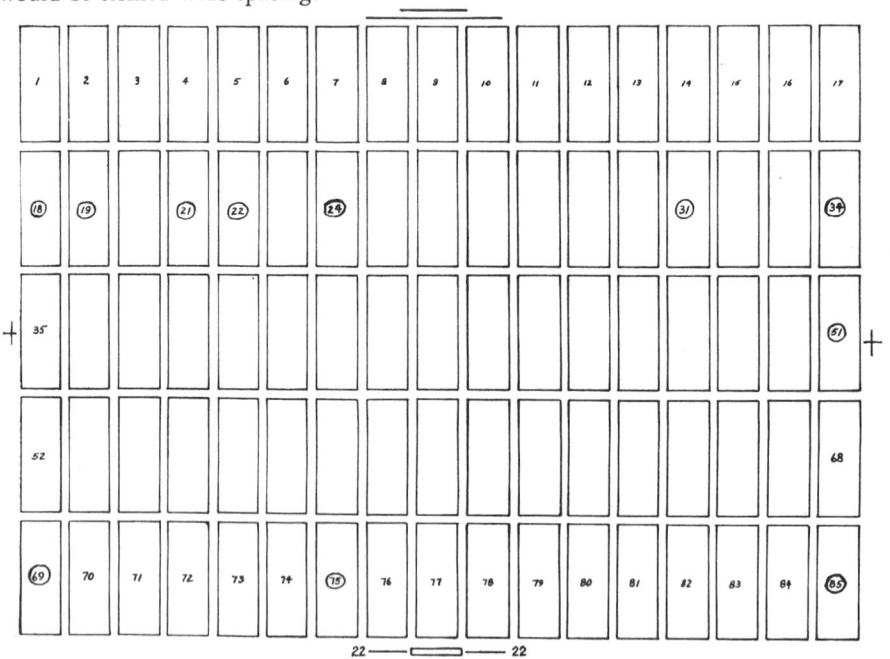

The rocking in was begun with the transfer roll at the upper right corner (as one views the printed sheet), to enter position #17 of the first horizontal row. Rocking was done from the top to the bottom of the design. The next position entered was #34 directly below, then #51, 68 and 85 followed in that order, to complete the right vertical row. Moving next to the second vertical row from the right, position #16 was entered. The process was repeated for each vertical row until all positions were entered; ending with #69 in the lower left corner of the sheet.

Additional dots are found on several positions. The added dot probably served some purpose in the layout of the plate. Their positions are listed so they may be definitely located.

Position   Description
1   Has a dot on the top line of the upper label, directly over the "T" of SIXTY.

2	Has an extra dot on the right edge of the upper right halberd.
17	Has a small dot on the top line of the upper label directly over the left arm of the "Y" of SIXTY.
18	Has a dot about midway from the point of the left halberd's edge to to the left edge of the upper label.
35	Has a dot to the right of the left halberd's point inside the right prong of this halberd.
52	Has a dot "on top" of the halberd's point.
69	Has a dot which is hardly discernible, it being exactly on the point of the left halberd.

These last four positions are all stamps from the left vertical row.

There are no marked varieties to be found in the vignettes, however some faint scratches do exist, but are not worthy of special attention.

One flaw has been found. There must have been a pit in the plate surface, as a spot of color (blue or orange) shows inside the upper label after the "Y" of SIXTY, about half way to the end of the label. This affords a means of recognizing one of the most difficult of the 70c relief positions.

There are a few other varieties which can be distinguished on the proof sheet. However, until actual stamps are found showing these characteristics it would be unwise to record them as existing.

All positions of the "double entry" 70c design have been seen on the actual stamps either in the Second or Third Issue colors. The error is also found on the inverted center proofs of this plate.

Dues Are Due

For your membership in the Unit have you sent your $1? We have had letters enclosing a dollar from the more enthusiastic members. Surely there are many more interested in revenues. We need your cooperation, so send along that $1.

SERIES 1940

Have you come across this new overprint? Mr. Colin MacR. Makepeace has forwarded the first copy, a $4 Stock Transfer with the additional overprint at the top "SERIES 1940" in small capital letters, 1.25 mm. in height. He also states he has seen the $10 of the same issue.

Inquiry indicates that the documentaries will also appear with this overprint. This will add a great many varieties if all the denominations appear thus overprinted.

We wonder if each year will likewise bear an overprint, perhaps somewhat similar to the Tax Paids that have the series changed each year. We presume this is being done for some record, or accounting to be kept by the Internal Revenue Bureau, or possibly it is to prevent subsequent re-use, because of cancellations being washed. More about this after further inquiry. Let us know what varieties you are able to find.

DOUBLE PRINT

Mr. Morton D. Joyce has shown us a fine double print on the 10c 1917 documentary (Scott #R-234). Other denominations have been listed on this series.

When at the Bureau, some time ago, we asked one of the older men who had charge of the presses, what caused such varieties. We learned that they had considerable difficulty with the feeding mechanism, and that it often became necessary to stop the presses. The paper might not have gone completely through the press rolls, and thus only a portion would be printed. Upon starting again the paper, if left in the press, might have moved slightly or due to the lag or drag of starting, the design would not key with that already on the paper. Or a sheet may have been pulled back and then re-fed. In any case a double print would result. Most of such copies that we have seen are markedly doubled, that is, the whole design is moved in one direction a considerable distance.

These double prints should not be confused with the newer type of "doubling" on the current Bureau of Engraving and Printing emissions. This latter shows the whole design "doubled" in both directions. That is, if you take a look at the frame line you will notice that there are smaller lines on both the outside and on the inside of this line.

Our check, thus far, reveals that these come from "polished" plates, plates that are deep etched (deeper than the first plates of the 1914 issue for example). Our theory is that the paper becomes depressed a greater degree into the deeper etched lines and receives ink from the edges as well as from the trough. Also by being depressed into the etch further a portion of the ink is squeezed out and is therefore taken up by the paper from along the edges of the etched line. Thus it is that you find lines—extra lines—on either side of a true design line. We are led to believe also that the term "polished" plate indicates the plate has been chrome plated to give a better wearing surface. This "polishing" may also introduce some effect that produces the extra lines.

We will be very glad to publish any views you collectors have on such "varieties" and shall open the column for a discussion.

NEW TAXES UNDER THE DEFENSE TAX BILL

Many increases in the tax rates have been made in the recently adopted Defense Tax Bill, in several instances they effect stamp collectors—and revenue collectors in particular. You had best be on the alert for these new denominations now, get in as they appear. Save them by all means, even though they may appear common.

It is our understanding that few actually new issues will be required. Yet one can not be certain, at this writing. Former changes of rate brought forth provisional surcharges and overprints and new denominations in some cases, they may appear again. However, it is generally understood that the "Series 110" is to be considered as indicative of the new rate, this is on TAX PAIDS in particular.

Keep your eyes on the watch for anything in your locality, and let us know what you find, also send along a copy so we may make the proper records.

Increases ranging from $16\frac{2}{3}\%$ to as high as $37\frac{1}{2}\%$ are noted for Tobacco, cigars, cigarettes, snuff, beer, distilled spirits, wines, etc.

Thus far we can report a new playing card stamp. The design has been changed —the value has been omitted (10c.) "One Pack" has been substituted. This will permit of the rate varying at any time, the increased amount being paid by the card manufacturer when he buys the stamps. The new rate is 1c more, a 10% increment, or total of 11c per pack of 52 cards. Mr. M. D. Joyce has seen Plate Nos. 143948 and 143950 for this new issue, which are engraved plates.

SERIES 1940

Another new denomination was sent us by Mr. Benjamin Cadbury, it is the 40c documentary. Who has found any others?

CATALOG DATA WANTED

During the past month, I had a fine discussion with Mr. Hugh M. Clark. In the forthcoming Specialized Catalog, an innovation is being introduced. All issues which bear an inclusive date are to be further annotatd indicating the exact year of issue for each denomination which appears subsequently to the first year of issue. As an example: the Future Delivery issue is listed as **1918-36** (catalog Nos. RC1 to 21), now it is known very definitely that all were not issued in the first year, 1918, as there was a rate change that occurred during the period that these stamps were current, or the Act was effective.

The present listing shows only the $100 (RC19) issued in the year 1936. What is wanted is the first year in which each denomination appeared.

If you will look over your copies for the earliest dates and send them to the writer, I will act as recorder and tabulate this information and compile the list for future publication.

Check up on all Revenue issues that bear inclusive dates. We want to make the listing as complete as possible. A reference to the catalog will show you the numerous issues, some of which are, Stock Transfers, Consular Fees, Revenue Stamped Paper, etc.

We tried to get Revenue Stitch watermarks re-listed, but so far without avail. Perhaps, if we all help with the inclusive date information, we can entice the Editor to replace the Stitches.

Let each one check, every one can have a part in this record of modern issues. Send along your lists, it will be very interesting to see who has these early dates.

Who has something new? No one has sent us a new variety—double transfer, stitch watermark, or imprint—in many months. Surely those who collect revenues must have found interesting items!

There are several new denominations appearing under the Defense Tax Law, and they have been noted in the weekly papers. The high values are to be red and overprinted with the Series of 1940. Mr. Joyce informed me that the $30 has the portrait of T. Corwin and the $100 that of D. F. Thomas. Can any collector supply the names of the other denominations?

Thus far the new "1 pack" playing card coils are reported as having the Bureau Overprint precancels as follows:

"B. & B."
"C. D. C. Co. Div. U. S. P. C. Co."
"U. S. P. C. Co." (small star).

Another rather new item is the K. P. P. C. Co. on both the 10c and "1 pack" issues of the perforated stamps. This, so far as we know, is a private cancellation and not applied by the Bureau. It is a brighter red ink and somewhat glossy, and the bars are spaced wider than on the regular Bureau Prints. This interesting new comer is found on the "plastic" cards of the KEM Plastic Playing Cards, Inc. products.

One member has sent us a long list of the dates of issue requested for the Specialized Catalog. Have you gone over your items yet? We need the assistance of all collectors. If you can advise us of those stamps, or rather denominations, of a set or series that did not appear under the first year as listed in the catalog we can soon make a list and have such information inserted in the catalog. Take a look at the 1941 Specialized, check up on this idea and see what you can supply in the way of more complete information.

Your Chairman would appreciate having some articles on revenue stamps, by some of the members, rather than supply all the data himself. It is a column conducted for your interests and expressions, so I would be glad to present something other than my "stuff." How about 20th Century revenue plate numbers? Or a list of the Rectified Spirit Porto Rico overprints? Write up what you have and we'll see if something can't be started.

Note the new address of your Chairman.

REVENUE UNIT

SURVEY OF UNITED STATES REVENUE STAMPS

or

What Comprises a Revenue Collection?

By George T. Turner, A. P. S.

Chairman Revenue Unit

It is by various and numerous channels that monies flow into Uncle Sam's coffers. Have you ever paused to consider how many of these methods employ stamps or have been checked by the use of stamps? These stampic evidences of taxation, which the government uses, are the basis for the philatelist's revenue collection.

One finds it quite an absorbing game to obtain just one stamp to illustrate each method used to collect revenue. The intensity of the game increases as one broadens out to find one stamp from every issue. Even so limited a general collection as just mentioned becomes a truly man-size job.

Because of the immensity of this field one usually finds that a collector specializes still further, or limits his collecting endeavors to a few groups in the field. In order to encourage each in his specialty, the Revenue Unit will broaden its scope to include a bit from all groups in the field of revenues. With this object in mind, we will welcome the assistance of all collectors in submitting odd, unusual, romantic or rare items around which short "interest stories" may be written and published in the Unit Column.

Without attempting absolute completeness, this article aims to give the reader a bird's eye view of the enormous scope of revenue collecting, known in detail to only a few, but currently attracting many collectors.

The diversified character of United States Revenues makes it necessary to consider separately each group into which they are most generally divided.

I **REVENUES BEFORE STAMPS**—Embossed Revenue Stamped Paper
  A—Colonial Issues—Massachusetts in 1755 and New York in 1757.
  B—British Revenues for Use in America, 1765 to 1766.
  C—United States Issues:
    a—First in 1798, Second in 1801, Third in 1814. Federal Issues and Licenses in 1794 and 1814.
    b—State Issues—Delaware in 1793, Virginia in 1813 and Maryland in 1818 and 1845.

All "stamps" of this group are embossed—that is impressed into the paper by means of a die—somewhat resembling a notary's seal (or similar to an envelope stamp without its ink).

A codfish, "Staple of Massachusetts," appears on the 2 pence of this Colony's first issue. Eagle and shield designs distinguish our government's first issues, more generally called Federal issues.

The "STAMP ACT" is recorded in our history as one of the outstanding causes of the Revolutionary War. Some of these "stamped papers" still exist and are highly treasured by their owners, but due to scarcity in number they can not become a popular line.

The collector who is able to browse through early files has a great opportunity to examine some of these embossed documents.

II DOCUMENTARY & PROPRIETARY ADHESIVES
A—Civil War Issues—1862-82.
B—Spanish-American War Issues—1898-1902.
C—"20th Century" Issues.
  a—1914, 1917, 1940 Documentary issues.
  b—1914, 1919 Proprietary issues.
  c—1918 Future Delivery issues.
  d—1918 Stock Transfer issues.
  e—1934 Silver Tax issues.

This group is found in almost every collection. It is the most popular and affords perhaps the greatest general interest, due in part to the fact that there are spaces provided for such stamps in most albums.

Widely different methods of specialization are found among enthusiasts in this group. Some of the specialties are:

Multiples—blocks or pairs	On Document
Shades	Cancellations
Plate Varieties	Insurance Companies
Cracks	Railroads
Double Entries	Printed
Plate Reconstructions	Pre-cancelled
Marginal Markings	Revenues used for postage
Paper Varieties	Postage used for revenue
Proofs	Oddities

Thus the collector is afforded a broad range in which to develop his interests. In this group are found some of the most beautifully designed and executed stamps that our country has issued. Those of the First, Second and Third Issues are superior works of the engraving art and the colors are a delight to behold. They were the work of Butler & Carpenter or Jos. R. Carpenter of Philadelphia, firms who were under contract to supply the government with its revenue stamps.

About 1875, when the 2c Liberty head issue was current, some of the plates were engraved and printed at the Bureau of Engraving and Printing. These might be termed "the first Bureau revenues". Since that time, with but one exception, all the revenue stamps have been the work of this government bureau.

All of the issues up to 1914 are engraved stamps. Since that time the low values, in general, have been produced by the offset process, while the high values have continued to be engraved. It is to be noted that a change has been made with the 1940 series of Documentary and Stock Transfer issues; they are all engraved stamps.

When the Civil War taxes were inaugurated hardly anything escaped taxation. The universality of this measure has been concisely described by Wells: "Wherever you find an article, a product, a trade, a profession, or a source of income, tax it." The numerous titles of the first issue stamps bear out this statement. One might say that the Act of July 1, 1862, established the taxing basis for our tax structure. It has been the basis and precedent for most of our taxation ever since.

The proprietary stamps were used on patent medicines, elixirs, perfumery, pills, cosmetics and other druggist's wares. They were also required for photographs and matches.

Most collectors include in their interests the Playing Card Stamps that appeared during the above periods. Much attention is given them when they are precancelled by the Bureau.

The narcotic overprints and the violet colored strip stamps should be added to the proprietary section. Perhaps the crowning variety of this set of "drug" stamps is that unique denomination, the $1.28 value.

III "MATCH & MEDICINE"—Private Proprietary Stamps.
a—Match stamps
b—Medicine stamps.
c—Perfumery stamps.
d—Canned Fruit stamps.
e—Playing Card stamps.
f—Labels, etc.

The popularity of this group continues to increase and several specialized collections are in evidence. The manufacturer, or seller, could have his private die engraved and stamps printed for use on his products. These stamps were considered effective advertising media, because most of the stamps have interesting designs and subjects expressive of the product or its proprietor. The designs are beautiful and appropriate, many bear the portrait of the fortunate inventor of some celebrated empirical remedy, like "Hembold's Buchu" or "Shenck's Sea Weed Tonic".

In some cases, upon repeal of the law, the stamps were altered in order that the fine designs might be continued as the label or wrapper. People had become familiar with such stamp "seals" and they were thought of as symbols of genuineness. All that was done was to eliminate the words "U. S. Inter. Rev." and "Proprietary" by substituting "Trade Mark", and 2 ounces replacing 2 cents, etc. These labels can sometimes be found and add interest to one's page of such stamps. Occasionally the old bottles or boxes turn up and they should be preserved to show how the stamps were employed.

Condition plays an extremely important role, because the stamps were so placed that they would be torn in opening the container, destruction being the accepted mode of cancellation, or of preventing re-use. Although pairs and multiples occur, they were not the rule, and should be saved as several specialists eagerly desire them in such form.

With certain exceptions, most of these stamps are reasonably priced and a goodly number under $1, for at least one of the four different paper varieties on which the majority exist. Therefore one is able to have an example of nearly every design for a modest sum.

IV STAMPS PRINTED ON DOCUMENTS—Revenue Stamped Paper
A—Civil War Issues—1862-1882
B—Spanish-American War Issues—1898-1902

There is a sufficient supply of these vari-colored, finely lithographed stamps on checks, notes, bonds, policies, receipts, etc. to enable almost every collector to possess a fine showing. Such items were used in lieu of adhesive stamps and may be said to bear the relationship that stamped envelopes do to adhesive postage. The stamp is printed directly on the instrument, so that the user does not have to affix an adhesive.

The design of the 2c Bank Check and 2c U. S. I. R. adhesive stamps along with the famous "Tape-Worm" strip are among the prime items in this group of revenues. In the '98 stamped paper, the milk checks, "Tom Thumb" checks and Pullman Car Tickets arouse the most interest and are difficult to locate.

V WINE STAMPS—Cordials, Wines, Etc.*
1914, 1916, 1933 and 1934 Issues.

While these are very popular and in good demand, they are somewhat "colorless" and rather unattractive looking. There are many unusual denominations, for example 1/5, 7½, 14-2/5, 36, 43-1/5 and 72 cents and $1.44 and $4.80 to mention but a few. The reason for so many denominations is the rate of taxation, which varies on a sliding scale with the percent of absolute alcohol per gallon. The brandies are taxed on the basis of proof gallons while champagnes and sparkling wines are taxed per half pint or fraction thereof.

---

* Treasury Department rulings make the sale, purchase or ownership of these stamps illegal, so the information given here is of purely academic interest—Editor.

VI TAX PAID STAMPS

Dating from the time of the Civil War Revenue Act, this large group of adhesive stamps, strips, labels, etc., has been continuously employed to collect federal taxes on various commodities. There are many who collect them all or as many as they can obtain. The earlier issues are all outstanding examples of engraving, done by such private concerns as Continental or American Bank Note. These were followed by work done at the Bureau of Engraving and Printing.

The stamps are large expanses of machine and hand engraving with skillfully produced portraits of eminent Americans, allegorical figures or plantation, dock and ship scenes. To mention just a few of the faces one can see—

Presidents: Van Buren, Fillmore and Harrison.
Secy. State: Clay and Seward.
Secy. Treasury: Hamilton, Corwin and Chase.
(The first) Commissioner of Internal Revenue: Geo. S. Boutwell.

One can find plate varieties without end, due in the main to such factors as:

a)—three reliefs often required for the one design.
b)—bi-colored, which necessitates two plates.
c)—vignettes usually from a separate relief.
d)—imprints and various legends not on the original transfer rolls, but added later.
e)—many plate positions lettered, so reconstructions can readily be prepared to study plate varieties and history.
f)—double transfers of vignette and each relief section individually or collectively with balance of design.

Tax Paid Stamps are always grouped together according to the subject or the commodity upon which the tax is applied. One could devote many pages to giving complete data on these remarkable stamps, but only brief notes can be mentioned here.

A—BEER STAMPS

This group has had a revival of interest since 1932, though always a popular sideline among collectors. First issued in 1866, they have been in continuous use up until National Prohibition and since repeal are again in use. The earlier issues, particularly, are wonderful examples of the engraver's art. All are large and showy, many being bi-colored with finely executed portraits of prominent Americans not found on the other issues. Some of the less familiar personages to be seen are:

Andrew Johnson—President after Lincoln's assassination.
Hugh McCulloch—Secretary of the Treasury under Lincoln after the resignation of Chase, and author of "Men and Measures of Half a Century."
Thomas Corwin—Secretary of the Treasury under Fillmore and Minister to Mexico.
Thos. H. Benton—First U. S. Senator from Missouri.
Silas Wright—Senator from N. Y. in 1833, and Governor of N. Y. in 1844.
Gen. Geo. H. Thomas—the "Rock of Chickamauga."

Lovers of unique values can not afford to overlook such values as $16\tfrac{2}{3}$, $18\tfrac{3}{4}$, $33\tfrac{1}{3}$, $53\tfrac{1}{3}$, $66\tfrac{2}{3}$ cents. The collector is not troubled by a deluge of new issues nor the "first-day-cover" racket. Those elegant Brewer's Permit Stamps should be included in a collection of Beer Stamps.

B—CIGARS (including Small Cigars)
Denominations include—3, 5, 7, 8, 10, 12, 13, 15, 20, 25, 50, 100, 200, 250 and 500 Cigars.

The first issue, in 1863, known as "Inspectors' Stamps," was continued until 1868 when the Tax Paid Stamps were introduced.

Here is a good place to explain the meaning of "Tax Paid." The rate of tax depends on the law in effect at the time, and is, in the case of cigars, an amount per 1,000 cigars. Therefore if the rate is $2.00 per 1,000 the money value of a 20 cigar stamp is 4 cents. The manufacturer purchases his supply of stamps and pays the then current rate, receiving such stamp denominations as he will use for the number of items he packs per box. He affixes these evidences of tax payment to each box so that you will know the tax has been paid.

About 1917 the schedules were changed a bit and various Classes, A through E, were introduced, which placed a different rate of tax per 1,000 cigars depending upon the sales price of the different grades or brands.

During several periods when the rates were changed, provisional stamps were issued; these all bear overprints or surcharges to indicate the rate having been effected by some Act of Congress. However, this was not done for the recent 1940 taxes under the Defence Tax measure.

One is very likely to spend a considerable time in hunting certain of these denominations. At one time the **"13 band"** was for display boxes used in show cases or on counters. Although it appeared to be full, it contained a false bottom and had only 13 cigars in the top row. It is understood that this has now been changed and that there are no real cigars in boxes.

C—CIGARETTES
Denominations include—5, 8, 10, 12, 15, 16, 20, 24, 40, 50, 80, 100 and 500.

The early taxes were collected by the Inspectors' Stamps and Cigar Stamps. A long strip for 500 cigarettes appeared in 1868 and those for the small denominations in 1879. Most of the values are still in use today, except the 500's. There are now two classes, A and B, blue and green stamps respectively. These denote the two price groups of cigarettes and the rate on the B class is over twice that of the A class. The 40 and 80 packages are by far the hardest to obtain and we have not seen any recently.

Another point which most of the tax paids have in common, is that one finds **"Series (number)"** appearing on these issues. In a general way this series number corresponds with each year to date, beginning with "Series 102" for 1932 and so on to "Series 110" for 1940-41. On the commoner denominations this is inscribed in the stamp design while on the less used stamps it is an overprint, usually in black ink, though some have been in red.

D—TOBACCO—manufactured, plug, rough cut, chewing, etc.
Denominations include—
ounce—⅛, ⅜, ½, ⅝, ¾, ⅞, 1, 1⅛, 1¼, 1⅜, 1½, 1⅝, 1⅔, 1¾, 1⅞, 2, 2¼, 2½, 2¾, 3, 3¼, 3½, 3¾, 4, 5, 6, 7, 8, 9, 10, 11, 12, 13, 14, 15, 16.
pound—½, 1, 1¼ 2, 3, 4, 5, 6, 7, 8, 9, 10, 11, 12, 14, 15, 20, 24, 30, 40, 50, 60.

Previous to 1868 tobacco was taxed, but no stamps were required. Two rates were established in that year, 16c per pound upon tobacco entirely or partly with stems and 32c per pound upon tobacco without stems. In general the ounce stamps are long strips and the pound values large rectangles. There are some very fine examples of engraving and many are choice items that will add beauty to any collection.

As a group, this is one of the largest in the Tax Paid field, because there are so many denominations for well over fifty different issues or series.

When collecting these strips one should check all the different types of tobacco—rough cut, ready rubbed, plug, chewing and other manufactured brands. Some of the denominations are rather scarce as they are used by but a few firms on some specialty brand or mixture. It is most unlikely that you can obtain every denomination in one shop.

Probably the most interesting items belonging to this group are the TIN FOILS. These are the complete foil wrappers from the packages of tobacco. They are like "printed revenues" because each tin foil wrapper bears the stamp already printed upon it in addition to the brand, name, manufacturer, etc. Some prefer to class them as "Private Tobacco Proprietary Stamps."

The first issued foils appeared in 1868, a half-ounce and one ounce denomination. More than 25 issues or series have appeared since that time and two brands of tobacco are still packaged in these foil wrappers. Most of the foils are for small packages of one-half, three-quarters or one ounce, however some two, four and eight ounce foils were used.

One finds many designs of particular interest. These are printed in gold, red, blue or black on plain foil. Some upon gold foil, while others are printed upon what is termed "ribbed silver."

To obtain even one specimen from each issue is a difficult task, and likewise each kind of foil printed with its different colors. Be content with some such simplified mode of collecting, as there are more than 1300 items if every brand is sought, and of certain ones but a single copy is known.

E—SNUFF

Denominations include—
ounce—nearly the same as for the tobaccos.
pound—½, 1, 2, 3, 4, 5, 10, and 20.

If you have the idea that this fad ceased years ago, just realize that 38,000,000 pounds of snuff were consumed in 1939, "believe-it-or-not!" Stamps for taxes on snuff began in 1870. The tobacco issues were used prior to that time. These have a great many interesting designs and subjects on the large stamps of the early periods. Most of the stamps between 1878 and 1910 bear the portrait of Seward. Since then a tobacco plant has been the characteristic subject.

F—LIQUOR—ALCOHOL—DISTILLED SPIRITS, etc.

1.—Distilled Spirits Stamps.
2.—Bottled in Bond—Case Stamps & Bottle strips or coupons.
3.—Rectified Spirits.
4—Alcohol—including denatured.
5.—Wholesale Liquor Dealers Stamps.
6.—Distillery Warehouse Stamps.
7.—Special Warehouse Stamps, etc.
8.—Brandy.
9.—Wines.

There are a great many of these stamps and the above list is an extremely meager outline. One should find a great deal of interest in this rather virgin field that would make a fine collection. Some information can be supplied to any one interested in this neglected group.

G—FOOD STAMPS
1.—Mixed Flour.
2.—Butter—process and renovated.
3.—Oleomargarine.
4.—Cheese.
5.—Meat Inspection.

Here is another group which needs the full interest of some serious collector. Most of these are comparatively recent issues, being established by the Revenue Act of 1898 or thereabouts. Some of these taxes are current today and labels, stamps or tags are used for the collection of the charges. From a historical viewpoint these stamps are worth saving and could in time be developed into a worthwhile group.

H—CUSTOM—IMPORTED—EXPORTED

While these stamps could be treated as a separate group, it is better to include them with each of the foregoing divisions, to which they belong. For example, the Customs Cigar Stamps should be placed with the Cigars. Most of these stamps have the appropriate inscription "For Exportation," "Imported" or "Customs," which fully indicates their purpose. Foreign brands of cigars, for instance, have a Customs stamp in addition to the proper tax paid stamp attached to the package. Manufacturers in this country who export cigarettes and similar items apply the export stamps to each pack to show tax exemption and prevent sale within the United States.

VII LOCK SEALS & HYDROMETER LABELS

Lock Seals were and still are (so it is understood) used by the internal revenue gauger or supervisor assigned to duty at distilleries, warehouses and breweries. Two sizes exist— the "tall" rectangular (18x48mm.) for the patented Slaight locks and the "small' rectangle (24x11mm.) for the Caton locks. Each type has a rectangular hole at one end which fits over the slot in the lock. The lock can not be opened without punching this paper seal which covers the key hole. Lock Seals are fine examples of engraving and are printed in a multitude of colors with various colored inks for the control numbers which appear on each. The Slaight type was printed 54 to the sheet (9 horiz. rows of 6 stamps each). Each one of the 54 positions was numbered, thus one has no difficulty in reassembling the sheet.

At one time, glass lock seals were tried, and occasionally one of these "window panes" ($23\frac{1}{2}$x$18\frac{1}{2}$mm.) turns up.

Hydrometer labels are nearly perfect examples of engraving. These labels were printed by the Bureau. The manufacturer of the hydrometer inserted them in the bulb of the glass instrument, while the graduated scale is placed in the stem portion. These standard hydrometers are issued to the internal revenue inspectors or gaugers for their use in determining the specific gravity of liquids, especially alcohol, liquor, etc., thereby providing a rapid method of determining the "proof" (alcoholic content) of such beverages. In this way, the basis is obtained for calculating the precise tax rate to be applied.

The labels are printed in black on white bond paper. All except two of the issues have the portrait of Washington in an oval frame in the upper left corner of the label. The words "Standard Hydrometer" appear on each.

Isolated copies appear in many collections and often in dealers' stocks. They are certainly worthy of attention.

VIII CONSULAR SERVICE FEE STAMPS.

These documentary issues are small and unobtrusive, yet served to usher in the period of "Dollar Diplomacy", so in the public eye years ago. First issued in 1906, printed by the Bureau, they have varied in perforation the same as the contemporaneous postage stamps. In size, they are identical with the 20c of the 1922 series and range in values from 25c to $10.00. There are three different types, each has a numeral as the chief motif. The first two differ only in the inscription, **Consular** service being changed to **Foregn** service. The third has a background of engine work.

The $9 is used on passports, while the other denominations are required on certain importation documents prescribed by the Tariff Acts. Most of the values in this small group are not difficult to obtain.

IX STATE REVENUES

Just as the Federal Government collects taxes by the use of stamps, so do most of the forty-eight state governments, and also the Territory of Alaska.

In this group is found the **Pioneer** ADHESIVE type of revenue stamp of our country. This emanated from California in 1857. More than 1,000 different stamps were issued, if one counts the surcharges and paper varieties from 1857 to 1873. Therefore, they antedate and over-lap the First Issue Revenues of 1862. Often one finds the two together on Western documents of the period.

While Delaware in 1793, Virginia in 1813 and Maryland in 1845 issued revenues, they were of the embossed type and are usually collected with the stamped paper group already mentioned rather than with these State Revenues.

Generally the State Tax issues are divided into three major classifications:

1—**Documentary** Taxes, which are applicable to mortgages, notes, insurance policies and other instruments. Some of these stamps bear specific designations as to what they tax, like: Tax on Seals, Intangible Tax, Investment Tax, Recordation or Stock Transfer.

2—**Excise** Taxes, which collect duties upon the consumption of such commodities as cigars, cigarettes, tobacco, cosmetics, liquor, beer, non-intoxicating beverages and oleomargarine.

3—**Inspection** Taxes, which are levies to cover the cost of inspections. Certain supervisory regulations have been established to maintain the quality of manufactured products, in order to protect the consumer. Inspections are made of gasoline, coal oil, or the ingredients used in preparing stock feeds or fertilizers, or the sanitary conditions in bedding, cushions and stuffing materials.

The complete list of items specifically named, or taxed, is quite extensive, and one finds Florida and Texas have taxes on Citrus Fruit, Tennessee taxes grass and clover seed, while other titles are Oysters, Scallops, Laundry-Cleaning & Pressing, Shells (ammunition), Eggs, Mechanical Games and one of the most recent is Canned Dog Food. The most "popular" item taxed is alcoholic drink in its various forms. The number of States having such stamps are listed here:

Beer	31	Beverage	7
Liquor	23	Alcohol	5
Spirits	13	Wine	19

Cigarettes are taxed in 18 different states, tobacco in 7 and cigars in 6.

New Jersey is the only State where no stamp taxes have been used to collect taxes.

A few of the stamps are engraved, others type-set, but usually they are printed by lithography or the offset processes. Decalcomanias now have an extensive usage, particularly for use on cellophane wrappings. "Decals" as they are generally called are simply stamps made upon specially prepared paper that are to be transferred to the package, similar to the children's "transfer pictures". The sizes and shapes vary greatly, ranging from the smallest 8x12mm to large labels the size of letter sheets. Some are gummed, others without gum as labels to be pasted on the package or even tags for use on sacks.

Meters are also used and form an integral part of this field. Similar to the Postage Meter, they are coming more and more into use, especially on cellophane cigarette packages.

Values range from ½ mill to $1,000 and many unique denominations occur, sometimes expressed decimally or as fractions, like: 8/60 cents $1.08½ or 10.888 cents or $.04839. Such odd values occur because the rates of taxation do not lend themselves readily to sub-division. To illustrate, $.07258 is the tax collected upon a case of twenty-four 12 ounce bottles of beer where the tax rate is $1.00 per barrel of 31 gallons.

Quite a number of these State stamps are hard to obtain and of some not a single copy has been saved. It is hoped that one collector can be found in each State who will act as State Chairman, to specialize in the local issues, in order that this phase of philately will not be neglected.

X COTTON STAMPS

During 1863-67, a tax stamp was employed for collecting the 3c per bale on cotton. The commonest form was a patented brass tag about 10 inches in length, which had a special barb for attaching to a bale. These tags bear a serial letter and number beside the inscription "U. S. Internal Revenue". There is one type of which very little is known, that is inscribed "U. S. Customs".

Unused remainders exist of a parchment type of tag, which has an eagle on a shield for the central design and the word COTTON beneath. A similar tag of canvas was employed and but a single copy is known.

Under the A. A. A., 1933-36, metal tags again came into use, along with certain certificate cards. There are three in number

a) Yellow, with inscsription U. S. I. R., Cotton, serial number, and 1933.
b) Gray (metal) with inscription U. S. I. R., Cotton, serial number and 1934-35.
c) Red with inscription U. S. Internal Revenue, 1935-36, and on the back Cotton Bale Tag.

These are small tags about 1⅝x1 inch with the right end rounded and a special patented feature for attaching to the bale at the other end.

XI POTATO STAMPS

Another commodity subject to regulations under the A. A. A. were potatoes. Two kinds of stamps were issued (1) for tax exempt potatoes—those allowed under the farmer's quota, and (2) for tax paid potatoes—those which the farmer sold in excess of his quota and for which he had to purchase stamps on the basis of 45c per bushel.

The "tax exempt" stamps were distributed free to the farmer in accordance with his quota allotment. They are small gray-black stamps with a large central numeral and were issued in booklet form, 12 stamps to the pane. The 2 and 50 pounds values are common, the 5 and 10 lb. rather scarce and the 25 and 100 lb. are not known in collectors' hands. When the Act was declared unconstitutional these remainders were offered for sale, but subsequently withdrawn.

The "tax paid" stamps, 13 in number, from ¾c per pound to $1.50 for 200 lbs. are described in the catalogue. These stamps were sold in sets to collectors by the Department of Agriculture, but are no longer available.

XII HUNTING PERMIT STAMPS—Duck Stamps.

Beginning with 1934 a stamp has been issued each year, which each hunter of wild fowl must purchase and attach to his license. The dollar tax so collected is used for maintaining bird sanctuaries, feeding grounds and refuges along the great flyways followed by wild ducks and geese. This rehabilitation of American wild life is administered by the Biological Survey of the Department of Agriculture.

By special enactment, stamp collectors may obtain these stamps at first and second class post offices. All unsold stamps are destroyed after June 30th of the hunting season for which they are issued.

The stamps are beautiful, distinctive engravings by famous etchers and artists of wild life subjects. They are an attractive small group in the field of tax stamps.

XIII REVENUES FOR U. S. POSSESSIONS & TERRITORIES

PUERTO RICO—The United States battleship revenue stamps of 1898 were surcharged by the Bureau and used in the Island. Following these the Bureau engraved a full set from 1c to $200 for use there. Many of the TAX PAID stamps are handstamped "Porto Rico" to show where the cigars or tobacco originated. Some of the current wine stamps have a surcharge "Rectified Spirits—Puerto Rico".

HAWAII—No special issues by the Government are known to have been prepared since the Islands came into our possession. However, many tax stamps of the Monarchy and former Hawaiian Government were used long after annexation, even as late as 1917. These could be classed as Territorial Revenues.

PHILIPPINES—None of the United States stamps are known to have been overprinted or surcharged for use in the Islands. New issues were prepared, many bearing the inscription United States Internal Revenue—Philippine Islands. There are many varieties and they follow the extensive Spanish schedules.

VIRGIN ISLANDS—Several varieties exist of United States Playing Card stamps surcharged for use in the Islands. In 1933 there was a Provisional Cigarette stamp issued due to nonarrival of the proper supply. These have the rate in "bits", the currency value in the island.

ALASKA—No issues of any kind are known for this Territory before the 1937 issues upon Beer or Malt Beverages, Wine and Liquor. It seems that nobody saved any of them.

CUBA and GUAM—No special revenue issues are known to have been issued by our government for either of these places.

This is an untapped field for research and it is hoped that some collector in each of these far distant Islands will cooperate and inform us of his studies on the revenue stamps that have appeared or are now used.

XIV U. S. REVENUES IN MEXICO

During the American occupation of Vera Cruz from April to November 1914, several revenue issues appeared. The first were surcharged locally on Mexican Stamps. These were followed in July by U. S. printings. Beside the usual Documentary stamps there were issues for Federal Tax, Cigarette, Cigar Boxes and Tobacco Taxes.

IN CONCLUSION

There are numerous other taxes, most of which bring in to the treasury a considerably greater amount of revenue than do the various "stamp taxes" noted above. Perhaps some of these others are more familiar, like Corporation and Individual Income taxes, Estate and Gift taxes, Excess Profits tax, Manufacturers' Excise taxes on gasoline, automobiles, electric energy or sporting goods and those miscellaneous taxes which include, telephone, telegraph, radio and cable facilities, admissions to theatres, concerts or cabarets, club dues or initiation fees and safe-deposit box leases. All such taxes combine to produce the income of the government, yet revenue philately deals only with such taxes as are collected by stamps.

It is not required that one become a "tax expert" in order to enjoy the hobby. Those who collect revenue stamps find, beside the mere fascination of collecting, a vast amount of information relative to the financial history of the United States from its very beginning to the present moment.

For those seeking additional information, the following standard sources will be of particular aid:

Historical Reference List of the Revenue Stamps of the U. S. by Toppan, Deats & Holland, Boston, 1899. Usually called the "Boston Revenue Book"; a classic work in the field.

Catalogue de Timbres-Fiscaux, by A. Forbin (in French) 3rd edition 1915. Long out of print and hard to locate, yet still the standard work for foreign revenues. Lists the U. S. tax paids and the M. & M. stamps are illustrated.

Catalogue of the State & City Revenue Tax Stamps, by Geo. D. Cabot—1940. (42 King Av., Weehawken, N. J.) The most up-to-date and complete listing of its kind.

Handbook & Check List of the U. S. Internal Revenue Stamps, Hydrometers and Lock Seals, by J. D. Bartlett & W. W. Norton—1912. A U. S. Revenue Society publication which is the best list of tax paids in general.

Metallic Tax Stamps For Cotton, by C. A. Nast in the 6th Annual number of the U. S. Revenue Society, 1912.

A List of the Beer Stamps of the U. S. by E. R. Vanderhoof, Reprint from the June, 1934, American Philatelist.

U. S. Private Tobacco Proprietary Stamps, by J. D. Bartlett & J. W. Prevost—1909; thoroughly covers the early Tin Foils.

Catalogue of U. S. Stamps—Specialized—Scott Publication Inc., 19th edition 1941; currently the best for the issues covered.

U. S. SERIES 1940-1941 REVENUES

After twenty-three years a new design appears on our revenue stamps. The vignettes are appropriate since they portray the Treasurers of the United States. These new stamps form a companion set to the Presidential series of postage stamps. One other outstanding change is that all denominations are printed from engraved plates. The issues are also inscribed for their particular use; therefore there are no more Stock Transfer or Silver Tax overprints.

However, in our enthusiasm over these new designs, we are getting ahead of the facts.

First of all there were issued the usual 1917-33 series of documentary stamps—offset printings 1c to 80c and engraved dollar values—with the respective overprints for Stock Transfer and Silver Tax, to which a second overprint reading "SERIES 1940" was added. Such a procedure usually constitutes and is known as a provisional series. They appeared late in 1940 and were designated for use under the Defense Tax rates, which imposed certain rate increases. No new values had to be printed as it was necessary only that the user attach the required amount in stamps as called for by the tax.

Practically every denomination has been reported.

1—**Types 1917-33** Overprinted in Black 'Series 1940'
Documentary—1, 2, 3, 4, 5, 8, 10, 20, 25, 40, 50, 80 cent
$1, 2, 3, 4, 5, 10, 20
Stock Transfer—1, 2, 4, 5, 10, 20, 25, 40, 50, 80 cent
$1, 2, 3, 4, 5, 10, 20
Silver Tax—1, 2, 3, 4, 5, 8, 10, 20, 25, 40, 50, 80 cent
$1, 2, 3, 4, 5, 10, 20

The high values $30, 60, 100, 500, 1000 are chronicled by Scott as appearing with a hand-stamped "Series 1940" in green ink. Definite advice on this will be appreciated by the writer.

2—**Types of 1940**— (engraved new design stamps) overprinted in Black **'Series 1940'**
   a) 1c to 80c, size: 19x22mm. 400 subjects to plate
   b) $1 to $20, size: 21½x36½mm. 200 subjects to plate
   c) $30 to $1000, size: 28½x42mm. 16 subjects to plate

  Documentary—(so inscribed in upper label) all denominations printed in carmine.
    1, 2, 3, 4, 5, 8, 10, 20, 25, 40, 50, 80 cent
    $1, 2, 3, 4, 5, 10, 20, 30, 50, 60, 100, 500, 1000

  Stock Transfer—(so inscribed in upper label) all denominations printed in bright green.
    1, 2, 4, 5, 10, 20, 25, 40, 50, 80 cent
    $1, 2, 3, 4, 5, 10, 20, 30, 50, 60, 100, 500, 1000

  Silver Tax—(none printed with "Series 1940" overprint).

3—**Types of 1940**—(same new design as above) overprinted in black **'Series 1941'**

  Documentary—1, 2, 3, 4, 5, 10, 20, 25, 40, 50, 80 cent
    $1, 2, 3, 4, 5, 10, 20, 30, 50, 60, 100, 500, 1000

  Stock Transfer—1, 2, 4, 5, 10, 20, 40, 50, 80 cent
    $1, 2, 3, 4, 5, 10, 20, 30, 50, 60, 100, 500, 1000

  Silver Tax—(so inscribed in upper label) all denominations printed in gray.
    1, 2, 3, 4, 5, 8, 10, 20, 25, 40, 50, 80 cent
    $1, 2, 3, 4, 5, 10, 20.

This makes a number of stamps to add to one's collection at one time. Our recommendation is to secure them now, at least the overprints **Series 1940** on both the old '17 stamps and the new designs. The **Series 1941** stamps are fast replacing the former. The overprint designates the year—calendar year—in which the stamps were sold, and they will be deemed valid for use for a period of two years.

To the above one must add the experimental ink overprints tried on the Types of 1940 having the **Series 1940** overprint. An indelible ink was used to print the overprint, which, if it becomes slightly wet, will run. This ink can be recognized if you are familiar with indelible inks, for it possesses a purplish cast with a gold sheen when held obliquely to the light, while the normal ink is bluish-black with a silvery sheen. Of course, if you wet or should soak them there can be no doubt of the "sensitive" ink. The object in issuing these was purely to obtain the reaction of the users and to try a possible means for the prevention of the resale of washed stamps, a deplorable "racket" which has been rather prevalent of late. No collector should become involved in such schemes as the penalties are severe. Only the Documentary denominations of 1, 2, 3 cent and $1, 2, 3, were overprinted with this sensitive ink.

The Cent Values, 1c to 80c, are sold in panes of 100 with unperforated top and bottom sheet margins. The plate numbers are usually cut off—though occasionally a small portion of the number shows. If anyone desires a list of these plate numbers it can be secured from the writer.

PLAYING CARD SERIES 1940.

A slight change has been made in these stamps to take care of the 10% tax increment. The expressed value, "10 cents," has been replaced in the central portion of the stamp with the designation "1 pack." Therefore, when the stamps are purchased the current rate per pack of 52 cards is charged, which under the Defense Act is 11c. Generally, such an item would be grouped among the Tax Paid stamps, since it indicates no specific monetary value but solely is an evidence of tax payment. The inscribed "Class A" stamps of 1918-19 are similar and have been included in the Standard Catalogues even though there was considerable argument at that time. Thus the new "1 pack" issue is catalogued, making for completeness in the playing card group of stamps.

INSURANCE CANCELLATIONS

By JERE HESS BARR

(At a recent meeting of the Revenue Unit at the A. P. S. Convention in Baltimore Jere. Hess Barr, a member of the Society, was asked to write an article on insurance cancellations on first issue Civil War revenues. Mr. Barr has been in the insurance business at Reading, Pa. for more than thirty years and is a General Agent for the Casualty Departments of the Aetna Life and Associated Companies; also the John Hancock Mutual Life Insurance Co.; has also represented the Hartford Steam Boiler Inspection & Insurance Company and a number of stock fire companies. The Agency of Essick & Barr is one of the largest in Pennsylvania. Mr. Barr's article follows.)

"A number of years ago, before there was any thought of a differential in price between pen-cancelled and hand-stamped revenue stamps, I sensed that the more attractive appearance of the hand-stamps would make them more desirable and I began to pick them up wherever possible. I soon found that a large number of the hand-stamped revenues had been used by insurance companies, and, being in that line of business, I began to look particularly for these cancellations.

The earliest check list which I was able to secure was from "The Insurance Blue Book for 1874" which was furnished me by our Aetna Home Office at Hartford, who sent me photostats of fourteen pages by States, giving the date of incorporation, location of the Home Office, and the lines of insurance written. Most of these companies dated back to the Civil War period or prior thereto, and therefore this list was very satisfactory. I was, however, very much surprised to find that the list comprised approximately 3,500 different companies writing principally life, fire, and marine insurance. Casualty insurance as we know it to-day was not being written, but a few companies did write accident, health, live stock, plate glass, boiler, and "guarantee" insurance.

Insurance company cancellations do not seem to be rare, but inasmuch as many of the companies at that time were very small, it is probable that intensive collecting by a number of people would soon exhaust the available supply. For instance, it was quite a while before I was able to secure a John Hancock Mutual Life and a Hartford Steam Boiler cancellation, although these companies are now very large; on the other hand companies like the Aetna Life and the Atlantic Mutual seemed quite common.

A few months ago I was quite interested in seeing a list of thirty companies in the United States having gross assets of over one billion dollars. In this list were eight insurance companies. Four of these antedated the Civil War.

  1842 Mutual Life Insurance Co. of N. Y.
  1849 New York Life Insurance Company
  1857 Northwestern Mutual Life Insurance Co. of Milwaukee
  1859 Equitable Life Assurance Society, N. Y.

Three of them began business during the period when the Civil War stamps were being used, and one during the period of the second issue:

    1862   John Hancock Mutual Life Ins. Co. of Boston
    1863   Travelers Insurance Co. of Hartford
    1868   Metropolitan Life Insurance Co. of N. Y.
    1873   Prudential Insurance Co. of America, Newark.

The Aetna Life began business in 1853 and might be included in this list since they have paid out more than a billion dollars in claims.

I believe that many companies may consider their original charters as dating back to this period since companies have been absorbed and names changed, but I am speaking of those which have maintained their original names.

Of the thirty-five hundred known companies, after many years of search I have been able to secure about five hundred different companies, many of them having hand stamps of various shapes, sizes, colors; some with and some without dates; also many of the companies had agencies and branch offices, each of which had their own stamps. Some of these include the names of the General Agent, Branch Manager or Branch Office.

A few of the stamps seem to have printed cancellations, and from several which I have secured on documents it is likely that some of the companies pre-cancelled their stamps. The Fire Association of Philadelphia apparently cancelled a whole sheet of stamps with an oval cancellation and then applied them to the policies.

There are a few banks which also conducted an insurance business such as Reading Fire Insurance & Trust Co. of Reading, Pa., and a few odd names are listed, such as "Pennsylvania Mutual Horse Thief Detective and Ins. Co. of York, Pa., St. Louis Floating Dock & Insurance Co., Insurers Own Fire Insurance Co., etc. Some of the same names are used in different states and therefore it is impossible to more than guess at the proper location, unless the name of the town is given. Some of the names are abbreviated and unless the stamps could be found on the original policies it would be impossible to check them.

The schedule of stamp duties or taxes for insurance companies was as follows:

Insurance, (Marine, Inland and Fire) each policy or renewal (or assignment of same) on which
    premium is $10.00 or less .... 10 cents.
    Premium over $10.00 .... 25 cents.

Insurance (Life) Policy (or assignment of same) not over $1,000 .... 25 cents.
Over $1,000, not over $5,000 .... 50 cents.
Over $5,000 .... $1.00.

Most of the insurance cancellations are found on 25 cent stamps; where found on two cent stamps they must be from bank checks; and the few which are found on $5.00 and $10.00 denominations, such as the New York Guaranty & Indemnity Co. and the New York Life Insurance Co. respectively, were probably used on mortgages, conveyances or other legal documents.

Cancellations are mostly black or blue; the Mutual Life Insurance Co. of New York used green in 1863 and red in 1869 but these colors are not common.

In closing I wish to say a word about the most frequently found cancellation: "A. M. INS. CO." I believe this is the Atlantic Mutual Insurance Co. which began business in 1842. Most of these cancellations are dated with pen and ink. The writer used a long flourish or curl upon some of the letters, and I find this same characteristic on several cancellations which are fully written out "ATLANTIC MUTUAL INSURANCE CO." I am assuming therefore that whoever dated these cancellations was the same person and that therefore "A. M. INS. CO." is "ATLANTIC MUTUAL."

A great majority of the cancellations are the conventional circle, oval, with either single outer line, or outer and inner line; a few are rectangular with corners curved inward; and there are a number of straight line, some of which look as if they were printed or pre-cancelled.

A great deal more could be written about this subject, and I hope some day a complete check list of cancellations in existence will be attempted, the same as has been done for the railroad cancellations."

SILK PAPERS

Mr. C. O. Powers, of Ames, Iowa, wrote us quite some time ago, saying that he was checking up on the silk paper and in particular trying to determine the exact date of its first appearance. The Scott catalogue only says *"about"* August of 1870, silk paper came into use. Mr. Powers has eight stamps on silk paper and they all bear dates prior to August:

R-24d— 1 March 1870	R-82d—20 June 1870
R-55d—28 April 1870	R-69d—25 June 1870
R-44d—29 April 1870	R-89d—11 July 1870
R-44d—20 June 1870	R-84d—12 July 1870

Check your silk papers cancelled in the year 1870 and see if you can add to this list, with earlier dates on these stamps or of the other silk paper varieties.

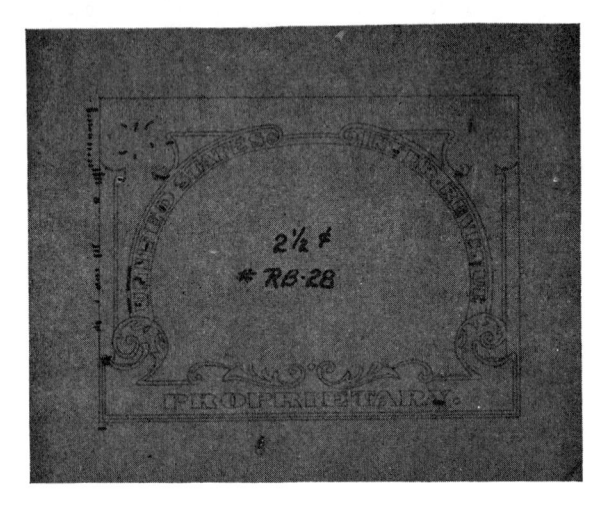

PROPRIETARY, 1898

We illustrate a very strong double transfer on the 2½c lake, (RB-28) which was sent in by Mr. H. M. Jones, who is famous for finding such varieties. This remarkable double is in a block of four and the stamp is to the left of the center line. Look over your copies of this stamp that have the line on the right margin; you may have a second copy of this fine variety.

PRIVATE PROPRIETARY—Edward Wilder, 4c

This year's catalogue lists a new variety under this stamp and we have seen the extremely fine copy owned by Mr. Howard E. Drummond of Westfield, N. J. The stamp has always been known die cut to shape in the vermilion (RS-267) and the lake (RS-269) shades. It has been listed imperforate only for the lake shade (RS-268). The copy Mr. Drummond has is a new discovery, a brilliant orange vermilion color on experimental silk paper and imperforate. This is believed to be the only copy and there has been no previous record of the same listed before. Scott now lists this as RS-266-A.

Mr. Drummond also has a copy of the 1c Wilder imperforate (RS-265) on experimental silk. This is new and is not now listed. The die cut variety on experimental silk has been listed for some time.

DESIGN PRINTED ON BACK

It has just come to light, "believe-it-or-not" after about 70 years in hiding. The rather common 2c THIRD Issue, orange and black, has been discovered with the orange frame printed on the back. Thus the paper was placed in the press three times, once each for the two sides to print the design or frame and the third time for the vignette. It is an interesting variety and has now been given catalogue listing, R-135. Two copies were found. So do not just look at the front of your stamps, look on the backs as well.

General:

I have not heard from many of the Revenue Collectors recently. Now that colder weather is coming, perhaps stamps will receive more attention than golf or outings. Drop us a line on new things you have acquired or discovered on your stamps; there is always space here to note them down. Feel free to write in at any time; your chairman will try and answer you or lend whatever assistance possible. Let's hope the mails are heavy.

SUBJECT INDEX

The following index is divided under several subheadings and a brief perusal should make the general arrangement clear to the user. Under each heading are listed specific topics in alphabetical order. Throughout use has been made of catalog number designations employed in the *Scott United States Stamp Catalogue Specialized*. After specific entries will be found page location in this volume and in brackets, volume, page and year of the original in *The American Philatelist*.

CHECK LISTS

Handbooks and Catalogs Pertaining to (U.S.) Revenue Stamps, 190-2 [52: 446-8, 1939].
Large multiples, first issue, 188-9, 193-5, 196-7, 199 [52: 359-60, 531-3, 723-4, 1069-70, 1939, resp.]; second issue, 200-1 [53: 55-6, 1939].
Postage Stamps Used for Revenues—Check List (Howard B. Beaumont), 149-52 [47: 85-8, 1933].
Printed and Other Pre-Cancellations of Playing Card Manufacturers on Civil War Issue Revenue Stamps (Morton Dean Joyce), 92-8, 99-105 [45: 126-32, 1931 and 182-8, 1932].
Stitch Watermarks, Check List of (C. H. Chappell), 11-13, 162 [41: 752-4, 1928 and 49: 253, 1936].

GENERAL AND MIXED CONTENTS

Bottling-in-Bond Act (of 1937) new amendment to, 171 [50: 703, 705, 1937].
Catalog, Sever & Francis, Mass. 1863, 60 [43: 452, 1930].
Check List of Handbooks and Catalogs Pertaining to (U.S.) Revenue Stamps, 190-2 [52: 446-8, 1939].
Defense Tax Bill, New Taxes Under, 211 [53: 813, 1940].
Double prints (how they come about), 210 [53: 537, 544, 1940].
First Issue: fraudulent use of, 147 [46: 619, 1933].
First Issue: indiscriminate use of, 168 [50: 488-9, 1937].
First Issue: research opportunities, 19-20 [42: 168-9, 1928].
Margin imprints, 125-8, 168 [46: 222-5, 1933 and 50: 448, 1937].
Insurance Co. Cancellations (Jere Hess Barr), 226-7 [55: 185-6, 1941].
King, Beverly S.—In Memoriam, 158 [48: 367, 1935].
Multiple Pieces: See under FIRST ISSUE and other specific headings.
Postage used as revenues, 21 [42: 170, 1928], 23, 33, 45 [42: 248, 594-5, 797, 1929], 121 [46: 72, 1932], 131-2, 133, 134, 137-8 [46: 325-6, 430, 485-6, 1933], 154 [47: 184, 1933], 170 [50: 601, 1937], and 174 [51: 381, 1938].
Postage Stamps Used as Revenue (Howard B. Beaumont), 123-4 [46: 167-70, 1932] and Check List (Howard B. Beaumont) 149-52 [47: 85-8, 1933].
Postage Used for Revenues (Trans-Mississippi issue) (F. Harrington) 117 [45: 551-2, 1932].
Precancelled revenues, 21-2 [42: 171-2, 1928].
Revenue Acts, Dates of Repeal of (Henry W. Holcombe), 138-40 [46: 486-8, 1933].
Revenues used for postage, 124 [46: 169, 1932], 129-30, 132, 134, 137, 142-5 [46: 261-2, 372, 430, 485, 572-5, 1933], 153-4 [47: 183-4, 1933] and 169, 170 [50: 568, 601, 1937].
Revenue Stamps Used for Postage (Howard B. Beaumont), 142-5 [46: 572-5, 1933].
Revenue Stamps, sale of (documentary) to collectors, 145 [46: 575, 1933].
Revenue Stamp Taxes, History of (Frank L. Applegate), 3-5 [41: 519-21, 1928].
Shinplaster (fractional currency) used as revenue stamp, 147-8 [46: 619, 1933].
Stitch Watermarks, 15-16 [42: 27-8, 1928], 25, 30, 46 [42: 322, 457, 798 1929], 61, 62 [43: 453, 494, 1930], 110, 116, 120 [45: 341, 550, 606, 1932], 135-6 [46:

431-2, 1933]. See also under FIRST ISSUE, CHECK LISTS, and other specific headings.
Survey of U.S. Revenue Stamps, or What Constitutes a Revenue Collection (George T. Turner), 213-23 [54: 391-2, 448, 455-6, 662-3, 671, 743-4, 810-13, 1941].
The Stamp Act (Harry M. Konwiser), 83-8 [44: 505-10, 1931].
The U.S. Revenue Society (its demise) (H. S. Ackerman), 61 [43: 485, 1932].

FIRST ISSUE: 1862-71

Bisects, 68-9 [44: 129-30, 1930], 75 [44: 255, 1931], 138, 148 [46: 486, 620, 1933].
Cancellations, Insurance Co. (Jere Hess Barr), 226-7 [55: 185-6, 1941].
Cancellations, Insurance (fire) (Robert F. Hale), 63-4 [43: 547-8, 1930].
Design, 19-20 [42: 168-9, 1928].
Dollar Denominations, Varieties of (Philip E. Hamilton), 28-9 [42: 455-6, 1929].
Double transfers, 13-15 [41: 805-6, 1928], 17-18 [42: 114-16, 1928].
Double transfers on miscell. varieties, 27 [42: 393, 1929].
Double transfers on proprietaries, 70 [44: 169, 1930].
Fifty cent denomination, varieties of, 73 [44: 217, 1931].
Foreign Entry: A Reworked Plate for the 1 Cent Express (C. W. Bedford), 111-13 [45: 393-5, 1932].
Imperfs, early cancel dates, 1-3, 8-9 [41: 451-3, 609-10, 1928].
Insurance Co. Cancellations (Jere Hess Barr), 226-7 [55: 185-6, 1941].
Insurance (fire) Cancellations Found on U.S. Revenues of 1862-71 (Robert F. Hale), 63-4 [43: 547-8, 1930].
Marginal marks, 169 [50: 568, 1937], 176 [51: 574, 1938].
Mint, value of, 7 [41: 599, 1928].
Multiples, large, 33 [42: 594, 1929], 52 [43: 194, 1930].
Multiples, Large—First Listing of Revenue Sheets or Large Blocks, 172-3 [51: 268-9, 1937].
Multiples, Large—Check List, 188-9, 193-5, 196-7, 199-200 [52: 359-60, 531-3, 723-4 1069-70, 1939].
Multiples, pricing of, 6 [41: 598-9, 1928].
On document, 46[42: 798, 1929]. See also entries under Bisects.
Paper, 24 [42: 322, 1929], 67 [43: 650, 1930].
Paper, first usage of silk, 228 [55: 255, 1942].
Plate numbers and marginal markings, 68-9 [44: 129-30, 1930] 179 [51: 790, 1938].
Precancels: Printed and Other Precancellations of Playing Card Manufacturers on Civil War Issue Revenue Stamps (Morton Dean Joyce), 92-8 [45: 126-32, 1931], 99-105 [45: 182-8, 1932].
Prices, 2-3, 7, 9 [41: 452, 598-9, 610, 1928].
Pricing based on type of cancel, 7 [41: 599, 1928].
Printed cancels, See Precancels.
Provisional, 50 cent Philadelphia, 187 [52: 259, 1938].
Proprietary, proposed (unissued) 50 cent, 68-9 [44: 129-30, 1930].
R1 Express, shift, 27 [42: 393, 1929].
R1 Express, A Reworked Plate for the 1 Cent Express (foreign entry) (C. W. Bedford), 111-13 [45: 393-5, 1932].
R3 Proprietary, plate numbers, 68 [44: 129, 1930].
R4 Telegraph, stitch watermark, 115 [45: 506, 1932].
R5 Bank check, double transfer, 14 [41: 805, 1928], 17-18 [42: 114-15, 1928].
R6 Bank check, 14 [41: 805, 1928], 17-18 [42: 114-15, 1928], 159 [48: 368, 1935].
R7 Certificate, double transfer, 14-15 [41: 806, 1928].
R8 Certificate, double transfer, See R 7.
R9 Express, double transfer, 14-15 [41: 806, 1928].
R9 Express, marginal inscriptions, 169 [50: 600, 1937].
R9 Express, R9 or R10 crack, 174 [51: 380, 1938].

R11 Playing cards, cracked plate, 187 [52: 331, 1939].
R13 Proprietary, double transfer, 14-15 [41: 806, 1928], 30 [42: 457, 1929].
R13 and/or R14, double transfer, 66 [43: 649, 1930], 135 [46: 431, 1933].
R14 Proprietary, double transfer, 14-15 [41: 806, 1928].
R15 USIR, double transfer, 14 [41: 805, 1928], 17-18 [42: 115, 1928], 135 [46: 431, 1933], 153 [47: 183, 1934].
R15 USIR, plate damage, 67 [43: 650, 1930].
R15 USIR, varieties, 44 [42: 797, 1929], 76 [44: 291, 1931].
R15 USIR, The Two Cent U.S. Internal Revenue (J. H. Train) 57-9 [43: 386-8, 1930].
R15 USIR, Plating—Double Transfers on a Full Sheet of 2 Cent USIR (LeRoy E. Shaw), 108-9 [45: 242-3, 1932].
R16 Foreign exchange, double transfer, 18 [42: 115, 1929].
R18 Proprietary, stitch watermark, 30 [42: 457, 1929].
R18 Proprietary, plate numbers, 68 [44: 129, 1930].
R19 Telegraph, double transfer, 18 [42: 115, 1929].
R22 Proprietary, double transfer, 60 [43: 453, 1930], 70 [44: 169, 1930].
R22 Proprietary, heavy scratch, 174 [51: 380-1, 1938].
R23 Agreement, double transfer, 116 [45: 550, 1932], 124 [46: 169, 1930].
R24 Certificate, double transfer, 18 [42: 115, 1928], 48 [43: 45, 1929], 56 [43: 312, 1930].
R24 Certificate, large imperf. multiple, 159 [48: 368, 1935].
R25 Express, double transfer, 135 [46: 431, 1933].
R26 Foreign exchange, double transfer, 18 [42: 115, 1928].
R27 Inland exchange, double transfer, 18 [42: 115, 1928].
R27 Inland exchange, plate crack, 59 [43: 388, 1930].
R27 Inland exchange, scratch, 30 [42: 457, 1929].
R27 Inland exchange, plating of, 74 [44: 254, 1931].
R27 Inland exchange, A 5 Cent Inland Shift, 60 [43: 452, 1930].
R27 Inland exchange, The Plates of the 5 Cent Inland Exchange (C. W. Bedford) 78-81 [44: 427-31, 1931], 106-7 [45: 240-1, 1932].
R29 Proprietary, plate number, 68 [44: 129, 1930].
R30 Inland exchange, stitch watermark 25 [42: 322, 1929].
R32 Bill of lading, plating, 153 [47: 183, 1933].
R33 Certificate, cracks and scratches, 30 [42: 457, 1929], 136 [46: 432, 1933].
R33 Certificate, Preliminary Data of Plating the 10 Cent Certificate, 163-5 [49: 303-5, 1936].
R34 Contract, double transfer, 18 [42: 115, 1928], 52, 55 [43: 247, 311, 1930].
R34 Contract, stitch watermark, 120 [45: 606, 1932].
R36 Inland exchange, bisect on cover, 75 [44: 255, 1931].
R36 Inland exchange, stitch watermark, 120 [45: 606, 1932].
R37 Power of attorney, bisect, 138 [46: 486, 1933].
R40 Inland exchange, double transfer, 18 [42: 116, 1928], 114 [45: 505, 1932].
R42 Inland exchange, stitch watermark, 120 [45: 606, 1932].
R44 Certificate, minor varieties, 44 [42: 720, 1929], 62 [43: 494, 1930].
R45 Entry of goods, double top frame line, 23, 29, 30-1, 36-7, 41-2 [42: 248, 457, 523-4, 655-7, 717-8, 1929], 62-3 [43: 494, 1930].
R47 Insurance, cracked plate variety, 136 [46: 432, 1933].
R48 Power of attorney, double transfer, 119 [45: 605, 1932].
R53 Inland exchange, double transfer, 18 [42: 116, 1928], 156 [48: 326, 1935], 182 [51: 1188, 1938].
R54 Conveyance, scratch plate and stitch watermark, 53, 66 [43: 248, 649, 1930].
R54 Conveyance, The 50 Cent Conveyance (W. W. Bradbury) 91 [45: 24-5, 1931].
R54 Conveyance, The 50 Cent Conveyance 118-19 [45: 604-5, 1932].
R55 Entry of goods, scratch, 27 [42: 393, 1929].
R55 Entry of goods, stitch watermark, 23 [43: 248, 1930].

R56 Foreign exchange, double transfer, 27 [42: 393, 1929].
R58 Life insurance, scratch plate, 133 [46: 373, 1933].
R59 Mortgage, cracked plate 24, 29-30, 32, 36 [42: 249, 457, 593, 655, 1929], 136 [46: 432, 1933].
R59 Mortgage, stitch watermark, 120 [45: 606, 1932].
R59 Mortgage, The 50 Cent Mortgage, A Stamp Replete with Interest (Warner S. Robison), 71-3 [44: 215-17, 1931].
R59 Mortgage, Replating the Cracks (C. W. Bedford), 89-90 [44: 566, 1931].
R59 Mortgage, Notes on the 50 Cent Mortgage (Justin L. Bacharach), 161 [49: 192-3, 1936].
R60 Original process, double transfer, 131 [46: 325, 1933].
R60 Original process, flaws, 160 [48: 369, 1935].
R60 Original process, reentry, 45 [42: 797, 1929].
R61 Passage ticket, scratch, 51 [43: 193, 1930].
R65 Foreign exchange, stitch watermark, 25 [42: 322, 1929].
R66 Conveyance, minor varieties, 29 [42: 456, 1929].
R67 Entry of goods, cracked plate, 75 [42: 798, 1929].
R68 Foreign exchange, extra line at top, 42 [42: 718, 1929].
R68 Foreign exchange, imprint, 110 [45: 340, 1932].
R68 Foreign exchange, recutting, 43-4 [42: 719, 1929].
R68 Foreign exchange, stitch watermark, 120 [45: 606, 1932].
R68 Foreign exchange, The One Dollar Foreign Exchange (Thomas H. Pratt), 50-1 [43: 192-3, 1930].
R69 Inland exchange, double transfer, 53 [43: 248, 1930], 133 [46: 373, 1933].
R69 Inland exchange, minor varieties, 29 [42: 456, 1929].
R71 Life insurance, minor varieties, 28 [42: 455, 1929].
R72 Manifest, minor varieties, 28 [42: 455, 1929].
R73 Mortgage, double transfer, 67 [43: 650, 1930].
R74 Passage ticket, minor varieties, 28 [42: 456, 1929].
R74 Passage ticket, printed cancel on, 69 [44: 130, 1930], 76 [44: 292, 1931].
R75 Power of attorney, minor varieties, 29 [42: 456, 1929].
R75 Power of attorney, plating, 90 [44: 566-7, 1931].
R75 Power of attorney, stitch watermark, 124 [46: 169, 1932].
R78 Inland exchange, double transfer, 33 [42: 594, 1929].
R81 Conveyance, stitch watermark, 47 [43: 45, 1929].
R82 Mortgage, stitch watermark, 47 [42: 798, 1929].
R85 Charter party, double transfer, 32, 46 [42: 594, 798, 1929], 62 [43: 494, 1930].
R94 Conveyance, double transfer, 56 [43: 312, 1930].
Shifted transfers: See Double Transfers.
Silk paper: see Paper.
Stitch watermarks, 10 [41: 683, 1928], 15-16 [42: 27-8, 1928], 25, 30, 46-7 [42: 322, 457, 798, 1929], 61, 64 [43: 453, 494, 1930], 115, 116, 120 [45: 505, 550, 606, 1932], 148 [46: 620, 1933] and 162 [49: 253, 1936]. See also under specific catalog numbers and CHECK LISTS.
Straight edges on perforated series, 9 [41: 610-11, 1928], 16 [42: 28, 1928].

SECOND ISSUE: 1871

Low Value Proprietary Stamps of 1871-1875 (plate varieties) (C. W. Bedford), 125-8 [46: 222-5, 1933].
Multiple pieces, check list, 200-1 [53: 55-6, 267, 1939].
Sixty Cent Stamp of the Second and Third Revenue Issues (George T. Turner), 203-9 [53; 465-71, 1940].
Stitch watermarks, 15 [42: 28, 1928], 135-6, 148 [46: 431-2, 620, 1933].

THIRD ISSUE: 1871-2

Pinkish paper, 34 [42: 595, 1929].
R135 Frame printed on back, 229 [55: 256, 1942].
Sixty Cent Stamp of the Second and Third Revenue Issues (George T. Turner), 203-9 [53: 465-71, 1940].
Stitch watermarks, 15 [42: 28, 1928]; on R135, 135-6 [46: 431-2, 1933].

ISSUE OF 1875-8

Scratch, 36 [42: 655, 1929].
Shift, 65 [43: 594. 1930].
Stitch watermark, 201 [53: 267, 1940].
The Two Cent Liberty (Beverly S. King), 158-9 [48: 367-8, 1935].

ISSUE OF 1898

R153, bisect on cover, 82 [44: 472, 1931].
R168, stitch watermark, 116 [45: 550, 1932], 176 [51: 574, 1938]. See Also CHECK LISTS.
R169, double transfer, 65 [43: 594, 1930].
R171, imperf, between, 51-2 [43: 193-4, 1930].
RB28 double transfer, 228 [55: 255-6, 1942].
Type R15, double transfers, 116 [45: 550, 1932].

ISSUE OF 1914

1/4 cent, double print, 46 [42: 798, 1929].
5/8 cent, double transfer, 30 [42: 457, 1929].
Stitch watermarks, 12 [41: 753, 1928].

ISSUE OF 1940-41

U.S. Series of 1940-1941 Revenues, 224-5 [55: 51-2, 1941].

CIGARETTE TUBES

RH1 Variety without period, 35 [42: 596, 1929].

CITY & STATE REVENUES

Florida State Revenue Stamps (David O. True), 183-6 [52: 75-6, 177-8, 1938].
Mass. Stock Transfer, cracked plate on 50 cent, 124 [46: 169, 1932].
New York City tax stamps, 180-1 [51: 983-4, 1938], 198 [52: 804-5, 1939].
South Carolina, The Revenue Stamps of the State of (Frank L. Applegate), 38-41 [42: 657-60, 1929].

EMBOSSED REVENUE STAMPED PAPER

The Stamp Act (Harry M. Konwiser), 83-8 [44: 505-10, 1931].

FOREIGN REVENUE

Postage Stamps Used for Revenues in Some British Countries (Gerard Gerardzoon), 25-6 [42: 319-20, 1929].
Italian revenues, 109 [45: 340, 1932].

PLAYING CARDS

New Precancels, 212 [54: 189, 1940].
New variety and precancels, 135 [46: 413, 1933].
Provisionals. See Joyce under CHECK LISTS.
RF1, cracked plate, 187 [52: 331, 1939].
Series of 1940, 225 [55: 52, 1941].

PRIVATE DIE PROPRIETARIES

Double transfers on RS286, RS290 and RS294, 65 [43: 594, 1930].
Double transfers listed, 120-1 [46: 71-2, 1932].
Private Die Matches Used on a Receipt (Henry W. Holcombe), 157 [48: 327, 1935].
Stitch watermarks on RS41b, 170 [50: 703, 1937], on RS107a, 167 [50: 568, 1937]. See also CHECK LISTS.
Stitch watermarks on match wrappers, 13 [41: 754, 1928].
Various varieties listed, 177-8, 181 [51: 662-3, 984, 1002, 1938].
Wilder, Edward: new variety, 228 [55: 255, 1942].

TAX PAIDS

Custom band for cigars, 147 [46: 619, 1933].
Imitation Sparkling Wine (Roscoe L. Wickes), 146 [46: 618, 1933].
Metallic Tax Stamps for Cotton (Clarendon Bangs), 141-2 [46: 571-2, 1933].
New Taxes Under the Defense Tax Bill, 211 [53: 813, 1940].
Sale of Tobacco Stamps to Collectors, 165-6 [49: 212-13, 1936].
Snuff stamps, values listed, 45 [42: 798, 1929].

U.S. POSSESSIONS

Guam and Puerto Rico provisionals, 124 [46: 169-70, 1932].

AUTHOR INDEX

Material appearing in Revenue Unit columns varied from titled and signed articles, to shorter notes, to quotes from letters to the secretary or editor from identified correspondents, and to miscellaneous pieces of information whose origin may be conjectural. The entries below are confined to titled and signed articles and notes of philatelic import.

Applegate, Frank: Revenue Stamp Taxes, 3-6 [41: 519-21, 1928]. The Revenue Stamps of the State of South Carolina, 38-41 [42: 657-60, 1929].
Bacharach, Justin L.: Notes on the 50 Cent Mortgage, 161 [49: 192-3, 1936].
Bangs, Clarendon: Metallic Tax Stamps for Cotton, 141-2 [46: 571-2, 1933].
Barr, Jere Hess: Insurance Cancellations, 226-7 [55: 185-6, 1941].
Beaumont, Howard B.: Postage Stamps Used as Revenues and Revenue Stamps Used for Postage, 122-4[46: 167-9, 1932].
  Revenue Stamps Used for Postage, 142-5 [46: 572-5, 1933].
Bedford, C. W.: The Plates of the 5¢ Inland Exchange, 78-81 [44: 427-31, 1931].
  The Three Plates of the 5¢ Inland Exchange, 106-7 [45: 240-1, 1932].
  A Reworked Plate for the 1¢ Express, 111-13 [45: 393-5, 1932].
  The Low Value Proprietary Stamps of 1871-1875. Plate varieties, 125-8 [46: 222-5, 1933].
Bradbury, W. W.: The 50 Cent Conveyance, 91 [45: 24-5, 1931].
Chappell, C. H.: U.S. Revenues Showing Stitch Watermarks, 11-13 [41: 752-4, 1928].
Gerardzoon, Gerard: Postage Stamps Used for Revenues in Some British Countries, 25-6 [42: 391-2, 1929].
Hale, Robert F.: Insurance Cancellations Found on United States Revenues of 1862-71, 63-4 [43: 547-8, 1930].
Hamilton, Philip E.: Minor Varieties of the $1.00 Values, 28-9 [42: 455-6, 1929].
Harrington, F.: Postage Used for Revenues, 117 [45: 551-2, 1932].
Holcombe, Henry W.: An Unusual Use of Private Die Match Stamps, 157 [48: 327, 1935].
  Dates of Repeal of Revenue Acts, 138-40 [46: 486-8, 1933].
Joyce, Morton Dean: Printed and Other Pre-cancellations of Playing Card Manufacturers on Civil War Issue Revenue Stamps, 92-8, 99-105 [45: 126-32, 1931 and 182-8, 1932].
King, Beverly: Revenues Used for Postage, 129-30 [46: 261-2, 1933].
  The Two Cent Liberty, 158-9 [48: 367-8, 1935].
Konwiser, Harry M.: The Stamp Act, 83-8 [44: 505-10, 1931].
Pratt, Thomas H.: The One Dollar Foreign Exchange, 50-1 [43: 192-4, 1930].
Robison, Warner S.: The 50 Cent Mortgage, 71-3 [44: 215-17, 1931].
Shaw, LeRoy E.: Double Transfers on a Full Sheet of 2¢ USIR, 108-9 [45: 242-3, 1932].
Train, J. H.: The Two Cent U.S. Internal Revenue, 57-9 [43: 386-8, 1930].
True, David O.: Florida State Revenue Stamps, 183-6 [52: 75-6, 177-8, 1938].
Turner, George E.: Preliminary Data on Plating the 10¢ Certificate, 163-5 [49: 303-5, 1936].
  The Sixty Cent Stamp of the Second and Third Revenue Issues, 203-9 [53: 465-71, 1940].
  Survey of United States Revenue Stamps or What Comprises a Revenue Collection, 213-23 [54: 391-2, 455-6, 448, 662-3, 671, 743-4, 810-13, 1941].
Wickes, Roscoe, L.: Imitation Sparkling Wine, 146 [46: 618, 1933].